Personality and Decision Processes

PERSONALITY

AND

DECISION PROCESSES

Studies in the Social Psychology of Thinking

ORVILLE G. BRIM, JR.
DAVID C. GLASS
DAVID E. LAVIN
NORMAN GOODMAN

STANFORD UNIVERSITY PRESS
STANFORD, CALIFORNIA

ERRATUM

The table on pp. 72–73 should read as follows:

EPISTEMOLOGICAL AND INSTRUMENTAL BELIEFS

Name and Number of Subtest	Items and t Values				
(1) Belief in animism	59 (8.4)	49 (7.8)	39 (7.1)	29* (7.0)	69 (5.4)
(2) Belief in supernatural causes	80 (8.8)	50 (7.1)	70* (5.0)	90 (4.7)	40 (4.6)
(3) Belief in fate	51 (6.2)	11 (6.1)	31 (5.0)	91 (4.6)	71 (4.1)
(4) Belief in predictability of life	27 (4.5)	17 (3.7)	67* (3.5)	57* (2.9)	47 (1.5)
(5) Belief in multiple causation of events	38 (8.3)	68 (3.8)	78 (3.3)	88 (2.9)	8 (2.8)
(6) Belief that good things will happen (OP++)	62 (7.8)	22 (6.7)	42 (6.5)	82 (3.6)	2 (2.6)
(7) Belief that good things won't happen (OP+−)	86 (5.1)	26 (3.8)	66 (3.2)	6 (2.6)	46 (2.4)
(8) Belief that bad things will happen (OP−+)	84 (6.1)	64 (5.6)	24 (3.8)	44 (2.6)	4 (2.1)
(9) Belief that bad things won't happen (OP−−)	14 (8.6)	54 (6.2)	74 (3.3)	94 (3.2)	34 (2.8)
(10) Future time orientation	1* (8.2)	61* (7.0)	81* (4.3)	41 (4.1)	21* (3.4)
(11) Anti-traditionalistic orientation	65* (3.9)	25* (3.2)	45 (3.1)	5 (2.8)	85* (2.7)
(12) Belief that events clearly are either good or bad	12 (5.3)	32 (5.3)	72* (3.7)	52* (3.0)	92 (2.8)
(13) Belief that events clearly are either highly probable or highly improbable	75* (6.7)	55* (4.7)	35 (3.7)	15 (2.7)	95 (2.6)
(14) Belief that actions have many consequences	93 (12.5)	73* (9.8)	13 (5.3)	33* (4.1)	53 (3.4)
(15) Belief in trying many actions in solving problems	96* (4.5)	56* (4.3)	16* (3.5)	76* (3.1)	36 (2.3)
(16) Belief in thinking before acting	3* (8.3)	43* (5.7)	83* (3.9)	63* (2.8)	23 (2.8)

Stanford University Press
Stanford, California
© 1962 by the Board of Trustees of the
Leland Stanford Junior University
Printed in the United States of America
ISBN 0-8047-0047-8
Original edition 1962
Last figure below indicates year of this printing:
87 86 85 84 83 82 81 80 79 78

ACKNOWLEDGMENTS

It is a pleasure to express our thanks to the organizations and persons who over the past several years gave support, cooperation, and personal sacrifice in bringing these studies to completion.

We are indebted to the Russell Sage Foundation, whose initial grant for a study of the education of parents provided the impetus for this more intensive analysis of the ways in which parents decide upon child-care practices. The Child Study Association of America, the host institution for the study referred to above, helped in every way possible to assure the success of this extension of the original plan by providing the space for research, and by assisting in planning the study. The Bureau of Educational Research of the New York City Board of Education, and the staff of the particular school from which our subjects were chosen, showed throughout their cooperation an astute grasp of the requirements of social research. The neighborhood settlement houses made it possible to extend the range of our inquiry beyond the traditional populations studied in social research, by serving as the source of some of our respondents and as the site of some of the research.

The particular persons who have helped us along the way are many. To those who over the years have done the painstaking typing and the meticulous searching out of errors, we give our many thanks; these are Mary J. Fleischman, Merle Fried, Anita O'Keefe, and Rachel DeWolf. For Ann Lee and Arla McMillan, who worked with us in the laborious analysis of data and the computation of statistics, we have lasting gratitude. We thank Mendel Hoffman for his invaluable aid in preparing and executing the computer analyses of a complex body of data. And last, we owe our gratitude to our respondents who gave generously of their valuable time in the spirit of furthering social science knowledge.

CONTENTS

Personality and Decision Processes

INTRODUCTION

The studies described in this book are concerned with how people make decisions. The studies are exploratory. They do not stem from a single general theory, nor was it our purpose to construct such a theory. Instead, the emphasis is on the development of new concepts and the refinement of old ones, and on the discovery of a few generalizations that might be used to describe the relation between decision making, personality, and social structure.

The studies have been designed and carried out from a sociological point of view, and reflect both the assets and liabilities of this perspective. But such merits and defects mark each approach to the study of decision processes, for each academic discipline has its own unique perspective. The biologist may contend that the intellectual processes of men should be studied as biochemical events, and that "behind every twisted thought lies a twisted molecule" [2]. The clinical psychologist or psychoanalyst may view the subject as his own private field of study and believe, as one has said: "A psychology which elects to study cognitive and apperceptive functions of man does not make contact at any point with sociology. The only psychology directly linked with sociology is one whose chief interest is the affective or emotional life of man" [3, p. 1]. The anthropologist may discount individual or group variability, and agree that "as far as we can ascertain, the intellectual processes themselves are the same for all normal human beings in all times and places . . ." [5].

It is true that sociologists have not been drawn in large numbers to the study of decision processes, and some would argue that it is not a proper subject for them to study. It seems to us, however, that research on decision making has been the poorer because of the absence of sociological contributions. For example, studies of value systems of different cultures [4] show there are basic differences in beliefs about the relation of man to nature. Beliefs about the ability of human beings to master their environment, and about whether it is right to attempt to master it at all, pervade the intellectual activities of a society and affect the traditional modes of attack upon problems faced by individual members.

In like manner, there are cultural differences in beliefs about the relative importance of immediate as against future satisfactions. A fundamental cultural emphasis on future time—a future orientation, as we say— leads to a concern with the consequences of decisions that lie far ahead, and not just with those of this hour or day. The span between cultural values emphasizing an immediate hedonism, on the one hand, and a delayed gratification of desires, on the other, is very great, and the typical decision processes of societies will reflect the degree to which one or the other value is stressed.

Moreover, when one goes on to consider the sources of individual differences in decision making, he is led to the study of early life experiences. Variations in child training, differing methods of formal education, the presence or absence of certain kinds of people in his environment, such as brothers, teachers, adult friends whom he might use as role models, all will influence the way in which each person defines his problems and attempts to make decisions. Clearly, some of the most important influences on human decision processes lie in the realm of sociology.

The actual decisions that we studied were parents' decisions about their children. It should be said at once that these are not studies of child-rearing practices. Although the decisions were about child care, we present no information on the nature of the practices parents actually chose, or their possible relation to child development. It is not the substance, but the general formal properties of the decision process that concern us.

Our interest in these decisions was an outgrowth of an earlier study, which evaluated the methods used in educating parents [1]. In the course of the study it became clear that parental decisions about children provided an interesting, manageable, and accessible class of decisions for the purposes of research. This is especially true in current times because the role of the parent is one of the few roles of fundamental importance in which habit and tradition have crumbled, and considerable autonomy is demanded.

The studies we report can be thought of as field studies. We collected information from 200 men and women, using tests of personality and tests of their decision-making processes. In our analysis of the results, we focused on the relations between the personalities of the respondents and their decision processes in various situations. We also studied the differences in decision making and in personality between mothers and fathers, and between middle-class and lower-class parents. In addition, we employed one experimental variation in which some of the parental couples made decisions together, in contrast to the other parents who made individual decisions. Because these studies include only observations made at one point in time, there are no analyses of developmental trends or of changes after experimentally introducing some stimulus. The strength of the studies is in their comparisons of the decision processes of different types of people, and in the description of the influence of personality on the decisions.

The organization of the book can be stated in this way. In Part I we describe the problem we set for ourselves, and show how our work relates to what has been done before. First, we clarify and refine the distinctions between various components of the decision process, so as to isolate them for study. We delineate six different phases of the decision process, two of which are the focus of our research: (1) the evaluation phase, which concerns the evaluation of alternative courses of action in terms of the probability of occurrence, the desirability and rapidity of the outcomes expected from each action; and (2) the strategy-selection phase, which concerns the choice among alternative actions and the selection of a sequence for their performance. In addition, we have identified ten characteristics of these two phases which we believe to be the elemental aspects of decision making. Among the ten are such familiar variables as optimism, future time orientation, and preferential ordering of alternatives according to expected utility. The ten together constitute the actual descriptive variables which we sought to relate to personality and social structure.

In Part I we also describe the social and personality characteristics that we studied. Our own cultural heritage of ideas about the relation of social and personality factors to decision making is, for the most part, a body of partial truths, myth, and prescriptions for cultivating good judgment. Our knowledge of the actual relations between character and decision processes is at best uncertain. Therefore we felt obliged to clarify the assumptions we had about the relations between these various characteristics and decision processes, and to define the kinds of personality variables we believed were important enough to study. An example of one of these is an autonomy-dependency dimension, isolated through factor analysis of a number of our personality tests. This ties in with prior work on fatalistic attitudes, on the sense of personal control, and on feelings of dependency and authoritarianism, and at the same time is related to some important aspects of the decision process.

In Part I we also set forth the logic that led us to choose our decision problems. We wanted them to represent different kinds of decisions that people must face, and to vary along certain theoretically important dimensions. An example is our use of a problem involving a boy's masturbation, for which the cultural solutions are ambiguous and which at the same time arouses strong feelings in the parents.

Parts II, III, and IV present the results of the different studies. In Part II the central study is presented. Correlations between personality characteristics, socio-economic characteristics, and decision making are described. An analysis is made of how the ten elements of the decision process are related to each other. The consistency of people in their methods of decision making as they move from one decision to another also is discussed. Sex and social class differences in styles of decision making are reported, and we show how they reflect the different cultural values of the groups. In Part III another study is introduced. It is concerned with how husbands and wives working together differ in their decision processes from husbands and wives individually solving child-rearing problems. In Part IV we use a traditional criterion of rationality to explore the degree to which human beings are rational; or, to put it differently, how well some of the current models for rational decision processes actually fit the men and women we studied.

The conclusions from these several studies interrelating personality, situation, and decision making have one of three forms. The first kind of conclusion relates personality or social characteristics to decision processes regardless of situational effects. For instance: highly dependent people are more optimistic than highly independent people about the results of their actions; they also consider a smaller number of possible outcomes of such actions. And again: there are no differences between the middle-class men and women in the characteristics of their decision making.

The second type of conclusion relates situations to decision processes regardless of the influence of personality. One example is that in the decision problem involving a son's disobedience to his parents, all groups of respondents, mother and father, middle and lower class alike, are less optimistic in their evaluation of possible solutions. In like manner, in the decision problem involving masturbation, the parents consider significantly fewer of the possible results of their actions than they do in other situations, and thus have a more limited basis for appraising the value of the different actions.

The third kind of conclusion concerns the effects on decision making of the interaction of personality with types of decision problems. For instance, the effect of the masturbation decision problem is to reduce the lower-class parents' consideration of long-range or distant consequences of their actions, but this is not true for the middle-class parents. Another conclusion about interaction effects is that in a decision problem involving stealing it is the lower-class mothers alone who become more extreme in their judgments. Still another finding of this kind is that persons with a strong generalized need for certainty, when confronted with the decision problem involving masturbation, tend to think only of consequences which have a high probability of occurrence. These conclusions, as well as those mentioned above as involving pure personality, social, and situational effects, are, of course, discussed in detail in their appropriate contexts. As examples at this point they serve to indicate the kinds of results one may expect to find in our studies.

In the Epilogue we have added a brief chapter which, in addition to summarizing the results of the different studies, suggests how we could improve upon our work now that we recognize certain mistakes that we made. In studies such as these the researchers certainly have learned more than the readers will learn, for properly there is much that is not presented in the highly distilled summary reports of the main results. In each of our studies there are things we would do differently if we had them to do over again, and since this wisdom about field research procedures themselves, rather than subject matter, rarely gets into the public domain, we have used this opportunity to comment on our own work.

PART I

Theory and Method

I

Characteristics of the Decision Process

As a result of learning, much of an individual's behavior becomes routine and habitual, based as it is on prior successful occasions of satisfying desires in given situations. There develop a great number of episodes in life in which an individual no longer needs to give deliberate attention to his behavior. Recognition of a situation as similar to or the same as one which has gone before results in performance of that act which the individual has learned is the best response. Where the situation is new, or where because of changes a prior solution no longer is successful, an individual's selection of an action cannot be routine. A problem must be identified; information must be gathered; new courses of action must be proposed; each action must be evaluated in terms of its probable success; some preferential ordering must be made; performance of one or more actions must occur.

Our organization of the components of the decision process reflects these demands of steps in problem solution, and can be put formally in the following way. The decision process consists of six phases customarily linked into a sequence: (1) identification of the problem; (2) obtaining necessary information; (3) production of possible solutions; (4) evaluation of such solutions; (5) selection of a strategy for performance; and (6) actual performance of an action or actions, and subsequent learning and revision. This formulation of the process will be a familiar one, for most of its components have appeared in decision analyses and descriptions of problem solving for many years. Consider the similarities between our view and several other formulations of sequences, selected to represent different intellectual traditions. Some collapsing and refinement of one or another phase is necessary as one moves from one formulation to the next, but the basic identity of the concepts is apparent.

Dewey's [13] sequence of phases probably is the best known. The phases are perplexity or doubt; then identification of the problem, research for facts, and the formulation of a possible solution; a testing of solutions and, where necessary, reanalysis of the problem; and last, the application of the correct solution.

A similar analysis appears in a recent book concerned with training in thinking and other personal characteristics [32]. The phases presented are recognition and definition of the problem; preliminary observation and collection of information; analysis of facts to see how they relate to the problem; formulation of possible solutions and evaluation of them; trying out the most promising solution; checking to see how the solution worked out; and last, being ready to make changes in the problem-solving plan.

A third example is a review article on recent research on thinking and problem solving [19], where the author classifies the research according to the phase with which it is concerned. In this instance the phases are reception of the stimulus situation; concept formation or invention; determining courses of action; decision making; and verification. One will note that the phrase "decision making" is used to designate what we consider to be only the fifth phase in the decision-making process, namely, the selection of a strategy.

Our last example comes from a review [2] of some three dozen studies, made during the past two decades, of the adoption of new farming practices. In the situations described by these studies, a farming practice such as the planting of a new crop or the use of a new insecticide or fertilizer in place of the old is recommended to farmers as a course of action different from their current practices. These studies are analyzed to show the phases which occur in the decision to accept or reject the new practice. The data indicate that the informants in the various studies do distinguish one phase from another, and can designate the points in time when they went through each phase. The identified stages are the awareness phase; the phase in which the farmer obtains information relevant to the problem; the evaluation phase; the trial phase; and, fifth, the phase of adoption. Note the absence of our third phase, the production of alternative solutions, which one would not expect to appear in these studies because a single course of action, alternative to their present solution, is presented to them.

Several matters remain to be discussed in regard to the phase formulation. First, it is not assumed that every decision need involve all of these phases; some problems may not require a person to obtain new information, or in others, such as in the final example above, the alternatives may be given.

Second, the conception of phases is suitable for use in analyses of decisions ranging in scope from solving a mathematical or chess puzzle to the choice of a college or of a husband or wife. In fact it is just this type of formal analysis of the basic phases of the process which permits one to see the similar nature of all decision problems.

A third question is the relation of this conception of phases to the general intellectual functions such as insight, judgment, and intelligence. Each of these seems to involve a process which may appear in all of the decision phases. For instance, in experiments on insight [15, 34], the situations used for the observation and analysis of problem-solving behavior may involve spatial or mathematical tasks, or the manipulation and combination of various implements in order to achieve an objective. The reports of such research on insight present data on all decision process phases, including sudden identification of the problem, sudden recognition of a probable solution, and so on.

Judgment, which appears in most lists of the components of thinking (e.g., [28]), also is involved in all problem-solving steps. The concept is vague, and what commonly goes by the name of "judgment" could refer to how one selects sources of evidence pertinent to the problem, or the degree to which one makes logical deductions from premises in formulating hypotheses, with how rationally one orders the alternatives in terms of their expected utility, and so on.

Since intelligence, when not defined as "what the test measures," is viewed as a measure of problem-solving capacity, one can ask to what extent the various measures of intelligence deal with different phases of the decision process. To answer this question adequately one might take the several leading tests of intelligence and assign their subtests to that aspect of the decision process to which they are relevant. This is not possible though, because too often the subtest areas are not clear. In the absence of satisfactory attempts to analyze tests of intelligence according to their adequacy in representing various components of problem solving, one only can surmise that the efforts made to develop new tests of some of the phases, such as tests of creativity and critical thinking, indicate a belief that current intelligence tests leave untapped some important components of the decision process. To look at things this way suggests the possibility of the ultimate development of a general intelligence test which deals not only with the properties actually measured, but also with the use of information, the evaluation of the information received, originality, and similar components.

Fourth, and finally, what is the relation of decision processes to problem solving? We see these two as much the same, and use the concepts interchangeably in this book. The differences between decision theory and problem-solving research are more differences of emphasis than of concern with different types of theoretical issues. Our studies are more closely related to studies of decision making than to studies of problem solving because of our concern with our respondents' beliefs about probability, future time, desirability, and other variables which rarely appear in problem-solving research.

Some will object, saying that problem solving is the more general term, and that the concept of decision refers only to the choice between alternative courses of action after preliminary steps in the problem solution have been reached. On the other hand, students of decision processes (among the social scientists) would argue that it is this term which is a more general one, since the traditional work on problem solving often has dealt with artificial and limited problems [47]. We believe that closer analysis shows that the puzzles or other types of contrived problems used in problem-solving research and the larger substantive problems such as planned parenthood and home purchases all have the same formal properties. The limitations of problem-solving research probably are matched by the limitations of decision research, since the latter is restricted by its traditional emphasis on utility theory and economic behavior. Both fields would profit by recognizing their similar theoretical interests.

This may be evident in the following examples of research on phases of the decision process. In these few pages we are not trying to summarize the research on the different phases, which would be a truly vast undertaking. Rather we attempt to clarify the distinctions between them, and to give some substance to each phase. The first phase of the decision process is that of the subject's recognition that he is confronted with a problematic situation which requires attention and definition. Typical studies report that there are consistent individual differences across different types of problems in the amount of time spent studying directions for a test [61], or that there are age differences in amount of concern with problem definition [60], or that instructions in regard to identification of the problem are effective in altering the process of solution [38]. In another quarter it is hardly necessary to cite the tremendous accumulation of clinical data showing that problem recognition is influenced by the degree to which the problem involves the unconscious components of personality. A person's defense against such a situation may be to deny the existence of any problem or to identify the problem incorrectly.

The second phase, acquiring information relevant to the decision, has been the object of different types of studies. Even so, in Miller's review of Bartlett's *Thinking* [43], he points out that the use of evidence is taken for granted in this work, without the author's recognizing that this evidence is hard to come by, and that to exclude the acquisition of evidence from the thinker's task makes everything seem to run too smoothly. Attempts to analyze the degree to which people seek information prior to problem solving have been studied by Glaser and his colleagues [23] and by Rimoldi [48]. Another approach is represented in the study by Katona and Mueller [30], which developed an index of deliberation about purchase decisions; one of the components of deliberation was the extent of information-seeking activity exhibited by the respondents. Studies of interpersonal influence also have focused on the way in which one obtains information prior to decisions, with particular reference to whom one approaches and the kind of information which is sought [31]. Another illustrative study of this phase is Marschak's [41] analysis of the cost of new information relative to the improvement of the over-all utility of the solution, and hence a specification of the conditions under which one is advised to obtain more information or to make decisions with the knowledge at hand.

The third phase, production of possible solutions, involves one immediately in a number of important research traditions. The work on this decision phase includes studies of originality, or creativity [7], or scientific invention [21]. The long history of work includes the inductive study of Wallas [59] on scientific creativity, with his description of the four stages of preparation, incubation, illumination, and verification, and at the present time is represented by the research on children's creativity by Getzels and his colleagues [20]. Two recent books [28, 57] review this history and indicate the continuing interest.

As for other types of work dealing with this phase, there are studies of induction of hypotheses from prior experience [64]; studies of logic [27]; and studies of "critical thinking" in the appraisal of data [22]. Recent work in computer simulation also is pertinent: attempts to formulate the problem-solving process in terms suitable for computer operation [44] have given special attention to the third and fourth phases, those of producing alternatives and their evaluation for probable effectiveness.

We will consider phases four and five (evaluation and strategy selection) together, since research has tended to deal with these two in combination. Other analyses often do not distinguish between these two phases: Gagné [19] refers to the two stages as the "decision" phase, as we mentioned earlier; and Foote and Cottrell [18, p. 86] have merged the two phases under the concept of judgment. Most work on these phases has come from those emphasizing decision making, rather than problem solving. This interest stems from economics and mathematical statistics [9, 37] in the forms of game theory and statistical decision theory. The fact is that traditional research on problem solving has not been much concerned with these two phases.

It is true that the basic analyses of conflict (e.g., [14]) and probably the work on level of aspiration can be viewed as applicable to the evaluation of alternative actions and their selection in terms of expected net satisfaction. Nevertheless, these have not been translated until recently into terms directly applicable to analyses of decision processes or problem solving. A notable example of the theoretical advances which can be made when this work is joined with the traditional interests of social psychologists is represented by Siegel's [51] interpretation of level of aspiration phenomena by means of utility theory, and his illustrations of the similarity of objectives of the two types of research and theory.

The sixth and last phase of the decision process, that of performance and subsequent revision, brings us to the area of learning in its broadest sense, including concept formation, reinforcement of expectations, and so on. One can do no more than call attention to the massive body of research on learning, and to point out that very little of this has been adequately related to the work on other problem-solving phases. It is thought-provoking to recognize that in the development of psychology, the study of thinking and specifically problem solving or decision making has been separated from the main body of research devoted to the learning process, and that this has divided work along two lines, one dealing with performance and revision, and the other dealing with prior phases in the over-all decision process. It is to be anticipated that a fully developed theory of the problem-solving process will draw upon the contributions of these different fields of interest.

TYPES OF DECISIONS

It has seemed to us that prior work on classifying decisions might be divided into that dealing with formal properties, as opposed to that which considers substantive characteristics of the decision. Formal properties refer to theoretical and abstract characteristics of decisions which are independent of content or the substantive nature of the problems. For example, the degree of risk involved, the information available, whether or not the decision is irrevocable, are formal properties. When one uses substantive characteristics, he speaks of economic problems, administrative decisions, career choices, mate selection, planned parenthood, investment decisions, and a number of others, with each class being identified by the activity it involves. These in turn might be viewed as subtypes of more general classes such as childhood, adolescent, or adult decisions, or religious, political, or familial decisions.

Classifications Based on Formal or Abstract Properties

Classifications based on formal attributes are large in number and vary in their generality and in the background from which they spring. They come from analyses of a formal mathematical nature, the works of philosophers and logicians, psychologists' studies of problem solving, and educators' programs on teaching how to think. For instance, Travers and his colleagues [56], in reviewing some classifications primarily from psychology and education, conclude that previous research has not established the relevant characteristics of problems that must be considered in studies on problem-solving effectiveness. They go on to suggest that important characteristics are whether or not the problem requires a unique solution, requires the discovery of essential principles, requires an evaluation of elements and their reorganization, and includes considerable essential data.

We have not attempted to develop an abstract ordering of the many decision characteristics mentioned in prior work. A theoretical classification which exhausts the characteristics of decision processes is a major undertaking—a study in itself. It is to be hoped that someone soon will turn his hand to this task.

What we have done is select a number of characteristics, drawn primarily from work in economics, which seem especially appropriate for describing our own studies (e.g., [29; 39, p. 14; 40]). Since our focus is on the fourth and fifth phases of the decision process (evaluation and strategy selection), we only discuss the characteristics which are applicable to these phases.

The first major property is the degree of certainty which characterizes the outcomes of the decision [1, 16, 37]. The term *certainty* applies to the condition when each alternative in a decision-making situation is associated invariably with a specific outcome; i.e., the outcome has a probability of occurrence of either 0 or 1. On the other hand, there is a condition of *risk* when each alternative is associated with outcomes whose probability of occurrence is less than 1 and greater than 0, and when the actual probability figure is known to the decision-maker. Finally, an *uncertain* condition exists when the probability of occurrence of outcomes is greater than 0 and less than 1, but when the actual probability figure is unknown to the decision-maker. This classification is cross-cut by whether or not the probabilities associated with outcomes are *objective* or *subjective*. Objective probabilities refer to outcomes whose probabilities are given as information by the experimenter. Subjective probabilities refer to outcomes whose probabilities are estimated by the decision-maker.

The second major basis of classification is the "state of nature." It is possible to conceptualize three states of nature: competitive, cooperative, and neutral. These serve to summarize the conditions or states under which decision making generally is carried out.

Decision making under competitive conditions is an example of *interest conflict* [16]. The major characteristics may be summarized as follows. A person is in a situation in which one of several outcomes will occur and with respect to which he has certain clear-cut preferences. Although he may have some control over the outcome, he does not possess complete control. When chance events may influence the final outcome, the problem is one of decision making under conditions of risk, where the risk results from random variation in events (nature). But, where lack of complete control over the outcomes is a function of the behavior of other individuals with conflicting preferences, the situation is one of genuine conflict or competition; e.g., a labor dispute, or a war between nations. This area has been the object of considerable description and explanation, the most familiar approach being the formal theory of games [17, 26, 63].

There is an intermediate condition between competition and cooperation, namely, the "non-strictly competitive situation" [37]. In this instance the situation differs, for there is at least one pair of alternative courses of action, A and A', such that one player prefers A to A' and the other (or others) does not prefer A' to A. Under these conditions a mutual benefit by some form of cooperation is possible [37, 58], and theories of coalition are being developed to describe this condition.

In regard to decision making under cooperative conditions, considerable formal analysis also has been carried out within a game-theory framework. Decision making under conditions of cooperation can be defined as a cooperative game in which the players can communicate prior to playing the game and form binding coalitions for their mutual benefits. One example of this class of cooperative games consists of bargaining problems [16].

The third state under which decision making occurs is the neutral state. In effect, we have here the case of decision making in which the decision-maker is not faced either by a malevolent opponent or by a friendly, cooperative decision-maker.

Five other properties of decisions merit mention at this time, although none of them has received the attention that has been given to degree of certainty and state of nature. The first of these is the type of cost involved; whether it is a wager or pay-to-play. This differentiation, as well as several which follow, has been suggested in a paper by Coombs and Beardslee [8]. In a wager decision, the subject's stake is forfeited in the event that he loses. In the case of pay-to-play, the subject pays a fee which he forfeits regardless of the outcome of the play. Buying a lottery ticket is an example of pay-to-play, while a bet on the outcome of a World's Series with a friend illustrates the case of a wager.

Another characteristic is that of repetitive play versus nonrepetitive performance. Under the "play once" condition, the decision is made only once, whereas under the repetitive play condition the decision is made a number of times, sequentially. In the latter case, there are several subdivisions as follows: The sequential choices may be the same or different; knowledge of success or failure may be immediate or delayed; and knowledge of the success or failure of the decision, i.e., whether the desired outcome was obtained, may affect the subjective probabilities and/or utilities which a subject assigns to the outcomes of sequentially presented alternatives.

A third characteristic is revocable versus irrevocable consequences of a decision. A physician's decision to amputate a gangrenous leg is an example of the choice which has irrevocable consequences; a decision to purchase a book "on approval" or to try a certain job before "committing oneself" can be revoked.

Fourth, there is the characteristic of method of choice versus single stimuli. In the method of "single stimuli" the subject is presented only with an alternative which he may accept or reject, an either-or situation. In the "method of choice" two or more courses of action are available and the subject selects from among them; that is, he makes a preferential judgment.

A final characteristic is whether the decision is betwen alternatives which can be compared on one, or more than one, significant classes of outcomes. In the former case the decision may be a choice situation in which the individual must decide between two or more political candidates whom he compares on one relevant issue, such as whether they will or will not raise taxes. In the latter case, the comparison of the alternative courses of action involves more than one such element. In the political instance, the candidates may be compared on a number of separate and distinct issues, or, to take another example, the parent in making a decision may review the outcomes of the various possible actions in terms of effects upon the child, his siblings, the mother or father, and other independent multiple consequences.

Classifications Based on Substantive Properties

Most classifications have been based on the social context or role in which the decision occurs. This is because roles include customs or rules for how one should attempt to solve a problem. For the scientist, his role provides him with a repertoire of alternatives, or tells him which consequences to consider. Parents, in making child-rearing decisions, are expected to consider only the effects upon the child, his siblings, and themselves. To be sure, the consequences might spill over into the marital relation and even further, but if the role did not restrict the range of consequences to be considered, or did not anchor the decision clearly within one interpersonal situation, the parent would have to consider too many outcomes to evaluate them adequately. Simon [52] stresses the point that decisions must be associated with particular positions in society, and that the associated role "institutionalizes" the decision itself. Decisions require frames of reference, objectives to be reached, legitimate alternatives to be used, classes of information to be applied, all of which are usual parts of role prescription.

One notes the existence of the large body of scientific information and folklore for the solution of different classes of problems. Each class in turn may constitute the realm of operation of a special profession. Each professional has a rich store of concepts and principles, which permits him to identify types of decisions and their important elements and to apply the various problem-solving processes for which he has been specially trained. Professionals are specialists in recognizing, labeling, and solving certain classes of problems which lie outside the day-to-day roles of other individuals. The professional is, in Everett Hughes' phrase, one who routinizes other peoples' crises.

Still, a review of occupational roles [55] shows that very little actually is known about the norms that regulate the decision-making process in different occupational roles. We know very little, also, of how the rules for solving problems in different roles are taught along with other content in socialization. We can see it most clearly in professional training, and the same must go on in a variety of nonprofessional roles, e.g., in the family, in political behavior, and so on. We have not found any child-development data, even among the studies of training children for thinking [50], which give evidence that there is deliberate training for decisions in different types of roles.

There have not been many attempts to analyze the characteristics of decision problems associated with different roles. To mention the best studies will indicate what has been done. Perhaps the most notable is the study by Cronbach and Gleser [12], which sets forth a taxonomy of decision problems in the special area of personnel management and test selection. The classification is relatively limited in scope and applies to the range of problems faced by personnel managers in their efforts to use test information to select job applicants. However, the authors indicate that this taxonomy should be applicable equally to problems of vocational and educational guidance. Of particular interest is the fact that the authors set forth suggestions of appropriate modes of decision making according to the different properties of the decision problem. This type of analysis, made in terms of the problems confronting the personnel administrator, is exemplary of what we believe could be done for other roles.

Another role which has been studied is that of the business executive. Reports on the actual decisions confronting him appear most frequently in informal analyses by the executive himself, such as Copeland [10],

Barnard [4], and others. Lazarsfeld, in his review [35] of sociological research on business, points out that the distribution of the types of decisions within organizations has not yet been systematically studied and that there is a need for research on this problem. One of Simon's ideas [52] is of special interest in this connection. He suggests that decision-making functions may be specialized among members of a business organization, and that analysis of decisions associated with different roles in business may show that the separate phases of a decision, or decisions with different formal properties, are allocated to certain roles. Research suggests that people differ in the kinds of problems they are good at solving [11, 56], so perhaps they find roles in organizations where the required decisions or decision phases are compatible with their skills.

Adolescent "career choice" also has been analyzed. It should be recognized at the outset that there is no single decision which can be called vocational or occupational choice. Instead, research (e.g., [3, 55]) makes clear that vocational development involves a series of decisions, each of which may demand consideration of long- as opposed to short-range consequences, estimating satisfactions over time, and other characteristics.

Another example is the role of the scientist. Conant [7] and Parsons [45], with others, have pointed out that the rationality of the scientist in his scientific role is an institutional pattern learned through socialization into that role and not necessarily a general mode of orientation or personality characteristic of the man in his other roles. Simon [52] points out that scientists deal with problems in which it is legitimate to consider simplified hypothetical conditions, rather than those which prevail in actuality, and may consider only isolated consequences, one at a time, rather than have to deal with the multiple consequences of real life. This contrasts with decisions of, say, political leaders, which cannot be so simplified.

We can mention briefly some other studies of types of decisions according to roles. Rose [49] indicates the differences between the decisions faced by a married woman as contrasted with a man, in that the former has to decide upon allocation of time and sequence of work, whereas for many men no decisions about allocation of time or work sequence are required during their working hours. Stryker [54] calls attention to the fact that people as family members, in contrast to their activities in other social institutions, face decisions which often are devoid of simple utilitarian rational elements found in economic decisions, and involve instead difficult estimates of desirability and probability of outcomes in influencing interpersonal relations of family members. Exemplary also are the recent analyses of decisions in government (e.g., [53]) and in regard to birth control [46, 62].

One must not, however, be misled into thinking that certain formal properties are always and necessarily characteristic of a given type of substantive problem; that a particular class of decisions must always have the same set of formal properties. It is possible to present the "same" problem under a variety of conditions which alter its formal properties. For example, the degree of uncertainty involved in a decision clearly is a function of individual or cultural ignorance, and is not inherent in the problem itself. In like manner, whether a decision problem is of a repetitive or nonrepetitive kind, with respect to investment in the stock market, depends upon the initial wealth of the individual and the degree to which he can tolerate a loss and still reinvest.

On the other hand, the classification of decisions by roles does suggest that within a given role a distinctive type of decision is accumulated, similar in its formal or abstract properties. For example, the typical decisions faced by a businessman, acting in his capacity as such, may be characterized by a relative ease of estimating desirability of outcomes because of the standardized measuring unit of money. In the end, of course, what is needed is an investigation in our particular society of the kind of empirical or substantive problems which actually exemplify different formal properties.

DEFINITIONS OF RATIONALITY

Students of decision processes have been interested in good thinking, in contrast to bad; in superior as contrasted with inferior solutions to problems; in decision characteristics which are of general significance in the affairs of men; in what might be referred to in a summary way as characteristics of rationality. But this leads one directly to the questions: How is one to distinguish between the better and poorer thinkers, between superior and inferior solutions? How is one to identify the characteristics of rationality? Discussion of these questions serves to extend and clarify further the context of our own research.

The first thing that strikes one in considering the problem of defining rationality is that it is an impossible task unless one states the conditions under which the definition can be applied. It is not sufficient, for example, to define rationality as "the selection of the most appropriate means to a given end after careful weighing of all available information" [53, p. 172] without first determining how the judgment of appropriateness is to be made; e.g., whether by external observers possessing the most advanced scientific knowledge, or by the actor himself given only limited information. Kochen and Levy [33] and Simon [52] argue effectively on the need for a continual qualifier to the term "rational." They point out that rationality must be regarded as a concept which has no meaning apart from a given set of rules.

In considering this problem, we thought it best to organize our discussion of definitions of rationality according to the two major types of definitions that appeared. The first type makes use of characteristics of the results of the decision. The criteria of rationality consist of such matters as the success of the solutions in satisfying the desires of the decision-maker, and other such consequence characteristics. However, the use of the characteristics of the outcomes as a basis for definition has received less attention than have the definitions of rationality that stress the actual process of the decision. The latter define rationality by reference to the specification of characteristics of the process such as taking into account long-range consequences, dealing with intermediate ranges of probabilities, selecting alternatives which maximize expected utility, and the like.

Definitions Based on Characteristics of Decision Outcomes

The use of outcomes of decisions as evidence of rationality depends on the assumption that these products reflect the prior decision process, and that one can infer from them whether or not the process was good or bad (rational or irrational). This can be done without any actual specification of what it was in the process itself which was good or bad. Using outcome criteria one can array individuals according to the degree of rationality alleged to have occurred in their decision process, as evidenced in the consequences. If one wished to go on and examine the process itself, the use of outcome criteria provides a possible starting point.

This approach has the merit of simplicity. But the problem, of course, is to specify which outcomes are indicative of good rational decision processes. There are a number of tests of decision-making results and Russell [50] has reviewed them. While many of them are inventive, and some have proved reliable, they still beg the question, since if the specification of criteria of rationality is only in terms of scores derivable from the tests, then one must ask the same question of the test score that was originally asked about the criteria in general.

Another shortcoming is that some of the test advocates elevate their testing of a single consequence of problem solving to the status of being commensurate with rationality as a whole, in spite of admonitions such as that of Guilford [25, p. 289] that we should stop looking "for any one function or process that is the *sine qua non* of all problem solving." Few students of the problem seem to be willing at this time to accept any one of these tests as measuring more than small and perhaps trivial portions of the outcomes of decisions, and the fact is there is no generally accepted test or set of tests appraising such outcomes as indicators of prior rational processes.

A second procedure is to use ratings by judges (as is sometimes done in studies of group problem solving) [36], of whether or not the decision outcome is good or rational. The drawback of this method is that the criteria used by the judges may not really come to grips with the question of what is rationality, and simply may reflect the judges' personal beliefs about what the outcomes of a given decision should be.

A third way of appraising the outcomes of decisions is to consider whether these result in success or failure for the subject's objectives; that is, whether they "maximize the individual's expected satisfaction," or fail to do so. Work on pilot failure, studies of career choice, of the evaluation of executive performance, of selection of marital partners, and of birth control, indicate that the success of any particular decision may not depend as much on man's rationality as on chance. Merton [42] argues that the success or failure of an action depends on luck, ignorance, and many other factors that lie outside the control of man no matter how much care he exercises in his choice. One solution, as Foote and Cottrell point out [18, p. 85] is "to require reference to a representative range of decisions and considerations within the history of the actor," that is, to appraise outcomes of a sample of decisions in a variety of a person's life situations.

Definitions Based on Characteristics of the Decision Process

There are a number of informal, heterogeneous endeavors to describe the characteristics of rational thinking and these are grouped together here not because of any communality in theory but because of their informal character and their source in cultural tradition. One class consists of the proverbs that cover a broad number of characteristics held to be desirable, such as planning ahead or being deliberate, which comprise society's collection of wisdom about problem solving. These maxims, bits of advice, rules of thumb, are found in the folk philosophy and literature of the society, and in the attitudes based on these. In our culture the values placed on long-range planning, suspension of judgment until the facts are complete, deliberation as against impulsivity, and others, have found their way into various studies of, and specifications for, human thinking (e.g., [6, 28, 50, 57]).

What are the deficiencies of this mode of specification of rationality? It is quickly apparent that any criteria for rationality advanced in such proverbial wisdom are matched by those of an equally cogent set of proverbs which maintain that just the opposite process of decision is the desirable one. Thus, "look before you leap" is contradicted by "he who hesitates is lost." It is of significance in this connection that in our efforts to develop a test composed of proverbs about thinking (described in Chapter 4) we found that in most instances one could match each proverbial prescription with a proverb about thinking which maintained the opposite.

In a better organized form are the practically oriented works on how to improve one's thinking, reviewed in Russell [50, Chs. 12, 13], which frequently appear in our culture and which seek to put into an orderly and succinct form some of the existing cultural prescriptions and blend them with formulations of scientific inquiry. But, these "how to" books, calling one's attention to deliberation, to the listing of alternatives, to consideration of distant outcomes, are contradicted by the equally well-formulated philosophical tradition which stresses spontaneity, the trusting of unique impulses, the expression of one's self, the supremacy of art over science, and the rejection of deliberate rational action as contrived, artificial, and, in the last analysis, impossible.

When one turns to the major formal effort in our culture, he finds, of course, that the development and expression of the scientific method is the dominant statement of rationality. The outlines of scientific methodology need no review here. It is desirable to point out, nevertheless, that attention in formulating the methods of science has been given unequally to the six phases of the decision process; primary attention has been given to what, in our terms, are the development of alternatives (hypotheses) from the available evidence, and to the last phase, the analysis of consequences and subsequent interpretation. It is of a special interest, therefore, to recognize that the models of decision processes derived from utility theory, both in its classical form and more recent development, are compatible with the existing framework of scientific method and indeed augment the work done heretofore by concentrating on a phase of thinking which has received less than its share of attention. In our judgment it is appropriate to think of formal utility theory and its specification for decision making as pertaining primarily to the fifth phase or the strategy-selection phase of the decision process, and as helping to complete an overall scientific methodology of problem solving.

In our own work we have been concerned with the characteristics of the decision processes of a number of men and women, and we have endeavored to describe their behavior with respect to characteristics we believe are of fundamental significance. Since we are of necessity strongly influenced by our own cultural specifications of optimal decision processes, we have leaned toward consideration of those characteristics specified by scientific method generally, and by decision theory in its more recent developments in particular. There are no other persuasive arguments for our having selected one or another definition to guide our inquiry.

Definitions of Rationality and Actual Decision Processes

In closing we must at least raise the question of how well the definitions of rational decision processes actually fit the behavior of men, how well they actually describe the way in which men make decisions. We must recognize that the definitions are at the same time specifications of optimum decision processes. They are, so to speak, an ideal to be sought after, a model to be followed by individuals, rather than being descriptions of an actual process.

Whether or not they are descriptive of what men do, whether men in fact even approximate them sufficiently to make their consideration as models worthwhile, leads to the historic debate on whether or not man is rational. Among those on the one side are Freud and Pareto; on the other Bentham and Malinowski; the current research on rationality in men shows the continuing interest of the social scientist [6, 56]. We cannot enter this debate. We only point out that the results of our studies do increase our knowledge of the degree of rationality in human decisions.

CHARACTERISTICS OF THE DECISIONS THAT WE STUDIED

All the decisions that we asked our subjects (who were parental couples) to make involved some aspect of child-rearing. Four decision problems were presented. Each problem involved the behavior of a boy about ten years old. Some of the problems probably are more serious than others. However, in every case the problems could be handled by the parents without outside assistance. The boy was to be viewed as a normal healthy child without any symptoms of serious maladjustment.

From the many problems which fit this description, the following four were selected: disobedience in the home, failure to attend to school homework, petty stealing, and masturbation. Each of these problems, and the rationale for their selection, is considered in detail in Chapter 2.

Now we want to relate our discussion of types of decisions, phases of the process, and selection of relevant variables to the characteristics of the child-rearing decisions used in our studies.

Formal and Substantive Aspects of Child-Rearing Decisions

We have stated that we believed that the formal characteristics of decision processes which seemed most pertinent to the decision phases we studied were certainty, states of nature, and the others mentioned above. Let us review these with reference to the child-rearing decisions which we studied. First, these decisions are characterized by some risk in regard to the effectiveness of alternative solutions. Second, in regard to the "state of nature," it is reasonable to believe that it is neutral; that is, it probably is not a cooperative or competitive situation. It is apparent, however, that in some families this characteristic may differ; parents may be at odds about a particular child-care solution, or they may try to satisfy each other's interests through their decisions.

The type of cost involved seems to be of the "pay-to-play" variety, in that the alternatives would have required at least some effort on the part of the parents which would have been expended without return if the alternative was unsuccessful. While it is true that the situations are hypothetical, this is not to be confused with the fact that the alternatives if they were performed would have required an expenditure of energy and time by the parent.

In terms of the earlier concepts, the decisions are not repetitive, but rather were to be made just once. Also, the decisions do not have irrevocable consequences in the sense given earlier, since if an alternative is not satisfactory, some other could be employed and the effects of a prior action could be mitigated through subsequent behavior. Nor do the decisions have a single solution, but more likely they have a preferential order of solutions with approximation to a so-called perfect answer. It seems, in addition, that the decisions involve a preferential judgment; i.e., a number of alternatives were offered and there was a need for choice among them, in contrast to the acceptance or rejection *in toto* of a single specified alternative. Finally, when the alternatives were compared, they were compared by most subjects on more than a single outcome or consequence.

Turning now to the substantive characteristics of the child-rearing decisions, it seems more difficult to attempt a description of their properties. We pointed out that little work has been done on this subject. In these studies, all the decisions lie within the context of the family, and more particularly within the parental role. The decisions pertain to a male child about ten years old, and the decisions should be regulated by whatever norms are operative with regard to the parent-child relation at this age. All of the normatively structured components of the decision, such as the objectives to be reached, the range of alternatives approved by society, the classes of information viewed as relevant, arise from the parental role norms.

With respect to the existence of norms for problem solving, there is only moderate agreement on well-defined principles for the solution of problems of child rearing [5, p. 19], in contrast to the problems faced in the role of the scientist or even of the businessman.

As to the other substantive characteristics, compared to decisions faced in other roles and even compared to other decisions faced by parents, the decisions we present may be of only moderate importance to the decision-maker. These are not big events in the parents' lives. The consideration of consequences seems to be limited to family members and it does not involve consideration of the ramifications through a network of extended interpersonal relations. With respect to the clarity of the elements involved in the decision, one can contrast these decisions with a typical decision in, say, economics, and conclude that attempts in the parental role to estimate desirability of outcomes, or probabilities of success or failure of different alternatives, are more difficult and subject to error. Finally, one must conclude that the parent himself is responsible for all of the phases of the decision process presented to him. This is not an organizational problem, where components of the decision process can be allocated to different individuals within the institution.

We do not expect that this delineation of formal and substantive aspects of the decisions used in our study can set rigorous limits to the generalizations from our results. Nevertheless, it will help to caution us against extending our concepts and generalizations to types of decisions which are obviously different from those with which we have been concerned.

The Evaluation and Strategy-Selection Phases

We have indicated that in our studies we were concerned with the fourth and fifth phases of the decision process: namely, those of evaluation of alternative solutions, and of selection among alternatives as a consequence of the evaluation. This means that we assumed that we adequately defined the problem for all of our respondents, that no new information was necessary for them to make an evaluation of alternatives, and that the alternatives presented were reasonable and within the realm of consideration by the respondents.

We now must consider any problems which we may have created by dealing with only a few phases of the decision process, and by presenting the other phases in standard form to all respondents. We have come to the conclusion that the major issue centers on our presenting alternatives to the respondents for their evaluation, in contrast to presenting a problem and then asking the subject to create alternatives and then evaluate them. For a while, at the beginning of our studies, we considered including within the scope of our work the decision process phase of production of alternatives. Originally, in a number of pretests we did ask subjects to name both good and bad actions in response to the problems which we presented them, and then to evaluate the actions. This turned out to be unprofitable, since the respondents seemed unable to name an alternative without evaluating it first. Hence, the alternatives which were named tended to be only the "good" ones. The evaluation which then followed was trite and commonplace, and did not indicate the true process which already had taken place prior to naming the action. We might have focused on the "producing alternatives" phase, and evaluated the solutions on their creativity or other characteristics, but we did not because we were more concerned with the evaluation process. To get the actual evaluation, we were forced to present our respondents with a standard set of alternative solutions, and to request them to make evident their evaluation processes by answering questions about each alternative.

There was a second important reason for presenting the subjects with alternatives to evaluate, instead of letting them name their own. Some of the characteristics of evaluation which we study, such as consideration of long-range consequences, or estimates of desirability of outcomes of an action, might be the result of the kind of solutions thought of by parents, rather than of their habitual evaluation processes. The only way to study individual differences in characteristics of the evaluation process was to standardize the alternatives themselves so that we could make some estimate of the typical process of evaluation, cutting across the influences of particular solutions. Therefore, we sampled opinion about the alternatives suitable for different situations and developed a set for each of the decision problems which seemed to represent an adequate range of variability, but which nevertheless controlled for the influence of idiosyncratic modes of solution. How we selected these is described in more detail in the next chapter.

Selection of the Decision Process Variables

Ten characteristics of the evaluation and selection of strategy phases of the decision process constitute the specific dependent variables in our studies. We selected those which in our judgment seem to show most promise of being significant in our understanding of rationality. Seven of the characteristics pertain to the evaluation phase and three pertain to the selection phase. The seven evaluation characteristics are those of desirability direction and extremity, probability direction and extremity, time direction and extremity, and the number of outcomes considered. The three strategy-selection variables are the number of actions selected, the degree to which the preferential ranking corresponds to the utility ordering of the alternatives, and the use of contingent and sequential courses of action. All of these are defined in Chapter 2.

We insist on retaining our skepticism about whether or not the characteristics we study actually are important components of rationality. Even these characteristics may turn out to be unimportant. Eventually it may become clear that the value placed on consideration of future consequences is simply a bit of folklore from the Protestant ethic. It may be that the statistical decision models prescribing certain modes of combination of probability and utility are in fact superfluous in the real world, and that something much simpler is all that is desirable. There is a possibility that some of the characteristics of the decision process viewed as indicative of rationality may apply to one situation but not to another. For the medieval peasant, a consideration of long-range results of action may be unnecessary, and even incapacitating. It is not that his actions would not have results, but that the results simply would be irrelevant to the satisfaction of the kind of desires which he has. Therefore, throughout these reports, when we speak of characteristics of the decision process which we have studied and imply that they are indicative of rationality, such statements always must be viewed as having the nature of hypotheses subject to validation in future research. It is still problematic whether these characteristics do in fact predict observable differences in outcomes which are agreed upon as being important to men.

However, in our work we must take the position that the variables which we study are the best candidates at the present time for characteristics of rational thinking. Some have a certain face validity; for example, the consideration of both long- and short-range consequences. Others have an exploratory status; for example, whether one takes an optimistic or pessimistic view of the outcomes of the actions which he takes. We must emphasize that given the present evidence no one of the variables we study is to be viewed as a better indicator of rationality than another. We stress this because at least one of the strategy-selection variables—namely, the ranking of the alternatives in preferential order according to their expected utility (designated later as S-scores)—is commonly viewed as being synonymous with rationality. While we recognize that this particular characteristic has this widespread acceptance as *the* definition of rationality, nevertheless this, in our judgment, is but one of many criteria of a rational process of problem solving.

In conclusion, one may appraise our analysis of the decision process and decide that we have fallen into the trap of naïvely rationalizing human thinking. But this would be wrong, because this apparently naïve rationalizing has not been done naïvely. We have decided that the approach we have used, which states a position with respect to what is worth studying, is a necessary clarification of the area of research on human decision processes. The process variables which we study are those which have been considered important to rational thinking for centuries. Current analyses continue to suggest the significance of such characteristics. True, it may turn out that the study of whether or not one considers long-range consequences, or multiple outcomes, or other such variables, is unimportant. This has yet to be demonstrated. It has seemed to us that it is only after such a demonstration that one should move on to the study of more esoteric aspects of human decision processes, and that our research, if it does little more, may suggest the degree to which this is necessary.

2

The Decision Process Test*

This chapter is devoted to a discussion of the major test used in the study. The chapter is divided into five parts: (1) a general description of the Decision Process Test; (2) a description and the scoring procedure of the evaluation phase of the test; (3) a description and the scoring procedure of the strategy phase of the test; (4) considerations of the test's reliability; and (5) considerations of the test's validity.

GENERAL DESCRIPTION

As stated in Chapter 1, we view the decision process as consisting of six segments, customarily linked into the following sequence: (1) identification of the problem; (2) obtaining necessary information; (3) production of possible solutions; (4) evaluation of such solutions; (5) selection of a strategy for performance; (6) the actual performance of an action and subsequent learning and reformulation. The Decision Process Test was designed to assess behavior in the evaluation and strategy-selection segments, i.e., segments 4 and 5. However, some of the decision process variables that we place in segment 5 are not conceptually pure. This will become evident when we discuss the strategy-selection variables.

This is a self-administering test, which takes about one hour and a half to complete, and consists of four booklets containing a different decision situation for parents. The decision concerns what action or actions the parent might take in each situation. These four situations describe a ten-year-old boy who is normal, healthy, and not in need of psychiatric assistance. The situations, each one an instance of deviation from commonly held social norms, are as follows:

Masturbation.† For some time now in a certain family a boy about

---

* See Appendix B for a copy of the Decision Process Test.

† During the course of the study, some subjects were troubled by the description of the masturbation decision. They felt that it would make a difference in their responses if the boy did not know his parents knew of his masturbatory activities. Consequently, we consistently told our respondents that the boy was unaware of the fact that his parents knew of his masturbation.

ten years old has been masturbating occasionally and in private. The parents know about his behavior.

Homework. For some time now in a certain family a boy about ten years old has been developing poor work habits in regard to his school homework. He leaves it until the last minute, and often does not get it done or does it carelessly.

Obedience. For some time now in a certain family a boy about ten years old has been very stubborn. He talks back in a rude and angry way when the parents ask him to do something, and often he refuses to do it.

*Stealing.** For some time now in a certain family a boy about ten years old has been stealing things from the local five-and-dime store. No one else knows about it but his parents.

The procedure for selecting the four decision problems was as follows: Nine child-rearing problems were selected which, on an *ad hoc* basis, seemed to represent the kind of child-rearing problems faced by parents of ten-year-old boys: sibling rivalry, honesty, religious practices, peer relations, money, obedience, health habits, work habits, and manifestations of sexuality. For each problem area we developed one hypothetical decision problem. The nine problems were then presented to 11 couples (22 individual respondents) from the upper socio-economic levels. These subjects were asked to state the actions they would take to solve these problems and the outcomes they believed would result from such actions. The responses were analyzed in terms of a series of categories, which included degree of affect or involvement in the problem, perception of own "potency" in handling the problem, whether or not the solution reflected normative clarity and the like. In selecting the problems to be used in the actual study, we attempted to maximize the differences in affect, "potency," and clarity by choosing those problems that best represented variations on these variables. Our analysis resulted in the selection of the four decision problems already described. We used only four because of the limitations of testing time and the probable declining motivation of the respondents as the length of the test increased.

In addition to the description of the four decision problems, the Decision Process Test includes six actions a parent might take. The six alternatives for the four problems were determined by presenting 200 parents with the problems and asking them to indicate two "good" things, two "bad" things, and two "neutral" things they would do if actually faced with this situation. As many as six actions appeared in each category,

---

* Two points should be noted with respect to the description of the stealing decision situation. First, in the stealing problem, the researcher made it clear to all subjects that the boy is aware of the fact that his parents know of his behavior. Also, the attention of all subjects was called to the fact that whereas the boy has been stealing for some time, the parents had discovered it only recently.

reflecting a wide range of solutions to each problem. We then selected the two most frequently mentioned items in the three categories and used these as our alternative actions. A total of six were used, in part because of the limits of time and subject interest, and also because this does not exceed the known span of comparability [14].

The six alternatives were presented in their respective booklets in the following randomly determined order.

Masturbation:
1. Interest him in other things such as hobbies, sports, and so on.
2. Tell him it is a dirty and shameful practice.
3. Explain the facts about sex to the boy.
4. Punish him in some way.
5. Give the boy more affection.
6. Ignore it; do nothing about it.

Homework:
1. Set a definite time each day for the boy to do his homework.
2. Ignore it; do nothing about it.
3. Help him with his homework.
4. Physically punish the boy if he doesn't do his homework.
5. Check each day to make sure if he has done his homework.
6. Explain the importance of developing good work habits.

Obedience:
1. Physically punish the boy when he refuses to do what you tell him.
2. Explain to the boy that there are certain things children must learn to do, and that it is the parents' job to make sure he does them.
3. Talk back to him in a rude and angry way.
4. Ignore it; do nothing about it.
5. Tell him that he will never get along with people if he keeps acting this way.
6. Forbid him to do things he likes when he disobeys.

Stealing:
1. Ignore it; do nothing about it.
2. Explain the end results of crime, and point out that "crime does not pay."
3. Spend more time with the boy and do more things together.
4. Threaten the boy with telling the police if he does it again.
5. Make the boy take back the stolen things to the store manager, and make the boy pay out of his own money for any that can't be returned.
6. Deprive the boy of television and movies for a month.

For each action (in each decision problem), the subject is required to write out the results he believes will occur if this action is taken. Space is provided for three results for the alternative courses of action, and the subject is required to write in at least one result. Having written his results, the subject then does three things: (1) estimates, on a five-point scale, how much he would like each of the indicated results to happen (desirability) ; (2) estimates, also on a five-point scale, the likelihood that the results will happen (subjective probability) ; and (3) estimates, again on a five-point scale, when he believes the results will happen (time orientation).

After evaluating the six actions in the preceding terms, the subject is then asked to rank them in order from the best to the worst action a parent might take. In addition, he is asked to indicate which action, or actions, he would take if actually faced with this situation. Finally, if he selects more than one action, he is asked whether or not the actions are to be performed in an ordered sequence. If the actions are to be performed in an ordered sequence, the subject is asked to indicate whether such actions have a contingency relation to each other, i.e., whether an action should be performed only if a prior selected act succeeds or fails.

Thus the test provides measures on several characteristics of the decision process. These characteristics have been divided into two general classes: *evaluation variables* and *strategy-selection variables*. The first class refers to the fourth phase in our conception of the decision process. i.e., the evaluation of alternative courses of action ; the second class deals primarily with the fifth phase of this process, i.e., the selection of a strategy for performance.

THE EVALUATION VARIABLES : DESCRIPTION AND SCORING*

The following variables pertain to the evaluation phase:

Number of outcomes.—The basic measure for this variable (Item A in the Decision Process Test) is the number of results given by a subject to each of the alternatives presented. The mean number of outcomes for a given decision situation is then calculated.

Probability.—Responses to this variable (Item B in the Decision Process Test) are scored in two ways : according to *direction* and according to *extremity*. With regard to direction, the following scale scores are assigned :

Highly probable	.95
Probable	.75
About half and half	.50
Improbable	.25
Highly improbable	.05

* For both the evaluation and the strategy-selection variables the following procedure was adopted for scoring "No answers" by the subjects : (1) Where the subject had given answers to four or five of the six questions (corresponding to the six alternatives) under a given item, e.g., probability direction, he was given the mean score (based on the four or five responses) for his "No answers." (2) Where the subject gave answers to three or less of the six questions under a given item, he was assigned the sample mean (for that item) for his "No answers." This procedure was

These scores may be viewed as an attempt to "guess" at the metric based in part on the findings of a study by Brim and Koenig [2].

The extremity measure is scored along a continuum ranging from 0 to 2, with the signs neglected. Thus the responses "Highly probable" and "Highly improbable" receive scores of 2, "Probable" and "Improbable" receive scores of 1, and "About half and half" is assigned a score of 0.

For the direction measure, a mean for a given decision problem is computed as follows: Probability estimates for each outcome listed under a given alternative are summed and divided by the number of outcomes. This is done for each of the six alternatives. These six averages are then summed and divided by the number of alternatives (i.e., six). This yields a mean probability direction score for the given decision situation.

For the extremity measure, means can be computed in like manner, bearing in mind that there are no negative values.

At this point the reader may question the procedure of treating one response in two different ways, since a correlation between direction and extremity measures might in fact be spurious. However, it can be shown that the direction and extremity measures are not necessarily correlated with one another. We illustrate this by setting up four hypothetical examples of probability scores. These examples show clearly that mean scores for extremity are not reproducible from a knowledge of mean direction scores. Although the extremity score can be reproduced for any given single direction score, we use only the mean scores.

EXAMPLE 1			EXAMPLE 2	
Direction	Extremity		Direction	Extremity
.05	2		.25	1
.25	1		.25	1
.95	2		.75	1
.75	1		.75	1
$\overline{X} = \overline{.50}$	$\overline{X} = \overline{1.5}$		$\overline{X} = \overline{.50}$	$\overline{X} = \overline{1}$

EXAMPLE 3			EXAMPLE 4	
Direction	Extremity		Direction	Extremity
.95	2		.50	0
.95	2		.50	0
.05	2		.50	0
.05	2		.50	0
$\overline{X} = \overline{.50}$	$\overline{X} = \overline{2}$		$\overline{X} = \overline{.50}$	$\overline{X} = \overline{0}$

Although we have shown that the same mean for probability direction can lead to different means for probability extremity, it does not follow

---

followed with each of the Decision Process Test scores and, unless otherwise indicated, with all the other tests used in this study. For a description of these other tests, see Chapter 4.

that the two measures are always independent of one another. The degree of independence of the measures depends upon the amount of variability in the direction scores. The smaller the amount of variability, the greater the relationship between direction and extremity. The greater the variability in the direction scores, the lower the magnitude of the relationship with the extremity measure. It should be noted that what we say here also applies to the desirability and time variables, discussed below.

Desirability.—The procedure for scoring desirability estimates (Item C in the Decision Process Test) is similar to the method used with probability in that both *direction* and *extremity* scores can be derived from the raw data. For direction, the following scale scores are assigned:

Strongly desire	+2
Desire	+1
Don't care either way	0
Do not desire	−1
Strongly do not desire	−2

The extremity measure is determined in precisely the same way as in the case of probability; i.e., "Strongly desire" and "Strongly do not desire" receive scores of 2, "Desire" and "Do not desire" receive scores of 1, and "Do not care either way" is assigned a score of 0. Again, as in the case of probability, means are computed for both direction and extremity across all outcomes for six alternatives associated with a given decision situation.

Time orientation.—Scores are obtained from the subject's estimate of when the results he lists will begin to happen (Item D in the Decision Process Test). As with the previous two variables, both the *direction* and *extremity* of the estimates can be computed. For direction, the following scores are assigned:

Within a week	5
A week to six months	4
Six months to a year	3
One year to five years	2
Five years or more	1

For extremity a 0-to-2 range is again employed. Thus, "Within a week" and "Five years or more" receive scores of 2, "A week to six months" and "One year to five years" receive scores of 1, and "Six months to a year" is assigned a score of 0. Means for both measures are computed in the manner described for the probability and desirability variables.

This scoring procedure fails to deal with results that occur fairly rapidly but whose effect continues over a long period. In the course of the study, this seemed to bother some of our subjects, who felt that the way the question was worded limited the kind of response they could make. This restriction on the meaning of time orientation may be an important limitation to the Decision Process Test, even though the other major aspects of time orientation were captured by the item used.

Expected utility index.—The basic proposition underlying the test is that in deciding between alternative courses of action, the outcomes of which have probabilities of occurrence between 0 and 1, a person will choose the alternative he perceives as yielding maximal satisfaction; i.e., he chooses from among the set of alternatives as if to maximize expected utility [4, 13, 20].

Expected utility is defined as follows: For each outcome listed by a given subject, one multiplies his probability direction score by his desirability direction (utility) score; the resulting products are then summed across the outcomes associated with a given alternative to yield the subject's expected utility value for that alternative. This means we must calculate every subject's expected utility value for each of the six alternatives in all four situations. For example, suppose a given subject writes in two outcomes for the first alternative in the masturbation situation. Suppose, further, that he considers both to be strongly desirable outcomes and very likely to occur. Under these conditions, we would compute his expected utility for this alternative as

$$E = (.95) \quad (2) + (.95) \quad (2) = 3.80.$$

Next we compute similar values for each of the other five alternatives in the masturbation situation; thus we have six expected utility values for our subject. The procedure is repeated in each of the other three decision situations.

One final point: Since some of the desirability estimates are assigned negative scores, it is possible for a subject to have a negative expected utility value for a given alternative. This seems reasonable, for it means the subject sees more dissatisfaction than satisfaction accruing to him from performance of that alternative.

We can introduce the time-orientation variable into the computation of expected utility. This constitutes an extension and modification of the concept of expected utility—which, in its original form, was taken directly from formal decision theory (e.g., [13]). The rationale for including the time variable utilizes the thinking and empirical findings of over a decade of social science research [1, 9, 11, 15, 18].

In examining the role of time orientation in social behavior, investigators (e.g., [1, 18]) have concluded that persons tend to choose between alternative courses of action in such a way that satisfaction will be forthcoming with the least possible delay; i.e., people select the means to a goal that seems to be the temporally most direct. This is not to say that persons are incapable of postponing immediate gratification to obtain a larger delayed gratification; however, given the choice of two or more paths to a goal, the person will tend to choose the one that yields "reinforcement" with the least delay in time. While such propositions are open to a variety of criticisms and qualifications, they are directly testable in empirical studies. It is with this end in view that we have introduced the time-orientation variable into the Decision Process Test.

It is assumed, therefore, that given two outcomes with the same expected utility, the subject will prefer the most readily attainable goal providing, of course, that his expected utility values are positive. On the other hand, when his expected utility values are negative, it is assumed that he will choose that outcome which is *not* most readily attained. Stated somewhat differently, the more readily accessible a negative outcome is, the less it will be preferred by the subject.

On the basis of the foregoing, a modified expected utility value, designated E', has been developed. This index is computed by multiplying the subject's probability, desirability, and time-orientation scores for each outcome he lists for a given alternative. If more than one outcome is listed, the products are summed across the outcomes. If, in the previous example, the subject had indicated that he believed both outcomes would begin to happen "Within a week," the E' for that alternative would be calculated as follows:

$$E' = (.95) \quad (2) \quad (5) + (.95) \quad (2) \quad (5) = 19.$$

As before, this procedure is repeated with every subject for each alternative in the four decision situations.

THE STRATEGY-SELECTION VARIABLES:
DESCRIPTION AND SCORING

In the strategy-selection phase of the Decision Process Test, the primary concern is with the characteristics of the subject's process of selecting actions from among those he has evaluated. There are four major procedures for scoring this phase of the decision process: (1) ranking the actions; (2) selecting the best action or actions; (3) relating the expected utility values (and E') to the ranking; and (4) the multiple, sequential, and contingency aspects of the choice of actions.

Before we go on to a discussion of each of these topics, a word must be said on the place of the strategy-selection variables in our conception of the decision process. It will be recalled that the strategy-selection variables were intended to correspond to a particular phase of the decision process, the selection of strategy for performance. Actually, the four variables composing the strategy-selection phase are not conceptually pure. The multiple, sequential, and contingency aspects of the choice of actions are variables that properly belong in the last segment of the decision process, the actual performance of an action and subsequent learning and reformulation. This follows from the nature of the items measuring these aspects of choice. In the questions on sequence and contingency, we are trying to find out the subjects' anticipated techniques for handling feedback; e.g., "if one action doesn't work, another will be tried." In effect, this is an attempt to measure how a chosen course of action is successively altered by feedback from the results of the chosen action. Feedback, in this sense, corresponds to what we have called subsequent learning and reformulation. In short, this means that the strategy-selection variables actually correspond to both the fifth and sixth phases of our conceptualized decision process. Initially, we had intended to measure only the fifth phase, but the unintended change arose in the course of our developing the Decision Process Test. However, the fact that we have an overlap of the sixth phase with the strategy-selection phase of the test turns out to be of small consequence because the results bearing on multiple, sequential, and contingency aspects of the choice of actions were of little value.

Let us return to a consideration of the four major phases of the strategy-selection aspect of the test.

1. *Ranking the actions.*—The subject is required to rank the six alternatives associated with a given decision situation from the single best action to the single worst action a parent might take. Scoring involves recording this preferential ranking so that it may be used for purposes of comparison with the E (expected utility) and E' values.

2. *Number of actions selected.*—This item of the test is scored by tabulating the number of actions chosen by a given subject. If he fails to select any of the six actions associated with a given decision situation, it is necessary to tabulate whether this is due to his inability to decide or to his rejection of the alternatives offered. Space is provided for the subject to check which of these possibilities apply to him.

3. *Relation of expected utility to the ranking.*—It was noted in our discussion of the computation of expected utility that the basic proposition underlying the test assumes that in deciding between alternative courses of action, the outcomes of which have probabilities of occurrence between 0 and 1, the subject chooses the alternative he perceives as yielding maximal satisfaction; i.e., he chooses among the set of alternatives as if to maximize expected utility. In addition, it is assumed that the subject's *rank order* of alternatives will agree with the *rank order* based on his expected utility values; i.e., the alternative with the highest expected utility will be ranked first, the alternative with the next highest expected

utility will be ranked second, and so on through the six alternatives. The same prediction is made for the E' values. In view of this proposed relationship, it becomes necessary to determine the degree of agreement or congruence between the actual ranking made by the subject and a criterion rank order based on his expected utilities for the six alternatives associated with a given decision situation. We can compute an agreement score for each subject that corresponds to the comparison of his actual ranking and the criterion ranking based on his expected utilities. A perfect agreement score would indicate perfect predictability of the subject's rank order on the basis of his expected utilities. However, scores somewhat less than perfect could also be treated as indicating substantial agreement between the two rank orders. It was decided that S, the numerator in Kendall's formula for *tau* [10], could serve as the measure of degree of agreement between actual and criterion rank orders.

Two reasons led to the selection of this index: (1) We needed a measure of agreement that would make it possible to determine when the relationship between the two sets of ranks should be taken seriously; i.e., when it is not a chance relationship. Since S is tabled for various significance levels, this score seemed to meet our requirements. (2) We needed a measure of agreement that also could be treated as a raw score for purposes of further analysis. Obviously S fulfills this function, and, in addition, is easily interpretable as a raw score.

The S-score (when N is equal to 6 alternatives) yields a range from -15 (maximum disagreement) to $+15$ (maximum agreement), with 0 indicating a random relationship between the two rankings being compared. Thus, we have in the S-score an index of the degree to which two rank orders are in agreement. This enables us to assess the extent to which a given subject's actual preferential ranking agrees with the criterion rank order based on his expected utilities for the six alternatives associated with a given decision situation. Accordingly, an S-score is computed for each subject in each of the four decision situations.

It will be recalled that for each decision alternative, we compute two expected utility values for each subject: (1) an expected utility value (E) based on the subject's desirability and subjective probability estimates; (2) an expected utility value (E') based on the subject's desirability, subjective probability, *and* time-orientation estimates. In view of the fact that there are two expected utility values $(E$ and $E')$, it becomes necessary to compute two S-scores, S and S', for each of the four decision situations. (The actual computational procedure is standard, and the reader is referred to M. Kendall [10] for the detailed discussion of the computation of S.) In this connection, it should be noted that when two or more E and/or E' values are tied, these tied values are given the average of the ranks they would have received if no ties had occurred. The same procedure is used when ties occur in the subject's actual ranking of the alternatives.

4. *Sequential and contingency aspects of the choice of actions.*—When subjects choose more than one action for performance, they are asked to indicate whether or not they would take the actions in some special order. Space is provided in the test booklets for the subject to indicate the type of "strategy" he would select. These responses are scored by tabulating the category that the subject selects; i.e., whether or not he indicates that the actions are to be performed in ordered sequence, and if so, whether a given action will be performed only if a prior act succeeds or fails.

RELIABILITY

Intersituational Correlations as Reliability Estimates

Examination of the Decision Process Test will reveal that it has a structural form which is designed to measure characteristics of the decision process apart from the particular substantive decision. Admittedly, the test must be given under certain conditions (i.e., with particular decision situations) that constitute the stimulus variations, which, therefore, affects the final results. However, this is analogous to the situation in intelligence testing in which an IQ test is administered under different conditions of motivation, which influence the final results but do not negate the concept of a general or situation-free intelligence.

Moreover, we have certain expectations concerning the effects of situational variations of the decision process; i.e., we expect that test performance may vary with the type of decision situation (stimulus condition) presented. This again parallels the situation in intelligence testing, in which, for example, one hypothesizes that the variations in test performance are a function of different levels of induced task motivation.

The relevance of traditional approaches to reliability will now be examined with this in mind. Since the Decision Process Test consists of four child-rearing problems, we might conceive of a universe of child-rearing decisions from which these four decision situations are a sample. This would enable us to treat the test as composed of four items, which are then split into part-tests such that the usual coefficient of equivalence (e.g., split-half) could be computed. However, a measure of internal consistency as an estimate of reliability is inappropriate, since a subject's score is hypothesized to be a function of both the decision situation (stimulus condition) and certain traits that are characteristic of the subject. Therefore, we would not expect the coefficient of equivalence to provide an accurate estimate of the reliability of our test scores.

The parallel forms approach to the estimate of equivalence is inappropriate for the same reason, namely, our conception of situational effects on test scores. This limitation also appears to hold for the equivalent forms method proposed by Thorndike [17] as well as the parallel tests approach suggested by Gulliksen [7]).

Another approach to establishing the reliability of the Decision Process Test would be to estimate the coefficient of stability by employing the test-retest approach and using the same stimulus conditions in both test administrations. Unfortunately, various practical exigencies (e.g., unavailability of the subjects) prevented us from retesting the subjects at a later date. Indeed, one might argue that it is frequently impossible to retest subjects in most social research situations, particularly when the subjects are not a "captive" audience, e.g., penitentiary inmates. Furthermore, a test-retest approach that employs the identical instrument on both occasions must be prepared to recognize and handle problems of memory, practice, and the like, which would presumably result in an overestimation of reliability.

We are thus faced with a situation in which we have data on the correlations between scores on the "same test" (Table 1)* under different stimulus conditions (decision situations), which, in turn, have been proposed as differentially affecting the test scores. The task is at least to determine lower-bound estimates of the reliability of these scores. One approach to obtaining such estimates is through intersituational correlations. The reader should note that the intersituational correlations from which we will estimate lower-bound reliability of our test scores constitute a familar situation in empirical research; e.g., they present an instance of Fiske's concept of *intra-individual response variability, Type III,* in which change in a subject's response is associated with objectively different stimulus situations and/or background situations [5].

Our interpretation of the data in Table 1 makes use of two separate but related lines of argument. The first derives from Guilford's discussion of the concept of test validity [6], in which he proposed what appears to be the limiting definition of validity: "A score is valid for predicting anything with which it correlates." Therefore, when two test scores show an intercorrelation greater than zero, the "what" that one of them measures is, in part, identical with the "what" that the other measures. In other words, these two scores share a certain amount of variance. This communality, or common factor variance, is what a test score measures in common with another test score (or scores). Under the "truth-error doctrine" of Spearman and Yule, common factor variance plus

* All tables are presented in Appendix A.

some specific variance (unique to the particular test score) make up the true variance, which is the basis of reliability; i.e., the proportion of true variance in the obtained test score variance. In the very unlikely instance of a test score that contains no specific variance, the reliability would be equal to the proportion of common factor variance in the observed test score variance. It would then follow that the reliability of a given test score would be equal to its correlation with another test score. However, since specific variance usually exists, it is perhaps more correct to state that the reliability of a given test score is equal to or greater than its correlation with another test score, i.e., its "trait validity."

If Guilford's limiting definition is applied to the intersituational relations between the Decision Process Test scores, we may say that the reliability of any of the test scores is equal to or greater than their intercorrelations with each other. For example, the variable "Number of Outcomes" (middle-class males) has a median intercorrelational value of .78, and therefore its reliability must be at least as high as this value. Similarly, the variable, S-score (individual males), has a median intercorrelational value of .08, and therefore its reliability must be at least as high as this figure. These median correlations are lower-bound reliability estimates, not reliability values in the sense of coefficients of equivalence. They underestimate the actual reliability because low reliability is but one reason why variables have low intercorrelations. They may be uncorrelated even though they are perfectly reliable. To examine this question, we turn now to a second line of discussion.

There are three basic ways in which one can generate correlation coefficients: (1) when the values of the two sets of scores are similar; (2) when the ranks of the two sets of scores are similar; and (3) when there are interaction effects, i.e., where the particular stimulus condition differentially affects test performance depending on the personality characteristics of the subjects involved. Each of these possibilities must be examined before one can conclude that low intersituational correlations reflect low reliability. It is precisely for this reason that the median intercorrelations reported in Table 1 must be viewed as lower-bound estimates of reliability. It may well be that some of the lower values in Table 1 (e.g., for the S-score) are due, not to low reliability, but, for example, to an interaction between the subjects and decision situations. To support this position, we present an analysis of a relationship that obtains between degree of manifest anxiety and the S-scores.* Table 2 summarizes the results of a 4×2 analysis of variance in which a significant inter-

* Taylor Manifest Anxiety Scale was one of the battery of tests used in the study. See [16].

action is found between the decision situation and level of manifest anxiety. Situations have a different effect on the S-scores, depending on the level of anxiety of the subject. For example, in the masturbation situation, S-scores are higher for "high-anxiety" subjects than for "low-anxiety" subjects, whereas the reverse is true in the homework situation (see Table 3).

These results, together with the line of argument which led to their presentation, illustrate the point that low intersituational correlations do not necessarily mean low test reliability. The position taken here is that the S-scores may well be reliable and that this is supported by the significant interactions found between the decision situation and the level of manifest anxiety.

Now let us consider the actual data relevant to reliability. In Table 1 it can be seen that for five of the ten Decision Process Test scores (for middle-class males) substantial intersituational correlations have been obtained. The same may be said for seven of the median correlations for the middle-class females and for six of the correlations for the group interaction subjects, also for seven of the correlations for the lower-class males and for three of the correlations for the lower-class females.

Communalities (h^2) As Reliability Estimates

In addition to the between-situation correlation values, h^2 values from factor analyses were used in estimating lower-bound reliability. In our earlier discussion we indicated that the reliability of test scores must be at least as high as their communalities, or common factor variance. This follows from a consideration of the "truth-error doctrine," from which, among other things, one may derive the proposition that common factor variance plus specific variance constitute the true variance in the obtained test score variance (reliability). Since common factor variance is represented by h^2, it follows that the *lower-bound* reliability of a test score is equal to its communality. That is, within the same sample of respondents, the correlation of a test score with a score obtained from, say, an alternate form could not be less than the test score's h^2. Note, however, that our use of h^2 as a lower-bound estimate of reliability puts our test scores to a severe test. The factor analyses on which the h^2 values are based, were carried out separately for sex and social class groups. A less severe test would have been to obtain h^2 values from an analysis performed on the total sample, since the argument of the study rests on the specificity of the situations, not on their similarity.

Table 4 records the communalities (h^2) for the Decision Process Test scores from eight parallel factor analyses: six 40×40 matrices and two 39 × 39 matrices, which included both personality and decision process variables. These matrices were used instead of the 10 × 10 matrices reported in Tables 49–53, and discussed in Chapter 6, since we felt that a more stable estimate of the communality would be obtained from a larger matrix. The analyses were carried out as follows: (1) four of the 40 × 40 analyses were performed separately on husband and wife data for both the middle-class and group interaction subjects; (2) two of the 40 × 40 analyses were carried out on husband and wife data only for the middle-class subjects; (3) the two 39 × 39 analyses were performed separately on husband and wife data for the lower-class subjects.

Table 4 presents the communalities for the Decision Process Test scores which were obtained from the factor analyses referred to above. These communalities constitute lower-bound reliability estimates for the decision process scores. For most of the variables, these data confirm reliability results based on intersituational correlations. For some of the other decision process variables (e.g., the S-score), the present analysis indicates that although they may have a low intersituational correlation, their lower-bound reliabilites are increased when their correlations with other measures are taken into account.

The reader will note that no data are presented that bear on the reliabilty of the sequential and contingency aspects of choice. Although these variables are derived from the Decision Process Test, we decided for several reasons not to estimate their lower-bound reliabilities by computing intersituational correlations. For one thing, it would have been necessary to compute different estimates for the subjects choosing two actions, three actions, four actions, and so forth. For another, if a subject failed to choose more than one action (which occurred in a number of cases), the sequential and contingency variables would not have been at all relevant. Finally, many of the subjects varied from decision situation to decision situation on whether they chose one action or more than one. This also would have necessitated several reliability estimates for each person. Since these variables were not included in any of the factor analyses, it was impossible to estimate their reliabilities by examining communalities.

We may conclude that the Decision Process Test scores show reasonably good lower-bound reliability. Although reliability estimates of the order of .50 may not be considered very high when dealing with tests of ability and intelligence for the purpose of *individual* decisions (e.g., diagnosis), they are certainly adequate for the purpose of the present study. Lower reliability estimates are more tolerable when the measures are being used for research purposes and only involve generalizations about groups "on the average" than when individual decisions must be reached as in diagnosis and vocational guidance [6, 8]. Besides, the final justification for the use of a measure rests on an empirical demonstration of its relations with other measures. Such relations are found for most of the Decision Process Test scores.

We used contrived "paper-and-pencil" tests of decision processes in order to make the data on the decision process comparable between situations and between subjects. For this reason we were unable to present the subject with a decision problem and simply say "Make a decision and give your reasons." This would not necessarily have brought forth the information or the characteristics we wished to investigate; if it had, it might not have been comparable from one instance to another.

We did not want to use subjective reports of the thinking process. The history of research on thinking shows this to be unprofitable, and a recent review by Travers *et al.* [19], points out that researchers are trying to increase the amount of observable behavior shown in problem solving. We have attempted to do this by forcing the subjects to be explicit about their evaluation of the alternatives and their choice among the alternatives.

A frequent criticism directed against paper-and-pencil tests is that they do not provide a basis for talking about behavior. In the present case, it might be argued that the Decision Process Test does not give one a basis for talking about parental decisions. It is true that we have no way of assessing the degree of congruence between the hypothetical problems and similar decision situations that actually confront parents. However, we view the relationship between the decision process scores and actual behavior in the following terms: The test provides optimum stimulation to the subjects to "think," and makes the assumption underlying many aptitude tests, which are designed to test under optimum stimulus conditions; namely, that it elicits optimum performance, but that individual differences under such conditions are highly correlated with individual differences in other less stimulating conditions.

A more specific criticism is that parental decisions involve unconscious emotional processes. The nonrational components of child-rearing decisions might emerge more strongly when parents are confronted with the behavior of their children that is emotionally distressing. Nevertheless, as Leeper [12] says, one should not restrict the meaning of thinking or decision making to any particular level of awareness or consciousness. It may be that some thinking is unconscious, in the traditional sense of the concept, but much thinking is conscious and hence worthy of study.

We do not have actual recourse to customary concurrent or predictive validity checks because they would involve some kind of behavioral criterion. That is, we have no way of assessing the relation between our subjects' evaluations of various alternative courses of actions and the alternatives they would use in *actual* child-rearing situations. Nevertheless, although concurrent and predictive validity checks are not available, we do have at hand measures of construct (trait) validity [3], that is, the relation of Decision Process Test scores to our measures of personality, beliefs, and social background characteristics. Thus if our predictions are that certain persons should have certain scores on the decision process variables, and in fact this prediction is supported, then to this extent we treat both scores as being valid. Of course if the hypothesis is not confirmed, then the source of error is difficult to locate. Either the prediction is wrong or the measures of personality are not relevant to predicting decision processes.

Data on the relationship between decision process scores and personality measures are presented in the succeeding chapters. These show that the Decision Process Test scores are related to the other measures used in this study, and therefore we have good grounds for assuming that the test has reasonably sound validity.

3

The Explanatory Variables

BASIC CONSIDERATIONS

Our studies of personality and decision processes are exploratory. They are designed to open up new areas of inquiry and to generate new concepts, not to make rigorous tests of carefully formulated hypotheses. This attitude toward our work guided our choice of personality and situation characteristics to use as explanations of variations in decision processes. We had no general theory of personality or of decisions which dictated our selection. Rather, our choice proceeded from a familiar set of assumptions which indicated that the choice should be made from several sets of explanatory variables.

First, there are variables pertaining to characteristics of the individual (his abilities, beliefs, attitudes, motives) which customarily are referred to as the individual's personality. Second, there are variables pertaining to the external, observable situations in which individuals may find themselves (e.g., being confronted with the fact of his child's stealing or refusal to do homework). Finally, there are variables which describe the momentary state of the individual resulting from the interaction of a specific situation with characteristics of the individual's personality.

Personality

Predictions from personality characteristics make several assumptions about such characteristics. One is that they are durable, or to put it differently, are relatively unchanging over time, so that a measurement at one time is a successful predictor of performance at a later time [21, 34]. We know little of how lasting such characteristics actually are, but fortunately this is not an issue in our studies because our measurement of decision processes occurs at the same time as our personality testing.

Another assumption is that a given personality variable has generality and that a measurement of it will predict behavior in many situations.

Two arguments usually are advanced in support of this view. The first is that the personality determinants of the individual's actions are so powerful that in fact external situations do not significantly influence his behavior. The other argument is that the situations an individual faces are so similar that their influence can be viewed as equivalent; i.e., situations in an individual's life span are so similar that for practical purposes any differences may be discounted. Arguments about lack of influence or the similarity of situations have been unable to stand up under the increasingly embarrassing lack of evidence that personality is constant from one context to the next [10].

The solution to the problem has been to make predictions from personality in one of two ways. The first is based on a test of some personality characteristic under study (e.g., dominance, or achievement motivation), which samples its expression in many different situations; an average is then computed, and this score is used to predict performance in subsequent situations. The second is based on a test of some characteristic as it is expressed in a specific situation almost identical with that which the researcher is trying to predict. Both procedures clearly have limitations. In the first instance what is gained in "generality" is offset by the loss of precision in predicting a given situation. In the second, what is gained in precision is offset by the loss of generality. These seem to be the empirical limits of attempts to predict from personality data alone.

In our own appraisal of personality variables we utilize both methods. That is, we use "general" tests of personality characteristics, and tests of the characteristics in specific situations as similar as possible to the actual decision process situations. Of course, these tests are not wholly satisfactory for the reasons stated above, and there remains much room for the effects of specific situations to influence the course of the decision process.

Situation

The attempt to make predictions of performance from knowledge of the situation presents some problems analogous to those of predictions from personality. In situational predictions some response is predicted from knowledge of an external (and oftentimes manipulated) situational characteristic or "stimulus variable." And, as with personality predictions, making predictions from knowledge of situations also requires assumptions. One is the assumption of equivalent individual reaction to specified situations. It is true that in earlier work, in psychology in particular, it was assumed that individual differences in reaction to the situation were of secondary importance. However, when the situational variables went beyond such things as light intensity or electric shock, and began to include the intensity of the group controls, the effects of success or failure, or exposing people to "fear-arousing" communications, to which there are very powerful acquired individual differences in reactions, then it was apparent that the equivalence of reaction assumption was unjustified.

Another assumption is that situational variables are powerful enough in their effects to override any possible individual differences in reaction to them. It has been said that if we could reduce the prevailing temperature enough, we would find practically everyone going about with his coat collar turned up about his ears. Probably, if it were cold *enough,* but the situational variables studied in social science often do not reach the level of intensity where individual differences disappear.

In our studies, we have made predictions about the effects on decision processes of certain properties of the decision situations which we employed. We assumed that some of these effects would be powerful enough to cut across individual differences in reaction and show up clearly in the decision processes. At the same time, however, we knew that personality characteristics would interact with most of the pressures of situations to produce different consequences for different individuals.

We may summarize now as follows: We have used measures of personality which estimate "general" personality characteristics from scores in several situations, and we have used personality measures which are situational or role-specific. For situations, we have tried to analyze and describe the characteristics of the situations used as predictive variables in our study, the most important being the four decision problems, and the presence or absence of the marital partner. But the measurement and use of these two sets of variables, without reference to each other, is not adequate. We need to use the concept of an intervening, momentary state, which results from their interaction.

Personality and Situation in Interaction

Historically, the analysis of situational variables has been as much a part of the tradition of psychology as has the emphasis on the individual. But, as Travers has pointed out [49], the early work in behavioristic psychology sought laws relating responses to situations, and it was not until it was integrated with the study of individual differences, which stressed enduring personality characteristics, that the modern period of psychology began.

In sociology, the division between situation and personality never reached the degree it did in psychology. It appears that from the outset most of the work in sociology stressed the relations between individuals and situations. Men such as Thomas, when postulating the existence of personality characteristics in the form of wishes or motives, at the same time stressed the need to take into account the influence of the situation [50].

What we have done in our analyses is to deal first with the direct effects of personality, regardless of the situation; second, to deal with the effects of situations, irrespective of personality; and third, to hypothesize that certain momentary states must have resulted from the interaction of these two sets of variables, and thus to look at the effects of interaction on the decisions. We cannot go beyond this at the present time, for we do not believe that the proposed momentary states are directly measurable. These have the status of hypothetical constructs whose parameters must be estimated either from some theory relating the antecedent sets of personality and situational variables to the intervening state, or by speculation about them based on the results they produce [47].

PERSONALITY VARIABLES

The actual personality characteristics we selected were chosen from diverse theoretical works. We believed all of them, however, would be related to decision processes, and it is this theme which ties together the seemingly eclectic approach. We have, for example, drawn on the research on time perspective and future orientation [11, 30, 31]. Following the leads in previous work on expectations [23, 29], we have stressed the appraisal of conscious beliefs about outcomes of actions. We relied on certain studies of decision making showing the influence of such things as probability preferences [15] and motivation [2, 4, 39]. Some of the variables are used simply as identifying or "marker" variables, chosen from previous studies of personality so that our own results can be related to them.

We have classified the personality variables we selected into three types, pertaining to abilities, motives, and beliefs. Let us now consider these in order.

Abilities

The first of our three major classes of personality variables is that of individual abilities. The relationship between intelligence and problem solving has been demonstrated in various studies to be of moderate to negligible size [18, 22, 33]. These data suggest that decision-making characteristics probably depend much more on individual differences in training, and on the effects of temperament or personality which regulate the use of various intellective factors, rather than on such factors themselves.

Our concern throughout the study is on the relation of nonintellective factors to the decision process. Nevertheless, as a matter of course we include a measure of intelligence. The discovery that measured intelligence is unrelated to the decision process characteristics studied here would be an important finding. On the other hand, if intelligence *is* related to such decision processes, then the relationship should be under control so that its effects will not confound our analysis of the relation of nonintellective factors to these same decision characteristics. We use a short measure of verbal intelligence described in Chapter 4.

Motivational Variables

In considering motivation, we begin by designating a concept of bodily tensions or energies which underlie and generate behavior. These drives in the individual impel him to act, and thus modify them to his satisfaction. We say "modification" advisedly, because as yet we know little of the degree to which subjective satisfaction involves increases or decreases in tensions. We use the concept of drive to refer to undirected level of affect.

These protean tensions become channeled and directed toward something specific, toward some state of affairs which the individual on the basis of experience has come to expect will modify the tensions in a satisfying way [26, 32, 34]. This formulation gives rise to three concepts: the individual's expectation about what are satisfying objects or events; the actual satisfying or dissatisfying object or event, which we call the goal or the end; and the tension in its form of being directed to this state, which we call the motive. Motive is thus defined as tension or energy directed toward a goal, but not such tensions in a diffuse form [3, 35].

It is apparent that we use a response-defined conception of motivation, with motives being named for the goals to which they are directed, but referring to the energy of the organism directed toward the goal. In simple discourse, the concepts of motive and goal are often used interchangeably, but this obscures a distinction necessary for the analysis of instrumental action. Our concepts must permit us to speak of the "ends which motivate us" (the goals expected to be satisfying), as well as the energies directed to them.

We now will consider the specific aspects of motivation that we studied.

1. *Level of drive.*—The first motivational variable is "drive strength," or level of affect of the subjects. We are interested in this because of prior speculation about its relation to performance in problem solving. Our level of analysis is like that of Hull [24], when he relates drive strength to amplitude of response, rather than some specific motive to some particular type of act.

(a) *Drive strength as a general trait.*—To speak of the general level of a given motivational trait such as drive implies that it is based on some averaging of an individual's behavior across a large number and variety of situations. Hull's definition of drive embodies just such an implication. He defines drive as an intervening variable determined by the summation of all extant need states irrespective of source and relevancy of reinforcement [24]. Current usage of drive (among Hullian learning theorists) rests on the assumption that the presence of this variable energizes whatever response tendencies exist in a given situation [16]. It is assumed that there are measurable variables manifesting this property of drive, and recently the most popular instrument used to capture it has been the Taylor Manifest Anxiety Scale, hereafter called the MAS [40, 42, 43, 44, 45].*

There is enough current ambiguity with respect to the relationship between drive level (as measured by the MAS) and performance so that few specific hypotheses about the effects of drive strength on decision processes seem warranted. But one proposition which seems tenable, the above notwithstanding, is that high drive level would be associated with a tendency in the decision process to make extreme judgments about the desirability or undesirability of outcomes.

In addition to using the MAS, we made one other effort to obtain a general measure of drive strength. In this we adapted a test of "general satisfaction" from another study in an effort to capture drive strength as expressed in tendencies to make extreme judgments about the desirability of different kinds of ends. A study by Jackson and Messick [27] suggests that a general tendency to like diverse things, although it might indicate response acquiescence, might also represent a capacity to relate strongly to one's environment. Others [18] also have argued that a personality trait related to "satisfaction" plays a crucial role in both cognitive and motivational processes. It was our thought that a tendency to view the world as differentiated into good and bad objects, as contrasted with its just being neutral, indicates a higher general level of drive, which in turn should be related to decision processes in much the same way as the MAS measure.

(b) Drive level in the parental role.—A role-specific conception of drive is not incompatible with the previous idea of a general level. One can speak of two individuals who differ in drive strength. For each of these individuals, also, there are social roles or other situations that arouse a greater specific drive level than do others. This is not to be viewed as a "motive," for no specific goal necessarily is involved; the goals in the situation, whatever they are, are strongly sought or rejected. The increase or

* The reader is referred to Chapter 4 for a detailed discussion of the MAS.

decrease caused by a situation is within a characteristic range of variation across situations, the mean of which is the individual's average or general drive level.

We have tried to capture specific drive level in two ways. We developed a test consisting of ten 5-item scales referring to different areas of child training. We are concerned with the degree to which the subject agrees or disagrees with certain statements about children. The test is predicated on the idea that a high drive level will result in a strong affective response, whether positive or negative. The strength of the response, not its direction, is the matter of interest. The use of this test of affect, in which responses are summed across the scales, gives us some indication of drive level with respect to the parental role area.

We have used one other measure of drive at this level, namely, the rejection factor score from the PARI [38], an inventory of parental attitudes. We employed this in part as a marker variable to tie our work to other studies of parents. It also seemed to be appropriate as a more specific test of affect. We are not concerned with the direction of affect implied in the rejection factor, that is, a rejection of the child and/or the parental role, but with the fact that rejection of this role often indicates underlying hostility. When this is unresolved it may tend to be displayed in a diffuse, undirected way within the parental role. The net result of repressed hostility toward parental role requirements, which would show up in part on a rejection scale, should be to generate a high level of affect about events of any kind occurring within that role.

Finally, we endeavored to measure affect at an even more specific level by using the ten subscale scores on the test of concern with child rearing just described. Our conceptions of general and specific drive strength lead to predictions about an individual's decision processes for any type of decision and for any parental role decisions, respectively. This even more specific level would thus lead to predictions about specific parental decisions, such as those involving a child's schoolwork, or disobedience.

2. *Desire for certainty as a motivational variable.*—We now consider a particular motive. On the basis of previous work, we conceptualized and measured a desire for certainty [20, 48]. One study [12] found that there are individual differences in strength of desire for certainty, that these differences are consistent from one test situation to another, and that the strength of this variable can be varied by frustrating or gratifying the individuals. This postulated need for certainty has analogs in other work on response set, intolerance of ambiguity, and need for cognition.

The importance of the need for certainty, so far as decision making is concerned, resides in the fact that it offers one approach to the interpretation of utility for risk, a variable which utility theory assumes to be either irrelevant or suppressed in analyses of decision making. Thus, willingness to take a risk may account for a large part of the variance in subjective probability estimates, but unless there is some way to assess these differences, this must remain an assumption. In particular, we would hypothesize that the higher an individual's need for certainty, the less likely he is to view the relations between events as having middle-range probabilities. Thus, he would tend to give more extreme probability estimates for the outcomes expected from his actions.

3. *Personality traits.*—Twelve personality "traits" were selected as being of relevance to decision making, and also as a means of relating our results to other studies of personality. While several of these are not strictly motivational variables, most seem to be of this nature, and hence all are discussed here. Nine of these variables were obtained from French's review of factor-analytic studies of personality tests [19]. Each of these had appeared in several prior studies as a separate factor. One of the remaining three variables is dominance, for which we developed our own set of items. The other two variables, orderliness and meticulousness, were selected from a study of psychosexual development [5], which found, among other things, that both variables loaded a factor suggestive of the anal-compulsive character type. In view of the supposed relationship between compulsiveness and rationality of the kind captured by some of our measures (e.g., the *S*-scores) we decided that these should be included.

We hazarded a number of specific propositions about relations of these traits to characteristics of thinking. The most important can be summarized as follows. We proposed that certain decision process characteristics, namely, the correct utility ordering of alternatives, a consideration of long-range consequences, and thinking of more than one outcome of a given alternative, are inversely related to impulsivity, emotionality, nervousness, and cycloid tendencies. This is on the assumption that "rational" decision processes require a calm, reflective person, not one who is nervous or given to ups and downs in moods. For the same reasons, we predicted that these variables would be positively related to interest in philosophizing and puzzles, confidence in one's ability to be successful, to orderliness and meticulousness, to persistence, and to preference for facing problems alone. In regard to the effects of autism on decision processes, it is generally agreed that the habit of using revery (i.e., autism) to escape from an environment which is perceived as challenging or threatening, tends to disrupt task-oriented behavior [17]. Given these views, one would not expect good solutions to decision problems, and thus we predicted that autism also would be inversely related to the kinds of decision variables mentioned just above.

4. *The effect of unconscious motivational factors.*—This section would

not be complete without a note on the way in which we deal with the influence of "unconscious motivation" of the subjects. We believe the general and important effects of unconscious motives occur through the influence of affect on the decision process, manifested in such characteristics of decisions as the improper utility ordering of alternatives, extreme desirability estimates, failure to consider long-range consequences, and other process characteristics.

If we were concerned with the content or the actual outcome of the decision process, rather than with the process itself, we would be negligent if we did not make an appraisal of the unconscious wishes of the subjects. But, for better or worse, we have studied general process and not specific content. Thus we are not interested, for example, in repressed hostility toward the spouse which may lead through displacement to a choice of punishment as a mode of discipline of the child. Instead, the important thing about unconscious motivation is that it is a powerful source of affect. This forms part of the general, diffuse, affective level which we have tried to assess in the several ways described above. We believe that our tests have captured the expression of conscious as well as unconscious desires of the individuals and have summed them up in a way which permits us to relate them directly to the decision process.

Beliefs

1. *General epistemological and instrumental beliefs.*—The third class of personality characteristics which we use as explanatory variables, in addition to abilities and motives, are beliefs. We use the concept of beliefs in a very general sense, and are concerned with two particular groups within the general class. The first group consists of epistemological beliefs, those concerned with characteristics of nature. The second group is that of instrumental beliefs, those concerned with the relations of means to ends. These issue logically from the first class, in that the former provides the epistemological framework from which the actual beliefs about appropriate behavior must be derived.

How are these related to the decision process? The evidence is thin and inconclusive, and we are unsure at the outset. For example, an experiment [39] indicates that values such as "fate orientation" have virtually no relation to variables such as degree of risk taken; yet it was found that subjects high in the theoretical and aesthetic dimensions of the Allport-Vernon-Lindzey measure of values also were those who were willing to take greater risks concerning large amounts of money. We are forced to rely on assumption, not evidence, and we assume that individuals have typical ways of making decisions. These are based, in part, on instrumental beliefs such as that it is good to consider long-range consequences, or to consider a number of actions for performance rather than just one. These beliefs in turn logically follow from one's beliefs about characteristics of the world, such as the degree of personal control one has over events, or whether the relation between events in nature is simple or complex.

We measure nine different beliefs of primarily an epistemological nature. These are grouped to represent different belief areas or dimensions. A few of these will seem new; most will be familiar because of their appearance in prior research.

Our first concern is with the degree of mastery which one believes he has over his environment. In its positive sense this can be thought of as a sense of mastery, while at the negative end the concept of fatalism seems appropriate. We endeavored to tap this belief area by a single scale, which we refer to as Belief in Fate. Other studies of this particular area of belief include Kluckhohn's [30] tripartite division of man's orientation to nature; that is, whether he views himself as being over nature, subject to nature, or one with nature. Also related is the work of Strodtbeck [41] on rational mastery, and his current work on perceived personal control. The large field study of child rearing carried on by the St. Louis County Health Department [28] makes considerable use of mothers' feelings of mastery over children's behavior. The analysis by Rainwater [37] of causes of successful fertility planning among different social classes probably is most important for our own studies because he reports some substantial differences between the social classes in their sense of fatalism.

The second basic set of epistemological beliefs is concerned with whether events occur through some natural order or whether they are caused by supernatural or mystical causes. We have two scales, one for Belief in Supernatural Causes and one for Belief in Animism. These were included because of their probable relation to fatalistic beliefs.

The third area is whether or not the world is viewed as predictable, and we measure this by a single scale on Belief in Predictability of Life. We expected this to be pertinent to decision processes in several ways. For example, in one study [25] it is indicated that when individuals are faced with a problem and believe the related events to be unpredictable, they tend to make stereotyped responses; whereas if they believe them predictable they will think more about the problem, try to solve it, and have a higher level of aspiration for success.

The fourth major area consists of beliefs about whether events which occur in the world are mostly good or mostly bad. We try to get at this domain of belief by four scales of optimism and pessimism. The optimism component can be broken down and measured by our two subscales, namely, Belief that Good Things Will Happen and Belief that Bad Things

Won't Happen. Similarly, the pessimism component is tested by the two subscales of Belief that Bad Things Will Happen and Belief that Good Things Won't Happen. We expected that these beliefs would be related primarily to desirability estimates in decision making.

The fifth type of epistemological belief pertains to the complexity of the causal relations between events in nature. We attempt to appraise the individual's view of causality by a single scale we call Belief in Multiple Causation of Events. As we state later, this should be related to the decision process variables of number of actions and number of outcomes.

We assumed that the more primitive views about the world influence problem solving indirectly through the instrumental beliefs to which they must give rise. We have appraised six beliefs of primarily an instrumental nature and one general instrumental orientation toward problem solving as a whole. The first of these instrumental beliefs concerns the emphasis which should be placed on consideration of future events, as against the past or present. We measure this with a scale we call Future Time Orientation. An orientation toward consideration of future consequences of one's actions reflects a prior epistemological view that the individual believes himself to be involved in and in part responsible for some of the outcomes and events in the world. He sees himself, that is, as having sufficient control over events actually to influence these distant consequences.

Another of the instrumental beliefs concerns the value placed on originality and creativity, and we measured this through a scale on Anti-Traditionalistic Orientation. This, like the consideration of future outcomes, seems to us closely related to a lack of belief in fatalism.

The next two beliefs are concerned with the degree of goodness or badness, and of the probability or improbability of events. The objective is to get at the individual's beliefs about the degree to which the world is an "either-or" type of environment, as opposed to one in which events are mixed blessings of uncertain occurrence. The work on probability extremity, which we appraise through the scale named Belief that Events Clearly Are Either Highly Probable or Highly Improbable, is the best known. It includes the work of Ojeman [36] on experimental teaching of probablistic conceptions of the world, and other studies of common ideas about probability [13, 14, 15, 46]. Beliefs about the value of outcomes, which we appraise through a scale named Belief that Events Clearly Are Either Good or Bad, are an attempt to extend this analysis of extremity into the area of value judgments. The beliefs should be related to the decision process through their effects upon the amount of consideration given to middle-range probabilities and to a mixture of good and bad outcomes, in contrast to extreme judgments of both in the evaluation process.

We test two other beliefs, which probably closely reflect the prior epistemological position regarding the degree of causal complexity in the environment, through a scale on Belief that Actions Have Many Consequences and a scale on Belief in Trying Many Actions in Solving Problems. In the first, the emphasis is on considering a number of outcomes of a proposed solution, rather than just the first or second that one thinks of; in the second, the emphasis is on selecting several potentially workable alternatives. Both of these should be related to the corresponding decision process variables.

The last instrumental belief is general and has to do with the value assigned to being thoughtful and deliberate in considering courses of action, compared with the value placed upon spontaneity and impulsivity. We test for this by a measure of Belief in Thinking Before Acting. The assumptions of our culture are that this approach to decisions should produce more concern with distant consequences, a more accurate preferential ordering of actions according to utility, and similar decision characteristics alleged to be indicative of careful thought.

2. *Other measures of individual beliefs.*—Two other measures of beliefs were employed in our studies.

(a) *Independence of judgment and cognitive complexity.*—Recent work on cognitive processes suggests a relation between how one solves problems and his view of the world as being complex or simple. The conception of complexity involved in these studies is defined by the scale items employed, but the more general common meaning across the studies is not clear. In an effort to make the best use of the work in this area, we utilize one such measure. In a series of studies of creativity, Barron [6, 7, 8, 9] has found that the more creative and original subjects prefer complexity and asymmetry in art, and they exhibit a clear-cut tendency toward independence of judgment in situations where group pressures are particularly strong toward conformity. For example, he shows that subjects who regularly perform in an original manner on tests of creativity also are independent in their judgments in the Asch-type conformity experiments. These "independents" also exhibit a generalized preference for asymmetry and complexity as revealed by the Barron-Welsh Art Scale [8]. This is reasonable, according to Barron, since in order to maintain his independence in the experiments, the individual must come to terms with the fact that he is suddenly at odds with his fellows in a situation where, by ordinary standards of experience, he should be in agreement with them. Only a subject who can live with complexity and contradiction, and who has confidence that an order lies behind the confusion, would be able to bear this kind of discord. An example of this type of individual would be the creative scientist who explores seemingly unresolvable areas.

In the course of his work, Barron [8] constructed a questionnaire designed to tap apparent correlates of independence of judgment. It was found that this questionnaire differentiated "independents" from "yielders" in the conformity experiments, and that furthermore, the high scorers (i.e., the "independents") also tended to score higher on the Barron-Welsh Art Scale, which is presumably a measure of cognitive complexity. The questionnaire was employed in the present study in an effort to explore the relations between independence of judgment and decision processes.

It is difficult to make any specific predictions concerning the effects of independence of judgment and cognitive complexity on decision making. From one point of view it may be argued that the more creative and independent person is likely to be more rational in his judgments. This on the assumption that such individuals are not constrained by the norms and values of their subculture, and thus they would tend to select the alternative which would yield the most desirable and most probable outcomes regardless of normative considerations; i.e., he would tend to make his decision as if to maximize expected utility.

On the other hand, it may also be argued that the more creative and independent person is likely to have a greater respect for the irrational and unconscious forces in himself and in others. To the extent that this is true, we would not expect such individuals to conform to the formal specifications of rationality, but rather to seek novel and original solutions to decision problems, particularly those problems which involve risky outcomes.

(b) PARI: dominance factor.—Use of the dominance factor from the PARI [38], like our use of the rejection factor mentioned earlier, provides a marker variable through which we can relate data from this study to other studies of parental attitudes. It differs from rejection in that the latter seems to us to be more motivational in nature. While no case is being made for the theoretical significance of the dominance factor, nevertheless it may reflect important syndromes of personal characteristics such as intolerance of ambiguity [1] which may be correlated with decision process characteristics.

SOCIAL CLASS AND SEX AS STRUCTURAL BASES
OF PERSONALITY DIFFERENCES

The next major group of explanatory variables are the descriptive characteristics of social groups: in these studies, the characteristics of sex and social class. The principle underlying their use is that individuals in the same social group will, by virtue of their prior similar experiences from birth on, have certain characteristic personalities and decision processes. This principle, demonstrated by scores of sociological studies of social class, ethnic, sex, community, and other social groups as determinants of personality, certainly needs no more than a sentence or two of explication. The early experiences of an individual during socialization, acting in conjunction with genetic influences, have a significant and apparently lasting effect upon his personality; and since social groups differ in the goals and techniques of socialization, they produce different personalities in their children as a consequence. Second, even the personality changes which occur in adult life are usually the result of participation in the recurrent social processes of education, marriage, occupation, and family role performance, all of which are tied to specific social groups. Thus, both early and late influences upon personality tend to be linked to social groups.

Our use of two social classes, and of males and females, is a deliberate effort to expand the range of variability in the personalities of our subjects. Although we anticipated a range of variation in the personality characteristics of our subjects by virtue of natural differences among them, we wanted to ensure the representation of different types of personalities by studying contrasting groups.

Concretely, we decided to study both males and females and so capture any personality differences between the sexes. This could have been done by using unrelated male and female respondents, but we decided to use husbands and their wives to permit the comparison of groups with individuals noted later.

In regard to social class, we had expected sufficient variation in education, occupation, and social status within our first group of subjects (described later) to provide variability. In fact it turned out to be a relatively homogeneous group, which we felt did not maximize the variation in personality reflecting social class membership. Therefore we added a lower-class group. We chose to maximize the variation along social class lines, rather than in religion, in the belief that the differences between the Jewish, Catholic, and Protestant groups at the middle-class level were of less import than were class differences within the same religion. Since the original basic group of subjects were almost three-fourths Jewish, we selected a comparable group of lower-class origin.

There is one point, in conclusion, which must be made, and to which we will refer frequently throughout the book. The theory leading to the use of these structural variations is that they have a probable relation to personality types, which in turn may be related to decision making. Nevertheless, it is important to realize that this assumed sequence of causality running from social structure to personality, and then to decision characteristics, may in some instances not appear because of inadequacies of measurement or because of a lack of articulation between the three panels of variables, in spite of our initial theory which led to their selection. We may discover some effects of class and sex upon thinking that operate through personality characteristics which we have not measured in our studies. These effects of class and sex bypass the panel of personality variables used in our studies, and would be evident in direct correlations of social structure with decision processes. On the other hand, we must expect to find correlations of social structure with parts of our personality test battery, but where neither of these is related to decision making. In both cases, important additional information about the relation of the three sets of variables is gained.

SITUATIONAL VARIABLES

We already have discussed how the prediction of performance must take into account characteristics of situations as well as characteristics of personalities. In this section we describe how we analyzed the characteristics of situations relevant to our studies, and introduced experimental variations in them.

Type of Problem

The first important way in which we sought to vary the effects of the external situation was our deliberate selection of child-rearing problems with different content, designed to maximize differences in their effects upon the parents serving as subjects of the study. One must realize that this variation does not refer to the formal properties of the decision problems, for in Chapter 1 we pointed out that these problems all have similar formal characteristics. Thus, the variability refers to the substantive properties of the decisions, as previously discussed. In our analyses, we appraise the effects of these different problems upon decision processes, regardless of the subject's personality, and in addition we deal with the effects of interaction between particular types of decisions and the personality characteristics of subjects.

We found it difficult to select *a priori* those substantive characteristics of situations which promised to be relevant to decision performance. After considering the results of our pilot study, described in Chapter 2, we chose four problems. Our objectives, in last analysis, were to select problems that differed in the degree to which subjects felt able to handle them (referred to as "potency"); that differed in the degree to which subjects would make the same choice of solutions (referred to as "normative clarity"); and that differed in the degree to which they aroused affect in the respondents. Of course, we hoped that in addition to these three, the situations would differ along other dimensions which would influence decision processes, and which we might discover from our analysis of results.

With respect to potency, the consideration is whether the subjects have a high regard for their abilities to solve the particular problem facing them. For example, where parents feel unable to handle adequately, say, children's refusal to do homework, one would expect a less rational solution because feelings of inadequacy may manifest themselves in muddled thinking.

The dimension of normative clarity in regard to appropriate solutions refers to whether there are specified and commonly-agreed-upon "rational" modes of handling the problem. The case in which there are relatively clear-cut norms for making a decision contrasts with the case in which parents are hard pressed to find an adequate, and socially agreed upon, solution. The contrast can be exemplified by comparing refusal to do homework with stealing from a local store.

In regard to the third characteristic—namely, the arousal of different degrees of affect—the selection of the four decision problems used in the study was based in part on our belief that the problems involving masturbation and stealing would arouse high affect, compared with the problems of disobedience and failure to do homework. The probable effects of high affect on thinking were discussed earlier.

Group Decisions

The second major situational variation was to require some of our husbands and their wives to make the child-rearing decisions together, in contrast to the subjects who made the decisions alone. This situational variation is most simply described as individual decision making vs. joint decision making with one's spouse. The fact that the couples who made the joint decisions are very similar in background to the respondents who made individual decisions means that we are able to compare the decision processes occurring in these two different situations and describe the special effects attributable to one or the other condition.

We made some attempt to study variability within the husband-wife relationship for each of these couples, with respect to relative dominance. To this end we used a pair of scales from the PARI [38], named Wife's Ascendancy and Complaint Over Wife's Ascendancy, for the wives and husbands, respectively.

It seems to us that this experimental variation falls within the tradition of research on group vs. individual problem solving. To our knowledge, however, it is the first instance in which this comparison has been made with respect to the decision *process,* as opposed to "outcome" variables. And we are very sure that this is the first occasion in which true social groups have been compared with individuals on the effectiveness of decision making; any prior studies have dealt with *ad hoc* groups, composed of unrelated persons. The study describing the effect of the group context on decision processes is described in Part III of the book.

Order of and Familiarity with the Problem

The third and fourth aspects of situational variability are by-products of our use of several decision problems, rather than being deliberate manipulations on our part. The first of these is the degree of familiarity which subjects have had with a particular decision problem. It is probable that the decision situations differ in regard to the experience subjects have had with them. This provides the chance to analyze the effects of novelty ("habit," "number of previous trials," etc.) upon the decision process. Our attempt to capitalize on this possible difference between our respondents took the form of asking them for self-appraisals of their familiarity with each problem, and the degree to which they had discussed it with their spouses.

The other situational variation which resulted from our use of different problems is the order of presentation. Since we have four different problems, one can ask whether or not the sequence of presentation influences performance on the problems. We presented the problems in the controlled, patterned sequence described in Chapter 5 to ascertain whether or not their order had any effect. The results for both order and familiarity are discussed in Chapter 8.

4

The Personality Tests

In this chapter we consider the various tests and questionnaires (other than the Decision Process Test) used in the study. We will attempt, as far as possible, to describe each test according to the typology set forth in Chapter 3. However, since this procedure would necessitate treating certain subtests of a given test separately, we shall not adhere strictly to this typology. The chapter will be divided into the following major parts: (1) Tests of Ability; (2) Tests of Affect Level, which, in turn, are divided into (a) tests of drive level, (b) test of desire for certainty, and (c) test of general personality traits; (3) Tests of Beliefs; and (4) the Social Background Characteristics Questionnaire. We discuss scoring procedures and reliability in connection with each test. Issues related to the various kinds of "response set" are dealt with at appropriate points in the discussion of the tests or the results. All tests considered in this chapter are either reproduced in Appendix B, or the publication in which they originally appeared is cited.

TESTS OF ABILITY

Vocabulary Screening Test of Verbal Intelligence, I.E.R. Intelligence Scale CAVD

The characteristics of the middle-class subjects were such that it was clear we were dealing with an intellectually superior group of adults. We required, therefore, an intelligence test with an adequate upper range. In addition, the exigencies of time demanded a relatively rapid screening device. Since the screening test of verbal intelligence based on the CAVD intelligence scale developed by E. L. Thorndike and his associates at the Institute of Educational Research, Teachers College, Columbia University, meets both of these requirements, we selected this instrument as our measure of intelligence [24, 25, 26]. This screening device consists of selections from the vocabulary section of the CAVD; i.e., two words were selected from each of the difficulty levels from H through Q. Two forms were developed, so similar that the investigator could use either one. In the present study only Form A was used.

The test involves four levels of difficulty, with twenty words being grouped into four classes according to level of difficulty. The subject is required to select one word from a group of five which most closely agrees in meaning with the word presented to him on the extreme left-hand side of the test sheet.

1. *Norms and standardization.*—The reader is referred to papers by Thorndike [24], Thorndike and Gallup [25], and a book by Miner [15] for detailed discussions of age, sex, and income norms of the test, as well as Otis mental age equivalents and A.C.E. percentile values.

2. *Reliability.*—The parallel form reliability coefficient of the vocabulary screening test is estimated to fall between .80 and .85 for a population of adult American voters [24, 25]. Table 5 presents the communalities of the IQ measure for each sample included in the present study. These values provide us with an estimate of the lower-bound reliability of the IQ test.

3. *Scoring.*—The scoring of the test items involves counting the number of words correctly defined. The subject's score is this total. The numbers of the correct responses to the 20 words (from the set of five alternatives) are as follows: 4, 2, 5, 5, 1, 4, 4, 3, 3, 1, 5, 4, 1, 5, 1, 5, 3, 3, 1, and 4. High score equals a high Otis MA equivalent.

TESTS OF AFFECT LEVEL

We employed three sets of tests in this area: (*a*) four tests designed to measure drive level, (*b*) one test designed to measure desire for certainty, and (*c*) a group of 12 subtests designed to measure traditional personality traits (e.g., emotionality).

Tests of Drive Level

At the most general level, we used three tests of drive level: (1) Taylor Manifest Anxiety Scale (MAS), (2) General Satisfaction Scale, and (3) Parental Attitude Research Instrument (PARI).

1. *Taylor Manifest Anxiety Scale (MAS).*—This test consists of 50 revised items originally part of a subscale of the MMPI. It was first devised by Taylor to serve as a measure of drive level in experiments testing some of the implications of Hullian learning theory; e.g., eyelid blink conditioning [21, 22]. The items are self-descriptive, but the reader should note that the fifty items were selected because they showed a high correlation with a larger set of 65 items. As the scale is usually employed, 160 buffer items from the L, K, and F scales of the MMPI are included.

However, in the present form of the test these items were omitted because of unavoidable restrictions on time.

(a) Reliability.†—Taylor reports test-retest correlations for a variety of populations ranging from college students to Air Force personnel. All correlation coefficients are of the order of .85 [22]. In addition, Table 5 presents the communalities for the MAS for each of our samples.

(b) Scoring.—All of the items involve a two-category response scale: "True" and "False." The numbers of the items are listed below; all *starred* items are scored 2 if the subject checks "False" (anxious response) and 1 if he checks "True" (nonanxious response). The procedure is reversed for the *unstarred* items. High score equals a high degree of manifest anxiety. All unanswered items are arbitrarily scored 1.

1*, 2, 3*, 4*, 5, 6, 7, 8, 9*, 10, 11, 12*, 13, 14, 15*, 16, 17, 18*, 19, 20, 21, 22, 23, 24, 25, 26, 27, 28, 29*, 30, 31, 32*, 33, 34, 35, 36, 37, 38*, 39, 40, 41, 42, 43, 44, 45, 46, 47, 48, 49, 50*.

2. *General satisfaction scale.* — This 40-item test was designed by Dr. Dale Harris, Pennsylvania State University, to assess the subject's general level of satisfaction in a variety of interpersonal and other areas. The items are self-descriptive. The test was included in the study because several predictions relate level of satisfaction to characteristics of the decision process, e.g., the S-scores.

(a) Reliability.—Data bearing on the lower-bound reliability of this test will be found in Table 6, in which we have presented the communalities for middle-class husbands and wives. Parallel data for the remaining subjects are not available. The communalities shown in Table 6 are based on the factor analyses reported in Chapter 12.

(b) Scoring.—Each of the test items involves a three-point response scale: "Satisfied," "Dissatisfied," and "Neutral." The subject receives two scores, one based on the number of items to which he responds "Satisfied" and one based on the number of his "Neutral" responses. A high

† The MAS has had extensive use in the last few years as a general measure of drive strength. As a result, a number of studies have been published attempting to assess the validity of the scale (e.g., [10, 13, 14]). We have taken the position that the construct (trait) validity of our tests can be directly assessed from their intercorrelations with one another. This point was discussed in detail in Chapter 2. However, since there have been extensive discussions of the validity of the MAS in recent years, a word or two in this connection should be said here. In general, data on the validity of the MAS are somewhat confusing in view of the conflicting results reported [11, 12, 19]. On the other hand, it is clear that the scale does differentiate between certain groups established on the basis of various criteria; e.g., Taylor reports that the distribution of scores for psychiatric patients differs radically from that of a normal group [20, 23]. In the light of this information, as well as the data collected in the present study, we feel justified in using the MAS as one of our antecedent variables.

"Neutral" score indicates low affectivity; a high "Satisfaction" score indicates high satisfaction.

3. *Test of parental concern with child rearing.*—This test consists of ten 5-item subtests corresponding to common child-rearing areas. The assessment of parental concern is based on the extremity of the subject's agreement or disagreement with an item, and not on the direction of his responses. High extremity is assumed to indicate high affect in a given area.

Comparisons between subjects can be made on the same subtest and on the total score summed across all ten subtests. Note that comparisons cannot be made for a subject or subjects on scores from different subtests, since the items on different subtests are not comparable.

The subtests, with items, are self-descriptive and were constructed especially for the present study. It should be noted that all items apply to a ten-year-old boy.

Name of Scale	Items
Obedience	1, 11, 21, 31, 41
Sex behavior	2, 12, 22, 32, 42
Health habits	3, 13, 23, 33, 43
Honesty	4, 14, 24, 34, 44
General child rearing	5, 15, 25, 35, 45
Peer group relations	6, 16, 26, 36, 46
Religious behavior	7, 17, 27, 37, 47
Work habits	8, 18, 28, 38, 48
Sibling relations	9, 19, 29, 39, 49
Economic behavior	10, 20, 30, 40, 50

In the present study, we used only four of the ten subtests, each corresponding to one of the four decision problems: obedience, sex behavior, honesty, and work habits. In addition, a total test score corresponding to over-all parental concern with child rearing was computed, based on the sum of the subject's scores on all ten subtests.

(a) Reliability.—An item analysis on an original pool of ten 10-item scales was carried out on a pretest sample of approximately 107 husbands and wives, all from upper socio-economic levels. All items were eliminated from each scale except those discriminating the upper and lower quartiles at the .05 level or better. On the basis of this analysis the ten 5-item scales described above were retained.

Total test score (sum of ten separate subtest scores) reliability (lower-bound) can be estimated from the communalities presented in Table 5. These values are taken from six parallel factor analyses on each of the six groups. The values in Table 5 are generally in line with a reliability coefficient computed on the pretest sample of 107 subjects. By the split-half method, the total score reliability was found to be .88, corrected by the Spearman-Brown formula.

Lower-bound reliability estimates for the four individual subtests used in this study (honesty, work habits, sex behavior, and obedience) are approximated by the communalities presented in Table 6. These communalities are for the middle-class husbands and wives. Parallel data for the remaining subjects are not available. The communalities shown in Table 6 are based on the factor analyses reported in Chapter 12.

(b) Scoring. — All items are scored with "Strongly agree" and "Strongly disagree" equal to 2, "Agree" and "Disagree" equal to 1, and "Uncertain" equal to 0. A "No answer" is scored 0. Scores on a 5-item scale thus range from 0 to 10, with a high score indicating a high degree of affect in that child-rearing area.

4. *Parental Attitude Research Instrument (PARI).* — This child-rearing attitude instrument consists of a series of separate 5-item scales, only eight of which were employed in the present study [16, 17, 18]. These particular scales were selected because they attempt to measure the three general personality areas with which the present study is concerned: dominance, rejection, and relative ascendancy of the husband and wife. For clarity of exposition, we are treating all three areas under the category of drive level, although conceptually we considered dominance and relative ascendancy to fall in a residual category with independence of judgment (see Chapter 3).

It should be noted that there are two slightly different forms of the PARI, one for fathers (30 scales) and one for mothers (32 scales). The scales for the mother's form were selected because of their high loadings on the two factors which the test constructors, Schaefer and Bell, extracted in their first factor analysis of the 32 scales. The scales constituting the father's form were selected so that they would parallel the mother's form. The only exception was Ascendancy of Wife, which required a complementary rather than a parallel scale in the father's form, namely, the scale Complaint Over Ascendancy of Wife. Subsequent factor analyses by Schaefer and Bell indicate that the factors they originally extracted were psychologically meaningful; that is, these additional studies resulted in substantially the same factor structure, although a third (somewhat weaker) factor was subsequently found. Further support for our reliance on these two factors as guides in the selection of scales from the original PARI may be found in the child-rearing literature over the past three decades, which repeatedly indicates the existence of the two factors in question: Dominance-Submission and Acceptance-Rejection [17].

The items constituting the eight scales used in this study may be grouped as follows:

		Mother	Father
(1)	Fostering dependency	3, 11, 19, 27, 35	1, 9, 17, 25, 33
(2)	Marital conflict	4, 12, 20, 28, 36	2, 10, 18, 26, 34
(3)	Rejection of homemaking role	7, 15, 23, 31, 39	3, 11, 19, 27, 35
(4)	Deification	2, 10, 18, 26, 34	4, 12, 20, 28, 36
(5)	Excluding outside influence	6, 14, 22, 30, 38	5, 13, 21, 29, 37
(6)	Irritability	5, 13, 21, 29, 37	6, 14, 22, 30, 38
(7)	(Complaint over) wife's ascendancy..	8, 16, 24, 32, 40	7, 15, 23, 31, 39
(8)	Intrusiveness	1, 9, 17, 25, 33	8, 16, 24, 32, 40

(a) Reliability.—Schaefer and Bell report coefficients of equivalence (K–R 20) and coefficients of stability for all the scales on the mother's form [16]. In addition, they report item validity indices for the scales on both the mother's and father's forms, thereby clarifying the procedure that led them to the final 5-item scales. Table 7 presents the reliabilities for the eight scales of the mother's form used in the present study.

Although Schaefer and Bell report no reliability data for the father's form, an item analysis of the 30 scales resulted in a reduction of the number of items in each scale to eight. In the present study, we used only 5-item scales, taking those five which correlated highest with the total scale score [18].

In our study, we also have lower-bound reliability estimates of the Dominance score (based on four subscale scores) for all six samples. For the Rejection, Wife's Ascendancy, and Complaint Over Wife's Ascendancy scores, we have lower-bound reliability estimates only for the middle-class subjects. As with the previously discussed tests, these reliability estimates are based on communalities from a series of factor analyses carried out as part of the larger study. Table 5 presents the communalities for the Dominance score within each of the six samples. Table 6 presents the communalities for Rejection, Wife's Ascendancy, and Complaint Over Wife's Ascendancy.

(b) Scoring.—All items in the PARI scales involve a four-point response continuum: "Strongly agree" (A), "Mildly agree" (a), "Mildly disagree" (d), and "Strongly disagree" (D), which are scored 4, 3, 2, and 1, respectively. "No answer" is assigned an intermediate value of 2.5. Thus the limits of the score range for any given 5-item scale are 5 and 20. High score means that the subject possesses a high degree of the indicated attitude.

In addition to the separate scale scores, we obtained two factor scores for each subject: a Dominance score and a Rejection score. These values were computed by summing the separate scale scores for all scales having high loadings on these factors. According to the original factor analysis by Schaefer and Bell [18], the structure of these factors is as follows:

	Mother	Father
Dominance factor	1, 4, 5, 8	1, 4, 5, 8
Rejection factor	2, 3, 6	2, 3, 6

The numbers refer to the scales listed in this section. Note that in the present research, we employed only the factor scores in the data analysis, although two separate scales (Wife's Ascendancy and Complaint Over Wife's Ascendancy) were also used in certain analyses.

Test for Desire for Certainty

This test is designed to assess individual differences in desire for certainty, and has been described in detail elsewhere [6, 7]. Briefly, the test consists of 32 statements about everyday events in the following form: "The chances that an American citizen will believe in God are about —— in 100." The subject fills in some probability value for each statement. In addition, subjects indicate how sure they are of their statements by rating the response on a 5-point scale ranging from 1 (Very Sure) to 5 (Not Sure at All). The test assumes that a strong desire for certainty is expressed in two ways: a tendency to set probability estimates near the extremes of 0 to 100, and a tendency to claim a high degree of certainty that these estimates are correct. The point of maximum uncertainty therefore is set at a probability estimate equal to .50, with the subject adding that he is "Not sure at all" about this. Deviations in the probability estimate in either direction, and more assurance that these are correct, are viewed as an increase in certainty in scoring the test. Therefore, in scoring, the distance of each probability estimate from its nearest endpoint (either 0 or 100) is multiplied by the associated certainty value. The products are summed and averaged for the 32 items. By this procedure, the lower the score, the higher the desire for certainty.

1. *Reliability.*—Brim and Hoff [7] report the reliability of the Desire for Certainty Test to be .81, based on an odd-even split and corrected by the Spearman-Brown formula. The sample on which this reliability estimate was based consisted of 50 male and female college students.

Data bearing on the lower-bound reliability will be found in Table 5, in which we present the communalities for husbands and wives based on factor analyses carried out with the middle-class and group interaction subjects. No parallel data are available for the lower-class subjects. These communalities are generally low, although the "group interaction males" and particularly the "group interaction females" showed h^2's of .48 and .70, respectively.

2. *Scoring.*—We have already described the scoring procedure used with this test. The test's format made it more appropriate to discuss scoring in connection with the description of the test.

Tests of General Personality Traits

We included only one test in this category: a set of 12 subtests which, for convenience, we named Test of Personality Factors. This test consists of 12 subtests corresponding to 12 dimensions of personality that we hypothesized as being related to the decision process. The majority of items for this measure were obtained from French's review of factor analytic studies of personality [8]. Either the items were used in the same form in which they appeared in this source, or their original phraseology was slightly modified. Subtests 10 and 11 were taken verbatim from another source [1]; subtest 5 was specifically constructed for this study. Brief descriptions of the subtests are as follows:

Autism. The habit of using revery to escape from an environment perceived as threatening and anxiety-provoking.

Cycloid tendency. Alternation between periods of normalcy and depression without any external reference.

Emotionality. Highly emotional disposition often accompanied by nervous fatigue and psychosomatic symptoms.

Interest in philosophizing and puzzles. Interest in serious happenings and discussions and liking for thinking out problems for its own sake.

Dominance. Tendency to have one's own way even in the face of opposition.

Nervousness. Emotional hypersensitivity to distracting or sudden stimuli. This is distinguished from the Emotionality subtest, since it pertains to the extent of emotional reaction to a stimulus rather than to the general level of emotionality.

Persistence. Willingness to stick to a task.

Self-confidence. Confidence in one's own ability to be generally successful.

Self-sufficiency. The ability and preference for facing problems alone.

Orderliness. Great concern with the minute details of task performance.

Meticulousness. Tendency to be systematic and orderly in one's personal routine.

Impulsivity-rhathymia. A tendency to act before considering the implications of the action. Freedom from care and lack of serious-mindedness.

Name of Test			Item Numbers					
Autism	1	12	23	34	45			
Cycloid tendency	2	13	24	35	46			
Emotionality	3	14*	25	36	47	56	59	62
Interest in philosophizing and puzzles	4	15	26	37	48			
Dominance	5	17	29	41	53			

Nervousness	6	28	39	50*	66			
Persistence	7	18*	40*	51*	67*			
Self-confidence	8*	19	30	52*	68			
Self-sufficiency	9	20	31	42	58*	61	63	64	69
Meticulousness	10	21	32*	43	54			
Orderliness	11*	22	33	44*	55*			
Impulsivity-rhathymia	16	27	38	49	57			

1. *Reliability.*—Data bearing on the lower-bound reliability of ten of the twelve subtests will be found in Table 5, in which we have tabled the communalities for husbands and wives in all groups. In the case of Meticulousness, parallel data are not available for either the group or the lower-class subjects. These communalities are generally high, the only exceptions being Self-sufficiency, Meticulousness, and Impulsivity. All three show low to moderate communalities in the middle-class husband and wife data. But even there, only Self-sufficiency is consistently low in both husband and wife data. Since the Orderliness and Dominance subtests were not included in any of our factor analyses, we are unable to present communalities for these tests. It might be added that neither showed any particular relationship with the decision process variables included in the study.

2. *Scoring.*—All *unstarred* items are scored with "True" equal to 2, "?" equal to 1, and "False" equal to 0. All *starred* items are scored in reverse manner. All "No answers" are given a score of 1. High score equals a high degree of the indicated trait.

TESTS OF BELIEFS

Following the classification set forth in Chapter 3, we divide our measures of beliefs into three categories as follows: (*a*) epistemological beliefs, or beliefs about the nature of the world; (*b*) instrumental beliefs, or beliefs about the means necessary to the attainment of goals; and (*c*) a residual category of beliefs, which consists of measures of independence of judgment and of dominance in parent-child relations. We divide this section into two parts: (1) Test of Epistemological and Instrumental Beliefs (which measures our first two categories of beliefs); and (2) Other Tests of Beliefs. In the latter category, we will discuss only our measure of independence of judgment, although strictly speaking the Dominance score of the PARI also belongs here. However, for purposes of exposition we discuss this score in the section devoted to the PARI.

Test of Epistemological and Instrumental Beliefs

This test consists of 16 subtests corresponding to 9 epistemological beliefs and 7 instrumental beliefs, each hypothesized to be related to the decision process variables. The following tabulation names the subtests, with their items. Note, however, that subtests 6 and 9 represent two facets of optimism and that subtests 7 and 8 do the same for pessimism. The item with the greatest discriminatory power for each test is given in the first cycle of 16 items, the item with the next greatest power is given in the second cycle, and so on. Thus if one wanted to use 3-item scales because of time demands, only the first three cycles of items should be administered. However, subtest reliability is likely to be reduced with attenuation in test length. We have no information on the reliability of the short form, and some estimate should be obtained before it is used in research.

EPISTEMOLOGICAL AND INSTRUMENTAL BELIEFS

Name and Number of Subtest	Items and t Values				
(1) Belief in animism	9	25	41	57*	73
	(8.4)	(7.8)	(7.1)	(7.0)	(5.4)
(2) Belief in supernatural causes.	10	26	42*	58	74
	(8.8)	(7.1)	(5.0)	(4.7)	(4.6)
(3) Belief in fate	11	27	43	59	75
	(6.2)	(6.1)	(5.0)	(4.6)	(4.1)
(4) Belief in predictability of life.	7	23	39*	55*	71
	(4.5)	(3.7)	(3.5)	(2.9)	(1.5)
(5) Belief in multiple causation of events	8	24	40	56	72
	(8.3)	(3.8)	(3.3)	(2.9)	(2.8)
(6) Belief that good things will happen (OP++)	2	18	34	50	66
	(7.8)	(6.7)	(6.5)	(3.6)	(2.6)
(7) Belief that good things won't happen (OP+−)	6	22	38	54	70
	(5.1)	(3.8)	(3.2)	(2.6)	(2.4)
(8) Belief that bad things will happen (OP−+)	4	20	36	52	68
	(6.1)	(5.6)	(3.8)	(2.6)	(2.1)
(9) Belief that bad things won't happen (OP−−)	14	30	46	62	78
	(8.6)	(6.2)	(3.3)	(3.2)	(2.8)
(10) Future time orientation	1*	17*	33*	49	65*
	(8.2)	(7.0)	(4.3)	(4.1)	(3.4)
(11) Anti-traditionalistic orientation	5*	21*	37	53	69*
	(3.9)	(3.2)	(3.1)	(2.8)	(2.7)
(12) Belief that events clearly are either good or bad	12	28	44*	60*	76
	(5.3)	(5.3)	(3.7)	(3.0)	(2.8)
(13) Belief that events clearly are either highly probable or highly improbable	15*	31*	47	63	79
	(6.7)	(4.7)	(3.7)	(2.7)	(2.6)

(14) Belief that actions have many consequences	13	29*	45	61*	77
	(12.5)	(9.8)	(5.3)	(4.1)	(3.4)
(15) Belief in trying many actions in solving problems	16*	32*	48*	64*	80
	(4.5)	(4.3)	(3.5)	(3.1)	(2.3)
(16) Belief in thinking before acting	3*	19*	35*	51*	67
	(8.3)	(5.7)	(3.9)	(2.8)	(2.8)

The items constituting the various subtests are for the most part adaptations of proverbs and adages. We should, perhaps, note the procedure used in writing these items.

The authors carefully reviewed two volumes of proverbs, compiling a list of some 800 that seemed relevant to "thinking." Some were selected because they appeared to correspond to certain theoretical dimensions we felt were related to the decision-making process. Others were selected not because of any *a priori* concepts regarding the thinking process, but because they seemed to point to new conceptual distinctions. After collecting the proverbs and assigning them to various categories, three members of the research staff independently re-sorted these items. In this way, the series of proverbs were finally allocated to sixteen categories under the two major headings of epistemological and instrumental beliefs. From the original proverbs, 10 to 12 test items for each category were devised.

A final point should be noted. For a number of the *a priori* categories it was not possible to find appropriate proverbs. This meant we had to construct items for these subtest categories without recourse to formal proverbs. The following subtests fall into this category: Belief that Actions Have Many Consequences, Belief in Trying Many Actions in Solving Problems, Belief that Events Clearly Are Either Highly Probable or Highly Improbable, Belief that Events Clearly Are Either Good or Bad, and Belief in Multiple Causation of Events. The failure to find any proverbs corresponding to these belief categories may argue against their importance in human affairs. On the other hand, it is not unreasonable to assume some beliefs may have escaped proverbial statement.

1. *Reliability.*—All subtests except 1, 2, 4, and 5 were pretested on 107 subjects from upper socio-economic levels. An item analysis of the findings from this pretest resulted in the selection of five items for each subtest which showed the greatest discrimination between upper and lower quartiles. All the items selected discriminated at the .05 level or better.

Item validity indices were also computed for subtests 1, 2, 4, and 5 based on a sample of 100 subjects similar in most respects to the other

107 subjects; i.e., they were primarily Jewish, white, and from the upper educational and occupational categories on the Hollingshead Index of Social Position [9]. On the basis of this item analysis five items were selected for subtests 1, 2, 4, and 5. All these discriminated the upper and lower quartiles at the .05 level or better (except item 71 in scale 1).

Data bearing on the lower-bound reliability of 12 of the 16 subtests will be found in Table 5, in which we have presented the communalities for husbands and wives in all groups. We report the communalities only for the middle-class subjects in the case of subtest 5, Multiple Causation of Events; parallel data are not available for the group and lower-class subjects. In the case of subtest 11 (Anti-Traditionalistic Orientation), we report communalities (Table 6) based on factor analyses of the middle-class subjects presented in Chapter 12. The remaining subtests (Belief that Good Things Won't Happen, Belief that Bad Things Will Happen, and Belief that Events Clearly Are Either Highly Probable or Highly Improbable) were not used in any of our major analyses and therefore communalities are not available.

The reported communalities are generally high, although this statement must be qualified for certain subtests in the case of the middle-class sample. Thus subtests 1, 4, 5, 10, 11, 12, 14, and 16 show only moderate to low communalities in the middle-class data; however, the high communalities displayed by these tests in the other two groups compensate for this, and we felt justified in including them in all our analyses.

2. *Scoring.*—All *unstarred* items are scored with "Strongly Agree" equal to 5, "Agree" equal to 4, "?" equal to 3, "Disagree" equal to 2, and "Strongly Disagree" equal to 1. All *starred* items are scored in reverse manner. Scores on a 5-item scale thus range from 5 to 25, with a high score indicating a high degree of the indicated belief.

Other Tests of Beliefs: Independence of Judgment

The test included here consists of 22 items specially selected, or written anew from an original pool of 200 items brought together because they were thought to be related to personality variables determinative of independence of judgment in the Asch-type conformity experiments [2, 3].

The rationale underlying the particular test items has been presented by Barron [3] and can be summarized as follows: (a) Independents (i.e., those subjects who do not yield in their judgments in the conformity experiments) value creative work and are receptive to new ideas;

(b) Independents are not fond of taking orders, and do not value strict discipline; (c) Independents tend to be intraceptive rather than extraceptive; (d) Independents prefer some uncertainty, and do not respond favorably to perfection.

Employing these general hypotheses as a point of departure, Barron selected 84 items (from the original 200) designed to measure the above-described characteristics. An item analysis with 100 college students was carried out. Criterion groups were formed of high and low scorers on a measure of esthetic preference and cognitive complexity [5]. This procedure was employed because of certain hypotheses that the author had concerning the relations between preferences for perceiving and dealing with complexity (as opposed to simplicity) and independence of judgment. Comparison of the two groups showed differences on 22 items that were significant at the .05 level or better.

Barron summarizes the pattern of responses to the questionnaire items [2], showing that preference for complexity is associated with artistic interests, unconventionality and creativity, political radicalism, and a desire for change and development. On the other hand, preference for simplicity is related to a dislike of modern art, emphasis on kindness and generosity, undeviating patriotism, preference for symmetry to asymmetry, friendliness toward tradition, categorical moral judgments, social conformity, and a tendency to believe that new inventions which temporarily cause unemployment should be suppressed. For additional correlates of Complexity-Simplicity, the reader is referred to two of Barron's papers cited above [3, 4].

In a later article [3], Barron reports another item analysis of the identical 84 items, again employing the same college students as his sample. This second analysis was designed to discover which particular questionnaire items discriminated Independents and Yielders most effectively. Therefore the criterion groups consisted of 43 Independents and 43 Yielders (i.e., those subjects who yielded in their judgments in the conformity experiments). The results again produced a 22-item test, with each item discriminating at the .05 level or better. However, it should be noted that of these 22 items only six overlapped with those included in the group of items yielded by the first analysis.

The 22-item scale we used is based on Barron's first item analysis, partly because of certain hypotheses concerning the relationship between cognitive complexity and the decision process variables; e.g., subjects who prefer complexity tend to think of more outcomes for each alternative course of action. Therefore we felt that those questionnaire items which had been validated against the Complexity-Simplicity criterion would be more appropriate for the present study.

1. *Reliability.*—Barron does not report any reliability data, but the communalities for the Test of Independence of Judgment are presented in Table 5.

2. *Scoring.*—The procedure for scoring the 22 items is as follows; 2 is assigned to items 1, 3, 5, 9, 12, 14, 17, 19, 22, if the response is "True"; 2 is assigned to items 2, 4, 6, 7, 8, 10, 11, 13, 15, 16, 18, 20, and 21 if the response is "False." If the subject responds to a given item in a manner opposite to the one given above, 0 is assigned to that response. All "No answers" are scored 1. High score indicates a preference for perceiving and dealing with complexity and a tendency toward independence of judgment.

SOCIAL BACKGROUND CHARACTERISTICS

The study employed a questionnaire which provides information on a variety of social and demographic characteristics. We obtained information on the following factors: age, sex, occupation, educational background, and religion; whether the respondent is self-employed or works for someone else; number, age, and sex of his children; number and sex of his siblings and whether they are older or younger than he is; and finally, the ethnic origins of his parents and grandparents. In addition, a derived index of social position was constructed using the Hollingshead two-factor index based on education and occupation [9].

5

Subjects and Procedures

This chapter deals with the procedures involved in the selection of subjects and with methods of data collection. Selection procedures are described in the first two sections under the following topics: selection of populations; methods of obtaining respondents from these populations; methods of securing subject participation in the research; the final disposition of cases; comparision of the descriptive characteristics of the subjects.

The selection procedures are described for three groups composed, respectively, of middle-class, group interaction, and lower-class subjects. The basis for our selecting these three different groups for study was set forth in Chapter 3. We deliberately sought two contrasting socioeconomic groups, represented by the middle- and lower-class subjects; we wanted to extend the range of variation in our respondents' personality characteristics, and also to permit the expression of effects of other characteristics associated with social class that we had failed either to identify or to measure. Similarly, we wanted to extend the range of variation in the kinds of decision situations we studied by asking one group of parents, the group interaction subjects, to make joint decisions, and by arranging for another group, the middle-class subjects, to make their decisions as individual parents.

It should be noted at the outset that the middle-class and group interaction respondents were drawn from the same population, and the procedures used for obtaining them were identical in most respects. They differ only in the administrative procedures used in the collection of data on the decision process. That is, they differ only with respect to the fact that the middle-class subjects were given the Decision Process Test as individuals, whereas for the group interaction subjects each husband and wife was administered the test as a couple. Thus, while the term middle class is equally applicable to both groups, we have labeled one set middle-class respondents and the other group interaction respondents only to emphasize the fact that they were exposed to different testing situations. Except as specifically noted, selection procedures for the middle-class subjects apply also to the group interaction subjects.

The last section of the chapter is devoted to the description of data collection methods.

SELECTION PROCEDURES: THE MIDDLE-CLASS AND

GROUP INTERACTION SUBJECTS

Selection of Populations

Arrangements were made with a specific public school located in a high income area near the research headquarters in New York City to furnish a list of parents of all boys in the fourth, fifth, and sixth grades. One hundred eighty-three comprised this list. No specific theoretical considerations were involved in limiting the population to parents of boys in these three grades. The age as well as the sex of the students was controlled so that the decision problems to be presented to the parents could be standardized. However, the decision to use males in this particular age range (nine to eleven years) was arbitrary.

Beyond the general criteria used to define the original population, further limitations on eligibility for participation in the research were imposed because we wanted to eliminate the effects of as many extraneous variables as possible. All couples who reported their child or themselves to be under psychiatric care were excluded. Further, the requirement was made that in all families both husband and wife must be alive and living together. Third, all nonwhite people were excluded. Finally, all subjects had to speak, read, and write English with sufficient fluency to understand testing directions and to respond to the questionnaires. Since school records did not provide data on these variables, these limitations could not be imposed until personal contact with the subjects had been made.

Methods of Obtaining Respondents from the Designated Populations

Having secured the list of 183 parental couples, we were able to select both middle-class individual and group interaction subjects. Two steps were involved in this procedure. First, the original list was ordered consecutively by a randomizing procedure. Second, every fourth couple was removed from this randomized list. These procedures divided the original population into two numerically unequal but randomly-assigned subpopulations. Population 1 (for selection of the middle-class subjects) consisted of all parents of fourth, fifth, and sixth-grade boys attending the New York City public school after every fourth couple had been removed subsequent to the randomization of the order. Population 2 (for selection of the group interaction subjects) consisted of all couples removed from the randomized list in accordance with the second step in the procedure. Thus, three-quarters of the original population fell into population 1, with the remaining one-quarter comprising population 2.

The original population was split into subpopulations for two reasons. First, a time interval of about three and one-half months separated the testing of the middle-class subjects and the testing of the group interaction subjects. Second, the original intention was to have 72 couples in the former and 24 couples in the latter group. Thus, the original population was divided into these proportions.

Methods of Securing Subject Participation

After dividing the original population into subpopulations, we sent a letter to all the couples in both of the populations. The letter stated the purpose of the project, the role of the school in furnishing a list of names, and the like. It stated also that a member of the research staff would personally get in touch with them in order to answer any questions raised by the letter and to make an appointment with the subjects to come to the research headquarters on a convenient evening to participate in the project.

Within a few weeks thereafter, a member of the research staff telephoned each subject couple in the middle-class population. The order of telephoning was predetermined as a result of the original random ordering of subjects. Aside from the purposes of the phone call that were made explicit in the letter, we also used this situation for a preliminary screening of the potential couples. It was made very clear that couples, but not individuals, were eligible to participate. We eliminated subjects who were divorced, separated, or widowed, or if one parent was not at home for some other reason. Furthermore, it was made explicit that the interest in the research was with normal everyday problems that parents face in rearing their children, and that we were not concerned with pathological behavior problems. In a few cases, this elicited replies that the child was under psychiatric care.

As a result of the initial telephone call, the case fell into one of four categories: (1) an appointment was made; (2) there was a refusal; (3) the subject was ineligible; or (4) a subsequent call needed to be made. Follow-up procedures were made until final disposition of the case occurred.

For the group interaction population, a new letter was sent two months later explaining why these subjects had not been called earlier and outlining again the purposes of the project. Subsequent to this letter the procedure for securing participation of subjects in this group was exactly the same as the procedure we have described for the middle-class group.

In the actual testing situation, any other factors affecting the definition of eligibility were assessed. If a subject did not meet the criteria, his questionnaires were discarded. When the screening and testing procedures were completed, the respondents who volunteered to participate in the research were English-speaking, white parents of fourth-, fifth-, and sixth-grade males between the ages of nine and eleven attending a certain New York City public school. As far as screening procedures could determine, neither parents nor children were suffering from any severe emotional or physical illness.

Final Disposition of Cases

Table 8 indicates the final disposition of cases. Several things may be noted about these data. First, the subject population totals to 200 rather than to 183, which it should have according to our original statement. Second, there are only 48 rather than 72 couples in the middle-class group. Finally, three-fourths of the cases are not found in the middle-class population.

The total population exceeded 183 because at a later stage in the research 17 additional cases who had enrolled in the school after the study was under way were included in the population. They were included to increase the pool from which the group interaction subjects were selected; otherwise, it would have been impossible to meet the required quota for this group.

As for the fact that 48 rather than 72 subject couples were used in the middle-class group, the original expectation had to be scaled down owing to the large number of ineligible and unlocatable cases.

The third discrepancy, the absence of the original proportionality in the final disposition, is due to two factors. First, 16 of the 17 new cases were added to the group interaction pool. Second, after it became apparent that it would be impossible to obtain 72 couples for the middle-class group, 16 cases—still outstanding after the 48 couples from this group had been obtained—were also added to the group interaction pool.

For the middle-class subjects, the acceptance rate runs at 55 per cent; for the group interaction subjects, the acceptance rate runs at 45 per cent (see Table 8). This difference is not significant. In all probability, even this obtained difference is due to the fact that the 16 cases from the individual population were allocated to the group interaction pool. These subjects were primarily parents who were not motivated to participate in the research and who chose to delay a definite commitment. When pressed to accept participation, they refused for one reason or another. These refusals were tabulated in the results for the group interaction subjects, but they could just as well have been included in the results for the middle-class subjects.

Comparison of Characteristics of the Subjects

Comparative characteristics for the two groups of respondents are given in Tables 9, 10, 11, 14, and 15, which present data on social class, occupation, education, religion, and age. These data indicate a lack of significant difference between the two groups on any of these descriptive variables. That is, the middle-class males are not significantly different from the group interaction males, and the same is true for the middle-class females vis-à-vis the group interaction females.

With regard to socio-economic position, both groups can be characterized as being predominantly in classes 1 and 2 on the Hollingshead Index of Social Position. Table 9 indicates that 88 per cent of the couples in the middle-class group and 71 per cent of the group interaction couples fall in classes 1 or 2. The χ^2 analysis shows that the two groups do not differ in socio-economic position.

Looking at education alone, no significant differences exist. Table 10 indicates that 90 per cent of the middle-class males and 76 per cent of the group interaction males have had at least some college training. Some 75 per cent of the middle-class males fall into categories 1 and 2, indicating that they are predominantly a college graduate and professionally trained group. The same may be said of 59 per cent of the group interaction males. Findings for females are of a similar nature: 63 per cent of the middle-class females and 66 percent of the group interaction females have had at least some college training.

Table 11 shows findings on the Hollingshead occupational index as follows: 84 per cent of the middle-class males and 71 per cent of the group interaction males are engaged in rather highly trained professional and administrative work or own large- to medium-sized businesses. No significant differences occur.

As for age, Table 14 indicates considerable similarity in mean ages for both groups.

Table 15 indicates that the groups are similar in religious affiliation and that both are predominantly Jewish. There is a smaller proportion of Jewish group interaction subjects, but the difference is not significant.

Despite the fact that no significant differences between the two samples have been revealed on these basic demographic characteristics, a further check using still other variables was carried out, since comparability of the groups is crucial for that aspect of the research comparing the decision-making performance of groups and individuals (Chapters 9 and 10).

Without such comparability it would be impossible to know whether any similarities or differences between individuals and groups on decision-making charactisterics were due simply to selection bias. The possibility of bias deserves special notice, since in the section on the final disposition of cases several departures from the original method of random assignment of subjects to individual and group subpopulations were noted. Consequently, three sets of additional comparisons were undertaken, using personality variables.

For the first comparison the middle-class males were contrasted with the group interaction males on a battery of 44 personality variables.* Only one difference reached significance at the .05 level, thus indicating that males in the two groups are not different in personality characteristics. The comparison of the middle-class females with group interaction females showed only three of the 44 differences to be significant. On a battery of variables of this sort, one would expect significant differences about 5 per cent of the time on a chance basis. Since the obtained proportion is only about 7 per cent, it is concluded that no true differences exist on personality characteristics between the two sets of female subjects.

Another comparison that is important within the present context concerns male-female personality differences in the middle-class group compared with male-female differences in the group interaction set (Table 46). For the middle-class group of 42 possible differences, 14 are significant at the .05 level. That is, in the middle-class group husbands differ significantly from wives on 14 out of 42 comparisons. For the group interaction respondents there are six such differences. A χ^2 test comparing differences and non-differences for both groups does not reach significance, although it does indicate a tendency toward significance ($\chi^2 = 3.21$; d.f. $= 1$; $.05 < p < .10$). In addition we find that of the fourteen differences in the middle-class group, five are *repeated* in the group interaction set. This indicates that the *pattern* of personality differences between males and females is similar for both groups. Furthermore, with regard to these significant differences, in only two cases was it found that the *direction* of differences was opposite for the two groups. In both of these instances this occurred when the difference was significant for the middle-class group but not for the group interaction set. In other words, no case was found where a significant male-female difference for each group went in opposite directions.

In short, the comparisons reported above furnish additional evidence that the two groups are similar, and they indicate that the later research results pertaining to comparative decision processes of individuals and

---

* Values of *t* for these middle-class and group interaction comparisons are not presented. The basic data for their computation are presented in Tables 44 and 45.

groups cannot be interpreted as any function of the non-comparability of the groups.

To summarize, the males in both groups may be described as composed predominantly of Jewish, upper-middle-class, college-trained business and professional people in their late thirties and early forties who have volunteered to participate in the research. The females are primarily of Jewish background and have had some college experience. In all cases, couples had a male child in the 9–11 age range.

SELECTION PROCEDURES: THE LOWER-CLASS SUBJECTS

Selection of Populations

Arrangements were made with two community centers situated in an area in New York City with a low mean reported income, to furnish a list of all Jewish boys between the ages of nine and eleven who were registered members. Only Jewish subjects were selected in order to make this group similar in religion to the middle-class group. The decision to use parents of boys aged nine to eleven was also a consequence of the desire to make the two groups comparable.

Beyond these general criteria used to define both populations, further limitations on eligibility were imposed on the lower-class populations. These limitations were identical with the ones imposed on the middle-class group. All couples were excluded who said that either they or their children were under psychiatric care. Further, the requirement was made that in all families both husband and wife must be alive and living together. Third, all non-white subjects were excluded. Finally, all subjects had to read and write English with sufficient fluency to understand testing directions and to respond to the questionnaires. Since school and community center records did not provide data on these variables, these limitations could not be imposed until later.

Methods of Obtaining Respondents from this Population and Securing Subject Participation

The procedure just described resulted in an initial list of 125 lower-class parental couples. As with the middle-class group, all couples were first approached by letter. The letter stated the purpose of the project and the role of the community center in furnishing their names. It stated that they would be called by telephone to make an appointment and to answer any questions. Within a few weeks, each subject couple was called. The order of telephoning was predetermined by an original random ordering of the list of names. Subsequent procedures followed in exactly the same manner as described for the middle-class group: phone calls were made, and ineligible subjects were eliminated, until the final disposition of cases was complete.

After the screening procedure was completed, the lower-class group was defined as follows: All subjects were volunteers. They were English-speaking, white parents of a boy in the fourth, fifth or sixth grade between the ages of nine and eleven. Each couple was Jewish and had a boy registered in one of two community centers in a New York City area. As far as screening procedures could determine, neither parents nor children were suffering from severe emotional or physical illness.

A Comparison of the Descriptive Characteristics of the Groups*

We now turn to the comparisons of the lower-class group with the middle-class group on eight characteristics. The first five (acceptance rate for participation in the study, social position, occupation, education, and generational status) are directly related to socio-economic status, and we expect the two groups to differ on them. The relevant data are presented in Tables 8 through 12. Two variables, birthplace of parents, and age, are not as directly related to socio-economic status, and we would not expect the two groups to differ in these areas. For the last variable, religion, an attempt was made to match the groups. Tables 13, 14, and 15 provide the relevant data on these three variables.

The comparisons on the first five variables show the groups to differ significantly as expected. Table 8 indicates the final disposition of cases. The two groups differ in the percentage of their members who volunteered to participate in this research. The acceptance rate for the middle-class group is 55 per cent; for the lower-class group it is 25 per cent. These data are in line with evidence indicating that middle-class people participate in more activities outside the home, such as social and business clubs, fraternal organizations, etc., than lower-class people [1, 2, 3, 6, 8]. It is reasonable to expect that this class difference would extend to participation in a research project.

With regard to social position, the data presented in Table 9 show that the middle-class group is located predominantly from classes 1 and 2 on the Hollingshead Index of Social Position. The lower-class group falls mainly into classes 3 and 4. The data indicate that the two groups differ greatly.

Tables 10 and 11 help to specify the meaning of the difference in social position. Table 10 indicates that while 90 per cent of the middle-class

* In the description of procedures for the middle-class group, data on the final disposition of cases were presented in a separate section. With procedures for the lower-class group, however, these data are significant as correlates of social class itself. We therefore treat them here.

males have had at least some college training, this is true for only 25 per cent of the lower-class males. For the females, 63 per cent of the middle-class and only 5 per cent of the lower-class women have had college experience.

Table 11 shows findings on the Hollingshead occupational index. These data indicate that 84 per cent of the middle-class males are engaged in high-level managerial, entrepreneurial, or professional work, but the same thing can be said for only 8 per cent of the lower-class males. The great majority of lower-class males are in relatively low-level white- and blue-collar occupations, while this is true for less than 20 per cent of the middle-class group.

Another variable closely related to social position is generational status, that is, whether or not a subject is native or foreign born. Since information on this factor was not directly available from our data, subjects were divided into the following two categories: (1) subjects having at least one parent born in the United States; (2) subjects having neither parent born in the United States. We assume that those in the first category are more likely to be native born than those in the second category.

The data presented in Table 12 indicate a significant difference between the two groups. In the middle-class group 50 per cent of the males and 46 per cent of the females had at least one parent born in the United States. This is true for only 4 per cent of the males and 13 per cent of the females in the lower-class group.

While our data suggest that there are differences in native as against foreign born place of birth, further analysis of the birthplace of subjects' parents who were not born in the United States was carried out. In Table 12 we have divided the subjects whose parents were born outside the United States into three groups: (1) those whose parents were born in Eastern Europe (Russia, Poland, etc.); (2) those whose parents were born in Western Europe (Germany, Austria, etc.); and (3) a residual group of all others. The distinction between Eastern European and Western European Jews has been found useful in understanding the differing orientations and cultural heritage of Jews in the United States [7, pp. 4–23, 45–94, 493–505]. As Table 13 shows, in both groups the foreign-born parents of subjects come predominantly from Eastern Europe. Thus the ethnic origin and cultural heritage of the two groups must be viewed as similar.

Table 14, which presents data on age, reveals that again the two groups do not differ. Middle- and lower-class males are both about forty-three years old; the mean age for women is about forty.

Table 15 indicates that 69 per cent of the middle-class males and 54 per cent of the females are Jewish. However, the major analyses of the middle-class data made prior to the selection of the lower-class subjects showed only one difference, and for males only, between the Jewish and non-Jewish subjects (reported in Chapter 12). Since one of our main concerns is a social-class comparison, this intra-class similarity, regardless of religious difference, lends support to the position that the presence of non-Jews in the middle-class group is not a factor that could account for social-class differences on decision processes. In addition, the literature provides evidence that in general Jews and non-Jews in the middle class are quite similar [7, pp. 138–47, 535–50].

It is true that when selecting the lower-class subjects we could have selected four Protestants and two Catholics and thus make both groups proportionally identical in religious composition. However, it seemed wiser to keep the lower-class group homogeneous with regard to religion, and not complicate the analysis by adding another major variable which might have an influence in the lower-class but not in the middle-class group. Therefore the fact that Table 8 indicates significantly fewer Jews, proportionally, in the middle-class than in the lower-class group was expected.

The question might be raised about the necessity for the foregoing comparison of the two groups. Since we examine social-class differences in parent decision processes, great care must be exercised in ascertaining whether the selected groups are in fact from different social classes. In addition, it is crucial that extraneous variables not be permitted to contaminate other data and so render more difficult an adequate explanation of later findings. Students of social class have long recognized that education, occupation, and generational status are among the most reliable and significant indices of a person's social-class position [2, 4, 5]. The data provided above indicate that these indices (as well as the Hollingshead Index of Social Position, which is a composite of the first two indices) significantly differentiate the two groups. At the same time, owing to the similarity of both groups in age, ethnic origin, and religion, we can confidently attribute any differences in results to differences in the social position of the subjects in the two groups.

To summarize, males in the middle-class group may be described as predominantly Jewish, upper-middle-class, college-trained business and professional people in their late thirties and early forties, who have volunteered to participate in the research. The females are primarily Jewish and have had some college experience. The males in the lower-class group may be described as predominantly upper-lower-class Jews with at least some high school education, who are employed in lower white-collar and upper blue-collar occupations, in their late thirties and early forties, and who have volunteered to participate in this research. The lower-class females are Jewish and have at least some high school education.

METHODS OF DATA COLLECTION

In this section the procedures involved in the collection of data are described. Procedures for the middle-class and the lower-class subjects are essentially identical. Procedures for the group interaction subjects are different and are separately described.

Middle-class and Lower-class Subjects

The basic procedure was to have the middle-class couples come to the research headquarters and the lower-class couples come to the community center for one evening of testing. On the average, testing took about three hours, with a brief intermission halfway through for relaxation. From one to five couples were scheduled for a given evening. The subjects were seated together around tables in one or two rooms. Husbands and wives were seated apart. No communication between subjects was permitted.

Administration of the test was preceded by brief remarks thanking the subjects for their cooperation, and describing the research as a study of decision making by parents when faced with everyday situations involving ten-year-old boys. No time limit was set on any of the tests but it was suggested that about fifteen to twenty minutes was the customary time taken to complete each of the four decision problems. Shortly after they began the actual decision tests, the researcher checked to see if the subjects understood the format and questions in the tests. When additional explanation was necessary the researcher provided it.

The sequence of tests and questionnaires given to the subjects was as follows:

1. Social Background Characteristics Questionnaire
2. General Satisfaction Scale
3. Test of Independence of Judgment
4. Decision Process Test
5. Test of Parental Concern with Child Rearing
6. Vocabulary Screening Test of Verbal Intelligence, I.E.R. Intelligence Scale CAVD
7. Test of Epistemological and Instrumental Beliefs
8. Parental Attitude Research Instrument (PARI)
9. Test of Personality Factors
10. Taylor Manifest Anxiety Scale (MAS)

With respect to the Decision Process Test, which used four problems involving different situations, it was considered important to control the effects of learning and fatigue upon performance. To avoid any systematic effects upon specific decision situations, the four decision problems were presented in all their possible sequences. These sequences numbered twenty-four in all. Since there were 48 couples, or 96 subjects in the middle-class group, each possible sequence of the four situations was used four times, twice for each sex. In the case of the lower-class group, which consisted of 24 couples or 48 subjects, each possible sequence was used twice, once for each sex. The assignment of a particular sequence to a given subject was made randomly.

Nine couples in the middle-class group were unable to come to the research offices and one couple in the lower-class group was unable to come to the community center for an evening; they wanted home visits. For these subjects the administration procedure was identical with the procedure used for the couples appearing at the research offices and the community center. The investigator stayed at the couples' homes during the evening while the tests were completed, and took the tests with him when he left.

Group Interaction Subjects

All subjects, except eight who wanted home visits, came to the research offices for evening testing sessions. Only one or two couples were tested each evening. Each couple was seated together in a private room. The brief introductory remarks described for the middle-class subjects were repeated with appropriate modifications for the Decision Process Test.

The sequence of tests and questionnaires given to the subjects was as follows:*

1. Social Background Characteristics Questionnaire
2. Test of Epistemological and Instrumental Beliefs
3. Vocabulary Screening Test of Verbal Intelligence, I.E.R. Intelligence Scale CAVD
4. Decision Process Test
5. Test of Parental Concern with Child Rearing
6. General Satisfaction Scale
7. Test of Independence of Judgment
8. Parental Attitude Research Instrument (PARI)
9. Test of Personality Factors
10. Taylor Manifest Anxiety Scale (MAS)

* The sequence of instruments administered to the group interaction subjects was different from the sequence administered to the middle- and lower-class subjects. The time required to complete the Decision Process Test in this group was longer than in the other two. Since we knew this as a result of pretests, it appeared that some couples would be unable to finish all the tests during one session. It was not feasible to arrange a second session, and our only alternative was to have the few couples who could not complete all the tests take the remainder home and, when finished, send them to us. Since we had no control over the home conditions, we wanted to ensure that those tests we considered the most important be finished at the research headquarters. For this reason we altered the sequence.

The Decision Process Test was administered one booklet at a time with instructions to discuss each situation and to answer the test according to their group decision. The description of the test and the monitoring of the initial responses was the same as for the middle-class subjects. Since 24 couples were used, all possible sequences of the four tests were given, with each couple having one of the 24 sequences. To guard against the possibility that the person who actually wrote the answers would have a greater degree of control over the situation than the person who did not write the answers, the husband and wife were required to alternate in writing the answers for the four successive decision tests. Moreover, whether the husband or wife did the writing on the couples' first situation was itself alternated for successive couples.

The couples' discussion of the four decision problems was recorded. Although the recording machine was located in another room and hence was not visible to the subjects, the microphone was visible on the table, and the subjects were told, as was true, that no one was listening to the discussion. The noticeable effects of the microphone's presence, e.g., "tension," disappeared after two or three minutes as the subjects got into the discussion. The home-visit sessions also were recorded. In these cases, the researcher remained in some other room in the house, where it was impossible for him to overhear the subjects' discussions.

PART II

Basic Influences on the Decision Process

INTRODUCTION TO PART II

Here we present our findings on the effects of personality, of social class and sex, and of types of situations on the decision processes of the parents. The data come primarily from the 48 middle-class couples and the 24 lower-class couples, although at several points we introduce data from the 24 group interaction couples to clarify our interpretations.

Chapter 6 concerns the relation between the personalities of the subjects and their decision process characteristics. The major analytic technique is factor analysis, because of the large number of personality and decision process variables. Six 39- or 40-item factor analyses were carried out, one for each of the six groups of subjects. The emphasis throughout is on the relation of personality to decisions within each of the six groups. Similarities and differences for the six groups in the influence of personality on decisions are noted.

Chapter 7 is devoted to the influence of social class and sex on decision making. The primary data are differences between them on their decision characteristics. The theory is that since the groups differ in the average personalities of their members, they will differ in their average decision processes. In addition, of course, we recognize that there are effects of social class and sex on decisions that have their influence through personality characteristics other than those measured in these studies, and thus there will be class and sex differences in decisions that we cannot explain directly by reference to any personality differences we have reported. Here we have to draw on other studies and speculate a bit.

Chapter 8 is concerned with the effects of situations on decisions and with the interaction of situations with personalities. We examine first the effects which are the same for all the subjects, regardless of class, sex, or personality. With this completed, we then describe the ways in which the influence of the decision situations combines with the influence of personality, social class, sex, and the group interaction situation to produce additional effects on decisions.

6

Personality Characteristics and Decision Processes

THEORETICAL BACKGROUND

The first step in our study of influences on decision making is to analyze the relations between personality and the decision process characteristics within each of the different sex and social class groups. Perhaps it will have been apparent by now that we would be confronted with what potentially could be an unmanageable body of information about our respondents. Fortunately, the availability of modern computers makes such a situation less formidable than it was a decade ago, when studies such as this would have been difficult to do. Even so, the more than 1,750 zero-order correlations that we obtained between the personality and decision-making variables for each of the social class and sex groups clearly are more than can be handled without further data reduction.

If our research had been guided by a set of carefully drawn and sharply stated hypotheses, whose validity could be appraised by the examination of simple correlations between certain variables, then perhaps this mass of information might have been of some immediate value. However, where previous scientific work has not provided a well-organized theoretical framework, and where the approach to the research is exploratory, some method of ordering the information is needed.

Our approach was to use factor analysis, since this enabled us to classify the large number of variables into a smaller number of clusters, which tied together decision characteristics with other personality characteristics. The results of the many factor analyses, along with their interpretation, are the substance of this chapter. Before we consider these, however, we shall discuss one further analysis that was logically necessary before we could move on to the factor analyses.

Analyses of Curvilinear Relationships

Our data on the zero-order correlations between variables would not reveal the existence of nonlinear relationships between pairs of variables. Therefore we analyzed the data on the middle-class males and females for possible curvilinear relations. For both groups of 48 subjects, we placed persons into one of three categories according to their position in the top, middle, or bottom third of scores on a given characteristic. This was done separately for each of 40 variables: 10 decision process variables and 30 selected personality variables. These variables are substantially the same as those listed in Table 21, and were selected because of their probable use in the factor analyses reported later.

Taking the middle-class males as the example, we see there were 40 variables on which the score distributions had been divided into thirds. The trichotomized distributions for any pair of variables then could be cross-classified to generate a 3×3 table. We did this for all possible pairings (about 750) of variables. We then examined each of the 3×3 tables to find those in which the distribution indicated a possible significant curvilinear relationship. Those that we identified as potentially significant were analyzed by a χ^2 test.

For both the male and the female groups, there were, coincidentally, 54 significant χ^2 values. However, if the variables simply had been random numbers, we would have expected to get a number of significant results. The 54 that we found are approximately 7 per cent of the total comparisons made within each group and are close to the 5 per cent range of sampling error. Furthermore, the impression that these may not be worthy of interpretation is brought home in a striking fashion by the fact that of the two sets of 54 significant curvilinear relations in the male and the female groups, only three involve the same pair of variables. Of these, two did not have the same kind of relationships between them, and the third had no apparent theoretical interpretation.

To sum up, an analysis of possible curvilinear relationships between 40 selected variables uncovered no findings of significance. We realize that this may be as much due to the crudity of the measurements we used as to anything else. In any event, we decided it was not worthwhile to analyze curvilinear relations for the other groups of subjects.

FACTOR STRUCTURE OF THE DECISION PROCESS VARIABLES

The foundation for our analyses in this and later chapters is the knowledge of how the decision process characteristics themselves join together to form the basic components of the decision process. Once these components have been established, we shall be able to examine the way in which they are related to and influenced by other personality characteristics.

We factor analyzed the mean scores (the average of the four situation scores) on ten decision process variables. These were: Number of Outcomes; Probability Direction and Probability Extremity; Desirability Direction and Desirability Extremity; Time Direction and Time Extremity; Expected Utility; *S*-scores; and Number of Actions. It will be noted that we have omitted Type of Strategy Selection because it cannot be ordered as meaningfully on a numerical scale and hence cannot be included in the correlational analysis.

The factor analyses were carried out separately for each of five groups of subjects: the middle-class males and females, the lower-class males and females, and the group interaction subjects. In the latter case, of course, there is only one set of decision process scores for each couple. The rotated matrices for the five groups are presented in Tables 16 to 20.

The factors were extracted using Thurstone's complete centroid method [5] and rotations were carried out by the Quartimax technique [3]. For all five groups, six factors were extracted. For the middle-class and the group interaction subjects four factors were retained for rotation, while five were retained for rotation for the lower-class groups.

The ordered factor tables accompany the discussion. All variables loading ± 30 or more were included in these tables. The order of presentation and the numbering of the factors are not necessarily the same as their order of extraction; some rearrangement was necessary to group together similar factors found for the five different populations.

Group I: Probability Direction and Probability Extremity

Probability Direction and Probability Extremity form a distinctive factor in all five of the groups, and we have brought these together as Group I. In Chapter 2, in discussing the scoring of the decision process test, we pointed out that the direction and extremity measures on the probability, desirability, and time variables were not necessarily dependent, even though both derive from the same response. The degree of independence of the two sets of scores is influenced by the amount of variability in the direction score, with the correlation between direction and extremity being inversely related to the amount of variability in the former.

A look at Table 36 shows that our subjects in their estimates of probabilities of outcomes had a mean estimate of about .75, their responses falling on the positive side of the equiprobability midpoint. To put it differently, the respondents tended not to think of outcomes with low probabilities. This restriction on the variability of scores on Probability Direction of necessity results in a high correlation with the Probability Extremity measure, since only half the scale is being used.

Clearly, this finding—namely, that in the evaluation process the outcomes of actions a person considers are, on the whole, more probable than improbable—is neither unfortunate nor spurious. Instead, it is an important discovery about the kind of human decision processes we are studying here.

Group I. Probability Direction–Extremity

Variable	Loading
Middle-class Males (Factor 1)	
Probability Direction	.96
Probability Extremity	.95
Desirability Extremity	.32
Middle-class Females (Factor 3)	
Probability Extremity	.74
Probability Direction	.64
Lower-class Males (Factor 3)	
Probability Extremity	.96
Probability Direction	.91
Lower-class Females (Factor 3)	
Probability Extremity	.94
Probability Direction	.77
Desirability Extremity	.50
Group Interaction (Factor 3)	
Probability Direction	.92
Probability Extremity	.87

The final point about Group I is that Desirability Extremity loads the factor for two of the groups, although not very strongly. Nevertheless, some indication is given here of the existence of a characteristic of extremity of judgment in decision making, a characteristic which may be manifested in more than just one of the evaluation variables. This shows up later on in the analyses of the relations between personality and decision characteristics.

Group II: Desirability Direction

The first point to be made in connection with the Desirability Direction factor, which shows up so clearly for all five groups, is that it is closely related to the Expected Utility characteristic, and that these two are in fact the defining variables. Why should these two be so closely related? At first glance the answer is obvious, since the characteristic of Expected Utility is an index based in part upon Desirability Direction. This is also true, however, of Probability Direction, since Expected Utility is a product of the two; yet Probability Direction does not appear in this group of factors.

An examination of the zero-order correlations between the variables shows that for the middle-class males and females the correlations between

Desirability Direction and Expected Utility are .82 and .90, but the correlations between Probability Direction and Expected Utility are only .13 and .06. This rather startling difference is the result of the greater curtailment of range in the Probability Direction variable in contrast to the Desirability Direction variable. The former, therefore, is contributing much less to the variance in the composite Expected Utility scores, and therefore neither influences it so greatly nor is correlated to such a large extent.

GROUP II. DESIRABILITY DIRECTION

Variable	Loading
Middle-class Males* (Factor 2)	
Expected Utility	.93
Desirability Direction	.87
Number of Outcomes	−.51
Middle-class Females* (Factor 2)	
Expected Utility	.65
Desirability Direction	.51
Number of Outcomes	−.42
Desirability Extremity	−.33
Lower-class Males* (Factor 1)	
Desirability Direction	.94
Expected Utility	.91
Lower-class Females (Factor 1)	
Desirability Direction	.99
Expected Utility	.93
Number of Actions	−.33
Probability Direction	.32
Group Interaction (Factor 1)	
Expected Utility	.96
Desirability Direction	.90
Number of Outcomes	−.72
S-scores	−.59

* Signs reflected.

The second observation to be made about these Desirability Direction factors is that Number of Outcomes appears in three of the five cases, and with respectable factor loadings. In all three it is negatively related to the estimation of outcomes being highly desirable or having high Expected Utility. Is this because each successive outcome that one thinks of in evaluating a course of action tends to be less desirable than its predecessor, or is there some other explanation? We analyzed the data for the two middle-class groups to see which of these is the better explanation.

For each group separately, all of the 1,052 alternatives which had been evaluated (six alternatives for each of the four situations multiplied by 48 subjects) were divided into one of three groups: Those for which one outcome was given, those for which two outcomes were given, and those for which three outcomes were given. There were about an equal number in each of the three classes. The mean Expected Utility was then computed for the outcomes in the single-outcome group; computed separately for the first and second outcomes in the two-outcome group; and separately for the first, second, and third in the three-outcome group. This made it possible to analyze the effects of total number of outcomes, as opposed to the effect of successive outcomes.

The mean Expected Utility for outcomes in the single-outcome group is $-.10$ for the males and $-.01$ for the females. In the two-outcome group, the scores for the males on the first and second outcomes are $-.08$ and $-.38$, for the females $-.06$ and $-.34$. Up to this point it looks as though the successive-outcome hypothesis is correct. However, the data for the first, second, and third outcomes in the three-outcome-group are as follows: for the males $-.32$, $.00$, $-.54$; for the females $-.42$, $-.38$, $-.31$. Thus, in the three-outcome case there is no apparent relation between the *order of production* of outcomes and decreased Expected Utility.

The alternative hypothesis is tested by looking at the grand means for the outcomes within each of the three groups, regardless of the order of their appearance. For the one-outcome case, the values are the same as above; for the two-outcome group, $-.23$ and $-.20$; and for the three-outcome group, $-.28$ and $-.37$. Here we find a clear progression toward decreased Expected Utility as the number of outcomes being considered increases.

Having eliminated one possible explanation, we are confronted with two alternatives. The first is that individuals differ among themselves in the degree to which they think *both* of undesirable outcomes and of a large number of outcomes. The second is that situations, and/or the alternatives differ in the degree to which they elicit in their evaluation both the large number and the less desirable outcomes; perhaps some are more thought-provoking than others. We will show that the former, not the latter, is the case. The supporting data appear later but can be summarized briefly here. In the first place, Chapter 8 reports instances of situational effects on decision processes showing that Number of Outcomes and Desirability Direction are not influenced in the same way. Thus, they are not necessarily related. Second, as we report in the latter half of this chapter, we find dimensions of personality that are related simultaneously to Desirability Direction and Number of Outcomes. We conclude, therefore, that personality, not the type of problem, brings about this correlation; that is, the people who tend to think of undesirable outcomes also tend to think of several.

A third observation about the Desirability Direction factor is that Number of Outcomes does not appear for the lower-class groups, and that a real difference may exist between classes in their styles of decision making.

Finally, we should point out that Desirability Extremity does not appear on these factors except for one group, and there only weakly. It emerges in a separate group of factors. This makes evident the lack of any necessary dependency between the directional and extremity aspects of the evaluation variable, and illustrates how the two vary independently when the whole range of the direction characteristic is used, as was the case for Desirability Direction.

Group III: Time Orientation

The third group is defined by Time Direction and Time Extremity. On Time Direction, the respondents tended to think of outcomes at the more immediate end of the time scale (the category "one week to six months" was the modal category). This restricted the variability of the scale scores, causing the Time Extremity variable to be highly correlated with Time Direction. This is, of course, the same relationship we found for Probability Direction and Probability Extremity.

GROUP III. TIME ORIENTATION

Variable	Loading
Middle-class Males (Factor 3)	
Time Extremity	.93
Time Direction	.79
Middle-class Females (Factor 1)	
Time Direction	.92
Time Extremity	.88
S-scores	−.33
Lower-class Males (Factor 2)	
Time Extremity	.94
Time Direction	.91
Number of Outcomes	−.45
S-scores	−.45
Number of Actions	.32
Lower-class Females* (Factor 2)	
Time Extremity	.85
Time Direction	.80
Number of Outcomes	−.49
Group Interaction (Factor 2)	
Time Direction	.97
Time Extremity	.96
Number of Outcomes	−.30

* Signs reflected.

In this case, however, the Time Extremity characteristic really has little theoretical significance, and was included initially because of the availability of the data as a by-product of the Time Direction variable. Because of its high correlation with Time Direction, henceforth we treat it as a shadow variable, of little importance.

Another characteristic, Number of Outcomes, appears in this group for the lower-class subjects. The absence of this variable on the Group II factors was noted. Here, Number of Outcomes is related negatively to Time Orientation, to a concern with immediate consequences of actions. The same relationship appears for the group interaction subjects, although in a weaker form.

This finding parallels the earlier finding that Number of Outcomes is related to Desirability Direction. Because of our previously reported analysis of the relation between those two characteristics, we have assumed here that this relationship means not that each successive outcome one thinks of lies further in the future, but instead that among the lower-class subjects, persons who are concerned with several outcomes in evaluating alternatives are the same persons who give the greater consideration to the future consequences of their actions.

Group IV: Number of Actions

The fourth group is defined by Number of Actions. On the whole this seems to be an isolate, with no systematic ties to other decision characteristics. There is no systematic difference along class or sex lines. The fact that no factor appears for the middle-class males seems to us to be just a reflection of the weakness of the factor, rather than either a social class or a sex difference.

GROUP IV. NUMBER OF ACTIONS

Variable	Loading
Middle-class Females (Factor 4)	
Number of Actions	.53
Desirability Direction	.32
Lower-class Males* (Factor 5)	
Number of Actions	.38
Lower-class Females (Factor 5)	
Number of Actions	.48
Number of Outcomes	.38
Group Interaction (Factor 4)	
Number of Actions	.63
Desirability Extremity	.58
S-scores	.43

* Signs reflected.

Group V: Desirability Extremity

The fifth group appears only for the middle-class and the lower-class males, with Desirability Extremity as the defining characteristic in each case. Two points should be noted about these factors. First, we said in connection with Group I that Desirability Extremity appeared in a weak form for some of the groups, suggesting that Group I in part captures a general characteristic of extremity of judgment. However, for these two male groups, in contrast to the female groups and the mixed group interaction subjects, Desirability Extremity emerges as a separate factor.

Group V. Desirability Extremity

Variable	Loading
Middle-class Males (Factor 4)	
Desirability Extremity	.52
Number of Outcomes	.34
Lower-class Males (Factor 4)	
Desirability Extremity	.61
Number of Outcomes	.57

Second, in both factors Desirability Extremity is associated with Number of Outcomes. We have seen already that for the middle-class groups Number of Outcomes and Desirability Direction are associated, whereas for the lower-class groups Number of Outcomes and Time Orientation are associated. Here we see the appearance of still a third relationship involving Number of Outcomes, occurring this time only for the two male groups. We see that among males, those who think of several outcomes in evaluating an alternative also are those whose judgments of the desirability of the outcomes tend toward the extremes.

Group VI: S-scores

The remaining variable in our set of decision characteristics is the S-score, which describes the degree to which the preferential rankings of alternatives is in accord with their utility ordering. The only instance in which this characteristic defines a factor is in the case of the lower-class females. The other variables appearing in this case are the ones we just noted as constituting the previous factors (Group V) for the two male groups; however, their loadings here are low and in our judgment of little consequence.

Group VI. S-scores

Variable	Loading
Lower-class Females (Factor 4)	
S-scores	.74
Desirability Extremity	.44
Number of Outcomes	.32

The *S*-scores for the other groups, where they do appear at all, have already been mentioned. For the middle-class females and the lower-class males, the *S*-score appears on the Time Orientation group; for the group interaction subjects, it appears in the Desirability Direction group, and to a lesser extent on Number of Actions; for the middle-class males, *S*-scores do not appear at all. In conclusion, it appears that the *S*-score has only a weak association with the other decision characteristics.

Implications

We have found that the ten decision process variables combine into four clearly defined factors, plus an additional fifth factor, which appears only for males, and a sixth and weaker factor, which appears only for one group. This has reduced the original number of characteristics, and has given us an understanding of the decision process by revealing the important components, the distinctive elements, of decision making.

Since there are separate factors, i.e., since not all the variables are intercorrelated, there is no reason to believe that any one person is equally proficient in all parts of the decision process. Instead the results suggest that some people may do well in one part of the process, whereas another person will do better in another aspect.

The discovery of these several factors also is of consequence for the analysis of personality correlates of decision processes; namely, that different personality characteristics may be associated with different decision process factors. The different components of the decision process may be related to different kinds of skill, or intelligence, or training. Some, for example, may be influenced primarily by motivation, another may be tied in with attitudes toward fate, and still another may vary with intelligence.

The results show such great similarity in the four major factors for the different groups that with few exceptions we can speak generally about a decision process factor structure that is the same for all groups.*

However, the differences on the fifth and sixth factors, and also on some of the items with smaller loadings on the other factors, indicate at least some differences in the style of decision making of different groups of people. There is the further implication that the relation of personality to decision processes may vary for different social groups, because the actual clusters of decision characteristics for which the correlates are sought show some differences.

---

* The similarity is evident from inspection of the data. In addition, a technique suggested by Cattell [1] allows us to compare factors on a statistical basis. Essentially, the technique involves converting all factor loadings on each factor to standard scores. We used this procedure in comparing the group interaction subjects with the two middle-class groups on the factors. The resulting intercorrelations of the factors are all over .90.

FACTOR ANALYSES OF PERSONALITY AND DECISION PROCESSES
IN CLASS AND SEX GROUPS

Theoretical Background

In this part of the chapter we present the results of factor analyses of the relations of personality characteristics to decision process characteristics. In this instance there are six major analyses, one for each of our six separate groups of subjects, since we include the separate sets of personality measures for the group interaction husbands and wives, and the relation of these to the common decision protocols can be studied.

The analyses for the separate groups are *intra-group* analyses of the relations between personality and decision making. At the same time, the analyses can be viewed as six replications in which we varied the characteristics of sex, social class, and group interaction. Since the test batteries are similar for the six populations, we also can make an *inter-group* analysis, comparing the factor structures of personality and of decision processes for each of the distinct subgroups. By comparing the factors, we can specify some of the limits of generality of the findings. For example, the characteristics which strongly influence estimates of desirability of outcomes may differ between the males and the females among our subjects; or, the influence of a given personality characteristic on time orientation may differ from one social class to the next. Therefore throughout our analyses we will look at factors with an eye for both the similarities and the differences in inter-group relationships.

In the analyses we used the same ten decision process characteristics as before, and an additional 30 personality characteristics selected from the larger number constituting our test battery. We recognize that this is a large number of variables, considering our small number of subjects. In four of the six analyses, there are more variables than subjects. The dubious feeling one may have about such a situation is allayed by the fact that six factor analyses were made, one for each group, and that in these replications, much the same factors were found for each group.

We used no more than 40 variables in all because of the increase in cost and difficulty of computer programming operations for larger factor analyses (at the time these were done). We chose the 30 personality characteristics for their promise of significant relationships with decision characteristics after we had inspected the zero-order correlations between all variables in our test battery. In our judgment very little was left out that would have altered the obtained picture.

The items used in the different factor analyses were not completely identical. The analyses were done at different times, and represented different stages of our thinking. We omitted the S-score and Expected Utility variables from the middle-class analyses because they had been included in another similar investigation, which is reported in Chapter 12. These two decision process variables were included in the group interaction and lower-class analyses, replacing in the latter instances the measures of "meticulousness" and "belief that actions have many outcomes." Another difference is that the variable "desire for certainty" was not included in the test battery for the lower classes because of the time pressures of the testing situation. Therefore scores were not available for inclusion in the analyses, and only 39 variables were factored. It should be noted that all rotations were performed mechanically, no adjustments being made by hand. As a result, whereas similar factors emerged in each successive replication, the magnitudes of the loadings tended to vary. The generally clear-cut picture, however, seems to indicate that failure to adjust was not too important.

Our procedure in handling the results was first to look for similarities in the factors emerging for the six different populations and to group them together. Then we named the groups by reference to one or another of the decision process factors described earlier.

The grouping of factors that were similar for the six populations can be summarized as follows. There were eight groups; we have labeled them by the letters A through H. The first three, A, B, and C, include the factors that involve Desirability Direction, S-scores, and Number of Outcomes, respectively. Groups D and E appear to be related, and involve Probability Direction–Extremity and Desirability Extremity, respectively. Groups F and G involve Time Orientation and Number of Actions, respectively. Finally, Group H contains factors incorporating sets of personality characteristics that are unrelated to the decision processes, but emerge with such strength and sharpness, and are so similar for the six groups, that they warrant discussion.

After the similar factors for the several populations had been grouped, a number of unidentified clusters of personality characteristics remained. They have little resemblence from one group to the next, and seem to be of small significance for the analysis of personality. These can be seen in Tables 21–29. These unnamed factors for the six populations are as follows: middle-class males, Factors 4 and 7; middle-class females, none; lower-class males, Factors 6, 8, and 11; lower-class females, Factors 3, 9, and 11; group interaction males, Factors 9 and 10; and group interaction females, Factors 7, 9, 10, and 11.

We now go on to a consideration of the factor groups themselves.

Group A. Desirability Direction

The characteristics associated with Desirability Direction comprise a fundamental dimension of personality. This dimension is the first factor extracted in all six analyses, and is defined in five out of the six cases either by belief in fate or belief in supernatural causes. In the sixth factor the Desirability Direction characteristic is the defining variable.

The positive pole is characterized by the variables of belief in fate, belief in supernatural causes, dominance in child-rearing attitudes, a general optimism about the outcomes of actions, and related variables. We will use the word *dependency* to describe this pole of the dimension, and compare it with the other pole of the personality dimension which can be described as *autonomy*. This latter pole would be defined by the personality characteristics appearing here with negative loadings, namely, future time orientation, independence of judgment, belief in thinking before acting, intelligence, and similar variables, which add up to a picture of a person whose attitude toward life is one of "rational mastery" or "perceived personal control" [4]. Henceforth we refer generally to this factor as the autonomy-dependency dimension of personality.

The general aspects of this dimension of personality are easily grasped, but some of the characteristics of the dependency end of the dimension require further interpretation. The appearance of the PARI dominance factor score with dependency variables leads to a review of the items in scales comprising the factor score (see Chapter 4 for discussion of the PARI, and Appendix B). Most of the items are expressions of attitudes lying along the autonomy-dependency dimension, but expressed in the form of prescriptions for autonomous or dependent behavior in children. A high dominance score says the parent believes that children should be dependent and submissive, a low score indicates that the parent believes that children should be independent and autonomous. Our results show that parents expect in their children's behavior a representation of the same philosophy of life which they, the parents, already possess. The autonomous person permits and encourages autonomy in his child. The parent scoring high in dominance is a parent who is submissive and dependent upon forces superior to him, and believes children should be the same. Thus, we see that child-rearing attitudes are consistent with other parts of the parents' personalities.

The two belief scales—the beliefs that "good things will happen" and that "bad things won't happen"—fall at the dependency pole of the factor. The decision factors of Desirability Direction and Expected Utility also are associated with dependency. How is one to account for this relation between "optimism" in both attitude and actual decision processes and a belief in fate, supernatural powers, and related variables? There is no reason to believe that life's circumstances really are happier, more to be desired, for persons scoring high in dependency. In fact, their perceptions of themselves as lacking control over their destinies suggest that, if anything, they are not able to achieve what they desire. Therefore we must view their optimism as "defensive." That is, their dependency on other people must cause anxiety, even fear, about events in the offing over which they have little control. This anxiety is allayed by an attitude that everything is all right, that whatever happens, it works out for the best. The optimism and the dependency fuse together into a nervous, rather than child-like, trust in a beneficent destiny.

In addition to the appearance of the Desirability Direction decision characteristic in this major personality factor, for some groups the decision characteristics of Number of Outcomes and the S-scores also appear. Number of Outcomes, of course, has shown up as part of the Desirability Direction decision factor in the earlier analyses, and so is not unexpected here. The S-scores appear on the Group A factors for three of the four groups where they were included in the factor analysis. It will be recalled that they were not included in the middle-class analysis. Both Number of Outcomes and S-scores are discussed fully in later sections.

Let us now consider the factor structures for the different groups, and make inter-group comparisons. The autonomy-dependency dimension, together with the Desirability Direction decision variable complex, is seen in its purest form in the group interaction females. The factor is defined by the Desirability Direction complex, and includes the key defining characteristics for the two poles of the factor.

Basically, the same is true for the group interaction males. In addition, both the S-scores and Number of Outcomes appear with substantial loadings, demonstrating that for this group of males much of the important variability in decision making is tied to this basic personality dimension. The Desirability Direction cluster appears also on a separate factor for this group, and it appears to have been pulled out of the larger factor because of the relation to "persistence" and Number of Outcomes.

Turning to the lower-class males, we see that here, too, the Desirability Direction unit is embedded in the autonomy-dependency dimension, along with Number of Outcomes. To this extent the lower-class males are similar to the group interaction males. But there also is an independent, and negative, association of Desirability Direction and Expected Utility with future time orientation and a belief in the predictability of life. The S-scores loaded positively on this factor, suggesting, on the whole, a "rationality" factor with which Desirability Direction has a negative relation. Moreover, the "rationality" pole of this small, sharply defined factor for the lower-class males is associated with higher social status, within this group. To sum up, this group of respondents are similar to the others in the major factor constituting Group A, but are distinctive in important ways. In Chapter 7, we shall see that the lower-class male is similar to

GROUP A. DESIRABILITY DIRECTION

MIDDLE-CLASS MALE Factor 1		MIDDLE-CLASS FEMALE Factor 4		LOWER-CLASS MALE Factor 1	
Belief in fate	.91	Belief in trying many actions in solving problems	−.72	Belief in supernatural causes	.93
Belief in supernatural causes	.75	Independence of judgment	−.65	Belief in thinking before acting	−.77
PARI: Dominance	.74	*Desirability Direction	.59	Belief in fate	.76
Optimism (belief that good things will happen)	.69	PARI: Dominance	.55	*Number of Outcomes	−.54
Belief in trying many actions in solving problems	−.51	Interest in philosophizing and puzzles	−.53	Independence of judgment	−.54
Independence of judgment	−.48	Belief that events clearly are either good or bad	.47	Belief that events clearly are either good or bad	.52
Optimism (belief that bad things won't happen)	.48	Verbal I.Q.	−.39	*Desirability Direction	.46
Impulsivity	.48	Social status	.34	PARI: Dominance	.45
Belief in thinking before acting	−.46	Optimism (belief that bad things won't happen)	.32	PARI: Rejection	.41
*Desirability Direction	.45	Autism	.30	*Mean Expected Utility	.39
Belief in animism	.45			Optimism (belief that good things will happen)	.36
Verbal I.Q.	−.45	Factor 1		Parental concern with child rearing	.33
Future time orientation	−.42	Belief in fate	.79	Impulsivity	.32
Belief that events clearly are either good or bad	.41	Belief in supernatural causes	.73	Social status	.30
Social status	.34	Parental concern with child rearing	.60		
Belief in multiple causation of events	.32	Belief in thinking before acting	−.46	Factor 7†	
		Optimism (belief that bad things won't happen)	.45	Social status	.70
		PARI: Dominance	.44	Belief in predictability of life	−.68
		Future time orientation	−.41	*Mean Expected Utility	.50
		Nervousness	.40	*Mean S-score	−.44
		Independence of judgment	−.39	*Desirability Direction	.42
		*Desirability Extremity	.37	Future time orientation	−.34
		Belief in animism	.30		

Factor 4†

*Desirability Direction .... .94
*Mean Expected Utility .... .93
*Probability Direction .... .36
Verbal I.Q. .... −.31

Factor 1

Belief in fate .... .93
Belief in supernatural causes .. .91
PARI: Dominance .... .64
*Number of Actions .... −.53
Self-confidence .... .50
Impulsivity .... .50
Verbal I.Q. .... −.49
Belief in animism .... .46
Independence of judgment ..... −.44
Belief in trying many actions in
  solving problems .... −.34
*Desirability Extremity .... .32
Persistence .... −.32

Factor 6

Optimism (belief that bad things
  won't happen) .... −.75
Optimism (belief that good
  things will happen) .... −.68
Social status .... .41
Belief in thoughtfulness ...... −.40
Self-sufficiency .... .31

Factor 1

Belief in supernatural causes .. .92
Verbal I.Q. .... −.88
Social status .... .88
*Mean S-score .... −.78
Belief in fate .... .74
*Mean Expected Utility .... .66
*Desirability Direction .... .61
PARI: Dominance .... .57
Belief that events clearly are
  either good or bad .... .53
Parental concern with child
  rearing .... .53
*Number of Outcomes .... −.52
Impulsivity .... .52
Religion .... .52
Optimism (belief that good
  things will happen) .... .47
Independence of judgment ..... −.46
Optimism (belief that bad things
  won't happen) .... .45
Belief in trying many actions in
  solving problems .... −.41
Age .... −.40
PARI: Rejection .... .38
Belief in thinking before acting −.38
Desire for certainty .... .30
Belief in animism .... .30

Factor 6†

*Mean Expected Utility .... .65
*Desirability Direction .... .59
Persistence .... −.50
*Number of Outcomes .... −.48
Nervousness .... .30

Factor 1

*Mean Expected Utility .... .96
*Desirability Direction .... .93
Independence of judgment ..... −.76
*Number of Outcomes .... −.68
Future time orientation .... −.59
Belief in fate .... .57
Belief in supernatural causes .. .52
PARI: Dominance .... .48
Interest in philosophizing and
  puzzles .... −.48
Optimism (belief that good
  things will happen) .... .46
*Mean S-score .... −.42
Verbal I.Q. .... −.36
Social status .... .33
Belief in trying many actions in
  solving problems .... −.32
Persistence .... .30

Note: In interpreting the factors in all groups, A through H, it must be remembered that some variables have unusual scoring. These are: Time Direction (high score is present time orientation); Social Status (high score is low social status); Need for Certainty (high score is low need for certainty); Religion (high score is being non-Jewish). Therefore, for example, a positive loading of social status on some factor means that high social status is negatively associated with the factor.

* Decision Process Characteristic.
† Signs reflected.

his wife in being more dependent than the middle-class population, but is similar to the latter in his decision processes. The separation of these elements in the factor analysis is corroborating evidence for the findings presented later.

The lower-class female is the next object of analysis. Here we find that the Desirability Direction decision factor has *no* important personality correlates. It seems to be an independent characteristic insofar as other components of personality are concerned. The autonomy-dependency factor appears clearly, but it picks up the decision variable Number of Actions. (We will discuss this later in connection with Group G.) Moreover, the optimism component of the autonomy-dependency factor is split off into a separate cluster, indicating that for these women dependency is not necessarily associated with the optimism that characterizes the other groups. All in all, we get here our first glimpse of a distinctive personality organization of this group of women, which emerges with greater clarity in subsequent chapters.

Last, we come to the middle-class males and females. It will be recalled that Expected Utility was not included in these factor analyses. Looking first at the males, we see that Desirability Direction is embedded in the basic autonomy-dependency dimension, although the loading is not as high as for the comparable group interaction subjects. Perhaps this is caused by absence of Expected Utility in the analysis; lacking the high correlation between the Desirability Direction and Expected Utility, the factor structure of necessity changes, and the former characteristic is less closely tied to these personality characteristics.

For the middle-class females the autonomy-dependency dimension has separated into two overlapping components, with the important common variables of independence of judgment, optimism, and the PARI dominance scores. The first emphasizes fatalistic attitudes. The second, on which Desirability Direction appears, stresses the intellective and independence components, indicated by the interest in philosophy and puzzles, the belief in trying many actions, and independence of judgment.

To sum up the inter-group comparisons, we find that a Desirability Direction factor appears for all six groups. Most importantly, for five of the six groups this decision characteristic is closely tied to a personality dimension of autonomy-dependency, with the more dependent persons in each group making higher estimates of the desirability of the results of their actions. We find that the lower-class females differ from the other groups in not showing this relationship. There are, in addition, the points that the lower-class males and the group interaction males both have other, smaller, factors in which Desirability Direction appears, and that the middle-class women, although recognizably similar to the other groups, have a slightly different organization in this area of personality.

Group B: S-scores

Group B contains the factor which includes *S*-scores, in addition to those already noted in Group A. All four groups are represented for whom *S*-scores were included in the factor analyses. Further, they represent, on the whole, idiosyncratic associations of personality variables with *S*-scores. It is as if certain elements among the characteristics making up the basic autonomy-dependency factor, in addition to their appearance there, had split off to form separate, smaller factors relating to *S*-scores.

With the group interaction females, we see that the *S*-score appears here as part of a separate, clear, social status factor, including intelligence.

For the group interaction males the additional *S*-score factor involves characteristics that indicate a degree of thoughtfulness or "cognitive complexity" similar to the Group A factor of the middle-class females. Note that for this group the *S*-score–social status complex has already appeared as part of the Group A factor.

GROUP B. *S*-SCORE

MIDDLE-CLASS MALE	MIDDLE-CLASS FEMALE
S-score not included in factor analysis	*S*-score not included in factor analysis

LOWER-CLASS MALE Factor 9		LOWER-CLASS FEMALE Factor 10	
Persistence	−.78	PARI: Rejection	−.76
Optimism (belief that good things will happen)	.60	Mean *S*-score*	.63
Belief in animism	.41	Belief in trying many actions in solving problems	.50
Mean *S*-score*	.38	PARI: Dominance	−.44
Optimism (belief that bad things won't happen)	.32	Desirability Extremity*	.37
Interest in philosophizing and puzzles	.31	Verbal I.Q.	.32
See also Group A		Probability Extremity*	−.31

GROUP INTERACTION MALE Factor 5		GROUP INTERACTION FEMALE Factor 3	
Interest in philosophizing and puzzles	.79	Social status	−.86
Mean *S*-score*	.49	Mean *S*-score*	.79
Optimism (belief that bad things won't happen)	−.47	Desire for certainty	.60
Belief that actions have many consequences	.39	Persistence	−.45
Self-sufficiency	.32	Religion	−.45
Self-confidence	.31	Self-sufficiency	.39
Desirability Direction*	.30	Verbal I.Q.	.37
		Belief in predictability of life..	.35
		Number of actions*	.32
		Parental concern with child rearing	−.30

Note: See note to Group A.
* Decision Process Characteristic.

For the lower-class males, also, the association of S-scores with social status has appeared already in Group A. In this group the special factor involving S-scores is defined by persistence. No particular explanation comes to mind. However, it is interesting to see that this factor, together with the smaller factor on which S-scores appeared in Group A, makes a cluster of variables quite similar to the group interaction female factor in this group; the persistence variable, the social-status component, the belief in predictability of life, all appear.

Last, for the lower-class females the S-scores appear here for the first time on a factor defined by the PARI rejection factor score, indicating that this decision process characteristic is associated with acceptance and affection for the child. We get an additional element added to our picture of these women as having a personality organization that differs from the other groups.

Group C: Number of Outcomes

This third group of factors also is complementary to the fundamental factors in Group A. We see, first that the factor does not appear for three groups. This is understandable in the case of the group interaction subjects, both males and females, for the decision characteristic factor analyses showed Number of Outcomes to be tied to Desirability Direction, and as was to be expected, it appeared with this variable in the Group A factors. For the lower-class males Number of Outcomes likewise has appeared in Group A, but for some reason other than the one just given, the earlier analyses showed no relation of it to Desirability Direction.

A Number of Outcomes factor appears for both the middle-class groups, and this is puzzling. Since the same reasoning applies to them as to the group interaction subjects, we would have expected this variable to appear on the Group A factors. However, it did not. The explanation may be that the absence of Expected Utility from these analyses reduces the correlation of Number of Outcomes, and frees it to appear as part of a different set of correlates. A Number of Outcomes factor appears for the lower-class females. In this case, there was no previously discovered relation to Desirability Direction, hence no reason to be surprised by this factor.

In all three of these groups for whom the factor appears, Number of Outcomes is positively associated with intelligence and social status: the brighter and higher-status respondents, within each of the three groups, consider more of the possible outcomes of their actions. We should note, in conclusion, that this is one of the few instances in which intelligence *is* related to the decision process; compared with some of the other personality variables, it does not appear to have much influence.

GROUP C. NUMBER OF OUTCOMES

MIDDLE-CLASS MALE
Factor 5

Number of Outcomes*	.67
Belief in predictability of life ..	.57
Social status	-.43
Verbal I.Q.	.38
Belief in multiple causation of events	.37
Interest in philosophizing and puzzles	.30

MIDDLE-CLASS FEMALE
Factor 5

Religion	-.60
Social status	-.59
Verbal I.Q.	.57
Number of Outcomes*	.39
PARI: Rejection	.36

LOWER-CLASS MALE

See Group A

LOWER-CLASS FEMALE
Factor 7

Number of Outcomes*	.82
Social status	-.51
Taylor Manifest Anxiety Scale	-.41
Number of Actions*	.39
Age	-.37
Verbal I.Q.	.36
Belief that events clearly are either good or bad	-.32
PARI: Dominance	-.32
Independence of judgment	.30

GROUP INTERACTION MALE

See Group A

GROUP INTERACTION FEMALE

See Group A

Note: See note to Group A.
* Decision Process Characteristic.

Group D: Probability Direction–Extremity

We now take up two groups of factors, this one and Group E to follow, which clearly are separate from the three preceding groups. A look at the factors in Group D makes it clear that in all six populations there is a sharply defined Probability Direction–Extremity factor. We pointed out in the earlier factor analyses of the decision characteristics that the respondents' tendency to employ only positive probabilities leads to a high correlation between these two decision variables.

At first glance, there seems to be no systematic relation across the groups between this decision process factor and the personality characteristics. Where similar variables do appear, such as the PARI dominance score, they load in opposite directions in the different groups. Apparently, variability in these decision-making characteristics is not tied to other personality traits.

GROUP D. PROBABILITY DIRECTION–EXTREMITY

MIDDLE-CLASS MALE Factor 3†	
Probability Direction*	.89
Probability Extremity*	.88
Desirability Extremity*	.49
Parental concern with child rearing	.43
Belief in trying many actions in solving problems	–.39
Desire for certainty	–.37
Time Extremity*	.37

MIDDLE-CLASS FEMALE Factor 6	
Probability Direction*	.57
Probability Extremity*	.56
Belief in multiple causation of events	.45
Optimism (belief that bad things won't happen)	.38

LOWER-CLASS MALE Factor 4	
Probability Direction*	.95
Probability Extremity*	.94
Desirability Direction*	–.47
PARI: Dominance	–.41
Age	–.40
Autism	.34
Self-confidence	–.34
Mean Expected Utility*	–.33
Mean S-score*	.30

LOWER-CLASS FEMALE Factor 5	
Probability Extremity*	.86
Probability Direction*	.75
Desirability Extremity*	.72
Parental concern with child rearing	.52
PARI: Dominance	.39
Impulsivity	.38

GROUP INTERACTION MALE Factor 4	
Probability Extremity*	.90
Probability Direction	.88
Belief that events clearly are either good or bad	.47
Belief in trying many actions in solving problems	–.30

GROUP INTERACTION FEMALE Factor 5	
Probability Direction*	.91
Probability Extremity	.86
PARI: Dominance	.50

Note: See note to Group A.
* Decision Process Characteristic.
† Signs reflected.

However, closer examination leads to a very different conclusion for two of the six groups: the middle-class males and the lower-class females. In these two we see the definition of a personality characteristic of which the Probability Direction–Extremity factor is an important part. We refer to the characteristic of extremity of judgment. It is seen most clearly in the middle-class males. In addition to the two probability variables there also appear variables of Desirability Extremity and Time Extremity. It is important to stress that the Time Extremity variable appearing here without the highly correlated Time Direction, demonstrates that this is a factor of judgmental extremity which is manifested in all of these major components of the evaluation phase of the decision-making process.

These decision process characteristics are related, in this factor, to two personality variables indicative of motivation, namely, high affect level in child rearing, and generalized need for certainty.* Both of these are related to extremity of judgment in decision processes in the way we expected them to be, as noted in Chapter 3, and give considerable support to our interpretation of this important personality–decision process relationship.

For the four other groups Desirability Extremity and the related measures show up as a separate factor. We now turn to this.

Group E: Desirability Extremity

The four groups for which the Group D factors did not indicate a general characteristic of judgmental extremity are represented in Group E by separate Desirability Extremity factors. In most instances, this decision characteristic is associated with the general desire for certainty or a high degree of concern over child rearing, indicating once again that these two motivational variables are associated with extremity of judgment in decision making. The fact that four groups are represented here shows that the basic component of the extremity characteristic is high affect and desire for certainty in association with extreme judgments about desirabilities of outcomes. In two cases, this factor is fused with judgmental extremity in probability estimates, to form an even more general complex of personality and decision-making characteristics.

An interesting additional variable which appears here is self-sufficiency. While absent for the group interaction females, and loading positively but weakly for the middle-class females, for the two male groups there are substantial negative loadings; viz., self-sufficiency is negatively related to the tendency to make extreme judgments in the two male groups represented here.

Group F: Time Orientation

Time Orientation, like Number of Actions (Group G), which follows, is a comparative isolate from either decision variables or personality characteristics. Examination of the factors in Group F clearly shows the close relationship between Time Direction and Time Extremity identified in the

* For the lower-class females, the test of need for certainty was not included in the test battery.

GROUP E. DESIRABILITY EXTREMITY

MIDDLE-CLASS MALE

See Group D

MIDDLE-CLASS FEMALE
Factor 7

Meticulousness .... .66
Desire for certainty .... .39
Age .... .37
Desirability Direction* .... .37
Belief in animism .... .34
Future time orientation .... -.32
Desirability Extremity* ...... .31
Self-sufficiency .... .31

Factor 8

Belief that actions have many
  consequences .... .49
Desirability Extremity* ...... .38
Belief in thinking before acting .37
Optimism (belief that good
  things will happen) .... -.32

LOWER-CLASS MALE
Factor 10†

Parental concern with child
  rearing .... .76
Desirability Extremity* ...... .72
Self-sufficiency .... -.62
Verbal I.Q. .... -.52
PARI: Dominance .... .45
Independence of judgment .... -.41
Future time orientation ...... -.40

LOWER-CLASS FEMALE

See Group D

GROUP INTERACTION MALE
Factor 7†

Desirability Extremity* ...... .74
Self-sufficiency .... -.50
Nervousness .... -.45
Belief in thinking before acting .44
Belief that actions have many
  consequences .... .42
Desire for certainty .... .37
Social status .... -.36
Optimism (belief that bad things
  won't happen) .... -.35

GROUP INTERACTION FEMALE
Factor 4

Desirability Extremity* ...... .74
Belief that actions have many
  consequences .... -.58
PARI: Rejection .... .41
Persistence .... -.32

Note: See note to Group A.
* Decision Process Characteristic.
† Signs reflected.

Group F. Time Orientation

MIDDLE-CLASS MALE
Factor 6

Time Extremity*	.75
Time Direction*	.66
Meticulousness	.48
Interest in philosophizing and puzzles	.38

MIDDLE-CLASS FEMALE
Factor 3

Time Extremity*	.85
Time Direction*	.83
Optimism (belief that good things will happen)	−.48
Belief in multiple causation of events	−.40
Religion	−.34
Meticulousness	−.33
Probability Direction*	.31
Persistence	−.31

LOWER-CLASS MALE
Factor 3†

Time Extremity*	.92
Time Direction*	.76
Optimism (belief that bad things won't happen)	.58
Future time orientation	−.58
Social status	.45
Desirability Direction*	−.43
Number of Outcomes*	−.42
Age	.42
Mean S-score*	−.36
Mean Expected Utility*	−.34
Belief in fate	.34
Verbal I.Q.	−.34

LOWER-CLASS FEMALE
Factor 8

Time Direction*	.89
Time Extremity*	.72
Age	.43
Persistence	.43
Self-sufficiency	−.37
Number of Outcomes*	−.32

GROUP INTERACTION MALE
Factor 2

Time Extremity*	.96
Time Direction*	.91
Nervousness	−.58
Cycloid tendencies	−.52
PARI: Rejection	−.47
Independence of judgment	.42
Future time orientation	.42
Desire for certainty	.40
Parental concern with child rearing	−.36

GROUP INTERACTION FEMALE
Factor 6†

Time Direction*	.95
Time Extremity*	.90
Number of Outcomes*	−.43
PARI: Rejection	−.36

Note: See note to Group A.
* Decision Process Characteristic.
† Signs reflected.

earlier analyses of decision characteristics, which is the consequence of the respondents' emphasis on short-run outcomes. We see also that in the two lower-class populations and the group interaction females, the decision characteristic, Number of Outcomes, loads the factor. This also corresponds to the earlier decision process analyses, where Number of Outcomes appeared on the time orientation factor.

We see no other common, significant correlates of the time orientation factor across the different groups. The belief in consideration of future consequences appears as one would expect, but only for two of the six groups, and without much strength in these. The optimism characteristics, supposedly equivalent forms of the same underlying belief structure, show up for the middle-class females and the lower-class males, and look interesting until one realizes that they load the factors in opposite directions.

In sum, we seem to have here a decision characteristic which simply is not related in a systematic way to the personality variables employed in this study. It is pertinent at this time to report that in Chapter 7 an important relationship is discovered between time orientation and the sex and social class of the respondents. This suggests that variability in time orientation is related primarily to cultural background, and presumably is expressed directly in the decision-making process.

Group G: Number of Actions

Number of Actions appeared as the defining variable on a separate, small factor for only the three male groups, and as a factor item for the group interaction females. This raises the question of the possibility of a sex difference in decision making. For the middle-class females, Number of Actions did not appear on any factor; for the lower-class females, it appears in Group A where it is associated with the autonomy-dependency personality dimension; for the group interaction females it appears in conjunction with the Group B, or S-score, factors, as well as here. This may suggest a weaker, less systematic relationship of Number of Actions to other variables for the women.

Still, when one reviews the three male groups, it is hard to find any personality correlates of Number of Actions which would have brought about this separation. True, in all three groups one finds an emphasis on animism and supernatural causes, but in one of the three the relationship is in the opposite direction from the other two. All in all, there seems to be little in common. Since the items themselves have only small loadings, compared with the other factors we have discussed, these may not be of much significance.

Group G. Number of Actions

MIDDLE-CLASS MALE Factor 8	
Number of Actions*	.56
Religion	.49
Belief in supernatural causes	.37
Future time orientation	.36
Age	−.34
PARI: Rejection	.32

MIDDLE-CLASS FEMALE

The decision process characteristic, Number of Actions, does not appear on any factor for the middle-class females.

LOWER-CLASS MALE Factor 5	
Number of Actions*	.65
Cycloid tendencies	.53
Belief in animism	−.53
Belief that events clearly are either good or bad	−.46

LOWER-CLASS FEMALE

See Group A

GROUP INTERACTION MALE Factor 8	
Number of Actions*	.50
Belief in trying many actions in solving problems	.49
Age	−.48
Parental concern with child rearing	−.41
Belief in animism	−.39

GROUP INTERACTION FEMALE Factor 8†	
Parental concern with child rearing	−.76
Number of Actions*	.54
Belief in fate	−.47
Belief in supernatural causes	−.42
Verbal I.Q.	.31
Religion	−.30

Note: See note to Group A.
* Decision Process Characteristic.
† Signs reflected.

Group H: Manifest Anxiety

This last group of factors is distinctive because the factors are made up solely of personality traits. They are not related to decision process characteristics. A very clear manifest anxiety factor emerges, with a number of identical variables across the six groups. It is the second factor extracted for five of the six groups, and the third factor for the remaining group. Evidently we have found a characteristic of the personalities of our respondents that is well organized and exists generally among different social classes and sex groups.

The factor is defined primarily by the Taylor Manifest Anxiety Scale. Each factor also includes the scales originally taken from French [2]. Emotionality, nervousness, autism, and cycloid tendencies show up with positive loadings, and self-confidence, self-sufficiency and persistence with

Group H. Manifest Anxiety

MIDDLE-CLASS MALE: Factor 2

Emotionality .... .92
Nervousness .... .82
Taylor Manifest Anxiety Scale .77
Autism .... .72
Cycloid tendencies .... .68
Self-confidence .... −.58
Persistence .... −.33

MIDDLE-CLASS FEMALE: Factor 2

Taylor Manifest Anxiety Scale .79
Emotionality .... .75
Cycloid tendencies .... .66
Autism .... .62
Self-confidence .... −.62
Nervousness .... .60
Persistence .... −.56
PARI: Rejection .... .51
Belief in multiple causation of
events .... .33
Optimism (belief that good
things will happen) .... −.33

LOWER-CLASS MALE: Factor 2

Nervousness .... .97
Taylor Manifest Anxiety Scale .92
Emotionality .... .90
Self-confidence .... −.73
Cycloid tendencies .... .57
Impulsivity .... .43
PARI: Rejection .... .43
Autism .... .40
Belief in predictability of life .. −.40
Belief that actions have many
consequences .... −.30

LOWER-CLASS FEMALE: Factor 2

Emotionality .... .89
Cycloid tendencies .... .89
Autism .... .83
Taylor Manifest Anxiety Scale .78
Nervousness .... .76
Persistence .... −.61
Self-confidence .... −.45
Impulsivity .... .43
PARI: Rejection .... .42
Belief in animism .... −.40
Optimism (belief that good
things will happen) .... −.36
Interest in philosophizing and
puzzles .... .31
Verbal I.Q. .... .31

GROUP INTERACTION MALE: Factor 3†

Taylor Manifest Anxiety Scale .82
Autism .... .82
Self-confidence .... −.68
Emotionality .... .66
Religion .... .65
Cycloid tendencies .... .58
Belief in thinking before acting −.54
Belief in animism .... .44
Belief that actions have many
consequences .... −.43
Belief in fate .... .40
PARI: Rejection .... .37
Nervousness .... .35
Optimism (belief that good
things will happen) .... .34
Persistence .... −.32

GROUP INTERACTION FEMALE: Factor 2

Taylor Manifest Anxiety Scale .95
Emotionality .... .89
Cycloid tendencies .... .88
Nervousness .... .84
Self-confidence .... −.81
Autism .... .74
Belief in supernatural causes .. .54
Self-sufficiency .... −.54
Belief in animism .... .46
Belief in fate .... .46
PARI: Rejection .... .44
Interest in philosophizing and
puzzles .... −.37
Belief that actions have many
consequences .... .31
Belief in trying many actions in
solving problems .... −.31

Note: See note to Group A.
† Signs reflected.

negative loadings. It appears that these various scales now could be combined to form a composite test of anxiety. It would be no longer than the whole Taylor Manifest Anxiety Scale, because the buffer items were omitted from this test, and it would include both positively and negatively scored scales.*

The other personality correlates of this manifest anxiety dimension are few in number. Even though there is a large literature on anxiety, showing its relation to other processes, little of a systematic nature shows up here. Intelligence is notable by its absence, as are the belief dimensions involving fatalism and the supernatural. The one characteristic that does appear to be of more than passing interest is the PARI rejection score, which here loads positively with anxiety in five out of the six groups. In our earlier chapters we suggested that rejection was partly an expression of a high degree of conflict generated in the child-rearing role; hence, it is to be expected that it would appear in connection with an anxiety syndrome.

Finally, and likely of most importance, is the fact that there are no relations with decision variables. This is very surprising, and in sharp contrast to our earlier findings about the relations of the measures of beliefs and values to decision making. It is the more interesting in view of the past studies describing relations between anxiety and apparently important cognitive processes such as rigidity and perceptual closure. We can only conclude, then, from our own analysis that the measures of anxiety employed here are simply not related to the characteristics of the decision-making process that we use in our studies.

SUMMARY

In the first half of this chapter we presented our factor analyses of ten decision process characteristics, and discussed the results. Six fundamental components of the decision process were identified through the factor analyses; each of these consists of one or more of the basic decision process characteristics.

These were considered to form the basic empirical units of the decision-making process. The next step was to investigate whether the variability on these factors was related to other personality characteristics of the respondents. In effect the problem was one of mapping onto the factor

---

* As we stated in Chapters 3 and 4, we selected items from French's review [2] to form the different scales measuring the personality traits. In this review, the different traits were identified in diverse factor analyses as independent personality dimensions. The fact that some of them constitute a single factor in this study is attributable to our use in the factor analysis of total scale scores, rather than the item responses. We believe that if we had dealt with the item scores, rather than the total scale scores, separate factors for these different traits would have emerged, much as they did in the earlier studies reviewed by French.

structure of the decision process a set of related personality variables that could serve as explanations of the differences in how people make decisions. The type of conclusions to be expected would be that people with certain personalities would, in their child-rearing decisions and perhaps generally in their decision making, tend to make decisions in certain characteristic ways. Our degree of success can be appraised as follows.

We found that the decision characteristics, Desirability Direction, S-scores, and Number of Outcomes, are significantly related to a personality factor we have labeled autonomy-dependency. The results show that people who stand toward the dependency end of this personality dimension will, in making their decisions, tend to be more optimistic over the outcomes of their actions, will consider fewer such outcomes in evaluating alternatives, and will be less "rational" in their preferential ranking of actions according to their prior evaluations. These three decision characteristics also were tied to other personality variables in several ways, the more significant of these being the positive relationship between S-scores, social status, and intelligence.

A second basic finding is that the decision characteristics, Probability Direction–Extremity and Desirability Extremity are significantly involved in a personality characteristic of extremity of judgment. The characteristic of making extreme judgments in the evaluation of the desirability, probability, and time characteristics of outcomes of actions was related to high levels of affect and to a generalized desire for certainty.

Last, the two decision characteristics, Time Orientation and Number of Actions, appear in these analyses to be decision variables essentially unrelated to those aspects of our respondents' personalities which we have measured in our research.

7

The Effects of Social Class and Sex Upon Personality and Decision Process Characteristics

INTRODUCTION

In Chapter 6 we demonstrated through factor analytic methods that although the two sets of variables (personality and decision process characteristics) are related to each other in several important ways, there are also independent clusters of characteristics in each set. As we go on to consider the relations of social class and sex with the personality and decision process characteristics, we shall expect to find some characteristics that are related to one or both of these structural variables. At the same time, we must expect to find some independent relations between the structural variables and personality, on the one hand, and independent relations between the structural variables and decision making, on the other.

The chapter is divided into three major parts. The first deals with the relation between social class, sex, and the personality characteristics. We note the relevant literature and discuss our own theoretical orientation to the problem. Following this, data obtained in the current study are presented. Last, we consider the degree to which our theories may account for the findings. The second major part of the chapter is concerned with the influence of social class and sex upon decision processes; the organization of the materials is the same as that above. The third and final section is devoted to a discussion of the relation between the differences in the social classes and sexes in personality and in decision processes. In this section we assess the degree to which the three panels of variables may be tied together.

THE EFFECTS OF SOCIAL CLASS AND SEX UPON PERSONALITY

We do not present a full review of the literature (e.g., [1, 10, 31, 35]) dealing with social class and sex differences in personality. We limit ourselves to those studies that include variables similar to ours.

We consider first the relation of social class and personality. Studies have shown that middle-class subjects tend toward more impulse suppression and emotional constriction than lower-class individuals [16, 18, 29, 30] and also have more orientation toward the future [21]; the two together thus give an impression of an emphasis on deferred gratification in the middle class.

Other findings reveal that lower-class individuals seem to have less confidence in their ability to control their personal destiny and environment [17, 27, 34], whereas the contrasting middle-class group is more self-confident [8], self-sufficient [26], and more dominant in their personal relations [5, 26]. Another well-known body of data presents the conclusion that middle-class subjects score higher than lower-class subjects on verbal intelligence tests, although this conclusion has been subjected to criticism because of the absence of any "culture-free" intelligence test (e.g., [12]). Related observations indicate that the middle-class group is better able to note and understand complexity [21] and abstractness [22].

Turning to the question of sex differences, we find that prior research has reported on several variables of possible relevance to the decision process. Some similarity in the variables mentioned in class differences and in sex differences will be apparent. One can note first that in our society women are stereotyped as being temperamental, frivolous, superstitious, i.e., generally irrational, whereas males are seen as shrewd, wise, and generally rational. Males are reported to be more dominant, self-confident, self-sufficient, meticulous, future-time oriented, and to be more interested in and to understand better complex events, and, in general, to have a greater personal control over their environment. In addition, women are reported as being more emotional, nervous, neurotic, and impulsive [3, 7, 13, 20, 32, 35]. These data are consistent with the view that through a variety of techniques males and females are socialized to behave differently in accordance with cultural expectations.

Most of the studies of sex differences in personality use college students as subjects, and further information about social class is not given. Thus one must conclude that in studies of sex differences in personality, middle-class (college student) subjects are the rule. Those studies that do present data by social class and sex show some interesting interaction effects [28, 35]. The effects of social class seem to be greater for females than for males, i.e., differential social class membership results in greater personality differences for females. For example, although middle-class women are less dominant and emotionally stable compared with men, they score significantly higher than the lower-class females on these variables. Therefore, though it is conceivable that for some purposes comparisons may be made between the sexes without controlling for social class, it seems the more sensible course in presenting our own data to compare males and females within each social class, and to compare the middle and lower classes for each sex separately. The analysis of the effects of sex and class separately sets the stage, of course, for an analysis of their interaction effects upon decision making and personality.

Differences in Personality Between the Classes

1. *Comparison of middle-class with lower-class males.*—The data in column 1 of Table 33 indicate that there are 12 significant differences among the 41 comparisons of average scores for the two groups.

Our confidence in these differences is strengthened by examining differences between the lower-class males and the group interaction males. Of the 12 differences, six are duplicated in the comparison of the group interaction subjects with the lower-class males (column 3). The remaining six differences are in the same direction for this comparison and also are of sufficient magnitude, although not significant, to support the original findings.

The middle-class males score higher than their lower-class counterparts on the characteristics of future time orientation, belief in the predictability of life, independence of judgment, and in verbal intelligence. The lower-class males are higher in their belief in fate, animism, and the supernatural, in believing that "good things will happen" as well as that "bad things won't happen," and in the dominance factor of the PARI. Quite clearly the personality characteristics are those of the autonomy-dependency factor identified in the previous chapter. These results show that while the same factor appears as an organizing principle for both the middle- and the lower-class groups, a comparison between groups, rather than within groups, shows that lower-class males fall toward the dependency end of the factor whereas middle-class males fall toward the autonomy pole.

In addition, middle-class males report significantly more satisfaction with their life situations (and a tendency to be less apathetic). These two variables were not included in the factor analyses reported in Chapter 6, but they easily might have appeared at the autonomy pole of the autonomy-dependency factor. One more variable differentiates the two groups; as one would expect, middle-class males score higher on dominance in interpersonal relations. Again, this was not included in the factor analyses, but in our judgment would have appeared at the autonomy pole.

It is of great interest to find that the two male groups do not differ on the traditional personality "traits" making up the manifest anxiety factor, identified in Chapter 6.

Further discussion and interpretation of these results will be withheld until we have completed presenting our findings with respect to the class and sex differences.

2. *Comparison of middle-class with lower-class females.*—Table 33

shows that there are 10 significant differences between the two female groups. As with the males, we compare the lower-class females with the group interaction females to see if the significant differences mentioned above were duplicated. Although none of the ten initial differences were duplicated at the .05 level of significance, all of them were in the same direction. Only two (the PARI rejection score and independence of judgment) were not large enough to support the initial finding. Whether the lack of support in these two cases reflects unreliability of the differences we have accepted as significant, or whether it results from a smaller number of subjects we cannot say. However, there is little doubt that the findings on the other variables are supported in the comparison with the group interaction respondents.

In general, the differences are similar to those for the males. The middle-class females are more intelligent, more satisfied, less apathetic, and score lower on the PARI dominance factor. They also are anti-traditionalistic, score higher on independence of judgment and on belief that actions have many consequences. Once again we find, as we did for the males, that the social classes differ on variables relating to the autonomy-dependency factor, with the middle class showing the higher degree of autonomy.

There are, in addition, three other variables, not primarily related to this factor, on which the lower-class females score higher; namely, orderliness, wife's ascendancy, and the PARI rejection factor. Finally, the results of the comparisons on the traditional "traits" in the anxiety factor show no material differences between the female members of the two social classes.

Differences in Personality Between the Sexes

1. *Comparison of middle-class males with females.*—The data in Table 32 reveal 12 significant differences between the two groups. We find a tendency for the males to be at the autonomy pole of the autonomy-dependency factor. We see this in the higher scores of the males on future time orientation, their lower scores on fatalism, and their generally lower scores on the optimism scales and their higher scores on the pessimism scales. On two related variables, dominance in interpersonal relations and general satisfaction, the males are higher and lower, respectively.

While we found no social class differences on the personality variables relating to the anxiety factor, sex differences do appear. The females have less confidence and less self-sufficiency, and tend to be higher on nervousness. In addition, the female scores are substantially higher on the need for certainty.

Two remaining variables unrelated to the above show the males to be more concerned about the children's work habits and to have a greater interest in philosophizing and puzzles, both of which seem easily under-standable on the basis of sex role-typing.

As we did previously, we look at the data from the group interaction subjects to see if it supports that obtained from middle-class subjects. The differences on the anxiety-related variables hold up, but the differences on some of the variables, such as belief in fate and future time orientation, do not, thus weakening the conclusion that the middle-class sexes differ on the autonomy-dependency dimension.

2. *Comparison of lower-class males with females.*—The relevant data in Table 32, column 2, indicate that there are no significant differences in 41 comparisons. The lack of sex differences in personality among the lower-class subjects is a very striking finding. Why this should be true, and what the implications of the differences between social classes may be, is a matter to which we now turn.

Implications of the Social Class and Sex Differences in Personality

When one considers the similarities and differences appearing in the personalities of the class and sex groups, a clear pattern emerges which can be described as follows. Both male and female lower-class groups differ from their counterparts in the middle-class in that they fall toward the dependency pole of the autonomy-dependency factor. The lower-class husbands and wives, however, do not differ from each other on this characteristic. The middle-class husbands and wives, on the other hand, do differ, with the former falling more toward the autonomy pole of the dimension.

These differences between the social classes lend support to Rainwater's view that "working class people tend to have a basic belief that what happens in the world is determined mainly by external forces against which their own energies are not likely to be effective" and that this group has "underlying uncertainties about the stability of the world and . . . feelings of inadequacy in coping with it" [28]. It appears that the middle-class respondents view themselves as considerably more autonomous and masterful over nature than do the lower-class groups. Such fundamental differences in personality may stem from earlier differences in socialization (assuming our subjects were born into the social class they now are in), but also may reflect their experiences as adults confronted by the world of affairs. The facts are that the lower-class males have less material resources for coping with obstacles ; in the occupational world, they are more likely to be in a subordinate position with no effective control over people or things. No one can doubt that these facts of life influence attitudes toward events and one's control over, or dependence on, them.

The differences between the sexes in the middle-class group are not paralleled by similar differences in the lower-class group. How might this have come about? It appears that the middle-class males either through earlier differential sex-role training, or through differences in later life experiences of success in occupational pursuits, have out-distanced their wives in the development of an autonomous personality. This in turn implies that there is either less difference in sex role-training in the lower-class group, and/or that the experiences of the lower-class males in their occupational pursuits do not lead to the development of greater autonomy.

With respect to the existing research data on sex differences in personality (which we noted previously), it must be mentioned again that virtually all of this prior work had been carried out on what must have been middle- or upper-middle-class respondents. The differences reported in the literature, which are congruent with our own findings for the middle class, must now be recognized as probably being limited to the particular social class from which the respondents came. We would make the prediction that subsequent research on sex differences in personality dealing with lower-class groups would find very few differences to report.

The other important discovery is, in our judgment, the absence of differences between the social classes on the traditional personality characteristics associated with the manifest anxiety factor reported in Chapter 6. The cluster of variables loading that factor, and dealing with anxiety, self-sufficiency, confidence, and so on, do not differentiate the social classes. Unlike the learned values that comprise the autonomy-dependency syndrome, these traits evidently are based on idiosyncratic and unsystematic experiences of individuals, i.e., events which are not related to the social stratification of society.

We have noted, however, that there *are* differences between the middle-class males and females in regard to this anxiety factor, thus paralleling the results of other research cited in the first part of this chapter. But, this difference between the sexes is limited to the middle class, for such differences do not exist between the lower-class males and females.

Correlations Between Husbands and Wives

Data on the correlations between husbands and wives on personality characteristics should deepen our understanding of their similarities and differences in personality, and provide a background for the discussion of correlations on decision characteristics that appears in Chapter 10. In addition, it hardly need be added that the data are of interest in their own right because of the contribution they make to our understanding of similarities in the personalities of husbands and their wives.

1. *Correlations between the same personality characteristics.*—The values of r in Table 34 indicate that the middle-class couples are significantly correlated on 9 characteristics. All the correlations are positive.

With one exception, the variables center on the autonomy-dependency factor, with both poles of the factor being represented by the characteristics involved. At one end, the couples are correlated on the beliefs that "good things will happen" and "that bad things won't happen," on belief in fate, and on the PARI dominance score. At the other end, they are positively correlated in intelligence, independence of judgment, and on the belief in trying many actions in solving problems. The general satisfaction scale also shows a positive correlation. The final variable on which the couples are correlated is the central variable in the manifest anxiety factor, namely, the Taylor Manifest Anxiety Scale.

Since the group interaction subjects and the middle-class subjects were drawn from the same initial pool of possible respondents, the data on the group interaction subjects may be viewed as providing a replication of the study of the middle class. On five of the variables, the same results occur, but on four of the variables—belief in fate, manifest anxiety, belief in trying many actions, and belief that "bad things won't happen"— the correlations between group interaction spouses are supportive but not significant. Once more, we cannot ascertain whether this lack of replication is due to the smaller number of subjects or whether it reflects an unreliability of the initial finding.

Table 34 reveals that the lower-class spouses are correlated on only one of the 41 variables, this being the measure of general satisfaction.

2. *Correlations on dissimilar characteristics.*—In the case of correlations between dissimilar variables, such a large number of relationships (1,724) are involved that many correlational values, due merely to the random fluctuation, will appear statistically significant. In order to ascertain which of the obtained significant correlations were least likely to be random findings, we again make use of the group interaction data. For the middle-class group there are 17 significant correlations between certain personality characteristics of the husbands and other characteristics of their wives, which are supported by the group interaction data (see Table 34). We limit our discussion to these.

No replication is possible, of course, for the lower-class subjects. For this group we obtained 51 significant husband-wife correlations, less than one would expect at the .05 significance level on the basis of random variation, from the total of 1,724 correlation coefficients. Therefore, we do not discuss any lower-class data in this section.

Turning to the data, we find for both the middle-class and group interaction respondents that high verbal intelligence of husbands is correlated positively with wives' independence of judgment (for the group interaction subjects r is just below the .05 level), and negatively with wives' scores on the PARI dominance factor.

In addition, the scores of the middle-class and group interaction husbands on the PARI dominance factor are negatively associated with the wives' verbal intelligence and their belief in thinking before acting. Conversely, the husbands' scores are positively associated with the wives' belief in ascendancy and belief that events are highly probable or improbable.

Manifest anxiety for both middle-class and group interaction husbands is positively correlated with the pessimistic belief of their wives that bad things will happen. Moreover, the husbands' belief in the multiple causation of events is correlated with their wives' belief that events clearly are either highly probable or improbable.

Not surprisingly, we find that the husbands' belief in supernatural causes is positively related to the wives' score on the PARI dominance factor and their belief in fate, and negatively related to wives' verbal intelligence and independence of judgment. For this latter variable, the relationship only approaches statistical significance for the group interaction subjects. For middle-class husbands, belief in fate is correlated with their wives' belief in ascendancy in the marital relationship, and negatively correlated with her independence of judgment. The latter relationship is not significant for the group interaction subjects. Middle-class husbands' belief in trying many actions in solving problems is negatively related to wives' score on the PARI dominance factor and the wives' belief in ascendancy in the marital relationship. Finally, future time orientation among middle-class husbands is positively correlated with their wives' belief in thinking before acting.

These data on correlations between the middle-class husbands and wives on dissimilar characteristics provide clear support for the tentative conclusion drawn from the correlational data on identical variables, namely, that these husband-wife pairs tend to be correlated on personality characteristics associated with the autonomy-dependency factor. The correlations just described—e.g., the husbands' belief in supernatural causes being positively correlated with the wives' belief in fate, and negatively related to wives' intelligence and independence of judgment—show that the same pattern occurs when we look at correlations between variables that are closely associated with each other as occurred on identical variables.

3. *Implications.*—The results show clearly that similarity in regard to at least the autonomy-dependency factor exists for the middle-class marital pairs. For these couples the results indicate that similarity in personality attributes was a consideration in the initial choice of marital partners, and (or alternatively) that convergence between the marital partners in their personality characteristics has occurred during the decade or more that they have been married. Personality characteristics certainly

are capable of change in adulthood from the influence of marital partners, and the theoretical basis for assuming that at least some convergence has taken place is presented in Chapter 9 in connection with the discussion of correlations on decision characteristics. Of course the relative contribution of initial homogamous mate selection and convergence in personality after marriage to present husband-wife similarity could be assessed only in a longitudinal study.

For the lower-class couples, from what we know, no systematic relationship exists between the personality characteristics of the spouses. There may have been a random pairing of personalities in the initial mate selection, at least insofar as the characteristics we have studied are concerned, and an absence of convergence of personality through interaction during their subsequent married life. In Chapter 10 we elaborate this point of view with respect to decision characteristics, and at that time refer back to these data.

As a final point, some comment is necessary about the implications of these findings for Winch's theory of complementary needs [36]. Winch's studies have reported that husbands and wives, during the period of mate selection and shortly thereafter, have complementary needs; e.g., if one member of the marital pair has a need to be dominant, the other member usually will have a need to be submissive. Our studies are replications of this earlier work, with some slight differences, and it is clear that the hypothesis one would have held on the basis of Winch's findings definitely is wrong for our subjects. Our results, obviously, do not suggest the existence of complementary needs.

However, there are two reasons that our results may not be fully comparable to Winch's, and they suggest that there is a more restricted area in which the hypothesis of complementary needs might be valid. First, Winch was dealing with unconscious needs obtained through projective techniques, whereas we are dealing with conscious self-reports. At the level of personality we dealt with, either homogamy or no relationship at all is the rule; however, at a deeper level some other relationship between other personality traits may exist. Second, the current study provides information on the personalities of marital partners after ten years of marriage, and if, as we believe, convergence in personality does occur through interaction, it follows that our results would differ from those obtained by Winch in studying couples who had been married less than two years, and who were childless. In fact, Winch points out that "the purpose of the latter restriction was to minimize the effect of marital interaction and thus keep personalities of our subjects as similar as possible to their patterns at the time of selecting their spouses." To sum up, then, our data disconfirm the hypothesis of complementary needs, suggesting that its validity does not extend beyond certain kinds of needs, and/or at certain periods of marriage.

THE EFFECTS OF SOCIAL CLASS AND SEX UPON DECISION PROCESS CHARACTERISTICS

Theoretical Background   ·

In contrast to the many studies of the relation between social class and personality characteristics, there are virtually no studies relating social class membership to characteristics of decision processes [11]. Although there is a study in which social class was a basis for subject selection, it limited itelf to subjects of a single social class; therefore, no class comparisons were made [14].

The situation is reversed for studies of the effects of sex. The research on sex differences in problem solving or decision making includes a number of important contributions, and they show rather clearly that prior training is an important determinant of performance. Research from a generation ago to the present reports that women are less efficient and produce inferior solutions to problem-solving tasks which involve logic, mathematics, and other formal analytic procedures [2, 6, 23]. More recent research suggests that the male-female differences in logical and other formal types of thinking are the result of differential training associated with male and female roles, and further, that when training approaches equality, the differences in decision making characteristics disappear. Thus, Milton, while reporting significant male-female differences of the usual kind, finds also that females who score high in masculine traits on the Terman-Miles M-F test are equal or superior in problem-solving skills to males who score low in masculine interests [23]. The author argues for the effects of masculine role identification in producing superior problem-solving ability, suggesting that the male role includes problem-solving skills to a greater degree than the female role. It is noteworthy that Morgan finds no sex differences on a test of logical reasoning for which the female sample was a highly selected, career-oriented group who clearly had left the traditional female role [25]. In an experimental study of improving subjects' attitudes toward problem solving, Carey finds that women make a significant improvement, thus suggesting an initial female deficit attributable to lack of training [9]. The author finds, moreover, a significant correlation between attitude and aptitude for females, but not for males; and he interprets this as consonant with the hypothesis that male problem-solving activity is role-determined and that men must claim a favorable attitude whether they feel competent or not, but that this is not true for women.

Milton in a later study found that sex differences in problem solving were a function of the role appropriateness of the task [24]. Bieri, studying cognitive behavior with Witkins' Embedded Figures Test, found, contrary to his expectations, no sex differences [4]. His subjects, like those in most of the other studies just reviewed, were all college students and presumably middle class. Kagan, Moss and Sigel likewise found no sex differences in conceptual style for middle-class subjects [19].

The research thus indicates that when customarily male tasks are presented, males will do better than females; but that females become equivalent to males in competence when masculine interests or training occur for them. Further, it suggests that where the problem-solving or decision-making task is either equally associated with, or novel to, both male and female roles, no sex differences should be found.

Overview of the Analysis

In the following sections data are presented on ten basic decision process characteristics:* Number of Outcomes; Probability Direction and Probability Extremity; Desirability Direction and Desirability Extremity; Time Direction and Time Extremity; Number of Actions; Type of Strategy Selection; and the S-scores.

The scores and standard deviations of each decision variable are reported in Tables 35 through 44 and 45 through 53, respectively. Data for each situation and the mean of the four situations are presented for each group of respondents. Inspection will show that, on the whole, the groups tended to think of between one and two outcomes of each action; to think of the more probable outcomes (average probability about .75); on the average, to think of as many desirable as undesirable outcomes; to consider outcomes that generally would occur within a week to six months; to select for performance about two different actions for each decision problem; and, quite clearly, to order the six alternatives in accord with their expected utility, as shown in the positive S-scores.

In the four basic comparisons (middle-class males vs. lower-class males, middle-class females vs. lower-class females, middle-class males vs. middle-class females, and lower-class males vs. lower-class females) we use the t test as our measure of difference. The values of t for differences in means and in situational scores for each variable are found in Tables 54 through 62.

In each comparison, we consider first the differences between the groups on the mean decision variable scores, and then we discuss any differences that may occur only in specific situations, i.e., any interaction effects.

---

* Expected Utility was omitted from the analysis because of its high correlation with Desirability Direction.

Differences in Decision Processes Between The Social Classes

1. *Comparison of middle-class with lower-class males.*—The data in Tables 54 through 62 show that there are a few variables for which significant differences occur.

First, the middle-class males regularly consider more outcomes of the various alternatives than the lower-class males. Number of Outcomes is correlated with the intelligence of our respondents, and socio-economic status also is correlated with intelligence. We hypothesized that the class difference in number of outcomes might be a spurious consequence of the correlations among these three variables. To test for this we matched each lower-class male with one middle-class male with an identical, or almost identical, intelligence score. We then compared these two matched groups on the mean Number of Outcomes, and the results indicated that there was no significant difference ($t = 1.31$). The remaining 24 middle-class males not matched for intelligence had, as expected, a higher mean score in intelligence than the lower-class groups ($t = 7.99$, $p < .01$). Thus it does appear that this difference is spurious.

There are two very interesting differences between these male groups in their handling of the masturbation decision. The first is that the lower-class males are significantly lower on the S-score variable. This variable, describing the degree of agreement of a preferred ranking of alternatives with the expected utility previously assigned to them in the evaluation process, is commonly taken as an index of rationality. It is implied that if S-scores are low, then some other, perhaps unconscious, concerns have entered the picture to produce the discrepancy between conscious evaluation and actual preferential ranking.

In this instance we may make the inference that the masturbation situation arouses more affect in the lower-class male which distorts the sensible relationship between his evaluation and his choice of actions. Strong support for this interpretation is provided in the studies of attitudes toward masturbation; the Kinsey report, for example, clearly shows that the lower-class attitude toward masturbation is one of severe negative sanction and undoubtedly arouses in the male—especially since his own son is the "deviant"—strong feelings of concern over social approval. In addition, in Chapter 12 an intra-class analysis of the relation of religion to S-scores shows that being Jewish is associated with lower S-scores in the masturbation situation. The lower-class group is one hundred per cent Jewish, in contrast to the middle-class group, as noted in Chapter 5. This would contribute further to the greater affect-arousing properties of the masturbation situation for the lower-class males. We cannot, in this work, tease out the relative contributions of the social class and religious factor in producing this important difference in S-scores.

The second and related difference between the groups in making the decision about the masturbation problem occurs on the Type of Strategy variable. Of the males in the two groups who said they would take more than one action (28 and 13, respectively, for the middle- and lower-class groups) 78 per cent of the middle-class males would employ these together, at the same time, while the comparable lower-class figure is 38 per cent. The other four response categories all refer to taking actions in some type of sequence, and the last two, essentially describing sequential trial and error, contain for all groups virtually all the responses not in the first category. Thus for purposes of analysis, we can compare frequencies in the first category with the combined frequencies of the other four categories. A χ^2 analysis shows the middle and lower classes to differ on this basis ($\chi^2 = 4.69$, d.f. $= 1$, $p < .01$).

We can say that the lower-class males are acting more in a trial-and-error fashion in regard to masturbation, trying first one thing then another, in contrast to the middle-class males' more intensive, multi-faceted attack on the problem. This does not reflect a general difference in thinking between the two groups, because it does not occur in the other decision problems. Instead, it appears that the lower-class male is able to deal with the masturbation situation only in a narrow and limited manner.

2. *Comparison of middle-class with lower-class females.*—The data in Tables 54 through 62 reveal significant differences between the two groups of women on Desirability Direction, Time Direction, and Time Extremity. The differences on Desirability Direction show that lower-class females think that more desirable outcomes will result from their actions than middle-class females. In regard to Time Direction, lower-class females are more present-oriented than are their middle-class counterparts. The differences on Time Extremity we consider to be an artifact of the high correlation between this variable and the more significant characteristic of Time Direction, a matter we discussed earlier in Chapter 6.

Two interaction effects occur. One involves the decision characteristic, Number of Actions. The lower-class women indicate (to a greater degree than do the middle-class women) that they would use more than just one of the alternatives in the stealing situation. We postpone our discussion of this until Chapter 8, where there are several similar findings involving Number of Actions.

The second involves Type of Strategy. Ninety per cent of the 22 lower-class women who would use more than one action would employ these one at a time, in some way, while for the 28 middle-class women the comparable figure is 54 per cent. The analysis gives $\chi^2 = 7.87$, d.f. $= 1$, $p < .01$. For some unapparent reason the middle-class females, when dealing with the obedience problem, take a more complex view of the matter and put into simultaneous operation a number of actions designed to improve the situation, whereas the lower-class women more often would use a trial-and-error approach.

A final point concerns the lack of differences between the female groups on Number of Outcomes. The two groups do differ in verbal intelligence, and in light of the results reported just above for the males, one might have expected the identical difference to have occurred. It is true that intelligence is correlated with Number of Outcomes to about the same degree in both groups (between .30 and .40). However, it will be recalled that in Chapter 5 we pointed out that in general the females of the two social classes were more similar than the males and in fact that the intergroup intelligence differences for the females are not as large as for the males. This smaller difference is reflected in the fact that although the middle-class women are higher on Number of Outcomes, as would be expected, they do not differ significantly from the women in the lower class.

Differences in Decision Processes Between the Sexes

1. *Comparisons of middle-class males with females.*—The results of these comparisons (Tables 54 through 62) reveal no sex differences in the middle-class on the mean scores on any of the decision variables.

There are two differences, on Desirability Direction and on S-scores, which arise in the refusal to do homework situation. In both cases it is the husbands who are higher on the characteristic; who are, for this decision, more optimistic and more "rational." No systematic explanation for this has occurred to us.

2. *Comparisons of lower-class males with females.*—The relevant data are found in Tables 54 through 62. The important but solitary difference in mean scores is that the women are more present-oriented than their husbands, i.e., they think more often of immediate outcomes. We view once again the difference on Time Extremity which shows up in the data as a reflection of its correlation with Time Direction.

Implications *

The main results were as follows: first, the middle-class males and females together with the lower-class males, differ from the lower-class females in that the latter are more present-oriented in the kinds of outcomes thought of in evaluating consequences of actions. Second, the middle-class males and females differ from the lower-class females on Desirability Direction, suggesting in this case that the latter group tend to think of the

---

* No husband-wife correlational data are presented here since they are not relevant to the analysis. These data are presented in Chapter 10, where they are of fundamental importance in the interpretation of the differences between the group and individual decision-making performance.

more desirable (and perhaps avoid thinking of the undesirable) consequences of their actions. Third, on this characteristic the lower-class males
fall between the middle-class groups and their lower-class wives and they
do not differ significantly from either of them.

As we did in the case of the personality comparisons, we will begin
with a consideration of the social class differences. Temporarily we will
disregard the lower-class male and will speak only of the lower-class female as the representative group from the lower class. We find what we
might have predicted from some of the previously noted personality differences, as well as from speculation in the sociological literature, namely,
that the lower-class respondents in their decision making seem to be concerned to a greater extent only with considerations of short-run pleasures,
rather than with giving attention to the more distant consequences and/or
the possible unwanted outcomes of their behavior. The class differences
show that the middle-class couples possess a different set of values, have
acquired a different set of habits in solving the problems which their day-
to-day life presents to them, and have learned to consider a broader range
of possible outcomes of behavior, which involve deferred gratification and
attention to the less pleasant possibilities of circumstance.

The greater consideration by the middle class of long-term consequences has been remarked on in previous studies, and it is of fundamental
importance that this characteristic, heretofore described in terms of values
or beliefs, actually should be manifest in decision processes. With reference to the greater middle-class attention to the less desirable aspects of
life, evidently no prior work has reported this social class difference and
so our results here must stand alone.

We now consider the results pertaining to the lower-class males. We
have found that these men differ significantly from their wives in their
greater consideration of long-range consequences of their actions and are
similar to the middle-class couples in this respect. They stand between
their wives and the middle-class subjects in their consideration of the
possible undesirable outcomes of their actions. Thus, they do not fall into
the expected pattern of social class differences [15] and it appears that
some additional force is at work.

We advance an explanation which makes special reference to Jewish
cultural tradition [33] in interaction both with sex role differentiation
and social class influence. Concretely, we believe that Jewish males in
both the middle and lower classes have received training leading them in
their approach to decision making to emphasize consideration of long-
term and possibly undesirable consequences of action. The traditional
emphasis for Jewish males is upon intellect and "rational behavior." The
norms for the Jewish male role place high value on his ability to renounce
impulses ("deferred gratification"), to engage in long-range planning, and

to establish rational means-ends relations. The absence of differences between the middle-class and the lower-class males is a consequence of the similar emphasis on rationality in the training of Jewish males of both classes.

To complete the picture, we now must consider similarities and differences between the sexes. At first one might think that any explanation must be based on the fact that in American society child rearing is primarily the responsibility of the mother, and that women are trained for this. However true this may be with respect to caring for the child, there seems to be no reason to believe that they are specially trained to make the decisions one faces in the parental role.

The answer instead is more complex, because of the differing results for the two social classes on the male-female comparisons; and is more general, because it involves more than just parental role training. Consider first the lower-class male-female differences in decision processes. This is readily explainable because the wife in lower-class Jewish culture has not received the same training as has the male. As Zborowski [37] points out, in traditional, orthodox Jewish culture there are sharp distinctions between the appropriate training for males and females in handling problems or decisions.

There is no difference, however, between the middle-class husbands and wives. This very significant finding indicates that whatever the early experiences may have been, both husbands and wives seem to have learned equally well the values and habits relating to decision processes, which set them off from the lower-class wife. Is this because the traditional sex role differentiation does not exist? Perhaps tradition does fade away under the impact of middle-class values about the female role, so that the middle-class wife's socialization has not differed from her husband's. Or, perhaps traditional socialization has occurred, but the later life-learning experiences of the middle-class women in college and career have destroyed any early differences between them and their husbands. Either or both are reasonable, and sufficient to explain the lack of middle-class sex differences.

IMPLICATIONS OF THE DIFFERENCES BETWEEN THE SOCIAL CLASSES
AND SEXES IN PERSONALITY CHARACTERISTICS AND IN
DECISION PROCESS CHARACTERISTICS

In this final section we return to the questions we posed in previous theoretical discussions concerning the relations between the different panels of variables used in our research. In the earlier parts of this chapter we presented our findings on similarities and differences in the personality characteristics and the decision processes of the various groups of respondents. Now we want to bring these results together, against the background of Chapter 6 and the information presented there, to make a composite picture of the effects of social class and sex.

The middle-class male stands out clearly as one who in his child-rearing decisions considers the long-term and possibly undesirable consequences of his actions, and who has basic personality characteristics—motives, beliefs, abilities—that establish him as self-confident and autonomous. His female counterpart has similar characteristics of decision making, and while she differs from him on a few of the personality traits indicative of the autonomy-dependency dimension, on the whole she resembles him in this respect. She does differ, it is true, on a few traits customarily related to the female sex role, e.g., less interest in "philosophizing and puzzles," but these have been shown to be unrelated to decision making. On the whole, the relations between social structure, personality, and decision processes are consistent for the middle-class groups, and are in accord with the conclusions of Chapter 6.

The lower-class male emerges from the preceding analyses as one who, like his middle-class male counterpart, gives attention to the possible long-range, undesirable results of his decisions. But a fundamental difference in personality exists, for the lower-class male has a fatalistic and dependent orientation toward life's circumstances that sharply separates him from the middle-class male. One gets the picture of a man who works through his decisions in a way that is no different from the middle-class males, but who lacks their characteristic autonomy and sense of personal control. Here, as before, the lower-class male seems to be a special case that does not fit easily into a pattern. However, we get our clue from the factor analyses of Chapter 6, for there we saw that the autonomy-dependency dimension appearing as a major component of the Group A factors for the other groups was split up for the lower-class males, indicating a possible separation of the personality and decision variables. This now is confirmed by the results of the inter-group comparisons of this chapter, in which the lower-class males are like their wives in their low autonomy, and like the middle-class in their decision making.

It remains for us to summarize the results for the lower-class females. They differ from the other groups both in decision processes and in other aspects of personality. The factor analyses of Chapter 6 showed that the characteristics on which they differ—Desirability Direction, Time Direction, and dependency—are not correlated for this group, so the differences should be viewed as results of different underlying factors, rather than the product of a single common factor. The lower-class wives are defined in the analyses as women who in their child-rearing decisions are more concerned with immediate consequences of a gratifying nature. In their personalities they, like their husbands, show a dependent, fatalistic approach to life.

8

Effects of Type of Situation on the Decision Process

Decision processes may be influenced as much by the characteristics of the problems themselves as by sex, social class, or personality. Up to this point, we have dealt primarily with average decision processes, using as variables the mean scores on decision characteristics, and have ignored the situational differences. In Chapter 3 we described how we selected four decision situations; we expected them to differ in the way they influenced decision making, because they would arouse different amounts of "affect," or would present different degrees of difficulty to the parents. Now we take up the effects of these decision situations on the decision process. First we describe the main effects of situations, i.e., those effects that are the same for all respondents regardless of personality or socioeconomic characteristics. In such instances the properties of the decision problems must be seen as powerful enough in their influence to overcome any individual or group variability in response to the problems. In the remainder of the chapter we analyze those effects of situations that depend on an interaction with specific personality or social group characteristics, and are therefore evident for some people, but not for others.

Before we turn to our main topics, there are two related aspects of situational influence that need brief discussion.

EFFECTS OF ORDER OF PRESENTATION

We were aware of the possibility that the order of presentation of the decision problems might have an effect upon subjects' performances, owing to practice and fatigue factors. For example, it might be that fewer outcomes are thought of on the last problem compared with the first. This could be due entirely to fatigue. Therefore, to eliminate the effects that the order of presentation might have on any particular decision problem, we arranged the problems into all possible sequences as described in Chapter 2.

To make sure that we had been successful in our effort to eliminate order effects, we analyzed the data for the middle-class males and females and for the group interaction respondents. We did not do the same for the lower-class groups because of these findings. The results are presented in Tables 65–67. The tables are read as follows: the values of r given in each cell are for the relation of order of presentation, 1, 2, 3, and 4, to the decision process variable score in the indicated situation. In the upper left-hand cell, we see that r is $-.33$; this means that Number of Outcomes in the masturbation situation is negatively correlated with the masturbation situation appearing *later* (i.e., toward position 4) in the sequence. Conversely, a positive value of r means that the decision variable score is positively related to later appearance in the sequence.

Examination of the findings shows the following: (1) While there are several significant correlations of order with a decision process score, few involve the effects of the order of a given situation on decision variables *within* the same situation; most of the order effects occur between the order of one situation and decision variables in the other situations. (2) In only two cases is the same order effect observed in different groups; virtually all of the effects differed for the three groups. The essentially random distribution among variables and groups of significant correlations led us to the conclusion that the correlations do not indicate systematic effects of order, but are attributable primarily to random variation.

EFFECTS OF FAMILIARITY WITH THE PROBLEM

In Chapter 3 we stated that familiarity with the decision problem might be an important variable, since it might be related to theoretical properties such as an increase in habitual behavior, and a greater feeling of competency or potency in dealing with the problem. For this reason we planned to study the effects of familiarity, and we deliberately included a question in the test battery that was designed to get the necessary data. We asked the subjects on each of the four decision problems to indicate whether or not that particular problem had ever occurred or was at present occurring in the family.

An analysis of the responses of husbands and wives showed that often they did not agree on whether or not the situation had occurred or was occurring. It is to be expected, therefore, that the data show no systematic effects. Table 63 presents the correlation values for three groups. It is apparent that familiarity has no consistent effect upon one kind of decision variable over different situations, and that there is no similarity in relationships for the three groups. However, the failure of method, i.e., the doubtful validity of our method of assessing familiarity, suggests that as yet we can conclude nothing about the effects of familiarity on decision processes.

In this section we are concerned only with those effects that are the same for all groups of subjects. Three of the four situations have consequences of this type. Our explanations of these effects, and also those that we describe in later sections, are based on assumptions about the differing properties of the four situations. A few of these assumptions, and related hypotheses about the effects of the situations, were made before the data were gathered and analyzed; in such instances the findings can be viewed as confirmation of the original views. The other assumptions have been made after the data were analyzed and the results studied; in these instances the explanations are *post hoc* and speculative.

The three main effects involve the masturbation, homework, and obedience situations, and the decision characteristics of Number of Outcomes, Number of Actions, Desirability Direction, and Type of Strategy. The basic data on situational effects for all situations and decision variables are in Tables 44, and 68–76.

1. *Masturbation situation and Number of Outcomes.*—Fewer outcomes are reported in the masturbation situation than in the other three situations. This is shown in Table 68. The difference is significant for the middle-class groups, and although it was not for the others, the similar *t* values for these groups led us to view this as a general effect.

Our explanation of this finding makes reference to our intention in the initial choice of decision problems. We included the masturbation problem with the expectation that it would arouse greater affect than the other problems because of its possible arousal of anxieties associated with early sexuality. Our explanation follows this view, since we interpret the obtained reaction as an avoidance response to the decision problem. The subjects desire to get through the task as quickly as possible; they do not want to think of the situation generally, and specifically do not want to consider another, and still another, possible outcome of their actions. They restrict the outcomes they think of, thus cutting down on the time and attention they must give to the disagreeable problem.

On first thought, the consistency of reaction across both social classes seems to contradict Kinsey's finding [2] about social class differences in attitude toward masturbation. We were forced to give more careful consideration to what was involved in the arousal of affect. This led to a distinction between two kinds of affect, each having different effects upon the decision process. One kind of affect comes from the arousal of anxieties that have their roots in unconscious conflict; the second kind comes from the arousal of quite conscious concerns over social criticism for deviance, which have their roots in the desire for social approval.

Kinsey investigated conscious attitudes regarding the "seriousness" of the problem and found that lower-class persons see masturbation as a more serious problem. The middle class, presumably, has a differing view of the social significance of masturbation and its relative placement on a scale of seriousness. This particular social-class difference made its influence felt on the decision process in the form of lower S-scores for the lower-class males in the masturbation situation, as we reported in Chapter 7.

Kinsey did *not* deal with the question of unconscious feelings that might be tapped by this situation, and we think that the middle-class person, for all his sophistication and understanding of the psychological nature of masturbation, is just as aroused at the unconscious level as the lower-class person. Thus the reaction is similar. When this affect-laden problem is presented, members of both classes desire not to think about it, and if this is not possible, then they try to get it over with quickly.

2. Homework situation and Number of Actions.—More actions are chosen by the subjects in the homework situation than in any of the others. This is shown in Table 75. The differences between situations are significant for all except the lower-class male group, for which the findings are very much the same.

This particular decision characteristic has had virtually no personality or social structure correlates in our previous analyses. Its variation seems to come primarily from situational influences. As a consequence, the meaning of variability in Number of Actions is less easy to interpret because we do not have the insights we have gained about the other decision characteristics from knowledge of their relations to other variables. It follows that where we are uncertain about the meaning of the result, it is also more difficult to specify the cause. In our explanation, then, we must make assumptions about both cause and effect.

We considered several interpretations. We might view the greater number of actions chosen as reflecting a lack of knowledge concerning the most efficient solution to the problem, and a consequent tendency to try many different ones. Or it might be that this problem has least affect associated with it, or is one that parents have met before, or is one that is easily handled in the ten-year-olds; all three sum up to giving the parents a feeling of mastery and potency. However, since the earlier analyses did not produce any important personality correlates of Number of Actions, it seemed less likely that ignorance or potency would be involved here.

We went on, instead, to a closer study of the situations themselves, and came up with a new property to use in describing the situations: the compatibility of alternatives. We examined the six alternatives we had presented for each situation to see if there were differences between the situations in the degree to which the alternatives were compatible; that is, if they could be performed at about the same time in response to the problem. Our criteria in making the judgments of compatibility were physical possibility, avoidance of psychological conflict, and other common-sense ideas about what seemed reasonable to expect of the respondents. One alternative common to all situations was that of ignoring the problem and doing nothing; clearly this is incompatible with the other five in each case. But for the remaining five, there were situational differences in compatibility. In the homework situation, all five could, and probably would, be employed by many parents. In the stealing situation, the parents who would notify the police would be unlikely to act in the other four ways also. The same can be said for the alternative of talking back in a rude and angry way, in the obedience situation. In the masturbation situation, incompatibility is even more clearly revealed as the alternatives split into groups of three (more interests, explanation, and affection) and two (punish him, tell him it's dirty).

In regard to the homework situation, the use of both a positive approach, involving the setting of work schedules, adult assistance, etc., and a negative approach, stressing threats of punishment, detailed checking of performance, etc., are complementary parts of the cultural complex involving the education of the young in school. There is no reason to believe that these are not also stressed at home. In fact, much of the advice given to parents by teachers includes all of these. Therefore we conclude that, when compared with the other situations, the effect of the homework situation on the decision variable of Number of Actions comes from the greater degree of compatibility among its alternatives.

One last point of interest is whether the greater compatibility is a result of our test construction, or whether it is somehow inherent in the social situation. One of the two "bad" alternatives for this situation was that of ignoring the problem, which appeared in all situations. The other was to help the child with his homework, and in retrospect we see that many parents might not view this as bad if it were associated with other efforts such as scheduling and punishment. Thus we may have unwittingly introduced into the study this aspect of situational variability, leading to a discovery of its influence upon decision making. Even so, one is left with the feeling that it might be more than just this: the pretest respondents were the ones who suggested the alternatives for the problems, and if they spontaneously produced a more compatible set for the homework problem, perhaps it reflects actual differences between the problems as they exist in nature.

3. *Obedience situation, Desirability Direction, and Type of Strategy.*
—Less desirable outcomes are thought of in the obedience situation: in

addition, the parents selecting more than one action for performance are more likely to utilize these one at a time.

Table 71 shows that all groups of subjects think of less optimistic responses in the obedience situation compared with the other situations. These results are significant for all except the group interaction subjects and for one comparison of the lower-class males. However, the group interaction data approach significance, and the nonsignificant lower-class comparison is in the same direction as the others.

Why should parents be less optimistic in handling disobedience than in handling other child-rearing problems? We suggest that they feel less competent, less masterful, and less assured of success, than in the other situations. Perhaps they are not, in fact, less successful than they would be in the problems of stealing or masturbation, but their analyses of these two lack the first-hand knowledge that must characterize their evaluations in the obedience problem. Certainly a reasonable case can be made for the assumption that problems of obedience are more often faced by parents than problems of masturbation or stealing. In the latter, the influence of wishful thinking probably appears in the higher estimates of success, whereas the less optimistic view in the obedience situation is a "realistic" response to a common situation which these parents have faced with their ten-year-old sons. Second, although the parents might know both equally well, we believe that obedience is a more difficult problem than homework. It is likely that the pessimism in the obedience situation derives from the very nature of the particular problem, which is inherently (at least in our culture) difficult to resolve. These factors combine to cause parents first, to be more realistic about the problem, and second, to see it as a difficult problem; the result is that they take a less optimistic view of the possible results of their actions.

The idea that the obedience problem causes feelings of inadequacy and lack of ability also is an explanation of the greater emphasis in this problem on step-by-step behavior among the users of more than one action. (The data appear in Table 44.) In Chapter 7 we concluded that this type of "strategy" is very similar to trial-and-error behavior, and is indicative of the subject's uncertainty about what to do.* This fits in with the view that the parents in fact are less successful in this problem, as shown in the Desirability Direction effect.

In summary, we found that on four of the ten decision variables, there was variability that could be attributed exclusively to the type of decision situation presented. The less optimistic outcomes and apparently more trial-and-error strategy appearing in the obedience situation suggests that

---

* Lower-class males in the masturbation situation; lower-class females in the obedience situation.

our subjects feel less able to handle this problem. The selection of more actions for performance in the homework situation is interpreted as indicative of a relatively greater degree of compatibility of solutions to this problem. Last, the listing and consideration of fewer outcomes in the masturbation situation is a consequence of the greater affect-arousing properties of this situation.

EFFECTS OF SITUATIONS IN INTERACTION WITH
SOCIAL CLASS AND SEX

Some of the effects of situations occur only for one of the specific social class or sex groups. These we consider here. We shall consider any interaction effects of decision problem with the group interaction situation in the last section of the chapter, rather than at this time. As we go along now in the analysis of personality, social group, and situation interaction, we should expect to find that the results complement what we have found in Chapter 7, and give us a more complete picture of interaction effects. We will note such points as they occur.

The effects we will consider are of two kinds: effects on content, and effects on variability. In the former case we are interested in knowing which particular decision variable is influenced by which particular situation; it is the kind of effect we have described in the first part of the chapter. In the latter case, the focus is on the variability of scores on decision characteristics from one situation to the next, and without regard to direction.

Effects upon Content

Three important, systematic interaction effects emerge from the analysis; they involve the masturbation and stealing situations, the decision variables of Desirability Extremity and Time Direction, and, of course, the different groups of subjects. (The basic data for the analysis are the same as in the previous section, Tables 68–76.) Two of the three results involve Desirability Extremity, and are explained by reference to the "desire for social approval" component of high affect, which we described in the prior section. The third result involving Time Direction leads us to formulate another new concept of situational differences to explain the findings.

1. *Stealing, lower-class females, and Desirability Extremity.*—In the stealing situation lower-class women are more extreme in their desirability estimates. We believe that a high score on the decision characteristic of Desirability Extremity is indicative of a high level of affect associated with the problem, which has its source in fear of social disapproval.

In the first place, a study [5] has been made of the attitudes of parents toward the relative seriousness of certain kinds of deviant behavior in children. The respondents were a large, well-selected sample of all socio-economic groups: Three of the four problems in our Decision Process Test were included in the list of problems used in that study (the homework problem was not included). The respondents ranked stealing as the most serious; disobedience was lower in the list, and masturbation still lower. Now, a look at Table 72 shows that for *all* groups, Desirability Extremity is highest in the stealing situation.*

There is another study that bears on the question of what most concerns parents. Kohn [3] asked parents from the middle and lower social classes to name the characteristics they desired in their children. Honesty was the most frequently mentioned trait in all groups, and by implication, stealing would be considered by these respondents to be a most serious offense.

Going on now to the specific interaction effects of the stealing problem, we find just the one: the lower-class women are higher in Desirability Extremity scores in this situation than in the other three. This did not occur for the other subjects. We believe this shows that the problem is more serious to the lower-class women than to the other groups.

We checked this assumption against Kohn's data. Kohn makes a comparison of women from the middle and lower classes on the value placed on honesty. We would expect the lower-class women to evaluate honesty more highly, because we have assumed they are more concerned. In Kohn's study, however, there is no significant difference. Confronted with this negative finding, we decided that our explanation of the lower-class females' greater Desirability Extremity in the stealing situation nevertheless was valid. In the first place, the concepts of "seriousness of problem" and of "most desired trait" are sufficiently different to permit this expression of class difference in one instance, but not in the other. Second, other data support our view that the lower-class women view this problem as a most serious one. We find later that within the middle-class group itself, social status is negatively related to Desirability Extremity—a strong supportive finding. We also note that the only significant differences between situations found for S-scores occur for the lower-class women. On the stealing situation they have lower scores, thus indicating that their utility ordering is less rational. We have already taken the position, in explaining other results, that reduction in S-scores is a consequence of a high level of affect deriving from concern over social disapproval. So, all in all, we believe our view to be correct in spite of divergence from the results of an earlier study.

* Another comparable study by the same author [4], in which teachers were the respondents, also showed that stealing was rated the most " serious" problem in children.

2. *Masturbation situation, middle-class males, and Desirability Extremity.*—In the masturbation situation the middle-class men are less extreme in their desirability estimates. This is, of course, what was to be expected from our knowledge of Kinsey's data, if the interpretation we have just given of Desirability Extremity was valid. In Kinsey's data it is the middle-class males as opposed to the lower-class males who see masturbation as a less serious problem, and this is manifested in our data in their less extreme judgments about the goodness or badness of consequences.

3. *Masturbation situation, middle-class males and females, and Time Direction.*—In the masturbation situation, the middle-class parents are more future oriented than the lower-class parents. Explanations of other effects of the masturbation situation have been in terms of its arousal of greater affect in the respondents. This does not seem to be involved in the present instance; something else, specific to the middle-class groups, is at work.

We believe that the masturbation problem differs from the other three in another respect, one that we formulated after considering these results. This problem has a higher degree of what we have called the "maturational component." We mean by this property the degree to which events in nature, independent of the decision-maker's efforts, work toward the eventual solution of the problem. Some problems may be solved only by the actor; others may solve themselves whether he acts or not; most, we expect, fall at varying points in between. In this case, of course, the "events" are the child's normal physical development and socialization, and time is on the side of the parent, while this may not be true in regard to homework habits, stealing, and disobedience. The higher setting on this maturational component leads the decision-maker to refer to the more distant working out of the problem. This was especially true for the alternative "ignore it, do nothing about it," in the masturbation situation.

The social-class difference is easy to understand. Clearly, whether or not a problem is viewed by the respondent as having a high or low maturational component depends on his knowledge and attitudes, quite apart from what the true case may be in nature. If he believes that only he can do something about the problem, then he will react differently from some other person who sees the problem as one that in large part will disappear with the passage of time. It is known [1] that middle-class parents to a greater degree than lower-class parents expose themselves to programs of education for child rearing. The content of these programs stresses that masturbation is not evil, that it is to be expected at certain developmental levels, and that maturation will bring its disappearance. This means that the middle class more than the lower class can view the masturbation situation as a maturational rather than moral problem, bringing in turn the greater attention to distant outcomes.

4. *Two other results for middle-class females.*—Two other effects of situations are specific to the middle-class women. We have grouped them here at the end because although we have speculated about what the results may mean, we have no preferred explanation. The first interaction effect is that the masturbation situation elicits high scores on Desirability Direction when compared with the other situations. There is an especially sharp contrast with the obedience situation. If we follow the line of thought we had earlier about the meaning of high and low Desirability Direction in the obedience situation, we can conclude that for this group the estimates of desirabilities of outcomes have a considerable amount of wishful thinking stemming from unfamiliarity with the problem.

The second interaction effect is that in the stealing situation these women take fewer actions than in the other situations. The difference is significant in only two of the three comparisons, so perhaps it is of lesser importance. In any event, following our previous interpretation, it suggests that the middle-class women find less compatibility of alternatives in the stealing situation than in the others.

Effects upon Variability

In our analysis of variability in decision processes, we use two bodies of data. One we have been using already: it is the intersituational mean differences, the t values being reported in Tables 68–76. The second is new, and consists of the correlations, between all pairs of situations, for the sets of scores for each decision variable. The values of r are given in Tables 77–85.

The number of significant mean differences, in the first body of data, can be used as a measure of the variability in performance from one decision problem to the next. The number of significant correlations, ignoring the sign of the r in the second body of data, can be used as a measure of the degree to which variability is patterned and predictable. A word more is needed on this. A significant correlation means that subjects in that particular group, when influenced on a decision variable by a situation, tend to change in the same direction and to about the same degree, so that their relative ranks on scores on the variable remain about the same. It means that for this group, if one knew an individual's position in the group in one situation, he could estimate what it would be in another situation. Hence we say that a large number of significant r's for a group indicates that the changes of its members are patterned and predictable. For both the t's and the r's we ignore the nature of specific variables involved, and consider the absolute number of significant instances.

An examination of Tables 68 through 76, presenting the t values, reveals that the middle-class males, the middle-class females, and the lower-class females have, respectively, 17, 16, and 13 significant intersituational mean differences out of fifty-four comparisons. The lower-class males, in contrast, exhibit practically no variability (two significant differences). The difference between this group and the one from which it is least different (the lower-class females) was tested by χ^2 and found to be significant beyond the .01 level ($\chi^2 = 7.74$, d.f. $= 1$).

Examination of the intersituational correlations (Tables 77 through 86) shows a different group alignment. Three groups of subjects, the middle-class males and females, and the lower-class males, have a similar degree of predictability of their decision process scores across the different situations. Of the fifty-four correlations, 47, 49, and 37, respectively, are significant. On the other hand, only 18 per cent of the lower-class females' intersituational correlations are significant. The difference between the two lower-class groups (considering only the comparison of the smallest differences, and hence most likely to be non-significant) was tested by means of χ^2 and found to be significant beyond the .01 probability level ($\chi^2 = 12.00$, d.f. $= 1$).

These results now can be combined to show how the four groups differ in the way they respond to pressures of varying decision problems. The discussion is facilitated by means of the accompanying chart.

		Number of significant Intersituational Correlations	
		High	Low
Number of significant Intersituational Mean Differences	High	A	B
	Low	C	D

The occupants of cell A exhibit many significant intersituational mean differences and correlations. This group many be considered quite adaptable, since they vary their decision processes in response to situational differences. Moreover, their variation is predictable from one situation to another. Both the males and the females in the middle class fall into this category.

Lower-class males occupy cell C in our table. They are characterized by little change in decision process responses to situational variation. As a consequence the responses of these people are relatively predictable inter-situationally. The conception of this group as being relatively inflexible is most compelling.

Finally, lower-class females occupy cell B. They exhibit a tendency to be responsive to situational differences and to vary in their decision processes. However, their variability is unpredictable, for there are few significant intersituational correlations.

All of this is reminiscent of Chapter 7. Again we find that the middle-class males and females do not differ in decision processes. Again we see that the two lower-class groups differ from each other and from the middle class. How is one to interpret this? The fact is that we are in the difficult position of having found some striking and important differences between social groups in variability in the way they make child-rearing decisions, but with no sharp, empirically based conception of what this variability means. Is it good, or bad; a sign of rationality, or not; is the less variable person consistent, or rigid; is the more variable person flighty and irresponsible, or is he adaptable and flexible?

What we can gain from this analysis, in the absence of promising hypotheses, might be summed up as follows. We find that the middle-class males and females are similar in their variability in decision making, and are this way presumably for the same reasons set forth in explanation of their similarity in mean scores on the decision characteristics: namely, the women in the middle class have had early socialization similar to the males or have made up for any differences through their later educational and occupational socialization.

If we take these two groups as a baseline, we can note that the lower-class women, when they change in the way they make decisions, change in an individualistic, unpredictable way. The different decision problems touch off idiosyncratic reactions in this group, shown in the variability in their decision making. We should point out that the explanation does not lie in the greater variability in personality of the lower-class group. The lower-class women in our studies were *not* more variable in personality than the middle-class women and although they differed on the average on some characteristics, the range within each group was just about the same.

Still using the middle-class groups as the baseline, we find that the lower-class males differ from them by handling all four situations in much the same way. Quite clearly they are less influenced by situational characteristics. Whether this is to be viewed as greater rigidity, or a commendable consistency in decision making, we cannot say.

EFFECTS OF SITUATIONS IN INTERACTION WITH PERSONALITY

We will consider now those effects of decision problems that depend on certain personality characteristics of the subjects. Important effects of situations may be hidden or masked and not appear as a main effect because subjects of differing personalities may be influenced by the same decision problem to change in quite opposite directions. For example, having to make a decision about her child's stealing may cause one mother with a certain personality characteristic to become more extreme in her judgments, whereas it causes another mother to become less extreme.

In a way, one could say that in this section we study the relation of situations to personality in the same way as we have just studied their relation to social class and sex groups. This time, however, we are making an analysis comparing individuals within a group, an intra-group analysis, rather than comparing the groups themselves as we did earlier. An important point is involved here: we should expect to find, in the intra-group analyses, some sign, some trace, of the relations between situations and group characteristics that we have noted previously. For example, if lower-class women are more extreme in desirability estimates in the stealing situation because of their greater concern, it follows that social status within each group of women should be correlated with Desirability Extremity. This would be an intra-group representation of the inter-group finding about the relation of status to desirability estimates in the stealing problem. Some of the earlier results may not appear here because of the restriction of range of the variables caused by studying just a single group. But where the results are duplicated, they must be viewed as a strong corroboration of the preceding findings.

In the analyses that follow we used only the data from the two middle-class groups of 48 males and 48 females. This decision was a practical one involving considerations of cost and best allocation of our resources. The first part describes the personality correlates of situational effects; the second part, by analogy with the section on situations and groups, will deal with personality correlates of individual variability.

Personality Correlates of Situational Effects

A traditional way of making the analysis presented here would be to divide the subjects within a group into those who are high and those who are low on a given personality trait, and then see if there were any situation effects that differed for the two types of subjects. This procedure is illustrated in Table 3, where in connection with the discussion of reliability of S-scores we carried out an analysis of variance. However, this procedure seemed to us to be less efficient for our purposes than a correlational technique of the following kind.

For a given decision process characteristic, say Desirability Direction, the respondents' scores in one situation are subtracted from their scores in another. The scores for the subjects range from a high positive value to a high negative value, indicating the degree to which the one situation elicits greater Desirability Direction than the other. This range of scores for the individuals comprising the group then are correlated (after adding a constant to remove all negative values) with selected personality characteristics. A significant positive correlation with, for instance, self-confidence, would mean that the one situation had the effect of eliciting higher Desirability Direction estimates than the other situation as the level of self-confidence of the subjects increases. Conversely, for subjects low in self-confidence, the first situation has the opposite effect. We end up, then, with correlational values showing the degree to which there are situational differences in decision characteristics which are contingent on individual personality characteristics.

In this analysis we used the following nine decision variables: Number of Outcomes, Probability Direction and Extremity, Desirability Direction and Extremity, Time Direction and Extremity, Number of Actions, and S-scores. There are six possible intersituational comparisons between the four situations. This gives, therefore, 54 variables representing the ranges in scores, six for each of the nine decision characteristics. These variables were correlated with the 30 personality variables used in the middle-class factor analyses (see Table 21). This was done separately for the middle-class male and female groups.

We report only those instances in which the situational effects in interaction with personality were strong enough so that in at least two of the three comparisons between a given situation and the other three, the resulting range of differences was significantly correlated with a personality variable. We are reporting, therefore, only the larger, systematic findings, and err on the side of omitting significant relationships in order to avoid considering those which may be the result of random fluctuations. The data for each situation are presented in the accompanying pages. For some reason there were no effects of the homework situation on decision making which depended on interaction with personality traits. This situation did have some main effects, of course, on Desirability Direction and Type of Strategy, as we reported earlier.

Six relationships stand out in importance. Four of them parallel the results we obtained in earlier analyses of situational effects. Two of them are new, and both involve S-scores. There are some other relationships which in our judgment are less important, and which we do not discuss.

1. *Stealing situation and Desirability Extremity.*—Among the women, those lower in social status are more extreme in their estimates of desirability of outcomes. This is an intra-group finding, directly paralleling the

results reported in the earlier section, in which the lower-class women, but not the other groups, were influenced by the stealing situation to make more extreme judgments. The explanation advanced there is suitable here; namely, that the greater concern of the lower social-status mothers about external manifestations of socially desirable behavior causes their desirability estimates to become more extreme in this situation.

STEALING SITUATION

Decision Characteristic Showing Increase	Personality Characteristic Associated with Increase	
	Males	Females
Probability Extremity	high in belief in fate	———
	high in animism	———
Desirability Direction	———	low in belief in predictability of life
Desirability Extremity	———	low in social status
	low in meticulousness	———
Number of Actions	low in belief in thinking before acting	———
	high in belief in fate	———
S-score	older age	———
	low on independence of judgment	———
	———	low in emotionality
	———	low in Taylor Manifest Anxiety Scale

2. Masturbation situation and Desirability Extremity.—The men are less extreme in desirability estimates in this situation if they are of higher intelligence. Lower intelligence is associated with extreme judgments. We already know that these middle-class males as a group are low in Desirability Extremity in this situation compared with the others; a finding explained by their lower concern or level of affect. They simply do not regard it as a "serious problem" at this conscious level. (Although, as we noted earlier, their avoidance responses to the situation, coming from deeper levels of personality, are the same as for the other groups.) The explanation is equally applicable to this finding: within the middle-class males, those of higher intelligence (and related status characteristics) are less concerned with the masturbation problem than with the other three, and this is expressed in their less extreme desirability ratings.

MASTURBATION SITUATION

Decision Characteristic Showing Increase	Personality Characteristic Associated with Increase	
	Males	Females
Number of Outcomes	———	high in belief that bad things won't happen
	———	low in independence of judgment
Probability Direction	high on independence of judgment	high on independence of judgment
	low in belief that bad things won't happen	———
	high in desire for certainty	———
	———	low in PARI dominance
	———	high in trying many actions in solving problems
Probability Extremity	high on independence of judgment	high on independence of judgment
	———	low on PARI dominance
	———	high in trying many actions in solving problems
Desirability Direction	low in meticulousness	———
Desirability Extremity	low in intelligence	———
	———	older in age
	———	low in social status
Time Direction	low in social status	———
	———	low in intelligence
	———	high in meticulousness
Number of Actions	———	low in social status
S-score	younger in age	younger in age
	non-Jewish	———
	high on independence of judgment	———
	———	low in self-confidence

The women show an effect on this decision variable resulting from the interaction of this situation with their age and social status. We note that the older, lower status women are more extreme in their judgments about masturbation. This very clearly is related to the foregoing and, indeed, really confirms the prior interpretation. The combination of youth and higher status as correlates of low extremity simply reflect the fact [1] that they not only are more educated about child-rearing than the lower status women, but also have been recipients of the more recent, permissively oriented advice regarding children's masturbation. Both combine to influence their attitudes toward the masturbation situation in the direction of not taking it so seriously.

3. *Masturbation situation and Time Direction.* We find that consideration of future consequences of actions increases among the males with increasing social status, and increases among the females with increasing intelligence. These findings very clearly parallel the inter-group discovery that the middle-class groups as a whole were more concerned with future consequences in this situation, whereas the lower-class groups were not. The earlier explanation was that the middle-class groups see the situation as having a maturational component. The present result is confirming: we have a within-class difference associated with social status and intelligence, caused by differential exposure to the developmental approach to the masturbation situation presented in educational materials for parents.

4. *Homework situation and Number of Actions.* Among the middle-class women, the number of actions selected is greater in the homework situation for those who are high in autonomy (or low in dependency), as

HOMEWORK SITUATION

Decision Characteristic Showing Increase	Personality Characteristic Associated with Increase	
	Males	Females
Desirability Direction	younger in age	———
	low in meticulousness	———
Number of Actions	———	low in belief in fate
	———	low in belief that bad things won't happen
	———	low in belief in supernatural causes
	———	low in PARI dominance
	———	high in independence of judgment

defined by the autonomy-dependency variables described in Chapter 6. The finding itself is evident enough; the interpretation that we made earlier for the greater Number of Actions in the homework situation could follow, namely, that the alternatives are more compatible. We would conclude that for some reason the women high in autonomy find the alternatives in the homework situation more compatible than they do in the other situations, and hence tend to use more of them. What the reason is, we cannot say. Even though there is no general relation here of autonomy to Number of Actions, it is well to recall that for the lower-class women, Number of Actions *was* generally related to autonomy in the group A factors in Chapter 6, and that this finding also remained unexplained.

5. *Masturbation situation and S-scores.* The older, Jewish middle-class males have lower S-scores in the masturbation situation than in the other three problems. This is not true, of course, for the younger, non-Jewish men. This important finding falls into place along with others concerning S-scores, and takes us a step further in our understanding of what influences this variable. We already have said that the lower S-scores of the lower-class males in the masturbation problem is attributable to their greater concern over the social undesirability of the problem; we have made the same point about the lower S-scores of the lower-class women in the stealing situation. We believe that the lower S-scores in the present instance are again the result of a heightened affect level based on a greater concern about the problem. Why, then, should the younger, non-Jewish males be less concerned? The age correlate is to be expected, since we know that younger parents have been exposed to the more recent advice about masturbation in children which would tend to reduce their concern about it as a problem to be taken seriously. We made this point earlier in describing the effects of the masturbation problem on Desirability Extremity. Note that the same age effect occurs for women, as one would expect. The non-Jewish correlate arises, we believe, because of the greater emphasis placed on avoidance of masturbation in the Jewish male culture. This point is developed more fully in Chapter 12, where we present an intensive study of correlates of S-scores.

6. *Stealing situation and S-scores.* The middle-class women who are high in emotionality and in scores on the Taylor Manifest Anxiety Scale have lower S-scores in the stealing situation than in the other three problems. This is the same finding we reported in Chapter 2 and in Table 3, where we were showing the effects of interaction of situations with anxiety in our discussion of S-score reliability. The explanation here appears to be straightforward. We know that middle-class women as a group are less concerned than lower-class women about the stealing problem, relative to the other three. Nevertheless, among the middle-class group those who are high in anxiety behave like the lower-class women: they view

stealing as more serious than the other problems, thus have a higher level of affect in dealing with it, and therefore are less rational in their ordering of alternatives.

This completes our discussion of the effects of situations that are contingent on the subjects' personality characteristics. We have not discussed all of the data, but feel that what has not been discussed is of less importance. The one exception may be that the effect on both males and females of the masturbation situation in increasing scores on Probability Direction and Probability Extremity depends on the subject's being high in independence of judgment. With no explanation, we can do no more than call attention to the result.

Personality Correlates of Individual Variability

Our method of analysis was a simple one. Since each subject was exposed to the same four decision situations, we could use as a measure of a subject's variability on each decision variable the difference between the highest and the lowest of his four situational scores on the variable. This gave us for each subject the response range for each variable. This simple index of variability then could be correlated with personality characteristics. We computed each subject's variability scores for the same nine decision characteristics used in the directly preceding analysis, and correlated these scores with their scores on the 30 personality variables used above. This method is not the same, of course, as in the preceding analysis, for there we were concerned with the direction of situational differences, while here the interest is in personality correlates of the size of differences without regard to direction.

We have reported in the chart accompanying this discussion all of the significant correlations of variability with personality. There are only a few, and on the whole probably are of little interest. However, they are presented to round out the analysis, and of those reported some can be singled out for comment.

1. *Number of Outcomes and autonomy.*—We note that for both sexes there is a negative relation between dependency and variability on Number of Outcomes. In addition to the significant correlations, several others defining this factor (e.g., fatalism for males) are close to significance.* We have no good explanation of this. Of course, we should find in our correlations here certain intra-group parallels to the inter-group differences in variability reported above. There we found that the lower-class

---

* This type of relationship does not mean, of course, that Number of Outcomes should have appeared in the Group A factors involving autonomy in Chapter 6, because the correlations used in the factor analyses were between personality and high or low Number of Outcomes, not variability as in the case here.

Decision Characteristic	Personality Characteristic Associated with Variability	
	Males	Females
Number of Outcomes	low in belief that bad things won't happen	———
	———	low in belief in fate
	———	low on PARI dominance
	———	low social status
Probability Direction	high on Taylor Manifest Anxiety Scale	———
	high on nervousness	———
	high in belief that events are either good or bad	———
	———	non-Jewish
Probability Extremity	high on Taylor Manifest Anxiety Scale	———
	high on nervousness	———
	high on emotionality	———
	high on autism	———
	low social status	———
Desirability Direction	high on emotionality	———
	high on nervousness	———
	———	high on concern over child rearing
Desirability Extremity	low on concern over child rearing	———
	———	high on impulsivity
	———	high social status
Time Direction	high in belief that good things will happen	———
	high in belief that bad things won't happen	———
	low in belief in future time orientation	———
	———	high in belief in trying many actions in solving problems
Number of Actions	low on PARI dominance	———
	———	high in independence of judgment
S-score	———	high in intelligence
	———	low in belief that bad things won't happen

men were generally low in variability for all decision characteristics. We might expect, then, in the middle-class males to find social status or intelligence associated with variability on at least a few characteristics. However, this does not appear in the data. The closest it comes is in the present instance, in which personality variables such as belief in fate, on which the social classes differed, are associated with variability. This leaves the question open to further consideration.

2. *Probability Direction and Extremity, Desirability Direction, and Manifest Anxiety.*—The key components of the manifest anxiety factor, which emerged in the analyses in Chapter 6, turn out to be positively associated with variability on three decision characteristics. Taylor Manifest Anxiety Scale scores, and scores for nervousness, emotionality, and autism appear in connection with one or more of the characteristics. The absence of any similar finding for the females is very clear. Here, as in the first point above, we are hard put to explain this result. This is especially to be regretted because this instance is one of the few ties of manifest anxiety to the decision process, and certainly the most systematic. It seems that males in the middle-class group who are higher in anxiety tend to move around in their evaluations of outcomes from one situation to the next: outcomes will happen, they won't happen; they will be good in one instance, bad in the next. While it may make sense to think of anxious men as being more variable in the way they make child-rearing decisions, one could have argued the reverse as well if the findings had been the other way; e.g., anxious men are more rigid in their child-rearing decisions. Perhaps the result fits easily into a broader picture of the relations of anxiety to performance, but we have not seen how to do it.

3. *Desirability Extremity and concern over child rearing.*—The third point is a minor one. For the males there is a negative correlation between high concern over child rearing and variability in extremity estimates. This is to be expected, since high motivation in child rearing generally should lead to extreme estimates, regardless of the situation, thus reducing variability. And we know from our earlier factor analyses that, for this group, their concern is in fact correlated with Desirability Extremity. This is logical, so far; but then we see that for the women the same personality variable is positively correlated with Desirability Direction.

EFFECTS OF SITUATIONS IN INTERACTION WITH GROUP

DECISON MAKING

In this section we are concerned with the differences in situational variation that occur for the group interaction subjects but not for the middle-class subjects. Paralleling the previous section, we deal with differences both in content and variability.

Effects upon Content

The data in Tables 68 through 76 reveal that there are no differences in decision processes resulting from the situational variation that occurs for the group interaction but not for the comparable middle-class subjects. Any influence of the type of situation, if it exists, does *not* depend on whether the decision is made alone or in interaction with one's spouse.

Effects upon Variability

The data reveal that there are only four significant, intersituational mean differences for the group interaction subjects. This number is much less than the 17 and 16 obtained from the comparable middle-class males and females, respectively. Tables 77–86 show a high number of significant intersituational correlations, similar to the middle-class groups. The variability of the subjects in the group interaction situation thus is similar to that of the lower-class males, and it differs from the patterns for the other three groups in the same way as the latter. Being unsure of the meaning of restricted variability, we could not explain the behavior of the lower-class males. In like manner, we should have little to say about the current finding. However, if we assume that the low variability in the lower-class males and group interaction subjects need not be attributed to the same cause, then we are able to advance what seem to be two sound, complementary hypotheses to account for the group behavior. In the group interaction situation there doubtless is a leveling effect that derives from the give-and-take involved in joint decision making, which serves to keep all responses at or near a modal level. In addition, the group decision situation involves a social relationship in contrast to the unregulated expression of wishful thinking and fantasies in the individual decision-making process. The variability of the individual, which comes from indulgence of his idiosyncratic reactions to the various stimuli in the problem situation, is significantly reduced by the influence of social controls exercised by the other person present in the direction of realism and attention to the task.

If this is true, we can return to our earlier findings, with the hypothesis that high variability is the result of greater expression of idiosyncratic, somewhat autistic and wishful reactions, whereas low variability indicates greater task orientation and impulse control. When we review the major finding on the relation of personality to variability, we see at once that the greater variability of the anxious, autistic males is understandable on this basis. The hypothesis thus allows us to tie together the results on variability for the middle-class populations.

This is not the explanation, though, for the low variability of the lower-class males. One could hardly assume that they have less autism, more impulse control, than the other groups, nor do the personality data show it. Something else unknown is at work in this case.

SUMMARY

The results of this chapter are too complex to be summarized in detail. We can touch on what we see as the high points in the analysis. We noted the occurrence of situation effects that were strong enough to overcome any group differences in reaction: the masturbation situation influenced Number of Outcomes; the homework situation, Number of Actions; the obedience situation, Desirability Direction and Type of Strategy. We also described the effects of situations in interaction, first with the four social class and sex groups, and second with the personality characteristics of the members within each group. We hypothesized that all of these effects, whether general or interaction effects, come from the differences between the situations on a few variables: arousal of affect coming from the unconscious; arousal of affect coming from the conscious concerns with social conformity; arousal of the feeling of inability or impotency to solve the problem; compatibility of actions; and the maturational component.

We also studied the differences between groups, and between individuals within groups, in the variability of their decision making from one situation to another. Although we are less sure here of the meaning of the results, we concluded that low variability for the middle classes was a reflection of greater task orientation and impulse control. Personality differences and the effects of individual versus group decision making may both be related to different degrees of this control, and hence to differences in variability.

PART III

*A Comparison of Individual and Group
Decision Processes*

INTRODUCTION TO PART III

The three previous chapters, constituting Part II, have been concerned primarily with the decision processes of individuals. Information about group decision making, however, was presented in several places to support or provide contrast with the data on individuals. Results for the group interaction subjects in regard to the factor structure of the decision variables, the relation of personality to decision processes, and the way in which situational effects depend on group processes, have been discussed in the prior chapters.

In Part III we extend our analyses of group decision processes by making a comparison of group with individual subjects on the basic decision characteristics such as time orientation and utility ordering of alternatives. Consideration is given both to general differences, and to the way in which group interaction effects may depend on certain kinds of decision problems.

Inasmuch as this is frankly an exploratory study, no attempt is made either to construct a hypothesis or to conduct a formal test of it. Instead, we examine relevant theory and research in sociology and social psychology with a view toward the implications which this literature may have for the interpretation of our findings.

Accordingly, Chapter 9 reviews the relations between the present study and previous research and theory, while Chapter 10 uses this work as a starting point for the analysis of the actual research findings.

9

Group Versus Individual Decision Making:
Theoretical Issues

REVIEW OF PREVIOUS RESEARCH

In this section we briefly review the relevant research on small groups, studies of the family, and research on decision making, and point out the implications which each of these may have for our investigation.

Relationship Between the Present Research and Small Group Studies

One important research area has been the comparative performance of groups and individuals on problem-solving tasks. These studies have been referred to as the "together and apart" research (i.e., comparisons of group and individual performance) [11].

1. Classification of research comparing individual and group performance.—A detailed review of research in this area has been carried out by Lorge and his associates [17]. This review indicates that studies comparing the performance of individuals and groups exhibit considerable variety along a number of classificatory dimensions. Specifically, these investigations may be classified with regard to: (1) the type of group used, (2) the nature of the task that is assigned, (3) the kinds of criteria used to evaluate group and individual performance, and (4) the particular types of comparisons which are made in order to assess relative performance in group and individual situations.

A number of characteristics are available for classifying groups used in these studies; for example, whether or not they have a formal leader, whether they are cooperative or competitive, what their size is. One convenient method used by Lorge *et al.* [17] for classifying types of groups employs two dimensions: (1) whether the group is a face-to-face aggregation, and (2) whether verbal interaction occurs. With these categories the typology of groups may be represented as follows:

Verbal Interaction

	Yes	No
Yes	1	2
No	3	4

Face-
to-
Face

Research comparing the performance of individuals and groups falls into cells 1, 2, and 4. Some of the work of Bavelas [5] falls into cell 3, but it is not relevant in the present context, since his focus is not upon the comparative performance of groups versus individuals. Furthermore, it should be noted that research within cell 4 does not study groups in any sociological sense of the term. Rather, it deals with statistical aggregations wherein the so-called "group" product is obtained by some method of averaging or combining individual products. Individual performance is then compared with this averaged performance.

Cell 2 denotes a situation where individuals work in the presence of others, but where no verbal interaction occurs. In what is perhaps the best known example of this type of investigation, Allport studied the ways in which working in isolation and in the presence of others affected performance [1].

Cell 1 portrays a situation characterized by verbal interaction in a face-to-face context. Research findings from this category are the most important for our research, since it is of this type.

Turning now to the classification of tasks, Lorge *et al.* [17] present a number of classificatory characteristics including memory, learning, judgment, and estimating. These may be reduced to two general categories: (1) tasks involving estimating or judging, and (2) tasks involving some more complex type of problem solving. A study by Jenness in which subjects estimated the number of beans in a bottle illustrates the first type of task [13]. A study by Watson wherein subjects were required to make as many shorter words as possible from the letters of a larger word is illustrative of the second kind of task [32]. In addition, a number of studies of problem solving using more complex tasks have been undertaken (e.g., [26, 28, 30]).

The third general dimension we noted in the classification of research comparing individuals and groups pertains to the criteria used for the evaluation of task performance. Evaluative criteria may be classified as *objective* or *nonobjective*. As Thomas [29] has pointed out, one important characteristic of any problem-solving task is the verifiability of the answer. High verifiability implies that there is a correct answer and that it can be easily distinguished from incorrect answers. The grounds for such verifiability may be physical (e.g., using a ruler to assess the correctness of a judgment about the length of lines) or formal (e.g., an accepted set of rules of logic or arithmetic operations for evaluating answers to arithmetic problems). When verifiability is high, we speak of the applicability of objective criteria for the evaluation of task performance, and where it is low, we refer to the use of nonobjective criteria for evaluation. A good example of the latter is found in the so-called human relations problem for which there is usually no clear-cut correct answer, and for which correctness is usually evaluated on the basis of the degree to which the answers agree with the judgments of "experts."

It should be noted that the literature on group versus individual performance is heavily influenced by an implicit value question, namely, whether groups or individuals are "better." While this kind of evaluation may be perfectly legitimate with tasks having high verifiability, it is a questionable procedure with tasks such as human relations problems, for which it is more difficult to identify the correct answer unequivocally. We believe that the emphasis should be placed upon the question of whether or not groups and individuals *differ*, rather than upon the issue of relative *superiority*, because the decision problems used here are of the complex human relations type for which there are no generally agreed upon criteria for correctness or adequacy.

The fourth and last consideration in the classification of studies comparing individuals and groups is the type of comparison which is made in order to assess performance. The usual procedure is to compare the *average* (mean) performance of the group with the average individual performance, although other kinds of comparisons are sometimes used. The various possibilities are presented below:

PERFORMANCE

	Highest Individual	Average Individual	Lowest Individual
Highest Group	1	2	3
Average Group	4	5	6
Lowest Group	7	8	9

The most frequently used comparison is illustrated in cell 5 of the table. Variation in types of comparisons between individuals and groups is an important consideration for any review of research results, since failure to take account of it may lead to lack of comparability and to discrepant findings from one study to another.

2. *Summary of results of comparisons of group and individual performance.*—When one examines the findings presented in extensive reviews [14, 17], an over-all conclusion is suggested, primarily because of the sheer number of findings, that groups are superior to individuals in problem-solving performance. However, a closer look makes it apparent that this conclusion needs severe qualification.

First, the results do not consistently indicate the superiority of groups. Some studies show no differences, and a few suggest the superiority of individuals.

Second, a number of the studies apparently supporting the thesis of group superiority exhibit methodological deficiencies that detract from the validity of the conclusions. The methodological shortcomings are of two basic types. Many of the studies use a design in which individuals perform a task, and then they subsequently perform the same task as group members. Any differences between the individuals and groups are then attributed to the group discussion. It is obvious that such a conclusion is not warranted, since the same result may well have occurred as a consequence of learning which took place from trial 1 to trial 2.

The other methodological weakness characterizing many of the studies revolves around the following question: If groups are found to be superior to individuals, can this superiority be attributed to the effect of the group, or is it merely an artifact based upon some combination of individual responses? For example, consider the frequent comparison of groups and individuals on tasks where there is either a right or a wrong answer (e.g., an arithmetic problem). If on this kind of task we find that groups arrive at a greater proportion of correct solutions than individuals, we might conclude that the former are superior on the task. However, Marquart has pointed out that in this kind of experiment a person working alone is considered to be the equivalent of one group [21]. But since the type of problem dealt with can be solved if only *one* of the group members can solve it, it becomes apparent that individuals are unduly penalized for failure to reach a solution. For example, consider that if a three-man group fails to solve a problem, this counts as only one failure, while if three individuals fail, this counts as three failures. In order to overcome this problem, Marquart has suggested that the individual performances be combined so that nominal three-man groups are constituted. Here, if any one of the individuals reaches the correct solution the nominal group receives credit for a correct solution. If there is still a difference after the nominal and actual groups have been compared in this manner, then it must be concluded that social interaction has some effect upon the efficacy of problem solving. A number of studies have compared groups with separate individuals rather than with noninteracting control aggregates. Hence, their conclusions are not valid.

The majority of the investigations in this area exhibit one or more of the weaknesses mentioned above, and the few which are beyond reproach in these respects also are not consistent in their findings. Several of these studies have shown [4, 9, 31] the superiority of groups over individuals, at least on some kinds of tasks. On the other hand, one study by Lorge *et al.* [18] indicated the superiority of individuals, while studies by Watson [32] and Marquart [21] showed no differences between groups and individuals.

In view of the great variety exhibited by these studies in terms of type of task, size of group, and kinds of criteria applied to the evaluation of group products, the absence of any consistent direction of findings should not be surprising. In fact, it would be appropriate to say that this whole area is characterized by vigorous research activity combined with a serious neglect of any concern with the systematic effects of the above-mentioned factors. This has resulted in a lack of comparability among studies, impeding the development of a cumulative body of knowledge. Thus any generalization that groups are superior to individuals on problem-solving tasks must be extremely tentative at best.

Another important point regarding these studies is that they are based entirely on investigations using *ad hoc* groups. Lorge *et al.* point out that the generalization of these findings to established groups is not warranted at the present time [17]. For this reason our research assumes importance, since it uses groups with an established tradition of working together. Furthermore, studies of individual and group problem solving have not dealt with the effects of sex composition of groups on their performance. That is, they have not taken into account the possible effects of having males and females combined in the problem-solving groups. The present investigation will provide data on this issue, since it utilizes married couples.

An additional characteristic of the together and apart studies is that they give attention primarily to the end *products* of group interaction rather than to the process of the *interaction* itself. That is, these studies tend to concentrate on the *outcomes* of group problem solving (i.e., the solution to an arithmetic problem or a human relations task), rather than on the group process which leads to these outcomes. There is a gap in our knowledge of the relations between the characteristics of interaction and the characteristics of the group product. While some studies state that the superiority of group as against individual performance is due to the fact that more information is available in the group, or that incorrect suggestions are more likely to be rejected in a group setting, these notions remain speculative and are not empirically grounded. There is, of course, an abundance of studies concerned with group process. Likewise, there are a large number of studies concerned with group as against individual problem-solving products, but it is rare that both interests are combined in one investigation.

In our study we have treated decision process characteristics as products, and we have concentrated mainly on the comparison of these products in groups and individuals. However, data having implications for group process will be presented also.

Relationship Between the Present Research and Studies of Husband-Wife Interaction

The major focus of studies on husband-wife interaction has been on relative influence [10, 12, 15, 16, 20, 27, 33]. The research leads to several generalizations concerning the characteristics of husband-wife interaction. In the first place the evidence indicates that cultural prescriptions regarding the distribution of power in husband-wife roles are related to the distribution of power when actual interaction is observed [20, 27]. Second, the findings suggest that couples are aware of the distribution of power, since considerable agreement has been observed between spouses with regard to their perceptions of relative influence in different decision areas [10, 33]. However, other work suggests that the preceding conclusion needs to be qualified, for it has also been found that husbands and wives are unable to predict their behavior with regard to one aspect of interaction that is related to influence : namely, who talks the most [15, 16]. This suggests that the degree of awareness and agreement concerning influence in husband-wife decision making varies with the particular measure used as the index of influence.

There are several important gaps in our knowledge about husband-wife interaction in decision situations. First, it is clear that only a very limited sample of types of decision-making areas have been used. With the exception of studies by March [20] and Herbst [12], the research deals primarily with decision making in economic areas. Little is known about the characteristics of husband-wife interaction concerning child-rearing problems, use of leisure time, areas of residence, and the like. Furthermore, the research on power relations tends to dwell too much on the question of who "wins" a decision, to the exclusion of questions regarding compromise and the processes by which compromise rather than outright victory is reached. Third, we have no data at all concerning whether decisions will be the same if they are produced individually rather than jointly. No research using a together and apart type of design has been conducted using married couples as subjects.

Relationships Between the Present Research and Decision Theory

At present no study exists which compares the applicability of decision theory models to individuals and groups. The research on group decision models has dealt primarily with the development of normative axioms for the ways individual choices may be amalgamated in groups to provide maximum satisfaction for all individuals [2], and any tests of decision theory models have limited themselves to the individual level. Although the main emphasis in Part III is not on a formal test of decision theory models, nevertheless some of the data, namely, the S-scores do pertain to this issue of the applicability of models.

A THEORETICAL BASIS FOR THE ANALYSIS OF RESULTS

In this section we present first a logically exhaustive classification of the types of results obtainable from comparisons between individuals and groups. In addition we point out that each type of result suggests a particular interpretation or hypothesis, and that one of these seems to be the most useful to us for the later interpretation of our data. This particular interpretation is then further explored in terms of current theory and research having relevance to it. However, as we shall see, no rigorous test of a hypothesis can be undertaken. For this reason we view the discussion in the following pages simply as a framework which will give meaning to the actual results.

Description of the Types of Possible Results

The classification below shows the results obtainable when the joint performance of husbands and wives in a group problem-solving situation is compared with the separate performances of husbands and wives in an individual problem-solving situation. To understand the classificatory scheme requires a brief review. The most important feature of the design for present purposes lies in the fact that subsamples of couples from the middle-class population have been drawn, one subsample being assigned to the individual decision-making situation and the other subsample being assigned to the joint decision-making situation. This allows us to analyze the data on decision process characteristics in terms of a basic set of comparisons in which the primary focus is upon the degree of resemblance between the group performance and the performance of each sex in the individual decision situation.

First, we compare the performance of husbands and wives (as we have done in Chapter 7). This we refer to as the individual male-female comparison. Second, the performance of the individual males is compared with the joint performance of husbands and wives in the group decision situation. Finally, the performance of the individual females is compared with the performance of husbands and wives in the joint situation. For each comparison the table indicates whether the groups are similar or different in performance. The criterion for similarity or difference is statistical significance.

Each set of the eight logically possible combinations of results suggests one or more appropriate theoretical interpretations. However, since we know from Chapter 7 that there are no sex differences in the middle-class sample, we will discuss only cells 1–4.

Cell 1 presents the situation in which there is no difference between the individual males and individual females. In addition there are no differences between the individual males and the group interaction subjects, nor are there any between the latter and the individual females.

At least three interpretations could be used to explain the findings of cell 1. The first of these holds that lack of difference in group as against individual decision-making behavior reflects a process of *convergence* between husbands and wives as a result of a history of interaction over decision problems similar to those used in this research. Due to this prior interaction, husbands and wives have grown alike in the characteristics of their thinking. This theory also requires that the individual husbands and wives be *correlated* on these characteristics. This is necessary because lack of difference between *males* and *females* does not necessarily signify lack of difference between *spouses*. That is, if the individual males and

MALE VS. FEMALE*

Similar				Different			
Male vs. Group				Male vs. Group			
Similar		Different		Similar		Different	
Female vs. Group		Female vs. Group		Female vs. Group		Female vs. Group	
Similar	Different	Similar	Different	Similar	Different	Similar	Different
1	2	3	4	5	6	7	8

* In the table the individual husbands and wives are referred to as the "males" and "females," respectively, while the couples in the joint decision situation are referred to as the "group." It should be kept in mind that separate "subsamples" of couples were drawn from the middle-class population, one sample being assigned to the individual decision situation, and the other sample being assigned to the joint decision situation. Thus, the same subjects were *not* exposed to both situations.

females do not differ, this in itself does not tell us that the individual husbands and their wives are similar. If, however, the individual husbands and their wives are correlated, then in conjunction with our prior knowledge concerning the absence of sex differences, we know that couples are similar. Thus, the convergence hypothesis requires the absence of differences on all comparisons, plus husband-wife correlations in the middle-class group.

Another hypothesis would interpret these data in terms of the original similarity of husbands and wives on characteristics of their thinking. That is, similarity in characteristics of thinking might be a basis for mate selection rather than a result of interaction. This explanation might be called a theory of *cognitive homogeneity* in mate selection. As with the convergence hypothesis, this explanation also requires that the individual husbands and wives be correlated on their decision process characteristics.

If the results indicated in cell 1 were to be obtained without the presence of husband-wife correlations, then a third interpretation would be called for. Here two separate hypotheses would be required, one referring to the absence of differences between the individual husbands and wives, the other referring to a type of interaction process in the joint decision situation. Specifically, the absence of difference between the individual males and females is interpreted as signifying a lack of differential sex-role training for child-rearing decisions. We wish to emphasize here that we refer to the absence of sex differences and not to the lack of difference between spouses. The absence of differences between the individuals and groups is then interpreted as a consequence of *compromise* in the group decision situation. That is, if there are no sex differences, but individual husbands and wives are uncorrelated, this means that any given couple will be different to some degree. Then, if such couples compromise their differences in the group interaction situation, there will be similarity between groups and individuals.

Cell 2 of the table describes a situation in which there is no difference between the individual males and females and in which the group resembles the individual males but is dissimilar to the individual females. This may be portrayed in terms of the following arrangement of means:

$$\bar{X}_g, \bar{X}_m, \bar{X}_f.$$

Here we assume that the distance between the individual males and females ($\bar{X}_m$, $\bar{X}_f$) is not large enough to reach significance, while the distance between the females and the group ($\bar{X}_g$) is large enough to be significant. Findings such as these would suggest that in the group decision situation, the slight difference between the males and females becomes accentuated as a result of interaction, and further, they suggest a consistent tendency for the males to influence the group decision. The results would thus suggest a theory of *emergent group performance* due to male influence. The results in cell 3 suggest the same theory except that it is the females who are most influential.

Cell 4 presents a situation in which the individual males and females are not different, and where the group differs from both of the former. Findings such as these also suggest a theory of emergent group performance as an explanation for the data. That is, if the individual decision-making performances of males and females are the same, but the group performance differs from these individual performances, it suggests that unique performance characteristics emerge as a consequence of group discussion. However, in contrast to cells 2 and 3 these emergent characteristics are not systematically related to the influence of either sex.

While we make no attempt in this study to undertake a formal test of a hypothesis, it is necessary to anchor our findings to some theoretical context. Although any one of the interpretations described above would furnish a starting point for the development of such a context, it is our opinion that a rather substantial body of research and theory points toward the convergence interpretation as the most reasonable framework for approaching our data. We turn now to the theoretical basis underlying this interpretation.

Convergence as a Context for Interpreting the Data

Briefly, this interpretation holds that as a result of prior interaction over child-rearing problems, husbands and wives will have converged in their method of solving such problems.

The fact that we were studying well-established married couples rather than *ad hoc* groups has direct implications for the convergence idea. The *ad hoc* group must solve certain organizational problems which the established group presumably has, to some degree, solved already. We refer to role differentiation as response to the need to fulfill instrumental and expressive functions, and to the elaboration of values and normative standards from which the role prescriptions are derived. Moreover, in the established group relatively stable sets of role expectations have been built up and are shared by the group members. Thus, in contrast to the *ad hoc* group, the members of the established group have internalized the responses of the other members. Under these conditions it is to be expected that the performance of the established group on a problem-solving task will exhibit considerable similarity to the independent individual performance of the constituent members if the task is similar to ones carried out in the normal course of the activities of the established group. In the present research the tasks to be performed (making decisions about child-rearing situations) are in fact ones that the parental couples customarily face.

In addition to the above there is a further basis for this expected convergence of the members of the established group, which is to be found in fundamental theory in sociology and social psychology. Beginning with the work of earlier theorists such as Baldwin, Cooley, and Mead, and continuing in the more refined formulations of Cottrell, Parsons, and others, a line of thought has developed which deals with the conditions required for the occurrence and maintenance of stable patterns of social interaction, and it is this which provides a context from which the convergence theory derives.

The work of the earlier theorists focused mainly upon the problem of conceptualizing the characteristics of self and the derivation of implications of this concept for the process of social interaction. In the thinking of Baldwin [3] and Cooley [7] the self is characterized as primarily a cognitive process. For Baldwin all thoughts of self exist in relation to thoughts of some alter, and the major implication of this for the process of social interaction is seen in the fact that the definition of the situation, or as Baldwin called it, the "self-thought-situation," tends to become identical for all parties involved in the interaction.

Cooley postulated that three elements are involved in the self process: (1) the imagination of ego's appearance to an alter; (2) the imagination of alter's judgment of that appearance; and (3) some kind of self-feeling or sentiment on the part of ego as a response to his perception of alter's judgment. These elements form the basis for a conception of social interaction. This conception views interaction as existing on the level of thought in the form of a kind of "self-dialogue" which can be described in terms of the three elements referred to above.

In the writings of G. H. Mead [22], the work of Baldwin and Cooley is amplified and extended to a considerable extent. Mead views the self as a process by which the person can be both subject and object. That is, ego can act and he can consider his act as if he were an outsider looking at himself. The critical factor determining this reflexive character of the self-process is language. The important characteristic of language is that it provides a set of symbols having universal significance. The term "universal significance" means a symbol calls out the same response in ego that it calls out in alter. In short, universally significant symbols are shared. Thus, it is through the medium of significant communication that the individual is able to view himself in terms of the attitudes with which others view him. This formulation is extended to relate it to a concept of social role. Here Mead states that the attitudes of others incorporated as part of the self become systematically differentiated with regard to different alters.

Recent theoretical work also has been concerned with these problems in a more systematic manner. For example, Cottrell has drawn on Mead and others in an effort to derive a set of propositions for the systematic analysis of social interaction situations [8]. He uses two basic assumptions. First, he postulates that any item of social behavior cannot be viewed in isolation. Rather, it must be viewed in relation to its function as a part of a situation composed of other individuals. Second, he assumes that any person not only develops his own response patterns, but also incorporates the responses of the others (in the interactive system) in his own reactive system.

On the basis of these two assumptions, Cottrell then develops a set of formal propositions for the analysis of interpersonal behavior. One proposition states that after an interactive pattern (involving two persons) has been repeated a number of times, it becomes possible for each person to carry out covertly the entire pattern alone. This proposition is of prime importance for a convergence theory.

One of Parsons' major interests has been in the analysis of social interaction situations [24, 25]. He postulates that in an interactive situation ego and alter serve as objects of orientation for one another. This premise is based upon the assumption that the outcome of ego's action (whether it is in some sense gratifying) is contingent upon alter's reaction to ego's behavior, since the latter's reaction can enhance or obstruct the movement of ego toward his goals. Consequently, ego becomes oriented to alter's expectations regarding ego's behavior. When interaction occurs over a period of time, this results in a tendency toward stability in the expectations of ego and alter and a consistent appropriateness of action and reaction. Such consistency tends to be maintained because each actor has some degree of control over rewards and punishments. Such orientation by ego and alter to the expectations of the other is reciprocal or complementary.

Parsons' analysis makes two things more explicit than they have been in the work of other theorists. First, he points out that it is the control over rewards and punishments which furnishes the motivation for ego and alter to become oriented to the expectations of one another. Second, he has made clear a distinction between mutual and complementary expectations. That is, in the stable interactive system the expectations of ego for alter and of alter for ego are complementary, whereas the expectations of ego for alter and of alter for himself are identical (mutual).

The major point emerging from the preceding discussion is that interaction results in the learning by ego of not only his own responses but also the responses of alters with whom he interacts. One implication of this is that ego should, under appropriate conditions, be able to reproduce alone the interaction pattern occurring between himself and alter.

Specification of Further Conditions Under Which Convergence Occurs

While these assumptions are necessary for deriving the idea that spouses converge in the characteristics of their decision processes as a result of prior interaction, they are not sufficient for the derivation of a convergence hypothesis. The process of convergence also requires the presence of additional conditions. In terms of this research we may state the problem as one of delineating the conditions under which husbands and wives exhibit similarity (convergence) in the characteristics of their thinking regarding child-rearing decisions.

There appear to be two conditions under which such convergence may take place. In the first place, the norms which individuals hold must demand convergence. We believe that child-rearing decisions represent a type of situation in which normative standards prescribe that mother-father consensus be achieved. If consensus is not achieved, this causes strain in the husband-wife interactive system, and in addition disrupts the separate mother-child and father-child systems, since a number of situations will occur in each of these latter interactive systems in which the expectations of each parent vis-à-vis the child are at cross purposes.

Consider a situation in which a child is disobedient to his parents, and they must decide what to do about it. In entertaining possible courses of action for handling this situation, the father may be concerned primarily with the long-range implications of the child's behavior, while the mother may be concerned mainly with the short-run, immediate consequences. If the parents differ in this way, conflict may ensue. First, the father may tell the mother that she is very "shortsighted," while she, in turn, may tell him to "worry about the present and the future will take care of itself." In addition, if the parents view the child's actions from different temporal perspectives, this may lead each to prefer entirely different courses of action for handling the situation. Thus, the father may prefer to be "rational" with the child, explaining to him the consequences that his disobedience may lead to if it continues when he grows up. On the other hand, the mother may want to spank the child when he disobeys. In this case, the mother may feel that the father allows the child to "get away with murder," while the father may feel that the mother is much too strict. To conclude, it seems reasonable to assume the presence of strong pressures on parents to achieve consensus regarding the ways in which they think about child-rearing decisions.

The basis of such normative demands for consensus is the fact that individuals usually have some degree of control over rewards and punishments affecting those with whom they interact. Brim [6] has defined power in terms of the control of rewards and punishments, and he points out that ego will adopt more of the characteristics of a more powerful alter in contrast to a less powerful alter, since it is more important to ego to be able to predict the behavior of the more powerful alter. In a similar vein, Maccoby [19] hypothesizes that the more power alter has over ego, the more ego will rehearse alter's actions in the absence of alter. Furthermore, in an investigation designed to test several alternative theories of identification in father-son relationships, Mussen and Distler [23] found that the masculinity of the son was significantly related to the frequency of interaction with the father and the degree to which he controlled both rewards and punishments.

It is true that these studies are concerned with situations of unequal power distribution, while the husbands and wives used as subjects in this study probably have equal power where child-rearing decisions are concerned; still it seems reasonable to think that the position they take also is applicable to a situation of equal power distribution. In the later case, both parties to the interaction have the capability of administering rewards and punishments to one another. Consequently, it is in the interest of each party to be able to predict and to conform to the expectations of the other.

Under a second condition, convergence may occur when ego recognizes that the behavior he enacts in a problem situation is not adequate to the demands of that situation. Given this possibility, it has been pointed out [6] that two processes can result in convergence. In the first process, there is a recognition by ego that alter is more successful than ego in some aspects of his behavior, and thus the appropriate elements of alter's behavior are consciously transferred to ego's role. We might call this a process of modeling or conscious imitation. Take the earlier example in which a couple is trying to decide what to do about their child's disobedience, and the father is concerned primarily with the long-range consequences of various alternatives, while the mother is concerned mainly with the short-range consequences. The mother may recognize that the father's long-range concern leads to a course of action for dealing with the child that is superior to the way in which she has previously handled it. Consequently, she may decide to use the father's solution. This process thus not only leads to convergence in the actions mother and father use in handling the child, but it also should lead to convergence in the manner in which mother and father think about the problem.

In a related process, but more complex than modeling, ego uses a trial-and-error approach to solving some problems for which his original responses have proved inadequate. Since he has the actions of alter in his repertoire, these are tried in response to appropriate cues, and if successful, will tend to replace the previous responses in the habit hierarchy. In this case, however, there is no necessary recognition that these responses were originally learned through previous interaction. For example, in our hypothetical case the mother may realize that her manner of handling the child's disobedience is ineffectual, but in seeking new solutions she may not be aware that she is, in effect, using her husband's responses in thinking about how to deal with her child.

All of the conditions presented above are presumed to lead to convergence. However, we can make no statement at this time concerning their relative importance.

We now can recapitulate. First, we have stated that interaction results in the learning not only of ego's responses, but also of alter's reactions to ego's behavior. Thus, with regard to interaction over any particular subject, ego has learned two sets of responses: his own and those of alter. An important implication of this is that under specified conditions, ego can reproduce the interaction pattern which has taken place between himself and alter, and he can do this in the absence of alter. Second, we have specified the conditions under which the responses of ego will become similar to those of alter. This will occur when (1) the norms governing the interaction between ego and alter demand it, and ego and alter each have some degree of control over rewards and punishments for each other; and (2) when ego and/or alter recognize that their own behavior is inadequate to the demands of the problem situation, and as a consequence they utilize the responses of the other which they have previously learned.

In this research we have not tested whether the necessary and sufficient conditions for convergence are present. Rather, we have tried to make a *prima facie* case that such conditions do hold for parents making decisions about child rearing. Nevertheless, the fact that we have not empirically established the presence of these conditions means that a truly rigorous test of a convergence hypothesis is impossible. It is for this reason that we view the preceding discussion as serving primarily to provide a theoretical context for the analysis of our results. Thus, while we approach our data with a point of view, we are not testing a hypothesis.

IO

The Comparison of Individual and Group Performance

The first part of this chapter presents comparisons of means on decision process variables, as well as data on correlations between husbands and wives. We make three types of comparisons: (1) a comparison of the middle-class males with females; (2) a comparison of the group inter-action subjects with the middle-class males; and (3) a comparison of the group interaction subjects with the middle-class females. In carrying out these comparisons, we focus on two kinds of effects. First, we assess main effects; i.e., those effects which are due to the situation of group, in contrast to individual, problem solving. Second, we assess interaction effects; i.e., those effects which are due to the influence of group vs. individual problem solving in interaction with the specific decision problems. For the analysis of main effects we use the average scores across the four decision problems, while for the analysis of interaction effects we use the scores for specific decision problems.

The second section of the chapter examines the findings in terms of their relevance for the convergence theory. A final section is devoted to further analysis and interpretation.

PRESENTATION OF RESULTS I: THE COMPARISONS

Comparison of Middle-class Males and Females

Data comparing middle-class males and females on the decision process variables were presented in Chapter 7. These results showed no significant differences.

Comparison of Middle-class and Group Interaction Subjects

Tables 54–60 present findings for significance of mean differences between middle-class males and the group interaction subjects and between middle-class females and the group. Tables 44, 61, and 62 show data for the strategy variables. Means and standard deviations for all groups are presented in Tables 35–43 and 45–53.

1. *Comparison of middle-class males with group interaction subjects.* —Let us take up first the seven variables for the evaluation phase. Tables 54–60 indicate that there are no main effects, since no significant differences on average scores across the four decision problems are observed. However, we do find three differences attributable to interaction effects. Two of these occur on the masturbation problem, in which the group subjects are significantly higher on Desirability Extremity and are less future time oriented on Time Direction. The third difference occurs on the obedience problem, in which the groups are significantly more likely to expect desirable outcomes on the Desirability Direction variable.

In addition there are two differences which approach significance ($.05 < p < .10$). One difference is a main effect occurring on the mean score for Desirability Direction across the four situations. Here the group interaction subjects tend to think of more desirable outcomes than the middle-class males. The second difference reflects an interaction effect occurring in the masturbation situation on the Time Extremity variable, where the groups tend to be more extreme.

The comparisons of the middle-class males with the group interaction subjects on the three variables of the strategy phase (Tables 44, 61, 62) indicate that there are no main effects for either Number of Actions or S-scores, since no significant differences on mean scores across the four decision situations were found. On Type of Strategy Selection, Table 44 shows what appears to be a fairly large discrepancy in the distributions for the homework situation: for those who chose more than one action for performance, 85 per cent of the groups and only 66 per cent of the middle-class males chose strategy a. However, this difference is not significant ($\chi^2 = 1.47, p > .05$).* Since this situation has the largest difference on this variable and is not significant, the other smaller discrepancies also are not significant.

While no differences at or below the .05 level have been found for any of the variables of the strategy phase, Table 62 does show that there are two differences on the S-scores which tend toward significance. One of these, a main effect, occurs on the mean S-score across the four situations. The other, an interaction effect, occurs in the masturbation situation. In both cases the group interaction subjects tend to have higher S-scores.

In summary, for the ten comparisons on means across the four decision situations which indicate the presence of main effects, no significant differences were found between the middle-class males and the group in-

---

* Categories b, c, d, and e, were collapsed, giving a 2×2 contingency table consisting of category a vs. the collapsed categories.

teraction subjects. On forty comparisons referring to interaction effects three significant differences were observed. In addition we have found two instances of a tendency toward a significant main effect, and two instances of a tendency for a significant interaction effect. We will take up the interpretation of these findings after the results of the comparisons between the middle-class females and the group subjects have been presented.

2. *Comparison of middle-class females with the group interaction subjects.*—Examination of Tables 54–60 shows that for the seven evaluation variables there is one significant main effect as well as two interaction effects. The main effect occurs on the mean score for Desirability Direction across the four decision situations, with the groups thinking of the more desirable outcomes. An interaction effect occurs also on Desirability Direction, with the group subjects thinking of more desirable outcomes in the stealing situation. The second interaction effect is found on Time Extremity, where groups are more extreme in their time estimates.

We also observe four differences which tend toward significance $(.05 < p < .10)$. The first is a main effect, occurring on the mean score across the four decision situations for the Time Direction variable. Here the groups tend to think of immediate rather than long-range outcomes to a greater extent than the middle-class females. The second difference is an interaction effect, wherein the group subjects are more present oriented than the middle-class females on Time Direction in the masturbation situation. The third and fourth differences are observed on the Desirability Direction variable. Here interaction effects are suggested since the group subjects tend to think of more desirable outcomes on the homework and obedience problems.

Turning now to the strategy variables, we see that Tables 44 and 61 show no significant difference between the middle-class females and the group subjects on the variables, Number of Actions and Type of Strategy Selection. On S-scores, however, there are three significant differences. The group interaction subjects have higher scores than the middle-class females on the mean S-score, indicating a main effect. The former are higher on this variable in the masturbation and homework situations. These, of course, are interaction effects.

Summarizing these comparisons, we find that the group subjects differ from the females on two of ten comparisons of means across the four decision problems. Thus, there are two significant main effects. On forty comparisons referring to interaction effects, four significant differences were observed. In addition we have found one instance of a tendency toward a significant main effect as well as three instances of a tendency toward a significant interaction effect.

Interpretation of Results

Two interpretations can be given to these results. One is that both sets of comparisons indicate an absence of differences between individuals and the group subjects. The other interpretation would assert that the results do indicate differences between individuals and groups, at least on some decision process variables.

Under the first interpretation it can be argued that the middle-class males do not differ from the group interaction subjects, since there were no significant main effects and only three significant interaction effects on a total of fifty comparisons. However, this argument has less justification when applied to the comparisons between the middle-class females and the group interaction subjects, since there are two main effects and four interaction effects on a total of fifty comparisons. Nevertheless, another argument can be presented to support the position that the differences obtained from these latter comparisons need not be taken seriously. This argument runs as follows: One of the differences between the middle-class females and the groups occurs on the same variable and in the same decision situation as was observed for one of the two significant sex differences between the middle-class males and females (S-score in the homework situation). The latter difference was previously discounted as due to random variation. Since any comparison between the middle-class females and the groups is not entirely independent of the earlier male-female comparison (i.e., the same mean for the middle-class females is used for both sets of comparisons), this suggests that the female vs. group difference can be discarded as a random finding. In addition, any situational score contributes to the average score across all situations, which suggests that the significant difference between the middle-class females and the groups on the mean S-score across all situations also should be discarded as random. If both of these difference are discarded, then we are left with only four significant differences, which is close to the number expected because of random variation. In short, this interpretation points to an absence of any differences between individuals and groups.

Under a second interpretation of the data it can be argued that in fact there are important differences between individuals and groups on some decision process variables. Here we assert that rather than the sheer *number* of differences, the crucial issue is really whether or not any *pattern* of differences is revealed. From this viewpoint we pay attention to those differences which approach significance (e.g., around the .10 level) as well as those differences which actually reach significance. If there seems to be no consistency, the differences being distributed in haphazard fashion, it would then be reasonable to conclude that the group subjects and the middle-class males and females are similar in the characteristics of their decision making. If, on the other hand, the observed differences do exhibit some pattern, then the opposite conclusion would be indicated. In order to examine this question, let us consider one decision process variable at a time in terms of the differences which have been revealed for the comparisons between the groups and the middle-class males and females, respectively.

For the first evaluation variable, Number of Outcomes, Table 54 shows that there are no significant differences for any decision situation or for the mean score across all four situations. The same thing may be said for the two variables Probability Direction and Probability Extremity.

Results for the Desirability Direction variable reveal six differences which are significant, or which tend to be significant, when the comparisons for the group interaction subjects with the middle-class males and females are combined. By and large, these differences are parallel for the group vis-à-vis the middle-class males and for the group vis-à-vis the middle-class females. In the obedience situation, the group interaction subjects differ from the middle-class males, and the difference between the former and the females is almost significant. In the stealing situation, there is a significant difference between the females and the group, while for the male-group comparison the difference approaches significance at the .10 level ($t = 1.58$).* On the average Desirability Direction score, across the four decision situations, the results also are parallel since for both comparisons the difference is significant or almost so. In the masturbation situation neither difference approaches significance, and for the homework situation the difference approaches significance only for the female-group comparison. The absence of parallel findings for this latter comparison may be attributed to the significant difference between middle-class males and females on this variable for this situation. In addition to the fact that these results tend to be parallel, it is also true that the direction of the difference is consistent in all cases. That is, for every difference which is significant or which approaches significance, the group interaction subjects have a higher score than either the middle-class males or females. In sum, the results support the conclusion that the group interaction subjects differ from the middle-class males and females on the Desirability Direction variable, and that this is a main effect of group vs. individual problem solving.

---

* It is true that the probability value for this latter comparison falls outside of the limits we have set in order that a difference can be considered as "approaching significance" (i.e., between the .05 and .10 levels). Ordinarily we would disregard such a finding. For example, for Number of Outcomes in the masturbation situation, the difference between the middle-class males and females falls almost within the "approach significance" zone, but in the absence of any other similar findings for this variable we disregard this difference. However, for the variable in question (Desirability Direction for the stealing situation) there is a general pattern which it fits; and therefore, we must consider it.

For the Desirability Extremity variable, the only significant difference observed was between the group interaction subjects and the middle-class male subjects in the masturbation situation. The t values for the other differences do not come close to the required level of significance, and the direction of the differences is not consistent. Thus, we conclude that the group interaction subjects and the middle-class males and females are similar on this aspect of the decision-making process.

For Time Direction the differences seem to fall into a pattern: In the masturbation situation, the group interaction subjects differ from both the middle-class males and females. For the male-group comparison, the difference is significant at between the .05 and .10 levels; while for the female-group comparison, the difference approaches significance at the .05 level. For the homework situation, no differences need to be considered. For the obedience situation both differences fall at about the .25 level of significance. In the stealing situation, the difference between the group interaction subjects and the middle-class females almost reaches significance at the .10 level ($t = 1.57$), whereas the group-male comparison yields a difference which only reaches the .25 level. For the mean score for the four decision situations, the group interaction vs. middle-class female comparison falls between the .05 and .10 levels whereas the middle-class male vs. group interaction comparison is almost at the .10 level. In every case (including the ones where the difference does not even approach significance) the mean for the groups is higher than the mean for either the middle-class males or the middle-class females.

These Time Direction data are equivocal. On the one hand, only one significant difference occurs out of ten comparisons on this variable, and in several instances only the slightest tendency toward a difference occurs (i.e., where a difference reaches about the .25 level). On the other hand, there appears to be an underlying consistency, since the direction of the differences is always the same. We feel that these results at least suggest that the group interaction subjects differ from the middle-class males and females on the Time Direction variable, and that this is a main effect of group vs. individual situations. The data indicate that the groups tend to think of short-range outcomes to a greater extent than do the middle-class males or females.

For the last evaluation variable, Time Extremity, the findings are similar to the results for Time Direction, although they are even less clear-cut than for the latter. However, the similarity on these two variables is to be expected, since they are highly correlated.

For the variables in the strategy-selection phase, no significant differences or tendencies toward significance occurred on the variables Number of Actions and Type of Strategy Selection. However, there are differences on the S-score variable. One of these occurs on the mean S-score, and the other is observed in the masturbation situation.* When we consider the direction of the differences on the S-score variable, in all cases (even where there is no tendency toward significance) the group interaction subjects have a higher mean than the middle-class males and females. These results indicate that the groups differ from the individuals on this variable.

Summary

We have compared the middle-class males and females with the group interaction subjects on means of decision process variables. Two interpretations have been offered for the findings. One interpretation has been concerned primarily with the sheer number of significant findings, and on this basis it can be argued that the individuals and groups do not differ. A second interpretation views the results in terms of whether or not any consistent pattern is revealed. Reviewed on this basis, the data suggest that the differences observed are not haphazardly distributed. Rather, they tend to be systematically associated with some decision process variables and not with others, they exhibit consistency with regard to their direction, and they tend to be parallel (i.e., differences between group interaction subjects and the middle-class males tend to be the same as those between the group interaction subjects and the middles-class females).

Substantively, the groups tend to think of more desirable outcomes (Desirability Direction), they tend to perceive these outcomes as occurring more often in the present (Time Direction), and they tend to have higher S-scores; i.e., their preferential rankings of alternatives are more consistent with their expected utilities for such alternatives. In short, for the group interaction subjects there appears to be a greater degree of the now familiar pattern of relative unconcern with the future, and possibly undesirable consequences of one's actions, which was characteristic of the lower-class females, but combined here with a greater amount of "rationality" in the traditional utility ordering sense.

Our findings that the conditions of group vs. individual problem solving do exert an effect upon some characteristics of the decision process lead to a consideration of the theoretical significance of these data, particularly in terms of the convergence framework outlined in the last chapter. However, since that theoretical position cannot be fully evaluated without data on husband-wife correlations, we now present those results before turning to the theoretical discussion.

---

* On the homework problem only the females differ from the groups. Regarding this finding, we feel that this should not be treated seriously, since it is probably an artifact of an earlier observed difference between the middle-class males and females which has already been dismissed as due to random variation.

PRESENTATION OF RESULTS II : CORRELATIONS OF HUSBANDS
AND WIVES ON DECISION PROCESS VARIABLES

Data on the correlations of the middle-class husbands and wives are presented in Table 86. For the first evaluation variable, Number of Outcomes, Table 86 indicates that all correlations are positive and significant. The correlations for Probability Direction are generally negative, but in no case is there a significant correlation. The same may be said of the correlations on Probability Extremity. For Desirability Direction the correlations are positive, and in three of the five cases, including the correlations on the mean score across the four decision situations, they are significant. For the remaining evaluation variables, Desirability Extremity, Time Direction, and Time Extremity, there are no significant husband-wife correlations.

For the strategy variables, one positive significant correlation is observed (in the stealing situation) for the variable Number of Actions Chosen. We interpret this as a random finding, since the other correlations are nonsignificant and inconsistent in direction. For the S-score variable it can be seen that there are no significant correlations. No correlational data are presented for the variable Type of Strategy Selection.*

In short, significant relationships have been found for only two variables, Number of Outcomes and Desirability Direction, leading to the conclusion that in general couples are uncorrelated in their decision-making performance. When we examine the findings on husband-wife correlations for the lower-class subjects (Table 86) we see that only Number of Outcomes has a significant value. Viewed as a replication, these results reinforce our conclusion regarding the middle-class subjects, i.e., that in general husbands and wives are uncorrelated. Nevertheless, the appearance of a correlation in both middle- and lower-class groups on the Number of Outcomes variable cannot be arbitrarily dismissed.

Discussion of Findings on Correlations

In the above connection we have tried to assess whether the observed significant correlations are spurious in the sense that scores on these decision variables are associated with personality factors on which couples are also correlated. To carry out such an analysis we could have used a formal

---

* No correlational data are presented for Type of Strategy Selection, because the number of couples is too small to carry out correlations. The questions on Type of Strategy Selection in the Decision Process Test are inapplicable to any respondents who did not choose more than one action, and there were not enough cases in which both husband and wife chose more than one action to permit an analysis of the relation between the two.

procedure, such as partial correlation, but the number of variables would have involved us in the very laborious task of computing partials of a very high order. Instead, we examined all significant zero-order correlations of personality and decision variables for the middle-class males and females. After isolating these correlations, we then examined our data on husband-wife correlations for personality variables. This examination showed in fact that a large number of personality variables on which husbands and wives were correlated also were associated with scores on the Number of Outcomes and Desirability Direction variables. This analysis suggests that the husband-wife correlations on these two decision variables probably are spurious.

However, before concluding that there are no husband-wife correlations, it is necessary to deal with another issue: namely, that there might be other factors operating to *attenuate* the correlations. At least two factors could attenuate the correlations. First, the reliability of the decision process scores could affect the magnitude of the husband-wife correlations. Second, the range of the scores could have an attenuating effect.

1. *Reliability of decision process scores.*—The reasoning behind the assertion that reliability is an important factor affecting the magnitude of correlation coefficients derives from Chapter 2 and may be stated as follows. The total variance of a set of scores can be apportioned into different components: (1) error variance and (2) true variance. Since error variance is assumed to be uncorrelated with true variance, we can define reliability as the proportion of true variance in obtained test scores [1]. In terms of the correlation between two sets of scores, we can see that this will be determined by the proportion of true variance which the two tests have in common, assuming that the error variances are uncorrelated.

Thus it follows that the reliability of the sets of scores sets limits upon the magnitude of the correlation between them. Specifically, it can be shown that the obtained correlation between two measures cannot exceed the product of the square roots of the two reliability coefficients [5]. However, the correlation between two variables will not usually be equal to the products of the square roots of the reliabilities, since true variance is composed of common-factor variance as well as specific or unique variance, i.e., that proportion of true variance which is specific to the test [1]. Only in the case where neither variable has any specific variance will the product of the square root of the reliabilities be equal to the correlation between the two variables. It follows, therefore, that the products of the square roots of the reliabilities will yield an upper-bound estimate for husband-wife correlations on decision tests scores.

Table 87 presents estimates of maximum possible husband-wife correlations and compares these with the correlations actually obtained. These data indicate that all estimates are considerably beyond the minimum significant husband-wife correlation (+.285), and these estimates are in general considerably higher than the actual husband-wife correlations. Thus the absence of husband-wife correlations cannot be ascribed to unreliability of the scores on decision process variables.

2. *Range of decision process scores.*—We now consider the possibility that the distributions of decision process variables are highly curtailed for husbands and/or wives. Curtailment in the range of scores as a factor attenuating correlation coefficients has been observed in a number of situations. For example, it is well known that correlations between intelligence and academic achievement are lower on the college level than on the high school level, and this is usually due to the fact that range of intelligence is more restricted on the college level. A similar line of reasoning is applicable to the problem at hand, i.e., the subjects used in this aspect of the research are primarily upper-middle-class, college-educated Jews. Consequently, it may well be that significant husband-wife correlations should not be expected because of the homogeneity of the characteristics of the sample.

In order to investigate the possible effects of range curtailment on husband-wife correlations some method of assessing restriction of range was needed. Although several formal statistical procedures are available, our data do not meet the assumptions required for their use. Therefore, we decided to assess the degree of curtailment of the various distributions of decision process variables through visual inspection of the distributions themselves. Frequency polygons for each decision variable were constructed for this purpose. This was done separately for middle-class males and females, and all polygons were based on mean scores across the four decision situations.

For the assessment of these distributions two factors were given primary attention. First, we were concerned with the degree to which the distributions cover the range of values provided by the scale. To the extent that only a relatively small portion of the scale values are covered, this indicates curtailment in the distribution. Second, we were concerned with examining the degree of kurtosis or peakedness of the various curves. To the extent that great concentration of scores is found around some scale values, this also indicates curtailment or lack of variability in the distributions.

Inspection of the frequency polygons from this point of view did not indicate curtailment either in terms of range restriction or extreme kurtosis. Thus, the absence of husband-wife correlations on decision process variables cannot be attributed to the effects of this factor.

The preceding analyses lend strong support to the conclusion that there are no husband-wife correlations on decision process variables.

Two sets of results have been presented: (1) comparisons between groups and individuals on means of decision process variables; and (2) correlations of husbands and wives on these variables. The group vs. individual comparisons indicated differences on four of the ten variables. The data on correlations showed an absence of significant associations between the scores of marital partners, and this absence could not be accounted for by the presence of attenuating factors. What are the implications of these results for the convergence theory?

In Chapter 9 we presented a classification of the kinds of results obtainable from comparisons between individuals and groups, and we pointed out that a particular kind of interpretation paralleled each type of result within the classification. In addition we attempted to show that on the basis of current theory and research, it seemed more reasonable to expect one type of result together with a particular interpretation; namely, convergence. Support for this interpretation requires the following results: (1) no differences on the comparisons between groups and individuals; and (2) correlations between the husbands and wives who made decisions as separate individuals. We now know that our data do not support a theory of convergence.

This could be interpreted in two ways. First, we could regard the theory as untenable. However, as we pointed out in Chapter 9, a number of conditions must be present before a convergence process can operate, and we feel that a more likely interpretation would be that if convergence has not taken place, certain necessary conditions were not present.

While we are unable to test for the presence of some of these necessary conditions, we can do so for one, namely that marital partners must interact over a decision problem before convergence can take place.

Effects of Discussion of Decision Problems

We know that couples differ in their reported familiarity with and discussion of the decision situations used in this research. Since prior discussion must take place before convergence can occur, it is to be expected that those husbands and wives who have faced a problem previously and report they actually have discussed it will be more highly correlated than those couples who report that they are unfamiliar with a problem.* Using

* We can only assume that subjects reporting they are not familiar with a problem have not discussed it, since we did not ask whether the problem had been discussed when it had not actually occurred.

these two sets of subjects, an analysis designed to answer this question was conducted.*

The results of these comparisons are presented in Table 75. The data indicate that among couples who report discussing the obedience problem the magnitude of the correlations is no greater than among couples who report that they are unfamiliar with the problem. The significant correlations found on two variables appear equally for both types of couples. We conclude, therefore, that familiarity and discussion of a decision situation is unrelated to the magnitude of the husband-wife correlation.

Why should this be the case? First, it may be that discussion of a decision problem simply does not result in convergence in the thinking of husband and wife. On the other hand, it may be that when husbands and wives discuss a decision problem, they do not discuss it in terms referring explicitly to the dimensions of the decision process used in this study. After all, these dimensions are abstract, and it is probably naïve to think that couples refer explicitly to items such as "estimating the probability that a given outcome will occur if a specific action is taken." We assume that people do take these kinds of dimensions into consideration when they must make a decision, but we do not assume that they are referred to explicitly. This is analogous to the point raised by Kluckhohn when he distinguished between explicit and implicit values [2]. Explicit values are clearly and habitually verbalized, whereas implicit values are only partially or occasionally verbalized and must sometimes be inferred on the part of the observer. In like manner, if the decision process dimensions in this research are used implicitly rather than explicitly, then it would seem reasonable that husbands and wives would probably not be correlated on these abstract characteristics of thinking.

Some support for this argument is provided in the investigations by Kenkel [3, 4] which indicate that spouses do not accurately perceive abstract characteristics of their interaction, since they cannot accurately estimate their contributions to the total amount of interaction. On the other hand, spouses show relatively more accuracy when asked to predict who will be most influential in the interaction (participation rates are closely associated with influence). This finding suggests the idea that spouses are not aware of the abstract characteristics descriptive of their interaction (i.e., participation rates) but that they are aware of more concrete characteristics (i.e., who will be most influential).

---

* The responses to the questions on familiarity with a problem and whether it was discussed were given by husbands and wives separately. Sometimes the responses of a particular husband and wife disagreed. These cases were eliminated from the analysis, and only couples who were in agreement were included. For this reason fewer than 48 couples were used. We made this analysis only for the obedience situation, because this situation is the only one with a sufficiently large N to allow computation of a correlation coefficient.

Thus we conclude that our results do not indicate the untenability of the convergence interpretation. Rather, they suggest that convergence may not have occurred because the couples did not interact over decision problems in terms explicitly relevant to the dimensions of the decision process used in this study.

EXPLANATION OF THE FINDINGS COMPARING
INDIVIDUALS AND GROUPS

Our original expections about the results of the group vs. individual comparisions on decision making were not fulfilled, and our general ideas about convergence were not supported. We are confronted, therefore, with results of an individual-group comparision which need further analysis and explanation.

By way of review, the results showed the following : (1) no differences between middle-class males and middle-class females ; (2) no differences between these individuals and the group interaction sample on six decision process variables ; (3) differences between the group and the individual subjects on four decision process variables. Our task now is to provide an integrated interpretation for these results.

The interpretation of findings regarding the absence of differences between the middle-class males and females was discussed in Chapter 7. That discussion is reviewed here as preliminary to the interpretation of findings on the comparisons between individuals and groups. In Chapter 7 we stated that the lack of differences between the middle-class males and females could be explained in terms of the absence of differential sex-role training for the dimensions of decision making used in this study. In support of this position we argued that there was no reason to believe that there has been a systematic difference in either the training or the experience acquired by males or females for decision making within the parental role.

Explanation of Findings Showing Absence of Differences
Between Individuals and Groups

We turn now to the six variables for which no differences were found between individuals and groups. These are Number of Outcomes, Probability Direction, Probability Extremity, Desirability Extremity, Number of Actions, and Type of Strategy Selection. This set of findings corresponds to the "type 1" result outlined in Chapter 9. By way of review, one interpretation of the "type 1" findings was that lack of differences between individuals and groups was a result of a process of compromise between uncorrelated spouses in the group decision-making situation.

Let us take up this interpretation in more detail by presenting an analogy. Assume that some characteristic of individuals, such as hair color, is not systematically related to sex. Assume also that hair color is not a basis for mate selection. Assume still further that the hair colors of spouses do not grow more similar over time, at least during the early years of the marriage.

In addition, let us assume that hair color can be measured on a ten-point scale with zero representing white and ten representing black. (For present purposes, we exclude red-haired individuals.) Now, if hair color is neither a sex-linked characteristic nor a factor which is systematically related to mate selection, nor one on which similarity increases, then several conclusions about different types of comparisons between husbands and wives are appropriate. First, there should be no difference between the mean hair color for males and the mean hair color for females. This must follow since we have stated that hair color and sex are only randomly associated. In addition, it is also apparent that among husbands and wives there should be no correlation on hair color scores. To illustrate these comparisons more clearly, we present some relevant hypothetical data.

HAIR COLOR SCORES

Column 1		Column 2		Column 3
Husbands	Wives	Husbands	Wives	Husbands + Wives /2
2	8	6	3	4.5
4	4	8	7	7.5
9	6	2	5	3.5
6	3	3	4	3.5
3	5	7	3	5.0
5	7	4	6	5.0
6	2	3	8	5.5
5	5	7	4	5.5
sum 40	40	40	40	40.0
$\bar{X}$ 5	5	5	5	5

Here it can be seen (from the results in column 1) that the means for the individual husbands and wives are not different. This is, of course, exactly the situation which was found with the decision process data when the middle-class husbands and wives were compared in Chapter 7.

It is also apparent from inspection of the hypothetical data that there are no husband-wife correlations on hair color scores. Thus, when one makes the assumption that scores are not sex-linked and are randomly distributed within couples, one finds that the hypothetical results concerning correlations as well as comparisons on means paralleled the actual findings obtained in this study using decision process variables.

In addition, we present hypothetical data on the joint hair color scores of husband and wife. Column 3 shows the score of husband plus the score of wife divided by two. From inspection of these data we see that the mean of the joint scores for husband and wife is not significantly different from the means of individual husbands and individual wives (in column 2). This is, of course, the situation found with six decision variables when the middle-class husbands and wives were compared with the group sample.*

Furthermore, the procedure for deriving the joint hair color scores serves as a model for a compromise interpretation of group process. That is, if compromise in a dyad is thought of as each person moving from his original position halfway toward the position of the other, then our arithmetic model of the joint hair color scores parallels this conception. While this interpretation is consistent with the results for six decision variables, we cannot completely establish that a process of compromise takes place. Since we know from the earlier comparisons that the middle-class males and females were not different, it follows that even if the husbands (or wives) were always the most influential, the group still would not have differed from the individuals. That is, since husbands as a class do not differ from wives as a class, then even if the husbands were always most influential in the group discussion, the group score would not differ from either the males or the females. Thus, we say that the present analysis has not proved the existence of the compromise process. Rather, it only suggests such a possibility. A *test* of the compromise model would require a different design from the one used in this research. Specifically, we would need a design in which we had individual as well as joint measures on the same subjects in group and individual decision situations. Then we could assess the nature of the group process more directly.

Explanation of Findings Showing Presence of Differences Between Individuals and Groups

The decision variables showing differences between individuals and groups are as follows: Desirability Direction, Time Direction, Time Extremity, and S-scores. On all of these variables the means for the group subjects were higher than the means for the middle-class males and females. These findings correspond to the "type 4" results referred to in

---

* It should be noted, however, that the presentation of the hypothetical data differs from the actual decision process data in that we do not have the scores for the *individuals* among the group interaction subjects. Nevertheless, the hypothetical data are appropriate as the model for the actual data, since the group subjects were drawn from the same population as the middle-class couples in the individual decision-making situation. Therefore, although the actual means for the husbands and wives *separately* are unknown in the group interaction situation, there is no reason to believe that they would differ from the means of husbands and wives in the individual situation.

Chapter 9, where they were interpreted as an expression of the emergence of unique decision-making characteristics when spouses interacted over a decision problem. However, to say that a process of emergence accounts for the individual vs. group differences is not really very descriptive, for we still have not characterized the nature of the presumed process. In order to be more specific we have developed a procedure for the further analysis of those decision variables where individuals and groups exhibited differences.

Our procedure differs from what has gone before. Up to now the groups have been compared with the middle-class males and females. Thus, the group subjects are compared with different sexes. Using a second basis of comparison, the means of the group interaction subjects could be compared with the means of the highest and lowest scoring spouses in the individual decision-making situation and also with the mean of the joint scores of couples in this situation. Here the basis of comparison cuts across sex. That is, the high-scoring spouse in one couple may be the husband; in another couple it may be the wife. The same is true when we consider low scorers. Since we already know that there are no sex differences, this means that about half the time high scorers will be husbands, and half the time the high scorers will be wives. Furthermore, since husbands and wives are uncorrelated in their decision-making performances, we know that there is no relationship between a husband's score and his wife's score.

When a comparison such as this is carried out, it becomes apparent that there are several alternative types of results obtainable. We portray these possibilities as follows:

COMPARISON OF GROUP SUBJECTS WITH HIGH, LOW AND
JOINT SCORES OF THE MIDDLE-CLASS SUBJECTS

Middle-class Subjects	Group Interaction Subjects	Type of Process
	< Group Mean	1—Emergent
Mean of Highest Scoring Spouses	= Group Mean	2—Influence
Mean of Joint Score of Spouses	= Group Mean	3—Compromise
Mean of Lowest Scoring Spouses	= Group Mean	4—Influence
	> Group Mean	5—Emergent

In the first column we show the rank order of means of the highest scoring spouses, the lowest scoring spouses, and the joint score of couples in the individual decision situation.* In the middle column we show the group interaction mean five times as it varies in its position vis-à-vis the means of the three classes in the first column. In the third column there is a postulated group process for each of the five types of results.

* The average joint score is derived by summing the husband and wife scores and dividing by two.

In the type 1 result the mean of the groups exceeds the means for the highest scoring spouse, the average score of spouses, and the lowest scoring spouse. Findings such as this would suggest that from group discussion new characteristics of group performance emerge. In this case the group performance exceeds the performance of the highest scoring individual. Thus, we might say that the group performance is an *emergent* characteristic.

In the type 2 result the group score equals the score of the highest scoring spouse, but it exceeds the average score as well as the score of the lowest scoring spouse. Since the group performance resembles the performance of the highest scoring spouse, this suggests that a process of *influence* or *leadership* accounts for the level of the group score.

The type 3 result shows the situation in which the group score equals the average score of couples but differs from the high and low scoring spouses. These results suggest the operation of the *compromise* process discussed earlier as accounting for the absence of differences in six decision process variables.

The findings depicted by the type 4 results show the group score to be equal to the score of the lowest scoring spouse and lower than the highest scoring spouse as well as the joint score of spouses. As in the type 2 result, these findings suggest a process of *influence*. In this case, however, it is the *low* scoring spouse who has the greater effect on the level of the group score.

In the type 5 result the group score is lower than the score of the highest, lowest, and average joint scores. This result is analogous to the type 1 findings for which we characterized the group performance as *emergent*. However, in the case at hand, discussion *reduces* the group score.

We have carried out the analysis described above, and the results are presented in Tables 89 and 90. It can be seen that for those variables in which the groups and individuals differed (Desirability Direction, Time Direction, Time Extremity, and S-scores) the means for the group subjects do not differ from the means of the high scorers in the individual situation. We find also that the mean for the group subjects is significantly greater than the mean for the low scorers on every comparison. Finally, compared with the average score for the individual husbands and wives, the mean for the groups is significantly higher for the variables, Desirability Direction and S-scores, while it approaches being significantly higher for Time Direction and Time Extremity. For these latter two comparisons the original differences between the groups and individuals were only suggestive, so it is to be expected that the present findings would not be clear-cut.

These data show that the performance of the group resembles the performance of the highest scoring spouse for these four characteristics of the decision process.* This indicates that on these four variables the highest scoring member of a couple has the greatest influence on the group product. Substantively, the group product most closely resembles the performance of the spouse who thinks of the more desirable outcomes (Desirability Direction), who is most present oriented (Time Direction), most extreme in his short-run time orientation (Time Extremity), and most "rational" in the sense that his preferential ranking of alternative actions shows closer agreement with his prior evaluation of these alternatives (S-scores).

Implications of the Analyses

Why is it that an influence process seems to operate on four variables (Desirability Direction, Time Direction, Time Extremity, and S-scores), while compromise occurs on the remaining variables? We can offer some explanations, but it should be noted that these are only speculative, and in no sense can the data presented in this study be utilized as a test of such interpretations.

On Desirability Direction it was found that the group resembles the spouse who thinks of the more desirable outcomes. It may be that in some sense it is less "punishing" to think of good things that may happen rather than undesirable things. Perhaps it is easier to convince a pessimist that "everything will be all right" than it is to convince an optimist that things are worse than he thinks they are. In short, the optimist may have his way because he provides support against the more threatening expectations of the pessimist.

As for Time Direction and Time Extremity, we found that the group performance most closely resembled the present-oriented spouse. Here we would guess that because of their greater immediacy, short-range outcomes have more "impact," while long-range outcomes are harder to think seriously about because they are less pressing; to put it another way, immediate concerns drive out more distant considerations.

On the S-score variable the group performance was closest to the individual who takes his prior evaluations into account when he states his preferences for alternative actions. It seems reasonable to think that among subjects (composed primarily of well-educated, successful business and professional people) it is not legitimate to act in an irrational or arbi-

---

* This same procedure could also have been used to analyze the comparisons for which no group vs. individual differences were found. However, it would have added nothing to the previous analysis for those comparisons. In addition, we should point out that in the case of the first analysis, where the presence of a compromise process was not clearly established, even if there were an influence process operating rather than compromise, there still would be an important difference between that analysis and the present one. Specifically, in the first analysis influence would be sex-linked, while in this second analysis, influence would be linked not with sex, but rather with the high-scoring member of a couple, regardless of sex.

trary manner when faced with an important decision. This same hypothesis, it will be recalled, was advanced in Chapter 8 to explain the greater group consistency from one decision problem to the next. Given this norm, it is to be expected that the most rational member of a couple will have the most influence on this aspect of the decision process.

We turn now to those variables for which the group scores suggested the operation of a compromise process in the interaction. For three of these, at least, one can speculate a bit. First, for Number of Outcomes, compromise may occur because it is not possible to proceed to the other aspects of the evaluation process until agreement has been reached on what the outcomes are. Thus, the pressure for agreement here may be greatest.

On Probability Direction, we have found that, by and large, subjects think only of outcomes which have fairly high probabilities of occurrence. Thus, the major problem in this aspect of the group discussion is to decide whether an outcome is highly probable or only moderately probable. It does not seem likely that there can be much disagreement between spouses when the question at issue is merely that of picking one of two adjacent response categories having essentially the same meaning.

A similar line of reasoning seems applicable to the variable, Desirability Extremity. Apparently, once a couple has agreed on whether an outcome is desirable or undesirable, there is little problem in deciding about the intensity of this rating.

In regard to Number of Actions, it is usually the case that those actions ranking highest in the preferential rank ordering are the ones actually chosen for performance. Here the major problem confronting spouses is whether to pick only the best action (i.e., the first-ranked action) or whether to pick a second or third best action also. Where one spouse would select more than one action, it seems reasonable that such a difference could best be resolved through compromise.

SUMMARY

We have seen that our results are not interpretable in terms of the convergence theory outlined in Chapter 9, because husbands and wives are uncorrelated on decision process variables, and because the group and individual subjects differed on some decision variables. However, it would not be accurate to say that the evidence indicates the untenability of the convergence formulation, for our discussion earlier in this chapter suggested that one condition which must be present before a convergence process can operate is not present in this study. Specifically, discussion by couples on the relevant decision dimensions is a requisite condition for convergence, and it apparently has not been met in this research.

We interpreted the results pertaining to group vs. individual differences in terms of two different kinds of group processes. For those decision variables on which the groups did not differ from the individuals, analysis suggested a process of *compromise* between husband and wife in the group decision situation. For those variables on which the groups were different from the individuals, additional analysis suggested that this is due to greater *influence* on the part of the *high-scoring spouse*. While the data are illustrative of these group processes, it cannot be said that our analyses constitute a true test of them. To carry out a more rigorous assessment would require a research design wherein the same subjects are exposed to both the individual and joint decision-making situations.

PART IV

*Application of Formal Decision Theory
to the Parents' Decision Processes*

INTRODUCTION TO PART IV

Formal decision theory and the related theory of games are concerned with the ways in which an individual makes a decision when faced with a set of alternative courses of action, the outcomes of which have probabilities of occurrence between 0 and 1.* Also, formal decision theory specifies how an individual who wishes to behave *rationally* can best choose among a set of alternatives. In these specifications for rational choice, rationality is considered to be an individual's selection of an alternative in a way which seems to maximize his expected utility. Expected utility, in turn, is defined as the sum of the products of subjective probability (the decision-maker's belief about the chances of a given outcome occurring), and utility (the desirability assigned to the outcome by the decision-maker) associated with each outcome resulting from a given course of action. We know little about the degree to which individuals do in fact approximate in their behavior these specifications for rational decision making. One can hypothesize that they do, however, and this hypothesis that individuals choose among a set of alternative courses of action as if they were attempting to maximize expected utility is known in decision theory as the *expected utility maximization hypothesis.*

Now it is readily seen that the decision theory models may be far removed from actual human decision processes because of the exclusion of some basic sociological and psychological assumptions. For example, Edwards [6, 7, 8] has found a genuine preference for outcomes with specific probabilities of occurrence and a real aversion for other probabilities, the subjects in his gambling experiment strongly preferring low probabilities of losing large amounts of money to high probabilities of losing small amounts of money. In addition, recent attempts have been made to discover some of the social and personality correlates of decision making [1, 2, 16, 21, 23] on the ground that formal decision theory alone is not adequate to account for choice behavior. On the basis of this work, it is now clear that decision making may be influenced by intelligence, need

* We make no attempt to present a systematic description of this theory. There are several excellent introductions to decision theory, some of which also discuss its implications for social science [3, 9, 11, 17, 19, 20, 22].

for success vs. fear of failure, value preferences, sex, age, and other factors. Moreover, a recent paper [26] has demonstrated that the utility and subjective probability aspects of decision making are correlated: individuals for whom the utility of success is greater also consider success to be more probable. It is our purpose in the first chapter in this part of the book (Chapter 11) to see how the expected utility hypothesis actually fits child-rearing decisions made by our respondents.

It turns out, as one might expect, that while the parents conform to the hypothesis to a significant degree, there are substantial deviations from it. What is the source of this deviation? We believe that an analysis of the influence of personal and social variables on decisions is especially important in an area such as child rearing, where these factors would be expected to exert a greater effect than in more highly formalized areas such as gambling decisions and economic choice behavior. The question thus arises whether or not such deviations are predictable from personality and social variables. Specifically, are decisions that deviate from expected utility maximization related to personal and social characteristics of the individual and to the nature of the decision situation confronting him? This question is the major focus of Chapter 12.

II

Tests of the Expected Utility Hypothesis

First we describe the procedures we used to test the expected utility hypothesis. The second section deals with the prediction of first choices made among the sets of child-rearing alternatives. The third section considers the prediction of the parents' rank orderings of child-rearing alternatives, and the last section presents a discussion of the findings and attempts to draw some general conclusions.

The subjects are the 96 husbands and wives (48 couples) whom we have called the middle-class subjects. All results are reported separately for husbands and wives, because the two groups are not independent and thus could not be combined, and also because it permits an analysis of sex differences.

Throughout the chapter we will be using the concepts of "utility" and "subjective probability," which are identical with the decision process characteristics of Desirability Direction and Probability Direction. We introduce this change in terms in this portion of the book because the former terminology traditionally has been used in other studies of expected utility, and their use here will aid in exposition. Now and then, we interchange the sets of terms just to stress their equivalence.

PROCEDURE

In Chapter 2, we described the computation of the subjects' expected utility. For each of the six alternatives presented with each of the four decision problems, the subjective probability (Probability Direction) scale value was multiplied by the utility (Desirability Direction) scale value for each outcome which the subject stated for a given alternative. If more than one outcome was listed, the products (subjective probability times utility) were summed to yield the subject's expected utility for the given alternative. Since utility estimates can receive negative scale values, it was possible to obtain a negative expected utility.

The subject's expected utility values for the alternatives were employed to predict two classes of data: (1) the action or actions he chose for performance in each decision situation; and (2) his preferential rank order of alternatives in each situation. As we shall see, both predictions served as tests of the expected utility hypothesis.

In order to test how well expected utility predicted the rank order of alternatives in each situation, it was necessary to determine the extent of relationship between the actual ranking made by the subject and a criterion rank order based on his expected utilities for the six alternatives. We use, of course, the S-score, whose computation is described in Chapter 2, and which we have included throughout as one of the ten basic decision process characteristics.

A perfect agreement score (S-score of 15) would indicate perfect predictability of the subject's rank order on the basis of expected utility. However, scores somewhat less than perfect could also be viewed as supporting, although in a lesser degree, the applicability of the expected utility hypothesis. It was decided that S, the numerator in Kendall's formula for *tau* [13], could serve as a measure of the degree of agreement between the actual and criterion rank orders. This score (when N is equal to 6 alternatives) yields a range from -15 (maximum disagreement) to $+15$ (maximum agreement), with 0 indicating a random relationship between the two rankings. Thus, in each of the four decision situations, an S-score was computed for each subject.

We recognize that the present analysis might be criticized (e.g., [5, 10, 18]) on the grounds that we failed to base our utility and subjective probability values on scales having a true zero point (i.e., ratio scales), and therefore are unable to make truly accurate predictions. Although we were aware of this limitation, we saw no way of readily overcoming it within the design of the present study. Moreover, we felt that this would not have serious consequences. Prediction in the social sciences has often violated this measurement assumption and still yielded reliable results. This is particularly true of field research using self-report techniques as are used in this study.

Before turning to the presentation of the results, we want to comment on still another methodological point. Considering the nature of our predictive problem, it might be argued that a one-to-one correspondence should obtain between expected utility values and the first choices and rank orderings of the subjects. This position would maintain that what we have done is to predict whether a subject would choose chocolate pie in a list of desserts by simply determining if the subject liked chocolate pie. This argument misses a crucial point in our research. If we had asked the subject which of the alternatives in a given situation he preferred and then had tried to predict which alternative he would actually choose, the results, admittedly, would not be important. However, our concern was the predictive accuracy of the expected utility hypothesis. Does the subject actually select the alternative from a list of alternatives that yields outcomes he both desires and believes are likely to occur? This is analogous to Lewin's level of aspiration model [15, 23], in which the problem is to predict a subject's level of aspiration on the basis of valence and subjective probability. In both cases, the attempt is to predict choice behavior from some composite index based on aspects of the subject's evaluative process. Thus the predictive problem is not a trivial one.

PREDICTION OF FIRST CHOICES AMONG THE

CHILD-REARING ALTERNATIVES

By scoring according to the methods previously outlined, each of the alternatives in the four decision situations was assigned an expected utility value for each subject. The expected utility hypothesis asserts that the subject should always prefer the alternative with the highest expected utility when he has to choose among a set of two or more alternatives. It is a relatively simple matter to compare this prediction with the choices the subjects actually made in each decision situation. Subjects were dichotomized in terms of whether or not they chose the alternative with the highest expected utility.* Table 91 shows this comparison separately for husbands and wives. One-sixth of the total number of predictions in each situation would be expected by chance. This follows from the fact that six alternative courses of action were associated with each decision problem, so that a subject had one chance in six of selecting the alternative with the highest expected utility, even if he was choosing at random. If there are 48 subjects, the probability of the total number of correct predictions by chance (i.e., selection of the alternative with the highest expected utility) is 1/6 times 48. Conversely, the probability of the total number of incorrect predictions by chance would be 5/6 times 48.†

---

* The number of subjects used in the various tests of the expected utility hypothesis was determined by the maximum number of usable cases for the class of data specified.

† Two or more alternatives may receive the same expected utility. This can arise from either one of the following two sources: (1) The subject's failure or inability to differentiate preferentially between alternatives; i.e., his indifference between the alternatives involved. (2) An artifact of the scoring procedure which is not sufficiently sensitive to distinguish between a slight degree of preference for one or two alternatives; e.g., the response "probable" is scored .75, even though a subject might mean .77 in one case and .73 in another. Similarly, the response "desirable" is scored +2, despite the fact that a given subject may mean +1.9 in one case and +1.6 in another. Under these conditions, two alternatives will receive the identical expected utility, although the subject may actually see them as different. Wherever such ties

While it is clear from Tables 91 and 92 that not all of the predictions were correct, there were more right predictions than wrong ones for both sexes in all four decision situations. By a χ^2 test with 1 d.f. the number of right predictions is significantly better than chance at the .001 level or better for all four decision situations, as well as for the mean across the four situations. The subjects did tend to select among the child-rearing alternatives as if to maximize their expected utilities.

Introduction of "Time Orientation" in the Expected Utility Index

The Decision Process Test yields measures of the subject's estimate of when the outcomes he lists will begin to happen. This variable of Time Direction can be used to extend and modify the concept of expected utility, which in its original form was taken directly from formal decision theory (e.g., [17]). The inclusion of a time variable in the expected utility index reflects the thinking and empirical findings of over a decade of social science research [4, 12, 14, 24, 25].

In examining the role of time orientation in social behavior, a number of investigators (e.g., [12, 25]) have concluded that persons tend to choose between alternative courses of action in such a way that satisfaction will be forthcoming with the least possible delay. In other words, granted that the goal has been set, when the subject is given the choice of two or more paths to the goal he will tend to choose the one that seems to be temporally most direct, i.e., the one that yields "reinforcement" with the least amount of delay. In light of this, it is proposed that given two outcomes with the same expected utility, an individual will prefer the most readily attainable one providing, of course, that his expected utility values are positive. On the other hand, when they are negative the individual will choose the outcome that is *not* most readily attained. Stated somewhat differently, the more readily accessible a negative outcome is, the less the subject will prefer it. To test this hypothesis, a modified expected utility value with Time Direction as a component and designated E', was constructed.*

The analysis of the data bearing on the predictive accuracy of the modified expected utility hypothesis parallels the method used with the original hypothesis. Thus, an E' value for each alternative was computed for each subject. The predictions based on the modified expected utilities

---

occurred, regardless of their source in the expected utility values, it became impossible to state whether or not a correct prediction was obtained. For example, if a subject selected alternative 1 and both alternatives 1 and 3 had the highest expected utility values, we could not justifiably count this as a correct prediction. Instead, we chose to eliminate such ties completely from the tabulation of right and wrong predictions. For this reason, the results in Table 1 have variable N's.

* Refer to Chapter 2 for a discussion of the rationale and construction of the E' index.

were then compared with the choices the subjects actually made. Tables 93 and 94 show these comparisons for husbands and wives. By a χ^2 test with 1 d.f., the number of right predictions is significantly better than chance at the .001 level for all four decision situations, as well as for the mean across the situations. It is concluded, therefore, that the expected utility hypothesis corrected for time predicts the child-rearing decisions made in this study substantially better than chance.

The next question concerns the relative predictive gain achieved by introducing the time-orientation variable into the expected utility index. Examination of Table 92 does not reveal any substantial increase in the number of right predictions using the modified index. In order to test this observation, we determined the number of right predictions based on the original expected utility (E) index, which were wrong predictions when based on the modified expected utility (E') index. Similarly, we tabulated the number of right predictions based on E', which were wrong predictions when based on E. The difference between these totals represents the comparative accuracy of the hypotheses using the two different indices. Tied predictions were eliminated from the analysis. By the binomial test, the totals for each decision problem did not differ significantly from what would be expected under the null hypothesis ($p > .05$, two-tailed). These results were found for both husbands and wives.

We conclude that introduction of time-orientation into the expected utility index does not give rise to an increase in the accuracy of prediction of the subjects' first choices. Although E and E' predict first choices better than chance, neither seems to have an advantage over the other.

Prediction of First Choices: Further Analysis

A frequent criticism of empirical predictions based on an index value is that the index may not be a better predictor than any one of the component elements alone. In the present study, we have used an index— expected utility—in an effort to predict parental choice behavior. It is desirable, therefore, to examine the predictive accuracy of each of the two variables that constitute the original expected utility index; i.e., subjective probability and utility. In other words, how well do utility and subjective probability taken alone predict the first choices made in each decision situation?

The fact that the components of the expected utility index (utility and subjective probability) are correlated with the index (see Chapter 6) indicates that the results of predicting the subjects' choices will reflect these correlations. Since utility is most highly correlated with expected utility, we would expect this variable to follow the predictive accuracy of expected utility more closely than subjective probability. Further it should be understood that we cannot unequivocally test the predictive accuracy of either variable in complete independence of the other. This, of course, would require holding the one constant while varying the other.

For each decision problem we tabulated the number of correct and incorrect predictions based on utility alone and on subjective probability alone. A choice was considered correctly predicted if the subject selected the alternative with the highest utility (or subjective probability) estimate. All tied predictions were eliminated. Tables 80 and 81 present the results for utility and subjective probability, respectively.

It is clear that the utility variable predicts first choices of the husbands and wives substantially better than chance (by χ^2 with 1 d.f., $p \leqq .05$). Subjects chose that alternative from the set of six which yielded the most desirable results; i.e., the alternative with the highest utility (Desirability Direction) value. Although this finding occurs for both husbands and wives, in the latter case the absolute number of incorrect predictions exceeds the number of correct ones in the masturbation and homework situations. These results seem to indicate that while the over-all picture is one in which utility predicts first choices substantially better than chance, the predictive power of this variable is not as great as the E or E' indices.

For subjective probability (Probability Direction), the data (Tables 97 and 98) indicate that we are unable to predict first choices very successfully. By χ^2 with 1 d.f., the subjective probability values for husbands did not predict first choices at better than chance level. While the number of incorrect predictions for the wives also exceeds the number of correct predictions, the χ^2 test revealed that the distribution was significantly different from chance. In other words, the wives tend to select alternatives whose outcomes have a *low* probability of occurrence. Since this same finding occurs for both males and females when later on we consider the predictions of rankings, some explanation is in order.

This unexpected result is understandable when we look at Table 38. The Desirability Direction (utility) mean scores for the middle-class males and females are negative. Thus, on the average, the outcomes associated with the alternatives had negative utility. By choosing the alternative whose outcomes have low probability, the subjects were behaving as if their selection of an alternative was determined by a tendency to select the one whose negative outcomes were least likely to occur. In other words, they wished to avoid negative outcomes, a strategy that complements the choice of alternatives whose outcomes are most desirable and most probable (maximization of expected utility).

In view of these results, we decided to test the comparative accuracy of expected utility, utility taken alone, and subjective probability taken alone. Following the method used earlier in testing the comparative accuracy of E and E', we found that utility alone predicted first choices as accurately as expected utility ($p > .05$). This conclusion should be qualified, however, since the number of tied alternatives was much greater in the case of utility alone (see Tables 82 and 83). This throws light on the important role that subjective probability may play in decision making, namely, it serves to "break" ties in expected utility and thereby makes a choice between alternatives possible. It follows that its inclusion in the expected utility index increases predictive accuracy.

A similar analysis for subjective probability alone revealed that expected utility was significantly more accurate in predicting first choices ($p \le .05$). In view of the earlier findings, this result was to be expected.

To summarize: The important conclusion to be drawn is that for the particular child-rearing decisions used and for the group of parents tested, expected utility, expected utility corrected for time orientation, and utility alone all predict first choices substantially better than chance. Moreover, on a probability basis, none of these values predicts more accurately than the other two. Nevertheless, while the absolute number of correct predictions is about equal for E and E', the utility variable taken alone yields somewhat fewer correct predictions. This is particularly evident in the case of the wives. Finally, subjective probability alone proved to be the least satisfactory predictor of first choices.

PREDICTION OF THE RANK ORDERINGS OF THE
CHILD-REARING ALTERNATIVES

In addition to selecting the single most preferred action from the set of six actions presented with each decision situation, the subjects also were required to rank all six in preferential order. A more rigorous test of the expected utility hypothesis can be achieved by attempting to predict these rank orders from a criterion rank order based on the subject's expected utilities for the alternatives. Accordingly, an agreement score was computed for each subject as a means of representing the degree of agreement between the actual ranking and the criterion ranking.

If subjects make their choices in accordance with the expected utility hypothesis, then their rank order of alternatives should follow the principle of expected utility maximization; i.e., the alternative with the highest expected utility will be ranked first, the alternative with the next highest expected utility will be ranked second, and so on throughout the six alternatives for a given decision problem. If a subject ranks the six alternatives in complete accordance with this strategy, we would expect a maximum S-score, since this means perfect agreement between the actual ranking and the criterion ranking based on the expected utility values for the six alternatives.

To test the prediction that subjects rank alternatives in a descending order of magnitude of expected utility (i.e., rank one is assigned to the alternative with the highest expected utility, and so on), the frequency of each S-score value was tabulated for each of the four decision situations. Kendall [13] has tabled the exact probability associated with the occurrence under the null hypothesis of a given value of S. Since the sample consisted of 48 husbands and 48 wives, the number of S-scores of a given value that would be expected under the null hypothesis is the probability of that score times 48. The resulting theoretical frequency was compared with the observed frequency of cases at each S-score level. Tables 82 and 83 present these results. A χ^2 analysis with 7 d.f. showed that the criterion rank orders predicted the subjects' actual rankings of alternatives significantly better than chance ($p \leqq .001$). This finding occurred for both husbands and wives. Thus the expected utility index predicts not only first choices among alternatives, but also the subjects' preferential rank orderings.

Introduction of "Time Orientation" in the Expected Utility Index

Following the procedure used in the prediction of the subjects' first choices, we analyzed the distribution of S-scores based on the modified expected utility value (E'); i.e., the expected utility value corrected for time orientation. It was proposed that in ranking a set of alternatives the subject would arrange these in a descending order of magnitude of E' values. S-scores were computed to represent the degree of agreement between the actual rank order of alternatives and the criterion rank order based on E' values. Tables 97 and 98 show the comparison of the observed and theoretical frequencies at each S-score level. By χ^2 with 7 d.f. the criterion rank orders predicted the subjects' actual rankings significantly better than chance ($p < .001$). This occurred for both husbands and wives.

In order to determine whether E' predicted the rank order of alternatives more accurately than E, we compared the two sets of S-scores for each subject in each decision situation. For every case in which S (based on E) was higher than S (based on E') a "plus" was given to that subject. Conversely, for every case in which S (based on E') was higher than S (based on E), a "minus" was given to that subject. All tied pairs were assigned a zero. The total number of pluses relative to the total number of minuses represents the comparative accuracy of one over the other. All subjects for whom the two S-scores were identical were eliminated from the analysis. Under the null hypothesis, we would expect the two totals to be approximately equal. Application of the sign test indicated that none of the eight pairs of sums differed significantly from what would be expected under the null hypothesis ($p > .05$, two-tailed).

One may conclude that the introduction of time orientation into the expected utility index does not lead to an increase in accuracy of prediction of the subjects' rank orderings of alternatives. Neither E nor E' seems to have an advantage over the other.

Prediction of the Rank Orderings: Further Analysis

Still following the steps taken in predicting the first choices, we next computed and analyzed the distributions of S-scores based on utility and subjective probability taken alone. How well do the criterion rank orders based only on utility and only on subjective probability agree with the actual rankings?

Tables 99 and 100 present the expected and observed distributions of S-scores based on subjective probability alone. For the husbands the distributions for the masturbation and stealing situations are significantly different from chance, and the scores tend to group at the lower ranges of the distribution. Subjective probability, then, predicts the rank orders better than chance for the males in two situations. The results indicate they order the alternatives so that the alternative with the *lowest* probability index is assigned rank one, the alternative with next lowest index is assigned rank two, and so on. This finding is even more clear-cut for the wives, where three of the four decision situations yield distributions of S-scores that are significantly different from chance. Thus both husbands and wives rank the alternatives so that the ones with the *least* probable outcomes are ranked first. The explanation of this was given earlier in the discussion of first choices.

If we now consider the utility variable only, it turns out that it yields S-score distributions that are significantly different from what would be expected by chance ($p < .001$). Tables 101 and 102 show these results. Examination of the over-all distribution of the S-score values indicates that they are, on the whole, lower than those obtained with the expected utility values (Tables 95 and 96). Thus, whereas utility alone predicts the rank orderings better than chance, there is some indication that it is not as accurate as the original expected utility index.

The foregoing results indicated a test of the comparative accuracy of expected utility, utility taken alone, and subjective probability taken alone. Comparisons were carried out separately for husbands and wives. Using the sign test, we first compared the S-score distributions based on utility alone with those based on expected utility. In each of the four decision situations the results indicated that the criterion rank orders based on the expected utility values were more effective in predicting the subjects' actual rankings of the alternatives than the criterion rank orders based on the utility variable alone ($p < .05$, two-tailed). This finding occurred for both husbands and wives. Thus one may conclude that the combination of subjective probability and utility in the expected utility index improves the accuracy of prediction of the subjects' rankings of the alternatives. We have seen that in predicting the subjects' first choices among the alternatives, although expected utility and utility alone were not significantly different, in absolute terms expected utility was a superior basis for prediction, just as it is for the rankings.

A similar analysis for subjective probability alone revealed that expected utility again was significantly more accurate in predicting the rank orderings ($p \le .05$, two-tailed).

To summarize: The results pertaining to the prediction of the rank orderings of child-rearing alternatives seem to parallel, in the main, those found in connection with the prediction of first choices. The distributions of S-scores based on E, E', and utility alone were all significantly different from chance. However, E and E' proved to be the more accurate predictors, with utility by itself being significantly less reliable. Finally, subjective probability was the least adequate as a predictor of the rankings for both husbands and wives.

The Effects of "Conflict" and of Imperfect Discrimination on the Rankings

In studying the relation between the rankings of alternatives and the respondents' expected utilities for these alternatives, we made two further refinements in the expected utility index, much as we did when we introduced time into the computation of expected utility and then tested to see if the altered index improved our prediction of the rankings.

The first refinement was made to take account of the possible effects of an alternative being viewed by the respondent as having both desirable and undesirable consequences. If the expected consequences are mixed (i.e., some desired and some not desired), then even though the expected utility for the alternative might equal the expected utility of an alternative whose outcomes are either all desirable or all undesirable, the alternative with mixed outcomes might still be displaced from the rank order one might expect. It seemed likely that an alternative with mixed outcomes should be ranked below an alternative of equal expected utility whose outcomes are all desirable, and yet be ranked above an alternative with equal expected utility whose outcomes were all negative. This expectation was based on the assumption that the anticipation of negative outcomes, even though offset in terms of over-all utility by the positive outcomes, would lead to an avoidance of performance and hence to a lower rank position. Similarly, when an outcome has a desirable consequence embedded in over-all negative expected utility, the desired outcome should lead to a greater tendency to perform than would be the case for which all outcomes were negative.

One would predict that the S-scores, the index of correspondence between ranks and expected utility, would be lower for those subjects whose expected utilities were more frequently based on mixed outcomes, since the latter would tend to increase the number of displacements of alternatives from their proper rank position. To test this hypothesis, we determined for each of the 96 subjects in the middle-class group the number of alternatives (out of a total of 24 for the four situations) for which mixed outcomes had been anticipated. We then computed correlations for the male and female groups between the number of such alternatives (ranging from 0 to 24) and the respondents' S-scores. Neither of the correlations for the two groups was significant, thus suggesting that within the limits of the methods used the expected utility index does not gain from making distinctions between over-all utilities based on pure as opposed to mixed sets of outcomes.

The second refinement concerned the effects of imperfect discrimination between alternatives because of insufficient differences in expected utilities. First, we plotted the frequency of misplacements in rank for each alternative (in terms of what would be predicted from the expected utility index) by the actual rank position of the alternative. This was done to see whether or not the errors tended to accumulate in the middle ranks and to be less frequent in the extreme ranks, i.e., the first and sixth. Our assumption in this instance came from psycho-physical studies of judgment, and was that extreme ranks serve as anchoring points, and errors in discrimination tend to be more frequent as one moves toward the midpoint of the scale being used. Nevertheless, the plotted curves showed no tendency for misplacements to be other than equally distributed among the six rank positions.

Next we tested to see whether the discrimination between pairs of alternatives with a small difference in expected utility was less perfect than discrimination between alternatives with a larger difference in expected utility. To do this, we selected pairs of alternatives with adjacent ranks that were inverted in their predicted rank order. For example, a pair might consist of two alternatives in the third and fourth position in which the one ranked third had a smaller expected utility than the one ranked fourth; these two were viewed as adjacent and inverted. For each pair that we found (there were about 40 such pairs for the total group of middle-class subjects) we selected from the subject's responses another pair of alternatives in the same rank positions as the inverted pair, but which themselves were ranked in correct order according to expected utility. We then computed for each matched set of pairs the difference in expected utility between the members of the two pairs. This was done to find out whether or not the difference in the inverted or misplaced pair was smaller, as predicted, than the difference between the correctly placed pair. Of the 42 sets of pairs, the larger difference in expected utility occurred just about as often in the correctly discriminated pair as in the imperfectly ranked pair.

Thus our attempts to refine the expected utility index to take account of the effects of varying size of the differences in expected utility between the alternatives produced no improvement in predictability of the rankings. This suggests that within the limits of the methods we have used, the size of difference in expected utility has little effect.

DISCUSSION AND CONCLUSIONS

Prediction of First Choices

In conclusion, we shall attempt to draw generalizations regarding the applicability of the expected utility hypothesis to child-rearing decisions.

First, the expected utility hypothesis appears to yield accurate predictions of the child-rearing decisions (i.e., first choices among the alternatives) made by our subjects. Both mothers and fathers selected among child-rearing alternatives as if they were maximizing their expected utilities. The fact that a formal decision theory hypothesis fits what some may consider to be a nonrational area such as child rearing makes the case for its general relevance *a fortiori* a stronger one than if it had been shown to apply to more highly formalized areas; e.g., economic choice behavior.

Second, the introduction of time orientation (Time Direction) into the expected utility index seemed to add little to the predictive power of this index. Whereas it was found that expected utility corrected for time predicted first choices substantially better than chance, an increased accuracy of prediction was not achieved. Apparently the subjects maximize their expected utilities whether or not this index is corrected for time. A tentative explanation for this finding is that E and E' values bear a direct relationship to each other; i.e., the alternative with the highest E value will also be the one with the highest E' value. This would follow, providing the majority of the subjects thought of outcomes that would occur only in the reasonably near future, since a present-oriented time estimate receives a higher score than a future-oriented time estimate. Under these conditions, if the subjects were maximizing expected utility corrected for time, as they were in fact shown to be, then there would be virtually no predictive gain of E' over E. Table 103 shows that the mean time estimates of the subjects tend toward the near future, and Tables 104 and 105 indicate high intercorrelations between E and E'. This indicates that where the subjects selected the alternative with the highest E value and then the alternative with the highest E' value there could be little predictive gain of E' over E.

Third, the use of the utility (Desirability Direction) variable alone yielded predictions of first choices that were almost as good as the predictions made on the basis of the expected utility values. This means that our subjects appear to have chosen the child-rearing alternatives that yielded the most desirable results (outcomes). However, the addition of subjective probability to form the expected utility index did yield some improvement in prediction, although this failed to reach statistical significance; i.e., expected utility was not a significantly better predictor than utility alone, but in absolute terms the number of successfully predicted first choices was greater for expected utility. It would appear that probability served to "break" ties between alternatives having the same utility for a given respondent, and hence permitted a choice to be made.

In addition to its role in the expected utility index, the subjective probability (Probability Direction) estimates alone also successfully predicted the first choices of the wives for some of the decision situations. This was not found to be the case with the husbands. That subjective probability was not as adequate as utility for the prediction of first choices is understandable if we recall that utility was very highly correlated with expected utility ($.82-.90$), whereas probability showed only a moderate correlation ($.06-.13$). We would expect, therefore, that utility would behave in much the same way as expected utility so far as prediction of first choices is concerned.

Predictions of the Rankings

The results pertaining to the prediction of the subjects' rank orders of alternatives seemed to parallel, in the main, those found in connection with the prediction of the first choices. Thus it appeared that the parents ranked the alternatives in a descending order of magnitude of their expected utilities; i.e., rank one was assigned to the alternative with the highest expected utility value, rank two to the alternative with the next highest expected utility value, and so on throughout the six alternatives. As with the first choices, expected utility corrected for time predicted the rank orderings no better than uncorrected expected utility. The reasons given for this in connection with the first choices would also apply here. When utility only was used, it turned out that the rank orders were predicted significantly better than chance. However, unlike the findings on predicting first choices, here the comparison of the predictive accuracy of expected utility and utility alone showed that the latter failed to predict the rank orders as well as the expected utility values. A tentative explanation for this finding is that in order to distinguish preferentially between six alternatives, subjects must consider not only their utilities for the outcomes but their degree of belief (subjective probabilities) that these outcomes will occur. On the other hand, the selection of one alternative from a set of six is a less complex task, and requires only consideration of the utilities involved.

The findings for subjective probability generally parallel those reported for this variable in the prediction of first choices. In the case of the rankings, however, subjective probability predicted at better than chance level for both husbands and wives in most of the decision situations. The explanation of these results was given earlier in our discussion of the prediction of first choices.

To conclude, the findings indicate that the expected utility hypothesis is a reasonable description of the considerations entering into child-rearing decisions by parents. We obviously cannot say that these are the only considerations, but they appear to be among the critical ones, for they enable us to predict the first choices and rank orders made by the respondents.

I2

Relations Between the S-scores, Personality, and Situational Variables

The expected utility hypothesis asserts that a decision is rational to the extent that it is made as if to maximize expected utility. This definition, we have seen, can be extended to the ranking of decision alternatives, and the S-score is a measure of the degree of rationality of that ranking. A maximum S-score for a given child-rearing decision can be viewed as a base line from which we can assess the extent to which parents depart from "rationality" in making this particular decision.

We have shown that predictions based on the expected utility hypothesis can account for the rankings of child-rearing alternatives made by the respondents. Nevertheless, there was considerable variation in the reported S-scores. We will now consider whether decisions that deviate from expected utility maximization can be explained by the personal and social characteristics of the decision-maker, and by the nature of the decision situation.

We have, of course, already given considerable attention to the correlates of the S-scores, but not quite in the same way as we will do in this chapter. In Chapter 6, for instance, we dealt only with mean S-scores in the factor analyses, not with situational scores. Moreover, the S-score was not included in the analyses for the middle-class males and females, which are the two groups to be reported on here. The best we could do would be to generalize from the results for the group interaction subjects, who are comparable in background. For them we found that mean S-scores were associated with an autonomy-dependency dimension of personality and, to a lesser degree, with social status and intelligence.

In Chapter 7 no major differences between the social groups appeared for the S-score variable. In Chapter 8, we found no main effects of type of decision problem upon this characteristic, nor interaction effects with the specific groups. We did find, though, some interaction effects of the

decision problem with personality; in particular, the S-scores in the masturbation situation varied inversely with the subject's age for both males
and females, and were inversely related to being Jewish for males only.

Because of the importance of the S-score variable in studies of decision
making, we undertook a special factor-analytic study for the middle-class
males and females of the personality and social correlates of S-scores for
each of the four decision situations. This study parallels the one discussed
in Chapter 6, which was concerned with the mean S-scores, but this one
differs by permitting us to see if the personality characteristics associated
with S-scores vary from one type of problem to another.

We used the factor analytic approach, which permits the organization
of a large number of personal, social, and decision-making variables into
clusters of independent content. The variables included the four S-scores,
based on the unmodified expected utility values corresponding to the four
decision problems, the expected utility scores for the four decision situations, and 32 personality and social variables (see Table 106). These
latter variables were chosen because of their assumed relevance to the
S-score measure of rationality.

METHOD

The 40 variables were intercorrelated separately for husbands and
wives. The correlation technique used was the Pearsonian product-
moment method. Each resulting matrix was factor analyzed by Thurstone's complete centroid technique [7], which resulted in 14 factors for
the husbands and 11 factors for the wives. Twelve of the male (husband)
factors and all of the female (wife) factors were retained and rotated by
the Quartimax Method [4]. Tables 107 and 108 present the orthogonal
rotated matrices for males and females.

As we move on to a discussion of the factors which were obtained for
the two groups of respondents, it should be noted that we expected them
to be similar to the factors already identified and reported in Chapter 6.
Some 30 or more of the 40 variables included in the present analysis are,
in fact, identical with those studied in the six major analyses described
earlier.

THE FACTOR STRUCTURE: HUSBANDS

In describing the factor structure, we list all ordered loadings for each
factor which are $\pm.30$ or higher. The titles given the factors are similar
to those we used in the previous chapters. Note that we have renumbered
the factors (the original order of the factors will be found in Table 107).

Factor 1: Autonomy-Dependency.—This factor is immediately recognizable as similar to the factors in Group A in Chapter 6. It is characterized on one pole by a fatalistic orientation to life, a belief in supernatural causes of events, a high degree of optimism, and attitudes of dominance toward children. At the other pole, this factor loads independence of judgment, intelligence, the belief in thinking before acting, future time orientation, and the belief in trying many actions in solving problems. The one *S*-score that loads this factor, although to a small degree, is the score for the masturbation situation. To this extent, then, rationality in masturbation decisions is related to the autonomy characteristic of the decision-maker. (It will be recalled that the mean *S*-scores for the group interaction subjects and lower-class males load this same autonomy-dependency factor.)

FACTOR 1. AUTONOMY-DEPENDENCY

Variable	Loading
Belief in fate	.96
Belief in supernatural causes	.77
PARI: Dominance	.68
Optimism (belief that good things will happen)	.64
Independence of judgment	−.53
Optimism (belief that bad things won't happen)	.48
Belief in trying many actions in solving problems	−.46
Belief in animism	.45
Future time orientation	−.44
Verbal I.Q.	−.44
Belief in thinking before acting	−.38
Belief that events clearly are either good or bad	.35
Parental concern with child rearing: honesty	.32
Expected utility: stealing	.32
General satisfaction (total score)	.32
S-score: masturbation	−30

Factor 2: Rationality in the masturbation decision problem.—This factor (originally Factor 4) has been given its title because of the relatively high loading in the *S*-score for the masturbation situation. Its appearance here suggests that it is more strongly associated with variables loading this factor than with those loading the autonomy factor. The heaviest loadings are in age (negative) and religion (non-Jewish), with two minor loadings in independence of judgment and belief in supernatural causes. The first two variables require comment. The age effect was evident in the earlier analysis of interaction effects in Chapter 8. It is explained by the fact that the younger parents generally are more sophisticated and more open in their approach to problems involving masturbation because of the change in social attitudes toward sexuality in children [2]. It is a

rather striking confirmation of the changes in attitudes toward such child-care practices to find this relation between age and the S-score, a measure specifically designed to capture clarity in thinking and the absence of emotional influences.

The positive loading in religion indicates that the non-Jewish fathers tend to be more rational in their solutions than the Jewish fathers. Since it is generally known that traditional Jewish codes attach severe sanctions to masturbation, it is not unreasonable to expect Jewish fathers, more than non-Jewish fathers and also more than Jewish mothers, to be particularly aroused when confronted with this situation. Moreover, Kinsey *et al.* [3] have pointed out that even among religiously less active Jewish males the severe cultural sanctions agaipts masturbation seem to exert some influence. It was hypothesized, therefore, that Jewish fathers, when faced with the masturbation situation, view the problem as more serious, and become much more aroused by it. Under these conditions we would expect their rank ordering of alternatives to be less rational than those of non-Jewish fathers. This, of course, is the same view we advanced in Chapter 7 when we were discussing the differences between middle- and lower-class males in their response to this decision problem, and in Chapter 8 in the discussion of interaction effects.

FACTOR 2.* RATIONALITY IN THE MASTURBATION DECISION PROBLEM

Variable	Loading
Age of respondent	$-.72$
S-score: masturbation	.54
Religion	.46
Belief in supernatural causes	.33
Independence of judgment	.30

* Signs reflected.

Factor 3: Rationality in the obedience decision problem.—The single appreciable loading for the obedience S-score occurs in this factor (originally Factor 5). Individuals who are high on this factor also are characterized by high verbal intelligence, a belief in the predictability of life, and a belief that events clearly are either good or bad. In our judgment, no general characterization of this factor can be made, and the three personality items that show loadings along with the obedience S-score will have to remain at the level of specificity represented by the factor title.

FACTOR 3. RATIONALITY IN THE OBEDIENCE DECISION PROBLEM

Variable	Loading
S-score: obedience	.56
Belief in the predictability of life	.54
Verbal I.Q.	.40
Belief that events clearly are either good or bad	.39

Factor 4: Rationality in the stealing and homework decision problems.—The two variables loading this factor (originally Factor 9) are the S-scores for the stealing and homework situations. This suggests that rationality in these two decision areas does not share appreciable variance with the personal and social variables included in our analysis, and that these S-scores essentially are unpredictable on the basis of the variables we have used.

FACTOR 4. RATIONALITY IN THE STEALING AND HOMEWORK DECISION PROBLEMS

Variable	Loading
S-score: stealing	.61
S-score: homework	.53

This completes the presentation of the factors on which the S-scores loaded. There were five other factors of some substance that dealt with independent clusters of personality traits not associated with S-scores (Factors 2, 3, 6, 7, and 8 in Table 107). On the whole, these other factors parallel in organization the structures found earlier. In particular, the factor of manifest anxiety, which appears so clearly in the earlier analyses, also is identified here.

Three remaining factors retained for rotation were poorly defined and need not concern us. These also are presented in Table 107 where they are listed as Factors 10, 11, and 12.

Discussion

The factors identified lead to the conclusion that the variance in S-scores is not, on the whole, related to the measures we have of the respondents' other personal and social characteristics. For two of the four S-scores, no correlates emerged in the analysis. For the S-score in the obedience situation, it is true that a factor was identified, but its general meaning is not clear. The S-score in the masturbation situation was related in an understandable way to the age and religion of the respondents, and to a minor degree to the personality dimension of autonomy-dependency.

At the risk of going too far beyond these results, one might offer the conclusion that the factor analysis has demonstrated that for the middle-class husbands the predictability of their rankings of child-rearing alternatives can be improved, at least in two of the four situations, by taking into account certain variations in personality. In particular, one would want to have some idea of the degree of affect engendered by the masturbation problem, since this problem seems to distort the actual ranking of alternatives from what would be expected on the basis of consciously estimated expected utility.

THE FACTOR STRUCTURE: WIVES

In presenting the factor structure for wives we follow the format used for husbands. We have renumbered the factors, and the original factor order will be found in Table 108.

Factor 1: Rationality in the masturbation and obedience decision problems.—This factor (originally Factor 4) appears to correspond to Factor 2 found in the male data. One may ask immediately whether or not any female factor appeared corresponding to Factor 1 in the male data. Such a factor did appear (Factor 1 in Table 108). However, the minor loading of the masturbation S-score, which appeared for the male data, was absent; hence this factor joins those clusters of personality traits which are not related to S-scores.

The first factor for the females corresponds to the second factor for the males in that the masturbation S-score is related to age of the respondent. On the other hand, it differs primarily in also loading the obedience S-score and in the absence of any relation with the religion of the respondents. The fact that the age relationship continues to hold (and in fact may even be stronger), is understandable, since it is primarily the mothers of children who have been exposed to the changing trends in attitudes toward restriction of infantile sexuality. The absence of any religious correlate also seems readily understandable, since it is primarily the Jewish male rather than the female on whom the concern about masturbation rests most heavily, and therefore he would be more disturbed when confronted with a decision involving this kind of problem.

The presence of the S-score for obedience, together with the belief that events clearly are either good or bad, suggests a possible fusion, for the females, of male Factor 3 with male Factor 2. We had no clear explanation of Factor 3 in the male data, it will be recalled, so it follows that the fusion of that factor with the factor loading the masturbation S-score is not clearly interpretable.

FACTOR 1. RATIONALITY IN THE MASTURBATION AND OBEDIENCE
DECISION PROBLEMS

Variable	Loading
S-score: masturbation	.80
PARI: Rejection	−.44
Age of respondent	−.44
S-score: obedience	.38
Belief that events clearly are either good or bad	.33

Factor 2: Rationality in the Stealing Decision Problem.—This factor, (originally Factor 7) which is defined by ascendancy of the wife, also loads the stealing S-score, dominance, rejection, and optimism. It appears to

have no clear parallel among the male factors. Indeed, the interpretation of the factor itself is by no means clear. Perhaps it makes some intuitive sense for the ascendant and dominant wife to be more rational in the stealing situation, but it seems fruitless to go beyond this.

FACTOR 2. RATIONALITY IN THE STEALING DECISION PROBLEM

Variable	Loading
PARI: Wife's ascendancy	.61
S-score: stealing	.47
PARI: Rejection	.47
PARI: Dominance	.44
Optimism (belief that bad things won't happen)	.42
Belief in thinking before acting	−.34
Belief in multiple causation of events	.31

Factor 3: Rationality in the Homework and Obedience Decision Problems.—This factor (originally Factor 9) parallels the male factor in which S-scores appeared without relation to other personality variables. Since the present factor is largely defined by the two S-scores, one can conclude that in these situations rationality fails to share much, if any, variance with the personal and social variables used in our study. It is true that the obedience S-score did appear on Factor 1, but this occurred with only a moderate loading.

For the males the decision problems that were isolated were homework and stealing, whereas in the female data we have seen that the stealing S-score loads an independent factor that included personality variables.

FACTOR 3.* RATIONALITY IN THE HOMEWORK AND OBEDIENCE DECISION PROBLEMS

Variable	Loading
S-score: homework	.75
S-score: obedience	.58
Belief in multiple causation of events	.42

* Signs reflected.

There are six other factors in the female data which consist of clusters of personality traits apparently unrelated to any S-scores. As we have pointed out, one of these parallels the autonomy-dependency factor found in our earlier analyses, and the anxiety factor also emerges again in identifiable form. The six factors in their original numbering (Table 108) are Factors 1, 2, 3, 5, 6, and 8.

Two other factors were retained for rotation, but these were completely unclear as to meaning; the reader will find these in Table 108, where they are listed as Factors 10 and 11.

Discussion

The over-all level of success in discovering correlates of S-score variations for the females is about the same as it was for the males, namely, some successes and some clear misses. The variation in S-scores for the masturbation situation again is related to age, with the obedience S-score also appearing in weak form on this factor. A factor loading the stealing S-score appears in strong form, but its meaning is ambiguous. A separate factor for the S-scores in homework and obedience also was found, suggesting that for these two scores we were generally unsuccessful in finding correlates of their variability.

CONCLUSIONS: THE EFFECTS OF THE INTERACTION OF PERSONALITY AND THE DECISION SITUATIONS ON THE S-SCORES

We have tried to find personal and social correlates of variations in S-scores, because the deviations in S-scores reported in Chapter 11 indicated that many respondents did not behave as if they were maximizing their expected utilities, and such deviations, it was hypothesized, should be related to personality characteristics of the respondents. What can we say now about the results of our attempt to find such correlates of S-score variation?

First, there is the inverse relation between rationality in the masturbation situation and the characteristic of being a Jewish male, which is explained by their greater concern about masturbation. Second, the relation between age of parent and rationality in the masturbation area is evident for both males and females and, in our judgment, reflects the difference in attitudes and beliefs about the control of infant sexuality that are held by the younger as opposed to the older parents. Third, for the males an obedience S-score factor appeared, and for the females a stealing S-score factor. However, in both cases the meaning of the personality traits associated with the S-score is ambiguous when one attempts to move beyond immediate description. That is, the traits themseves add up to no clearly interpretable set of general personality characteristics. Last, for both males and females there appeared to be S-scores that were unrelated to the personal and social variables used in this study. However, the important point to note is that the homework S-score was the only one of the four rationality measures that was not found to be associated with any major cluster of personality or social variables in either the male or the female data. This indicates that whatever underlies variations in the homework S-score was not included in this study.

Apart from the specific relationships, perhaps the most significant conclusion to be drawn from the factor analytic findings is that deviations from expected utility maximization in the respondents' rankings depend in part on the nature of the specific decision problem. We saw in Chapter 6 that there is a general, or average, variability in S-scores, associated with certain personality characteristics. Now we see in addition a situation-specific variability, associated with different sets of personality variables. The situational S-scores do not appear to be associated with any single constellation of personal and social traits, but rather with different ones in different types of problems. Thus we conclude that any assessment of degree of rationality, as measured by the S-score, must look to the interaction of the individual's personality with the particular decision situation that is involved.

While the over-all results of the effort reported in this chapter may not bulk large, nevertheless they must be viewed as more than merely suggestive but as demanding full consideration in any use of the expected utility index (cf. [1, 5, 6]). Certainly the findings here, together with those of previous chapters, warrant the general conclusion that formal decision theory can be improved as a model of decision making by the inclusion of personal and social variables that are related to measurable departures from rationality as defined by expected utility maximization.

END OF PART IV

EPILOGUE

These last few pages represent neither conclusions nor summary. The conclusions of the studies all have been presented within the preceding chapters, and the results are too complex to permit a separate summary. Instead, in the spirit of the traditional epilogue, we intend to comment briefly on our own work. First we shall note what in our judgment are the most significant assets and defects of the procedures we used. Then we shall review a few selected findings that we believe to be the most interesting of the results of the studies.

COMMENTARY ON THE PROCEDURES

We studied the relations between a large number of variables, more than half a hundred, and we collected data on these from approximately 200 subjects. This provided the information for the subsequent analyses and led to conclusions that decision-making variables are, in fact, significantly influenced by personality and social structure. The research cannot be viewed as an experimental investigation in the customary sense, with specific hypotheses and a limited number of variables studied two or three at a time. In this kind of exploratory investigation one must undertake a more loosely organized field study. Now that this is done, the path is cleared for more intensive experimental investigation of the relations of decision processes and personality. A number of experiments could be undertaken now that would give a more sharply defined picture of some of the relationships found in our work. For example, would the same social class differences have occurred if non-Jewish subjects were used? Also, we could design studies in which antecedent personality or situational variables are manipulated in specified ways, as for example, the effects of anxiety on expected utility. Perhaps we could then speak in a conclusive way about the effects of levels of anxiety on the decision-making process.

Our exploratory field studies were made more powerful by introducing into the investigation certain variations in the social context in which the studies took place. To this end we introduced deliberate variation in the characteristics of the respondents, the problems to which they responded, and the procedures by which their decisions were reached. These planned variations can be viewed as experimental manipulations of the conditions governing the decision-making process. In general, through such controlled variation the design of field studies can be expanded to maximize the range of information that is obtained.

Consider now the test of decision processes used in the studies. Although this test was devised particularly for the current work, it has more general applicability. It is a useful device for measuring individual and group differences in those particular characteristics of the decision-making process which generally have been viewed as important, such as probability, desirability, and time orientation. Moreover, the particular decisions studied need not be limited to child rearing, as in the current research. The test is just as suitable for studying management decisions in industry, personnel decisions, etc., by altering the content of the test.

If one were interested in using a test such as this, there are certain characteristics he might wish to alter. Some of these are of more general import and deserve comment. One could work more carefully on the decision characteristics involved in "type of strategy." We had it overformalized, and it lacked an appropriate metric. Also, the probability and desirability scale values we used perhaps were too restricted in range; seven- or nine-point scales might be better. One might also alter the sequence in which *parts* of the test were given, to permit evaluation of the effects of different sequences. By forcing explicit evaluation of alternatives prior to the strategy-selection phase, one may be forcing a greater conformity to the expected utility hypothesis than would otherwise occur.

In considering the personality tests we used, we can make a general point about exploratory field studies: the design should not employ new measures alone for both the dependent and independent variables. Rather, one or the other panel of variables should be anchored to prior research through the use of well-validated measures of the variables. This not only enables one to tie his own research to earlier studies, but gives him much more power in interpretation of the results. In our own work, we found very few existing tests that were suitable to include in our investigations. However, we included a few to accord with the above objective; we used tests of intelligence, anxiety, child-rearing attitudes, and certain other traits, which had wide prior acceptance.

The tests we ourselves developed for the studies proved to be of general interest and should be valuable in subsequent research, particularly the tests of general cultural orientations such as fatalism, optimism, and time orientation, which along with some other characteristics comprise the autonomy-dependency dimension of personality.

The study design called for the use of contrasting social class and sex groups. Our use of parallel factor analyses for the six different sex and social class groups is noteworthy; its value emerges clearly in our research.

Basically, factor analysis is an important method of identifying relationships between large numbers of variables in exploratory studies. When several known and contrasting populations are used, as in our own case, the value arises both from showing the stability of factor structures for the several groups, and in pointing to important differences between the groups in the personality organization of the members. When each of the subgroups is small, as in this case, the stability of the factor structure always is in doubt. However, when the results hold up across all groups, or across one subgroup of theoretical significance, such as for males, then the results may be viewed as cross-validated. Where these results appear time after time, one is forced to conclude that the relations really do exist in the nature of things.

Another important procedure we used was to confront the parents with different decision problems so we could study the effects of the problems upon their thinking. We gave considerable attention in our theory chapters to a conceptual analysis of the types of decision problems, in regard to both their formal and substantive properties. It was difficult to translate this analysis into operational terms in selecting the problems to be used. We could not rank the four situations very clearly along the various theoretical dimensions—such as affect arousal—prior to their selection and use. However, given this kind of exploratory investigation of the consequences of a set of problems, deliberately chosen to maximize differences in the decision processes they elicit, one now has a clearer conception of the theoretical properties of different situations and thus, in subsequent research, a firmer grasp on the nature of the experimental induction which he is introducing into the decision-making process.

The other basic alteration of the situational context in which the decision making occurred was in our use of joint husband-wife decisions in contrast to the individual parental decisions. This constitutes, to our knowledge, the only study comparing individual and group thinking processes, in which social groups having a history, a future, and norms regulating their behavior are compared with individual counterparts, and an appraisal made of the differences in their decision processes. The theory underlying our expectations of differences was a theory of convergence in personality characteristics through interaction of individuals. Described in Chapter 9, it brings to bear on the process of convergence the relevant data from several disparate fields of inquiry.

There were alternative ways of designing this particular study, some of which would have made it possible to test consequences of group decision making other than those we studied. For example, if we had measures on the same couples in both individual and group interaction situations, then we could have analyzed the ways in which differing personality factors in husbands and wives worked to produce specific interaction processes. In addition, we might have used problems that both husbands and wives explicitly agreed had been discussed by them as problems of child rearing, rather than having confronted them with problems we believed (but without certainty) they might have discussed.

But to have made the first change would have led us beyond our resources of time and ability to motivate the respondents. In the second case, we would have been led to a quite different study, in which we would use decision problems that were not comparable from one person to the next. We chose to use the identical situations for all our subjects, and in the recognition that not everything can be done in one investigation, this points the way to subsequent studies comparing the decision-making processes of significant social groups and their comparable individual members.

Finally, the characteristic of our procedures that stands out in our own judgment as important, although we may not have given sufficient recognition to it in the earlier chapters, is our method of handling the effects of interaction of personality and situation upon decision making.

Many studies of interaction effects do not actually deal with interaction but instead, confronted with personality variables and external situation variables, sum up the effects of the two individual forces and discuss the probable results as if they were an interaction effect. In contrast, we dealt with the effects of personality and social group characteristics that are contingent upon the nature of the decision situation, and, in turn, with the effects of situations that depend on the presence of specific personality or social group characteristics. We can say that we dealt with the interaction effects of situations with the characteristics of our respondents in two ways. First, we considered the interaction of situations with the existence of certain group characteristics, e.g., whether the respondent was male or female, middle or lower class. Second, we looked at the effects of situations that depend on the personality characteristics of the individual parents, i.e., the variability in personality within these specific social groups.

All in all, the procedure permits us to extract the last bit of information from our data about the interaction effects of personality and situation; it seems to us to be a paradigm for the analysis of a wide range of problems in social psychology and in particular for the analysis of interaction effects, which is the mark of a mature social science.

COMMENTARY ON THE RESULTS

Since this work did not attempt to test a general theory, one can hardly comment on "implications for the hypotheses," because there were no formally derived propositions to test. Instead, our objective was to generate some new concepts, and to lay the basis for some generalizations about the relation of decision making to personality and social structure. At this time we feel justified in speculating a bit beyond the more cautious conclusions set forth in the earlier chapters.

It seems to us that our conceptualization of the decision process will be an important contribution to the analysis of this aspect of personality. Our designation of the six phases of the decision process, and furthermore of the characteristics of the evaluation and strategy-selection phases, takes us a good distance beyond earlier attempts to analyze the decision process. Not only does it provide important units of analysis for studies of the process, but it provides a means for relating the recent studies of decision making to the more traditional studies of thinking and problem solving.

We did not limit our conception to the traditional view of rationality, viz., the preferential ranking of alternatives in accord with expected utility. We pointed out that the decision-making process is much more complex than this, and tried instead to present a more general concept of rationality. Much must have entered into a "good decision" prior to the simple act of utility ordering. Each of the six major phases themselves may exhibit different degrees of rationality, according to the way in which each operation is performed. We went on to note that within the evaluation phase itself, the considerations of multiple outcomes, low probabilities, outcomes of differing degrees of desirability, and both present and distant consequences, all must be viewed as being fundamentally important in any definition of rational decision making.

The study of the decision process shows that the respondents come close to, but do not reach, what is commonly viewed as "perfect" decision making. The number of outcomes considered, on the average, falls short of the three which the respondents might have considered within the context of our test (not to speak of additional ones that would be pertinent). The consequences with low probabilities of occurrence were overlooked. The concern with the more distant consequences of an action was, on the whole, minimal. The intensive study of the relation of expected utility to preferential ranking of alternatives (the S-scores) indicates that although the expected utility hypothesis fits the actual choice process, the departure from maximization of expected utility is nevertheless a substantial one.

Even though the respondents fall short of what is generally regarded as optimal rationality, there were significant individual differences in the way in which decisions were made and in the degree to which these decisions approximated the formal models. Whereas it is hardly new to report that persons differ in the way they make their decisions, it is of value to measure such differences and to lay the base for an analysis of the reasons for these differences. The actual differences that were found are important ones. Consider the characteristic Number of Outcomes. A difference here of .50 between the average number of outcomes considered (where the maximum number that could be considered is three outcomes), means at the very least that the subjects who consider a higher number of outcomes are considering from 15 to 20 per cent more outcomes in making their decisions. Similarly, a difference in the Time Direction characteristic of the order of .50 means that some of the respondents are, on the average, considering results that lie from two to six months beyond those being considered by their more present-oriented peers.

The consideration of just one more consequence of an action frequently might lead to the choice of one as opposed to another alternative action, and to the avoidance of a "bad decision." The same is true of the other decision variables, such as the consideration given to the less probable outcomes of action, or to those that are more likely to occur in the future. When one multiplies initial differences between subjects in decision characteristics by the actions considered in each decision, and then by the number of child-rearing decisions made day after day by the subjects, one must recognize that the subjects rapidly diverge in the significant, cumulative consequences of their customary decision-making procedures.

The factor analyses for the differing social class and sex groups showed that the factor structure of the decision process was virtually the same for all groups of subjects. The analyses reduced the units of the evaluation and strategy-selection phases to a smaller number of clusters of characteristics, associated with desirability estimation, probability estimation, time estimation, and certain other processes. These now must be viewed as the basic elements of these phases of the decision process. These decision process factors constitute the newly defined set of dependent variables which can be used in studies relating antecedent personality and situational characteristics to the decision process.

Looking at the conclusions about the effects of personality and cultural background on decision-making, we should stress that the research has demonstrated that there are characteristics of the decision-making process which are influenced by the personalities and the social background of the decision-makers. We can hardly study the characteristics of thinking and of cognitive functioning generally without considering their determination by these other characteristics.

The analysis of the determinants emphasized both the personality characteristics of the individual and his characteristics defined by membership in a specific social class or sex group. This method of analysis, commonly referred to as a consideration of intra- and inter-group variability, is a worthwhile procedure in exploratory work because the two sets of variables thus identified may not be coextensive. Thus the concern with both personality and social group variability extends the range of determinants that are considered.

The analysis of the personality determinants of decision making primarily emphasized factor analytic techniques, and the following conclusions resulted. First, the factor analytic study of variability in S-scores shows that the discrepancy between actual performance and the expected utility hypothesis is in part understandable by reference to the personality and social background characteristics of the respondents. This implies that research which uses the expected utility hypothesis must consider variations in the personalities of the subjects. From the factor analyses, we can also note the identification of an extremity of judgment factor, involving estimates of desirability and probability extremity. However, it seems to us that the most important finding involving personality and decision processes was the identification of the autonomy-dependency dimension of personality in all of the six subgroups, and the parallel finding that for five of the six this basic characteristic was closely related to the way in which the subjects evaluated the desirability of outcomes. Also, for some of the subgroups the characteristic correlated with the number of outcomes which the subjects considered, and with the degree to which they "maximized expected utility."

At the outset of the study we understood that our personality measures probably could appraise only a limited portion of the differences in personality that would exist between the subject populations. Therefore, we expected to find some differences in the decision processes of different groups which came from underlying differences in personality that were not captured by the personality tests we employed. This was the case; there were significant effects of both social class and sex upon the way in which decisions were made. For example, in the lower class, there were differences between the sexes: the lower-class women differed both from their husbands and from the middle-class subjects in that they considered the more immediate and optimistic outcomes of their behavior, rather than the more distant and possibly undesirable consequences of their actions. At the same time, we found no differences where they might have been expected, and this is at least of equal significance; e.g., the middle-class males and females did not differ in characteristics of their decision-making.

From both of these modes of analysis one provocative conclusion can be drawn: general values and orientations toward life, together with the cultural background of the respondents, seem to account for more variability in decision making than the more traditional personality traits. Indeed, it is noteworthy that verbal intelligence had a negligible relation to the decision process characteristics, and that the much-studied personality characteristic of manifest anxiety seems unrelated to whatever cognitive processes are involved in making decisions. Instead, it is variables such as belief in fate, being a lower-class female, or being socially concerned about the undesirability of masturbation, that are the powerful influences upon thinking, and that tie basic differences in social background to the day-to-day decision-making process.

The other fundamental set of forces operating on a person are those of the external situation. In each case the variations in the external context, experimentally introduced, produced differences in the performance on the decision-making tasks. The decision problems themselves turned out to be powerful influences upon the decision process, as was seen with special clarity in the masturbation decision problem in its arousal of both conscious and unconscious affect. In the group decision-making process, decreased variability in response to differing decision problems, increased S-scores, and consideration of more present and desirable outcomes were evident.

Interesting as these conclusions may be, their importance lies not so much in the demonstration of the significant effects of external pressures, or in the specific propositions that issue from the studies. Instead, it is the ability of the investigations to demonstrate the effects of interaction of the situational demands with personality and social group characteristics that merit a retrospective comment. The use of both intra-group variability in personality and inter-group differences in socio-economic characteristics as predictors of decision processes led to a fuller understanding of those effects of situations that were contingent upon the characteristics of the respondents. Both group membership characteristics and individual personality characteristics are valuable in the analysis of the effects of situations. Thus we see that in some instances there are parallel inter- and intra-group interaction effects with situational determinants. A case in point is the influence of the stealing situation upon the S-scores. The situation caused a lowering of S-scores, but only for those of lower social status. This effect appeared in the comparisons of the middle- and lower-class S-scores in the stealing situation, and also within the middle class as a function of the intra-group social status variation of the respondents.

In other cases, there are distinctive sets of social group and personality characteristics, each of which exercises separate influence on the effects of situations upon decision making. We find, for example, that within the middle-class female group, those who are high in emotionality and manifest anxiety have lower S-scores in the stealing situation. We also find, for example, that in the lower class, but not in the middle class, the effects of the masturbation situation are to increase the consideration of long-range consequences.

APPENDIXES

APPENDIX A

TABLE 1. MEDIAN CORRELATIONS OF THE DECISION PROCESS TEST SCORES
BETWEEN THE FOUR DECISION SITUATIONS

Variable	Middle-class Subjects*		Lower-class Subjects†		Group Interaction Subjects†
	Males	Females	Males	Females	
Number of Outcomes	.78	.72	.78	.83	.79
Probability Direction	.62	.52	.55	.20	.42
Probability Extremity	.55	.55	.58	.43	.37
Desirability Direction	.40	.51	.46	.21	.50
Desirability Extremity	.51	.71	.45	.58	.45
Time Direction	.51	.50	.33	.32	.61
Time Extremity	.41	.38	.39	.29	.45
Number of Actions	.34	.45	.66	.18	.50
S-score	.08	.24	.41	.30	.20
Expected Utility	.34	.48	.34	.30	.49

* $r \geqslant .29$ is significant at the .05 level or better.
† $r \geqslant .41$ is significant at the .05 level or better.

TABLE 2. ANALYSIS OF VARIANCE OF S-SCORES OF HIGH- AND LOW-ANXIETY
SUBJECTS UNDER FOUR DIFFERENT DECISION SITUATIONS

Source	Sum of Squares	d.f.	Mean Square	F
Between groups: HA, LA	5.56	1	5.56	n.s.
Between subjects in same group	869.14	50	17.38	
Total between subjects	874.70	51		
Between situations	47.88	3	15.96	1.68
Situations × groups	78.24	3	26.08	2.75*
Pooled subjects × situations	1420.88	150	9.47	
Total within subjects	1547.00	156		
Total	2421.70	207		

* $p < .05$ with 3 and 150 d.f.

TABLE 3. MEANS OF S-SCORES FOR DECISION SITUATIONS AND ANXIETY LEVELS

Level of Anxiety	Decision Situations			
	Ma	Hw	Ob	St
High	10.15	8.35	8.96	7.73
Low	9.08	10.08	8.27	9.08
Differences	1.07	−1.73	.69	−1.35

TABLE 4. COMMUNALITIES FOR MEAN DECISION PROCESS TEST SCORES
BY SEX AND SOCIAL CLASS

Variable	Middle-class		Lower-class		Group Interaction	
	Male	Female	Male	Female	Male	Female
Mean Number of Outcomes	.59	.30	.69	.87	.69	.85
Mean Probability Direction	.83	.46	1.00	.77	.85	.92
Mean Probability Extremity	.82	.50	.92	.90	.89	.85
Mean Desirability Direction	.37	.53	.92	.98	.91	.93
Mean Desirability Extremity	.54	.46	.69	.79	.64	.72
Mean Time Direction	.55	.75	.86	.87	.86	.96
Mean Time Extremity	.75	.73	.97	.89	.95	.89
Mean Number of Actions	.39	.16	.65	.69	.45	.72
Mean S-score	.55*	.56*	.63	.57	.98	.92
Mean Expected Utility	.63*	.65*	.90	.90	.91	1.00

* These are estimates of the communalities for the mean S-score and the mean expected utility, based on the mean of the communalities for the four separate decision situations as reported in Tables 107 and 108. All others are from factor analyses reported in Tables 21–29.

TABLE 5. COMMUNALITIES FOR PERSONALITY TEST SCORES
BY SEX AND SOCIAL CLASS*

Variable	Middle-class		Lower-class		Group Interaction	
	Male	Female	Male	Female	Male	Female
Future time orientation	.40	.36	.74	.87	.76	.78
Optimism (belief that good things will happen)	.60	.64	.69	.79	.72	.80
Belief in thinking before acting	.48	.42	.74	.56	.74	.65
Belief in predictability of life	.41	.16	.74	.66	.67	.58
Belief in multiple causation of events ..	.38	.55	...†	...	...	...
Belief in animism	.45	.43	.67	.81	.65	.85
Belief in supernatural causes	.74	.64	.97	.88	.97	.85
Belief in fate	.88	.69	.96	.93	.77	.86
Belief that events clearly are either good or bad	.34	.42	.65	.67	.82	.54
Belief that actions have many consequences	.40	.39	.83	.78	.81	.66
Optimism (belief that bad things won't happen)	.59	.49	.76	.78	.64	.83
Belief in trying many actions in solving problems	.54	.64	.76	.68	.70	.68
Parental concern with child rearing ...	.50	.43	.79	.75	.80	.76
PARI: Dominance score	.75	.56	.84	.93	.76	.76
Desire for certainty	.34	.29	...	...	.48	.70
Autism	.70	.64	.74	.85	.79	.78
Cycloid tendencies	.50	.58	.65	.95	.78	.91
Emotionality	.88	.62	.86	.91	.73	.90
Interest in philosophizing and puzzles ..	.57	.43	.62	.66	.74	.84
Nervousness	.71	.62	1.00	.77	.83	.97
Persistence	.58	.52	.72	.90	.79	.79
Self-confidence	.79	.56	.85	.56	.73	.91
Self-sufficiency	.11	.21	.70	.62	.70	.69
Meticulousness	.32	.61	...	...	...	...
Impulsivity	.60	.25	.95	.80	.69	.65
Independence of judgment	.84	.61	.78	.74	.64	.77
Taylor Manifest Anxiety Scale	.71	.72	.92	.93	.93	.96
Verbal I.Q.	.49	.56	.75	.93	.91	.77

* All communalities presented in this table were derived from the factor analyses reported in Tables 21–29.

† Three dots (...) means test not used.

TABLE 6. COMMUNALITIES FOR PERSONALITY TEST SCORES
MIDDLE-CLASS SUBJECTS*

Variable	Male	Female
Anti-traditionalistic orientation	.32	.42
Parental concern with child rearing:		
Sex behavior subtest	.53	.64
Honesty subtest	.69	.73
Work habits subtest	.68	.65
Obedience subtest	.80	.60
PARI: Rejection score	.77	.62
PARI: Ascendancy of wife	...†	.75
PARI: Complaint over wife's ascendancy	.69	...
General satisfaction scale	.50	.57

* All communalities presented in this table were derived from the factor analyses reported in Tables 107–8.
† Three dots (...) means test not used.

TABLE 7. COEFFICIENTS OF EQUIVALENCE AND STABILITY

Scale	Coefficient of Equivalence*	Coefficient of Stability (Test-Retest)
Fostering dependency	.75	.71
Marital conflict	.67	.64
Rejection of the home-making role	.74	.62
Deification	.71	.72
Excluding outside influences	.72	.72
Irritability	.69	.79
Ascendancy of wife	.77	.60
Intrusiveness	.81	.63

* These values represent approximate averages based on five samples of mothers from the better educated strata.

TABLE 8. DISPOSITION OF CASES:
MIDDLE-CLASS, LOWER-CLASS, AND GROUP INTERACTION SUBJECTS

	Middle-class		Lower-class		Group Interaction	
	N	%	N	%	N	%
Could not locate	11	9	10	8	5	6
Refusals	39	31	71	57	29	38
Ineligibles	26	21	20	16	18	24
Secured	48	39	24	19	24	32
Total	124	100	125	100	76	100

Acceptance rate, the proportion of secured to the total of secured plus refusals, is 55% for middle-class, 45% for group interaction, and 25% for lower-class subjects. A χ^2 analysis of differences between the groups in the number of secured in relation to the number of refusals gives the following results:
Middle-class vs. Group Interaction: $\chi^2 = 0.62$; d.f. = 1, n.s.
Middle-class vs. Lower-class: $\chi^2 = 15.76$; d.f. =1; $p < .001$.

TABLE 9. COMPARISON OF MIDDLE-CLASS, LOWER-CLASS, AND GROUP INTERACTION
SUBJECTS: HOLLINGSHEAD INDEX OF SOCIAL POSITION

Class Position	Middle-class N	Middle-class %	Lower-class N	Lower-class %	Group Interaction N	Group Interaction %
1	20	42	1	4	8	33
2	22	46	1	4	9	38
3	4	8	9	38	3	12
4	2	4	10	42	4	17
5	0	0	3	12	0	0
Total	48	100	24	100	24	100

Middle-class vs. Group Interaction: $\chi^2 = 1.98$; d.f. =1, n.s. (χ^2 based on Classes I and II vs. III, IV, V).

Middle-class vs. Lower-class: frequencies make χ^2 inappropriate; inspection indicates two groups differ greatly.

TABLE 10. COMPARISON OF MIDDLE-CLASS, LOWER-CLASS, AND GROUP INTERACTION
SUBJECTS: HOLLINGSHEAD INDEX OF EDUCATION

Education	Middle-class Male N	Middle-class Male %	Middle-class Female N	Middle-class Female %	Lower-class Male N	Lower-class Male %	Lower-class Female N	Lower-class Female %	Group Interaction Male N	Group Interaction Male %	Group Interaction Female N	Group Interaction Female %
1. Professional	27	56	7	15	0	0	0	0	10	42	2	8
2. 4 yr. college graduate	9	19	15	31	2	8	1	4	4	17	6	25
3. 1–3 yrs. college	7	15	8	17	4	17	4	17	4	17	8	33
4. High school graduate	4	8	14	29	5	21	12	50	0	0	2	8
5. 10–11 yrs. of school.	0	0	1	2	7	29	6	25	2	8	3	13
6. 7–9 yrs. of school ..	1	2	2	4	5	21	1	4	3	12	3	13
7. Under 7 yrs. of school	0	0	0	0	1	4	0	0	1	4	0	0
No Answer	0	0	1	2	0	0	0	0	0	0	0	0
Total	48	100	48	100	24	100	24	100	24	100	24	100

Middle-class vs. Group Interaction: Male: $\chi^2 = 1.21$; d.f. = 1, n.s.; female: $\chi^2 = .58$; d.f. = 1, n.s. (χ^2 based on 1 and 2 vs. 3–7.)

Middle-class vs. Lower-class: Male: $\chi^2 = 27.80$; d.f. = 1; ($p < .001$); female: $\chi^2 = 9.51$; d.f. = 1; $P < .01$. (χ^2 based on 1–3 vs. 4–7.)

TABLE 11. COMPARISON OF MIDDLE-CLASS, LOWER-CLASS, AND GROUP INTERACTION SUBJECTS (MALES) : HOLLINGSHEAD INDEX OF OCCUPATION

Occupation	Middle-class		Lower-class		Group Interaction	
	N	%	N	%	N	%
1. Higher executives, proprietors of large concerns, and major professionals	20	42	1	4	9	38
2. Business managers, proprietors of medium-sized businesses, and lesser professionals	20	42	1	4	8	33
3. Administrative personnel, small independent businesses, and minor professionals	5	10	6	25	3	12
4. Clerical and sales workers, technicians, and owners of little businesses	1	2	5	21	0	0
5. Skilled manual employees	2	4	5	21	4	17
6. Machine operators and semi-skilled employees	0	0	4	17	0	0
7. Unskilled Employees	0	0	2	8	0	0
Total	48	100	24	100	24	100

Middle-class vs. Group Interaction: $\chi^2 = .85$; d.f. $= 1$, n.s. (χ^2 based on 1 and 2 vs. 3-7.)
Middle-class vs. Lower-class: frequencies make χ^2 inappropriate; inspection indicates two groups differ greatly.

TABLE 12. COMPARISON OF MIDDLE-CLASS AND LOWER-CLASS SUBJECTS: GENERATIONAL STATUS

Birthplace of Parents	Middle-class				Lower-class			
	Male		Female		Male		Female	
	N	%	N	%	N	%	N	%
At least one parent born in United States	24	50	22	46	1	4	3	13
Neither parent born in United States	24	50	26	54	23	96	21	87
Total	48	100	48	100	24	100	24	100

Frequencies make χ^2 inappropriate; inspection indicates two groups differ greatly.

TABLE 13. COMPARISON OF MIDDLE-CLASS AND LOWER-CLASS SUBJECTS: BIRTHPLACE OF SUBJECTS' PARENTS WHO WERE BORN OUTSIDE OF THE UNITED STATES

Birthplace of Parents	Middle-class				Lower-class			
	Male		Female		Male		Female	
	N	%	N	%	N	%	N	%
Eastern Europe	42	75	36	63	35	79	35	81
Western Europe	2	4	6	11	3	7	1	2
Other	12	21	15	26	6	14	7	17
Total	56	100	57	100	44	100	43	100

Male: $\chi^2 = .09$; d.f. $= 1$, n.s. (Eastern Europe vs. all others).
Female: $\chi^2 = 3.12$; d.f. $= 1$, n.s. (Eastern Europe vs. all others).

APPENDIX A 245

TABLE 14. COMPARISON OF MIDDLE-CLASS, LOWER-CLASS, AND
GROUP INTERACTION SUBJECTS: AGE

| | Middle-class | | Lower-class | | Group Interaction | |
	Male	Female	Male	Female	Male	Female
Mean age	42.9	39.8	42.8	38.7	44.2	38.5

TABLE 15. COMPARISON OF MIDDLE-CLASS, LOWER-CLASS, AND
GROUP INTERACTIONS SUBJECTS: RELIGION

| | Middle-class | | | | Lower-class | | | | Group Interaction | | | |
| | Male | | Female | | Male | | Female | | Male | | Female | |
Religion	N	%	N	%	N	%	N	%	N	%	N	%
Jewish	33	69	31	65	24	100	24	100	13	54	14	58
Protestant	7	15	7	15	0	0	0	0	5	21	8	33
Catholic	5	10	5	10	0	0	0	0	3	13	2	8
None	2	4	4	8	0	0	0	0	2	8	0	0
Other	1	2	0	0	0	0	0	0	1	4	0	0
No Answer	0	0	1	2	0	0	0	0	0	0	0	0
Total	48	100	48	100	24	100	24	100	24	100	24	99

TABLE 16. ORTHOGONAL ROTATED FACTORS, DECISION PROCESS VARIABLES
MIDDLE-CLASS MALES ($N = 48$)

Variable	1	2	3	4	h^2
1. Number of Outcomes	−.22	.51	−.01	.34	.43
2. Probability Direction	.96	−.11	.14	−.00	.95
3. Probability Extremity ...	.95	−.12	.15	.06	.95
4. Desirability Direction ...	.08	−.87	.20	.14	.83
5. Desirability Extremity...	.32	.06	.06	.52	.38
6. Time Direction	.14	−.24	.79	−.09	.70
7. Time Extremity	.25	−.13	.93	.07	.96
8. Number of Actions	−.11	.07	.11	.20	.07
9. S-score	−.24	.08	−.16	.14	.11
10. Expected Utility	.05	−.93	.10	−.05	.88

TABLE 17. ORTHOGONAL ROTATED FACTORS, DECISION PROCESS VARIABLES
MIDDLE–CLASS FEMALES ($N = 48$)

Variable	1	2	3	4	h^2
1. Number of Outcomes	−.02	.42	−.08	.00	.18
2. Probability Direction	.22	.12	.64	.08	.48
3. Probability Extremity ...	.20	−.17	.74	−.05	.62
4. Desirability Direction ...	.04	−.51	−.25	.32	.42
5. Desirability Extremity...	.11	.33	.12	.23	.19
6. Time Direction	.92	.06	.06	.08	.87
7. Time Extremity	.88	.05	.12	−.03	.80
8. Number of Actions	−.05	.09	.03	.53	.30
9. S-score	−.33	−.15	.24	.23	.25
10. Expected Utility	−.14	−.65	.10	−.08	.46

TABLE 18. ORTHOGONAL ROTATED FACTORS, DECISION PROCESS VARIABLES
LOWER-CLASS MALES ($N = 39$)

Variable	1	2	3	4	5	h^2
1. Number of Outcomes	.16	−.45	.06	.57	−.10	.56
2. Probability Direction	.23	.24	.91	−.04	−.00	.95
3. Probability Extremity	.23	.05	.96	.04	.05	.98
4. Desirability Direction	−.95	−.11	−.28	−.01	.05	.99
5. Desirability Extremity	.03	−.02	.04	.61	.07	.38
6. Time Direction	.01	.91	.06	.06	−.08	.84
7. Time Extremity	.24	.94	.16	−.08	.06	.97
8. Number of Actions	−.12	.32	.01	.03	−.38	.26
9. S-score	.30	−.44	.28	−.28	−.21	.49
10. Expected Utility	−.91	−.01	−.20	−.02	−.00	.86

TABLE 19. ORTHOGONAL ROTATED FACTORS, DECISION PROCESS VARIABLES
LOWER-CLASS FEMALES ($N = 24$)

Variable	1	2	3	4	5	h^2
1. Number of Outcomes	−.24	.49	−.16	.32	.38	.57
2. Probability Direction	.32	.04	.77	.16	.18	.76
3. Probability Extremity	.02	−.19	.94	−.14	−.08	.94
4. Desirability Direction	1.00	−.06	.09	.04	−.04	1.01
5. Desirability Extremity	.12	.02	.50	.44	−.15	.48
6. Time Direction	.17	−.80	.06	−.07	.04	.68
7. Time Extremity	−.13	−.85	.17	−.04	−.04	.77
8. Number of Actions	−.32	.06	−.18	.11	.48	.38
9. S-score	−.18	.17	−.09	.74	.06	.61
10. Expected Utility	.93	−.00	.12	−.08	.06	.89

TABLE 20. ORTHOGONAL ROTATED FACTORS, DECISION PROCESS VARIABLES
GROUP INTERACTION SUBJECTS ($N = 24$)

Variable	1	2	3	4	h^2
1. Number of Outcomes	−.72	−.30	−.15	.10	.64
2. Probability Direction	.06	.12	.92	.02	.86
3. Probability Extremity ...	.12	−.07	.87	.03	.78
4. Desirability Direction ...	.90	−.09	.07	.06	.83
5. Desirability Extremity ..	−.14	−.01	.12	.58	.37
6. Time Direction	−.02	.97	.04	−.09	.95
7. Time Extremity	−.04	.96	.10	.09	.93
8. Number of Actions	.04	−.05	−.11	.62	.41
9. S-score	−.59	.10	.23	.43	.59
10. Expected Utility	.96	−.01	.08	.07	.94

TABLE 21. VARIABLES USED IN FACTOR ANALYSES OF PERSONALITY AND DECISION PROCESS CHARACTERISTICS; MIDDLE-CLASS MALES AND FEMALES

Number	Variable
1	*Mean Number of Outcomes
2	*Mean Probability Direction
3	*Mean Probability Extremity
4	*Mean Desirability Direction
5	*Mean Desirability Extremity
6	*Mean Time Direction
7	*Mean Time Extremity
8	*Mean Number of Actions
9	Religion
10	Age
11	Independence of judgment
12	Parental concern with child rearing
13	Verbal I.Q.
14	Taylor Manifest Anxiety Scale
15	Desire for certainty
16	PARI: Dominance
17	Social status
18	Autism
19	Cycloid tendencies
20	Interest in philosophizing and puzzles
21	Emotionality
22	Nervousness
23	Persistence
24	Self-confidence
25	Self-sufficiency
26	Meticulousness
27	Impulsivity
28	Future time orientation
29	Optimism (belief that good things will happen)
30	Belief in thinking before acting
31	Belief in animism
32	Belief in predictability of life
33	Belief in multiple causation of events
34	Belief in fate
35	Belief that events clearly are either good or bad
36	Belief that actions have many consequences
37	Optimism (belief that bad things won't happen)
38	PARI: Rejection score
39	Belief in trying many actions in solving problems
40	Belief in supernatural causes

* Decision Process Characteristic

TABLE 22. ROTATED FACTORS; PERSONALITY AND DECISION PROCESS VARIABLES
MIDDLE-CLASS MALES ($N = 48$)

Variable	1	2	3	4	5	6	7	8	h^2
1	−.26	.17	.15	−.04	.67	−.14	−.07	−.01	.59
2	.10	−.01	−.89	.04	−.12	.10	.05	.03	.83
3	.14	−.09	−.88	−.03	−.01	.13	.00	−.02	.82
4	.45	.10	−.15	−.03	−.09	.27	.16	−.16	.37
5	−.15	.17	−.49	.23	.23	.01	.25	.28	.54
6	.17	.15	−.22	.07	−.06	.66	.01	.03	.55
7	.07	.12	−.37	−.03	−.08	.75	−.16	.07	.75
8	−.06	.04	.13	−.06	.11	.18	−.08	.56	.39
9	−.08	.09	−.23	−.35	−.10	.09	.08	.49	.45
10	.13	.19	.26	.31	.10	.25	.21	−.34	.44
11	−.48	.16	.17	−.68	.14	−.20	−.10	.10	.84
12	.20	.18	−.43	.29	.27	−.28	−.07	.01	.50
13	−.45	−.13	.27	−.17	.38	.10	.11	−.01	.49
14	.25	.77	−.09	.05	−.04	.14	−.14	.08	.71
15	−.01	.05	.37	.10	−.21	−.27	.22	.18	.34
16	.74	.14	−.26	−.06	−.14	.13	.08	−.27	.75
17	.34	.09	−.19	−.04	−.43	−.11	.18	.17	.42
18	−.02	.72	.19	−.20	.06	.28	.14	−.01	.70
19	.07	.68	−.07	−.06	.08	.03	.04	−.10	.50
20	−.08	−.21	−.14	.04	.30	.38	−.50	−.13	.57
21	.11	.92	−.05	−.04	.06	−.06	−.04	−.03	.88
22	.03	.82	.02	.04	−.07	−.08	.15	.01	.71
23	−.27	−.33	−.09	.61	.01	−.06	−.08	−.01	.58
24	.05	−.58	−.29	.05	.03	−.03	.58	−.15	.79
25	.00	.00	−.18	−.01	.12	−.06	.05	−.22	.11
26	.01	−.03	.06	.26	.02	.48	.12	−.03	.32
27	.48	.25	−.20	−.42	−.23	−.16	.08	−.03	.60
28	−.42	.04	−.11	.09	.17	.13	.14	.36	.40
29	.69	−.03	−.06	−.24	−.14	−.01	−.18	−.06	.60
30	−.46	−.14	.03	.34	.28	−.06	.19	.14	.48
31	.45	.27	.06	−.04	−.16	.14	.35	−.04	.45
32	−.04	−.04	−.04	−.19	.57	−.13	−.15	.07	.41
33	.32	.14	−.16	.05	.37	.19	.16	.18	.38
34	.91	.12	.07	.12	.12	.04	.07	.07	.88
35	.41	−.21	−.26	.06	.10	−.06	.19	−.10	.34
36	.03	−.05	−.18	−.27	−.08	.01	.52	−.08	.40
37	.48	.17	.04	.50	−.19	−.05	−.17	−.05	.59
38	.18	.18	−.12	−.27	.04	.26	.05	.32	.32
39	−.51	.08	.39	−.25	−.22	−.06	−.04	.11	.54
40	.75	.11	−.02	.10	.05	−.08	−.10	.37	.74

TABLE 23. ROTATED FACTORS; PERSONALITY AND DECISION PROCESS VARIABLES
MIDDLE-CLASS FEMALES ($N = 48$)

Variable	1	2	3	4	5	6	7	8	h^2
1	−.10	−.14	−.01	.27	.39	−.15	.03	.16	.30
2	−.10	−.01	.31	.16	.00	.57	−.05	−.00	.46
3	.17	.04	.28	.12	−.26	.56	−.04	.00	.50
4	.01	−.10	−.02	−.59	−.06	−.16	.37	−.06	.53
5	.37	−.08	.19	.04	.15	.13	.31	.38	.46
6	−.04	−.09	.83	−.11	.18	.09	.02	−.01	.75
7	.03	−.01	.85	.06	.03	.02	−.09	−.01	.73
8	−.14	.26	.02	.04	.08	−.06	.17	.15	.16
9	.07	.10	−.34	.22	−.60	−.01	−.23	.04	.59
10	−.19	.17	−.09	−.24	.15	.04	.37	−.11	.30
11	−.39	−.02	−.09	.65	−.08	.09	−.05	.05	.61
12	.60	−.07	−.05	.08	.01	.06	.20	.15	.43
13	−.02	−.18	.04	.39	.57	.00	−.10	.20	.56
14	−.03	.79	.06	.01	−.28	.02	−.08	.04	.72
15	.08	.19	−.14	.06	.10	−.19	.39	−.18	.29
16	.44	−.03	−.17	−.55	−.02	−.10	.06	.15	.56
17	.05	−.08	−.14	−.34	−.59	.08	.09	.16	.54
18	−.16	.62	−.23	−.30	.16	.23	.04	.00	.64
19	−.21	.66	−.17	−.17	.01	−.03	.18	.10	.58
20	−.25	.04	.03	.53	−.07	.07	.27	.03	.43
21	.08	.75	−.01	.01	−.09	.20	−.00	.03	.62
22	.40	.60	.15	−.02	.06	−.22	.00	−.12	.62
23	.13	−.56	−.31	−.15	−.03	.26	−.04	−.05	.52
24	.06	−.62	.13	−.01	−.08	.27	.20	.19	.56
25	−.12	−.12	−.04	−.10	−.03	.27	.31	.06	.21
26	−.12	−.14	−.33	−.00	.06	−.02	.66	.17	.61
27	.18	.11	−.12	.17	−.00	.24	−.18	−.27	.25
28	−.41	−.08	.00	−.01	.13	−.02	−.32	.26	.36
29	.27	−.33	−.48	−.23	.10	.12	.21	−.32	.64
30	−.46	.14	.11	.16	.11	.10	.01	.37	.42
31	.30	.20	−.15	−.19	−.20	.03	.34	−.28	.43
32	−.01	−.07	−.17	−.08	−.19	−.18	.01	.24	.16
33	.12	.33	−.40	.19	.14	.45	.07	−.01	.55
34	.79	.07	.13	−.15	−.01	−.04	−.12	−.03	.69
35	−.06	.21	−.22	−.47	−.03	−.07	−.27	.17	.42
36	.11	.11	−.29	−.02	−.06	−.06	.18	.49	.39
37	.45	.04	−.15	−.32	.04	.38	−.06	−.08	.49
38	.24	.51	.10	.04	.36	.09	−.07	.10	.48
39	−.18	−.18	−.08	.72	.19	−.14	.04	.06	.64
40	.73	−.05	−.11	−.28	−.07	.02	−.06	.11	.64

TABLE 24. VARIABLES USED IN FACTOR ANALYSES OF PERSONALITY AND DECISION PROCESS CHARACTERISTICS; LOWER-CLASS MALES AND FEMALES

Number	Variable (1)
1	*Mean Number of Outcomes
2	*Mean Probablity Direction
3	*Mean Probability Extremity
4	*Mean Desirability Direction
5	*Mean Desirability Extremity
6	*Mean Time Direction
7	*Mean Time Extremity
8	*Mean Number of Actions
9	Religion
10	Age
11	Independence of judgment
12	Parental concern with child rearing
13	Verbal I.Q.
14	Taylor Manifest Anxiety Scale
15	PARI: Dominance
16	Social status
17	Autism
18	Cycloid tendencies
19	Interest in philosophizing and puzzles
20	Emotionality
21	Nervousness
22	Persistence
23	Self-confidence
24	Self-sufficiency
25	*Mean S-score (2)
26	Impulsivity
27	Future time orientation
28	Optimism (belief that good things will happen)
29	Belief in thinking before acting
30	Belief in animism
31	Belief in predictability of life
32	*Mean Expected Utility (3)
33	Belief in fate
34	Belief that events clearly are either good or bad
35	Belief that actions have many consequences
36	Optimism (belief that bad things won't happen)
37	PARI: Rejection
38	Belief in trying many actions in solving problems
39	Belief in supernatural causes

* Decision Process Characteristic
(1) *Desire for Certainty* was not included in this analysis; see text.
(2) Replaces *Meticulousness* used in the middle-class factor analysis; see text.
(3) Replaces *Belief in Multiple Causation of Events* used in the middle-class factor analysis; see text.

TABLE 25. ROTATED FACTORS: PERSONALITY AND DECISION PROCESS VARIABLES
LOWER-CLASS MALES ($N = 39$)

Variable	1	2	3	4	5	6	7	8	9	10	11	h^2
1	-.54	.08	.42	.13	.07	-.02	.25	.11	-.21	-.27	.06	.69
2	.08	.19	-.22	.95	.04	-.06	-.00	.02	.09	.01	.02	1.00
3	.04	.09	-.04	.94	-.01	-.05	.09	-.05	.06	-.07	.12	.92
4	.46	-.21	.43	-.47	.21	.06	-.42	.14	-.01	-.02	.10	.92
5	-.16	.04	.12	.04	.13	-.23	-.03	-.12	-.16	-.72	.16	.69
6	.24	-.26	-.76	.13	.25	.08	.03	.24	-.03	-.01	-.10	.86
7	.19	-.05	-.92	.26	.06	.06	-.02	-.03	-.10	-.02	-.05	.97
8	.03	-.04	-.21	-.02	.65	.12	-.04	-.09	.24	-.09	-.31	.65
9	...	...	...	...	...	...	...	...	...	...	...	...
10	-.06	-.09	-.42	-.40	.18	-.39	-.04	.21	-.25	.19	-.04	.68
11	-.54	.24	-.07	.03	.12	-.22	-.02	-.43	.03	.41	.07	.78
12	.33	.09	.05	.14	.06	-.10	.04	-.07	.24	-.76	.04	.79
13	-.19	-.23	.34	-.16	.14	-.31	.26	.04	.06	.52	-.25	.75
14	.16	.92	.04	-.15	.03	-.04	-.05	-.08	-.03	-.09	.02	.92
15	.45	-.08	-.21	-.41	.09	-.08	-.08	.24	.20	-.45	.31	.84
16	.30	.19	-.45	-.25	.02	.07	-.70	-.02	.05	-.08	.14	.90
17	-.06	.40	-.17	.34	-.04	-.45	-.29	-.04	.28	-.12	-.20	.74
18	.07	.57	.05	-.07	.53	.03	.04	.08	.10	-.03	.10	.65
19	-.16	-.02	-.22	-.04	.05	.11	-.05	-.12	.31	.18	-.62	.62
20	.10	.90	.11	.10	-.01	.02	.04	.12	-.01	-.08	-.00	.85
21	.06	.97	-.01	.19	-.00	.02	.03	-.03	-.05	.04	.14	1.01
22	-.05	.00	.01	-.28	-.10	-.10	.08	-.04	-.78	.02	.07	.72
23	.22	-.73	.02	-.34	.11	.27	.17	.06	-.11	-.12	.12	.85
24	-.11	-.05	-.27	.07	.26	-.14	.10	-.32	.06	.62	.12	.70
25	-.07	.16	.36	.30	-.02	.10	.44	.02	.38	.17	-.07	.63
26	.32	.43	-.02	.21	-.13	-.07	.00	.08	.18	-.20	.72	.95
27	-.07	-.08	.58	.04	.21	.22	.34	.11	-.08	-.40	.07	.74
28	.36	-.01	.16	.10	.06	-.24	.17	-.15	.60	-.11	.19	.69
29	-.77	-.18	.00	.07	.08	.14	.20	.22	.00	-.02	-.08	.74
30	.14	.27	-.00	.03	-.53	.03	-.10	.34	.41	.01	.00	.67
31	-.08	-.40	.12	-.08	.19	.05	.68	-.02	-.02	.06	.21	.74
32	.39	-.23	.34	-.33	.27	.19	-.50	.32	-.03	-.00	-.00	.90
33	.76	.24	-.34	.14	-.08	-.27	-.03	.24	-.11	-.19	-.05	.96
34	.52	-.00	-.02	.01	-.46	-.10	.09	.33	-.08	-.17	.05	.65
35	-.14	-.30	-.04	-.17	.13	.77	-.09	.14	.04	.13	-.17	.83
36	-.16	.16	-.58	.09	-.26	-.07	-.07	.30	.32	.13	.27	.76
37	.41	.43	-.24	.26	-.01	-.36	-.22	.24	.14	-.00	.04	.74
38	-.27	-.02	.25	.16	.12	-.09	.10	-.72	.01	-.04	-.20	.76
39	.93	.14	-.14	.10	.12	.12	-.03	-.01	.11	.02	.12	.97

TABLE 26. ROTATED FACTORS: PERSONALITY AND DECISION PROCESS VARIABLES LOWER-CLASS FEMALES ($N = 24$)

Variable	1	2	3	4	5	6	7	8	9	10	11	h^2
1	.02	.11	-.02	.20	-.10	.08	.82	-.32	-.01	.15	-.07	.87
2	-.06	-.00	-.15	-.36	.75	-.14	.05	-.04	.11	-.01	-.10	.77
3	-.03	.03	.12	-.06	.86	-.09	-.16	.11	.03	-.31	.05	.90
4	.18	-.18	.01	-.94	.14	.01	-.08	.07	-.06	.01	.02	.98
5	.32	.03	.01	-.03	.72	.11	.05	-.02	-.13	.37	-.02	.79
6	.16	-05	.01	-.09	.06	.02	-.11	.89	.08	-.11	-.03	.87
7	-.08	.13	.49	.09	.13	-.10	-.26	.72	.02	-.10	.02	.89
8	-.53	-.08	-.14	.24	-.15	.05	.39	.08	-.01	.08	-.38	.69
9	-.53	.25	.12	.08	.32	.19	-.07	.14	-.29	.28	.13	.70
10	.20	.17	-.21	-.19	-.01	.02	-.37	.43	.11	-.12	-.14	.52
11	-.44	.28	-.01	-.20	-.08	.22	.30	.01	.08	.04	.53	.74
12	.12	-.00	-.38	.15	.52	.10	-.24	.29	.20	.01	-.34	.75
13	-.49	.31	-.13	.31	-.21	.15	.36	.15	-.40	.32	-.13	.93
14	.22	.78	-.13	.13	.20	.11	-.41	.06	.00	-.03	.13	.93
15	.64	.09	.20	-.01	.39	-.05	-.32	.07	-.04	-.44	-.11	.93
16	.26	.08	.12	.20	.06	.41	-.51	.14	-.05	.06	-.03	.59
17	-.17	.83	.09	.08	-.27	.08	-.02	-.19	-.05	.02	.03	.85
18	.10	.89	-.26	.15	-.01	.15	.09	-.03	.08	-.11	-.03	.95
19	.11	.31	.22	.01	.21	.07	-.28	-.18	.23	.02	.54	.66
20	-.08	.89	.10	.09	.05	.09	.21	.14	-.08	.06	-.10	.91
21	-.08	.76	.06	.02	.02	-.18	.12	.14	-.18	-.26	.10	.77
22	-.32	-.61	.11	.03	-.22	.02	.25	.43	-.24	-.09	-.21	.90
23	.50	-.45	.06	.02	-.01	-.09	.28	.14	-.00	-.03	-.03	.56
24	.27	.15	.38	-.06	-.03	.31	.28	-.37	.00	-.22	-.14	.62
25	-.07	-.07	.04	.17	.08	-.17	.23	-.15	.10	.63	-.09	.57
26	.50	.43	.16	-.23	.38	-.22	-.01	-.20	-.19	-.15	-.08	.80
27	-.17	.24	-.83	.12	-.02	-.03	-.06	-.17	-.21	-.09	.02	.87
28	.11	-.36	.17	.01	.13	-.68	-.18	.09	.24	.06	-.20	.79
29	-.25	-.26	-.15	-.07	-.09	-.40	.27	.00	.23	.28	.18	.56
30	.46	-.40	.10	.14	.14	-.00	.11	.13	.59	-.10	.00	.81
31	.10	-.16	.33	.12	.03	.10	-.13	.21	.61	.24	.01	.66
32	.08	-.11	.03	-.93	.06	.07	-.04	-.00	.03	-.12	.04	.90
33	.93	.15	.06	-.15	-.08	.07	.04	.04	-.03	.03	-.00	.93
34	.19	-.10	.57	.07	-.21	.17	-.32	-.05	-.22	-.25	-.03	.67
35	.20	.10	-.12	-.03	-.24	.29	-.17	-.03	-.07	-.18	.71	.78
36	.05	-.26	-.13	.16	.09	-.75	.00	-.04	-.21	-.06	-.21	.78
37	.10	.42	-.12	-.15	.23	.02	-.03	.27	.02	-.76	.12	.94
38	-.34	.26	-.36	-.17	.02	.28	.03	.06	.04	.50	.07	.68
39	.91	-.07	-.07	-.04	.01	.04	.04	.13	.09	.08	.10	.88

TABLE 27. VARIABLES USED IN FACTOR ANALYSES OF PERSONALITY AND DECISION PROCESS CHARACTERISTICS; GROUP INTERACTION MALES AND FEMALES

Number	Variable
1	*Mean Number of Outcomes
2	*Mean Probablity Direction
3	*Mean Probability Extremity
4	*Mean Desirability Direction
5	*Mean Desirability Extremity
6	*Mean Time Direction
7	*Mean Time Extremity
8	*Mean Number of Actions
9	Religion
10	Age
11	Independence of judgment
12	Parental concern with child rearing
13	Verbal I.Q.
14	Taylor Manifest Anxiety Scale
15	Desire for certainty
16	PARI: Dominance
17	Social status
18	Autism
19	Cycloid tendencies
20	Interest in philosophizing and puzzles
21	Emotionality
22	Nervousness
23	Persistence
24	Self-confidence
25	Self-sufficiency
26	*Mean *S*-score (1)
27	Impulsivity
28	Future time orientation
29	Optimism (belief that good things will happen)
30	Belief in thinking before acting
31	Belief in animism
32	Belief in predictability of life
33	*Mean Expected Utility (2)
34	Belief in fate
35	Belief that events clearly are either good or bad
36	Belief that actions have many consequences
37	Optimism (belief that bad things won't happen)
38	PARI: Rejection
39	Belief in trying many actions in solving problems
40	Belief in supernatural causes

* Decision Process Characteristic
(1) Replaces *Meticulousness* used in the middle-class factor analysis; see text.
(2) Replaces *Belief in Multiple Causation of Events* used in the middle-class factor analysis; see text.

TABLE 28. ROTATED FACTORS: PERSONALITY AND DECISION PROCESS VARIABLES
GROUP INTERACTION MALES ($N = 24$)

Variable	1	2	3	4	5	6	7	8	9	10	h^2
1	−.52	−.29	−.06	−.20	.09	.48	−.04	−.16	−.01	.14	.69
2	−.08	.18	.05	.88	−.00	−.12	.13	−.06	−.06	−.06	.85
3	.15	−.04	.05	.90	−.10	−.00	−.16	−.01	.04	.08	.89
4	.61	−.08	−.12	.15	.30	−.59	.00	−.06	.18	−.13	.91
5	−.22	.05	.02	.09	−.03	−.00	−.74	.13	.06	−.14	.64
6	−.05	.91	.14	.06	.05	.01	.02	.02	.03	.05	.86
7	−.09	.96	.07	.08	.08	−.03	−.01	.04	.04	.02	.95
8	−.26	−.05	.05	−.01	−.09	−.24	−.17	.50	−.14	−.12	.45
9	.52	.24	−.65	.09	−.02	.26	.02	.11	.03	−.02	.84
10	−.40	−.12	.14	.05	−.19	−.15	−.07	−.48	.05	.12	.51
11	−.46	.42	−.21	.17	−.09	.23	.27	.03	−.01	−.19	.64
12	.53	−.36	−.09	.27	.22	.06	−.04	−.41	.30	−.03	.80
13	−.88	−.04	−.23	.11	.03	.11	.09	.14	.05	−.19	.91
14	.29	−.25	−.82	−.23	−.00	.00	−.22	.03	−.08	.01	.93
15	−.30	.40	−.07	−.06	.00	−.22	−.37	.09	−.15	−.03	.48
16	.57	−.14	−.29	.02	.18	.18	.17	−.03	−.44	−.20	.76
17	.88	−.01	−.01	.10	−.19	.20	.36	−.08	−.02	.02	.99
18	.03	−.20	−.82	.04	−.15	−.07	−.04	−.05	−.01	.16	.79
19	.11	−.52	−.58	.13	.19	−.11	.12	.06	.24	.13	.78
20	−.14	.16	.13	−.11	.79	−.16	.14	−.02	−.00	−.02	.74
21	.11	−.10	−.66	−.23	.13	−.10	.29	−.12	.29	−.11	.73
22	.14	−.58	−.35	−.04	−.07	−.30	.45	.18	.14	−.05	.83
23	.14	.15	.32	.06	.03	.50	.04	−.05	−.07	.61	.79
24	.08	.01	.68	−.14	.31	.07	−.11	.08	.12	.34	.73
25	.13	−.23	−.06	.03	.32	.25	.50	.06	−.04	.46	.70
26	−.78	.02	.09	.21	.49	.12	−.12	.09	−.20	.00	.98
27	.52	−.22	−.24	−.12	.11	−.07	.25	.17	.44	.06	.69
28	−.22	.42	.28	−.17	−.01	−.03	−.04	.15	−.04	−.64	.76
29	.47	−.06	−.34	.08	.08	−.05	−.12	−.12	.58	−.04	.72
30	−.38	−.08	.54	.24	.02	.19	−.44	−.03	.07	.08	.74
31	.30	−.24	−.44	.14	.28	−.15	.07	−.39	−.15	−.11	.65
32	−.28	.23	.19	−.11	−.02	−.11	.11	.04	.06	.68	.67
33	.66	−.01	−.04	.15	.12	−.65	−.09	−.06	.01	.11	.91
34	.74	−.07	−.40	.15	−.13	.07	.03	.10	−.05	−.01	.77
35	.53	−.27	.19	.47	.23	.16	−.16	.26	.01	−.16	.82
36	.20	−.22	.43	−.13	.39	−.21	−.42	−.15	−.08	.33	.81
37	.45	.05	−.09	.08	−.47	−.10	.35	.17	−.15	−.13	.64
38	.38	−.47	−.37	.18	.25	.15	−.01	−.01	−.50	.03	.87
39	−.41	.26	.24	−.30	−.20	.02	−.13	.49	.11	−.06	.70
40	.92	−.12	−.21	−.09	.10	−.03	−.11	.14	−.08	−.09	.97

TABLE 29. ROTATED FACTORS: PERSONALITY AND DECISION PROCESS VARIABLES
GROUP INTERACTION FEMALES ($N = 24$)

Variable	1	2	3	4	5	6	7	8	9	10	11	h^2
1	−.68	−.02	.28	−.01	−.11	.43	.22	.19	−.14	.11	−.07	.85
2	.04	.11	.06	−.03	.91	−.20	.05	−.10	−.04	−.08	.12	.92
3	.10	.04	−.08	.16	.86	.03	−.16	.09	.03	.09	−.11	.85
4	.93	.07	−.08	.02	.07	.10	.18	.07	.02	.05	.02	.93
5	−.07	.06	.34	.74	.07	−.01	.05	.08	.11	.03	−.15	.72
6	−.02	−.19	.05	−.07	.04	−.95	−.01	.01	−.02	−.02	.02	.96
7	−.04	−.12	.06	.07	.08	−.90	.14	−.02	−.03	.18	−.06	.89
8	.06	.26	.32	.28	−.15	.04	−.01	−.54	.01	.33	−.18	.72
9	.24	.28	−.45	−.11	.09	−.08	.29	.30	.44	−.04	−.01	.72
10	−.04	−.17	−.06	−.07	.08	−.08	−.10	−.24	−.63	−.08	.15	.54
11	−.76	.10	−.00	.24	.06	−.03	.27	.08	−.11	.05	−.15	.77
12	.02	−.07	−.30	.21	−.06	.04	−.13	.76	.14	.01	−.02	.76
13	−.36	−.07	.37	.21	.06	−.09	.51	−.31	−.20	−.10	−.20	.77
14	.07	.95	.05	.03	.15	.05	.08	.04	.01	.01	−.11	.96
15	.22	−.20	.60	−.10	−.14	−.07	.01	−.27	.26	−.15	−.22	.70
16	.48	.18	−.24	−.26	.50	.24	.01	−.04	.20	−.04	−.10	.76
17	.33	−.07	−.86	−.11	.15	.12	.00	.10	.06	.03	−.05	.92
18	.18	.74	.07	.05	.06	−.02	.13	.04	.20	.14	.33	.78
19	.13	.88	.08	−.24	.08	.03	.02	−.17	.02	−.15	.05	.91
20	−.48	−.37	−.03	−.12	.21	−.04	.29	.08	−.13	−.46	−.30	.84
21	.00	.89	−.02	.09	.12	.16	−.10	.06	.16	.09	−.15	.90
22	−.01	.84	−.23	.02	−.00	−.05	−.15	−.15	−.06	−.11	.39	.97
23	.30	−.16	−.45	−.32	.03	−.28	.09	−.20	.34	−.35	−.01	.79
24	−.02	−.81	−.12	.00	.18	−.09	−.02	.01	.39	.12	.18	.91
25	.20	−.54	.39	.01	.12	−.06	.32	−.10	−.05	−.26	.00	.69
26	−.42	−.01	.79	−.03	.24	.01	.08	−.05	.01	.18	.13	.92
27	.19	−.00	.15	.07	.11	.14	−.71	−.05	.12	.18	.01	.65
28	−.59	.00	.17	−.11	−.06	−.01	−.39	.19	−.03	.40	−.19	.78
29	.46	−.06	−.19	.16	−.05	.12	−.12	.20	.47	−.49	−.01	.80
30	−.04	−.12	.17	−.08	.12	−.28	−.23	−.22	−.01	.43	−.46	.65
31	.18	.46	−.07	.03	−.08	.21	−.09	.17	−.02	−.71	.10	.85
32	.17	.04	.35	−.17	−.21	−.16	.16	.15	−.49	.03	−.20	.58
33	.96	.16	−.15	.06	.09	−.02	.02	.03	−.16	.02	−.08	1.02
34	.57	.46	.19	−.16	−.08	−.06	−.18	.47	.03	.01	.04	.86
35	.04	.13	.05	.15	.02	.13	.04	−.28	.04	−.61	−.13	.54
36	−.04	.31	.09	−.58	−.19	−.08	.05	.01	.05	.32	−.27	.66
37	−.17	.21	−.19	.00	.12	.01	−.77	.14	−.22	−.21	−.02	.83
38	−.12	.44	.02	.41	−.06	.36	.08	.08	.14	.44	.19	.77
39	−.32	−.31	−.20	.04	−.04	.00	.14	−.01	.07	−.09	−.63	.68
40	.52	.54	−.14	−.10	−.09	.19	−.03	.42	.04	−.17	−.07	.85

TABLE 30. MEAN SCORE ON PERSONALITY VARIABLES

Personality Variable	Middle-class Males	Middle-class Females	Lower-class Males	Lower-class Females	Group Interaction Males	Group Interaction Females
Verbal I.Q.	15.65	15.31	12.67	12.96	14.96	14.12
Taylor Manifest Anxiety Scale	12.56	12.58	14.21	16.67	13.04	14.12
Harris Total Score	50.33	53.50	44.21	45.33	50.04	50.00
Harris Neutral Score	5.58	6.17	8.50	8.83	7.96	6.88
PARI: Dominance Score ..	45.33	43.69	53.17	52.67	46.83	46.96
PARI: Rejection Score ...	40.10	40.17	42.58	44.58	40.29	43.67
PARI: (Complaint over) wife ascendancy	13.17	10.77	13.71	12.58	12.79	11.62
Parental concern with child rearing: Total score	59.75	58.08	57.83	58.54	56.21	56.00
Parental concern with child rearing: Sex	6.54	6.10	6.38	7.04	5.75	6.46
Parental concern with child rearing: Honesty	7.19	7.40	7.83	7.75	7.04	7.12
Parental concern with child rearing: Work	5.85	5.19	5.33	4.79	5.25	4.79
Parental concern with child rearing: Obedience	5.38	4.98	5.58	5.17	5.42	5.08
Desire for certainty*	75.75	91.50	...	...	77.83	91.00
Autism	2.60	2.50	2.08	3.33	3.42	2.58
Cycloid tendencies	3.69	4.02	3.46	4.08	4.42	4.50
Emotionality	4.92	6.92	5.25	6.58	4.83	6.75
Interest in philosophizing and puzzles	7.31	5.90	6.46	5.46	5.92	6.46
Dominance	6.67	4.90	5.33	4.79	7.17	5.67
Nervousness	2.06	3.04	2.54	3.38	2.50	3.71
Persistence	7.40	6.79	7.50	6.71	8.33	7.33
Self-confidence	8.06	6.62	7.75	6.46	8.04	6.79
Self-sufficiency	9.50	7.12	8.00	7.42	10.58	9.50
Meticulousness	5.69	5.08	6.08	5.04	5.92	5.42
Orderliness	5.40	4.69	6.46	6.75	5.17	5.46
Impulsivity	4.98	6.23	5.29	6.33	5.17	5.46
Future time orientation	15.77	14.46	13.75	13.58	14.79	14.62
Optimism (belief that good things will happen)	15.50	16.69	17.71	17.54	15.54	15.67
Belief in thinking before acting	17.58	17.00	16.58	15.92	17.42	16.62
Optimism (−+)	17.00	16.08	16.54	16.46	17.29	16.54
Anti-traditionalistic orientation	15.46	15.31	14.50	14.04	15.50	15.12
Optimism (+−)	16.50	15.62	17.00	15.75	16.46	15.62
Belief in predictability of life	17.85	17.77	16.42	17.29	17.50	17.08
Belief in multiple causation of events	19.23	19.62	19.04	19.12	19.92	19.04
Belief in animism	11.90	17.08	16.33	16.12	14.04	14.58
Belief in supernatural causes	12.25	15.23	15.62	14.58	13.38	14.12

(Continued on p. 258)

* High score indicates low desire for certainty. Dots mean test not used.

TABLE 30. MEAN SCORE ON PERSONALITY VARIABLES (*Continued*)

Personality Variable	Middle-class Males	Middle-class Females	Lower-class Males	Lower-class Females	Group Interaction Males	Group Interaction Females
Belief in fate	12.21	13.54	16.50	14.92	13.54	14.50
Belief that events clearly are either good or bad	13.25	13.71	14.12	14.04	13.42	13.88
Belief that actions have many consequences	14.42	14.88	14.50	13.38	14.62	14.25
Optimism (belief that bad things won't happen) ...	17.10	18.33	18.75	18.21	17.00	18.08
Belief that events are probable or improbable	14.52	13.81	15.21	14.00	13.58	14.42
Belief in trying many actions in solving problems	14.42	14.75	14.58	14.25	14.58	14.46
Independence of judgment ..	19.42	18.94	15.58	15.33	18.54	15.92

TABLE 31. STANDARD DEVIATIONS ON PERSONALITY VARIABLES

Personality Variable	Middle-class Males	Middle-class Females	Lower-class Males	Lower-class Females	Group Interaction Males	Group Interaction Females
Verbal I.Q.	3.35	2.36	2.79	2.92	3.41	3.07
Taylor Manifest Anxiety Scale	7.82	7.32	10.64	11.80	5.99	8.19
Harris Total Score	10.06	8.99	11.28	12.66	10.56	7.63
Harris Neutral Score	4.43	5.08	6.38	3.48	6.35	4.96
PARI: Dominance Score ..	8.73	10.71	7.83	11.87	8.70	9.75
PARI: Rejection Score ...	4.44	7.42	5.51	6.88	4.60	5.14
PARI: (Complaint over) wife ascendancy	2.00	2.97	2.05	3.16	2.20	2.32
Parental concern with child rearing: Total score	9.60	11.26	10 59	10.67	11.72	8.12
Parental concern with child rearing: Sex	1.51	1.69	1.63	2.05	1.94	1.29
Parental concern with child rearing: Honesty	1.82	2.09	1.80	1.90	1.79	1.79
Parental concern with child rearing: Work	1.40	1.83	1.31	1.55	1.74	1.38
Parental concern with child rearing: Obedience	1.15	1.41	1.60	1.34	1.73	1.44
Desire for certainty	21.57	24.08	....*	....	17.82	3.07
Autism	2.12	2.23	2.14	2.66	2.10	2.36
Cycloid tendencies	2.14	2.93	2.02	2.66	2.61	2.61
Emotionality	3.87	6.42	4.84	4.34	3.20	4.20
Interest in philosophizing and puzzles	2.06	2.71	2.98	1.91	2.61	2.22

(Continued on p. 259)

TABLE 31. STANDARD DEVIATIONS ON PERSONALITY VARIABLES (*Continued*)

Personality Variable	Middle-class Males	Middle-class Females	Lower-class Males	Lower-class Females	Group Interaction Males	Group Interaction Females
Dominance	2.40	2.63	2.66	2.52	2.32	1.65
Nervousness	2.32	2.77	2.80	2.67	2.24	2.94
Persistence	2.48	2.69	2.25	2.54	1.86	2.49
Self-confidence	2.01	2.74	2.14	2.66	1.37	2.10
Self-sufficiency	4.35	4.90	4.52	3.80	3.34	4.02
Meticulousness	2.34	2.52	2.04	2.39	1.68	2.69
Orderliness	2.91	2.70	2.25	2.24	2.90	2.64
Impulsivity	3.68	3.60	2.98	3.84	3.22	3.29
Future time orientation	2.56	2.45	1.66	2.36	3.70	2.56
Optimism (belief that good things will happen)	2.44	2.36	2.73	2.64	2.60	1.75
Belief in thinking before acting	2.64	2.57	3.41	2.86	2.53	2.75
Optimism (− +)	2.06	2.37	2.61	2.25	2.96	2.41
Anti-traditionalistic orientation	2.24	2.41	2.14	2.21	2.38	2.45
Optimism (+ −)	2.76	2.37	3.04	2.44	3.01	2.45
Belief in predictability of life	2.86	2.55	2.81	1.43	2.80	2.40
Belief in multiple causation of events	2.36	2.29	2.56	1.74	2.10	1.72
Belief in animism	4.06	19.68	2.88	2.79	4.34	2.77
Belief in supernatural causes	4.02	14.33	3.71	4.54	4.47	4.20
Belief in fate	3.89	3.83	4.11	4.05	4.88	4.14
Belief that events clearly are either good or bad	2.19	2.22	2.09	2.46	2.38	2.22
Belief that actions have many consequences	2.80	2.86	2.93	2.41	2.41	2.37
Optimism (belief that bad things won't happen)	2.72	2.93	2.37	3.43	3.48	2.60
Belief that events are probable or improbable	2.51	2.24	2.75	2.24	1.98	3.08
Belief in trying many actions in solving problems	2.16	2.08	2.61	2.44	2.71	2.81
Independence of judgment	7.30	6.26	6.05	5.59	5.66	6.07

* Dots mean test not used.

TABLE 32. VALUES OF *t* FOR DIFFERENCES IN MEANS BETWEEN
SEXES ON PERSONALITY VARIABLES

Personality Variable	Middle-class Males vs. Middle-class Females	Lower-class Males vs. Lower-class Females	Group Interaction Males vs. Group Interaction Females
Verbal I.Q.	0.71	−0.41§	1.35
Taylor Manifest Anxiety Scale	−0.02	−0.79	−0.58
Harris Total Score	−2.11*	−0.46	0.02
Harris Neutral Score	−0.65	−0.23	0.70
PARI: Dominance Score	1.04	0.21	−0.07
PARI: Rejection Score	−0.05	−1.07	−2.76†
Parental concern with child rearing: Total score	0.87	−0.22	0.10
Parental concern with child rearing: Sex	1.40	−1.30	1.60
Parental concern with child rearing: Honesty	−0.59	0.16	−0.21
Parental concern with child rearing: Work	2.27*	1.41	1.34
Parental concern with child rearing: Obedience	1.56	1.02	1.16
Desire for certainty	−3.97†	....‡	−2.61*
Autism	0.25	−2.04	1.58
Cycloid tendencies	−0.72	−0.96	−0.12
Emotionality	−1.77	−0.99	−1.80
Interest in philosophizing and puzzles	3.25†	1.33	−0.68
Dominance	3.58†	0.75	3.02†
Nervousness	−1.94	−1.00	−1.93
Persistence	1.21	1.02	1.71
Self-confidence	3.35†	2.01	2.42*
Self-sufficiency	2.91†	0.44	1.05
Meticulousness	1.31	1.62	1.03
Orderliness	1.33	−0.39	−0.66
Impulsivity	−1.75	−1.03	−0.26
Future time orientation	2.77†	0.32	0.21
Optimism (belief that good things will happen)	−3.03†	0.23	−0.25
Belief in thinking before acting	1.13	0.83	1.30
Optimism (− +)	2.12*	0.12	1.50
Anti-traditionalistic orientation	0.29	0.73	0.58
Optimism (+ −)	1.68	1.91	1.38
Belief in predictability of life	0.15	−1.43	0.69
Belief in multiple causation of events	−0.82	−0.13	1.68
Belief in animism	−1.88	0.24	−0.54
Belief in supernatural causes	−1.40	0.94	−1.08
Belief in fate	−2.24*	1.57	−0.78
Belief that events clearly are either good or bad	−0.32	0.12	−0.64
Belief that actions have many consequences	−0.72	1.31	0.52
Optimism (belief that bad things won't happen)	−2.64†	0.53	−1.16
Belief that events are probable or improbable	1.60	1.49	−1.10
Belief in trying many actions in solving problems	−0.93	0.40	0.17
Independence of judgment	0.50	0.18	1.70

* Significant at .05 or less.
† Significant at .01 or less.
‡ Dots mean test not used.
§ In Tables 32 and 33 a negative *t* value indicates the first group has a lower mean than second group.

TABLE 33. VALUES OF *t* FOR DIFFERENCES IN MEANS BETWEEN SOCIAL
CLASSES ON PERSONALITY VARIABLES

Personality Variable	Middle-class Males vs. Lower-class Males	Middle-class Females vs. Lower-class Females	Group Interaction Males vs. Lower-class Males	Group Interaction Females vs. Lower-class Females
Verbal I.Q.	3.92*	3.36*	2.49†	1.32
Taylor Manifest Anxiety Scale	−0.66	−1.52	−0.46	−0.85
Harris Total Score	2.21†	2.77*	1.81	1.51
Harris Neutral Score	−1.97	−2.57†	−0.29	−1.55
PARI: Dominance Score	−3.78*	−3.07*	−2.60†	−1.78
PARI: Rejection Score	−1.88	−2.46†	−1.53	−0.51
PARI: (Complaint over) wife ascendancy	−0.33	−2.30†	−1.46	−1.17
Parental concern with child rearing: Total Score	0.73	−0.17	−0.49	−0.91
Parental concern with child rearing: Sex	0.41	−1.90	−1.18	−1.15
Parental concern with child rearing: Honesty	−1.41	−0.71	−1.50	−1.15
Parental concern with child rearing: Work	1.53	0.94	−0.18	0
Parental concern with child rearing: Obedience.........	−0.56	−0.54	−0.34	−0.20
Desire for certainty	....‡	....	....	....
Autism	0.96	−1.30	2.13†	−1.01
Cycloid tendencies	0.44	−0.09	1.39	0.54
Emotionality	−0.29	0.26	−0.34	0.13
Interest in philosophizing and puzzles	1.23	0.78	−0.65	1.64
Dominance	2.04†	0.16	2.49†	1.39
Nervousness	0.71	−0.48	−0.06	0.40
Persistence	−0.18	0.13	1.37	0.84
Self-confidence	0.58	0.24	0.55	0.47
Self-sufficiency	1.32	−0.27	2.20†	1.81
Meticulousness	−0.73	0.07	−0.30	0.50
Orderliness	−1.68	−3.38*	−1.69	−1.84
Impulsivity	−0.38	−0.11	−0.14	−0.83
Future time orientation	3.96*	1.44	1.23	1.43
Optimism (belief that good things will happen)	−3.29*	1.31	−2.76*	−2.84*
Belief in thinking before acting	1.24	1.54	0.99	0.86
Optimism (− +)	0.74	−0.64	0.91	0.12
Anti-traditionalistic orientation.	1.73	2.20†	1.50	1.57
Optimism (+ −)	−0.67	−0.20	−0.61	−0.17
Belief in predictability of life ...	2.00†	1.00	1.31	−0.36
Belief in multiple causation of events	0.30	1.02	1.27	−0.16
Belief in animism	−5.26*	0.33	−2.11†	−1.88
Belief in supernatural causes ...	−3.48*	0.28	−1.86	−0.36

(Continued on p. 262)

* Significant at .01 or less.   † Significant at .05 or less.   ‡ Dots mean test not used.

TABLE 33. VALUES OF *t* FOR DIFFERENCES IN MEANS BETWEEN SOCIAL
CLASSES ON PERSONALITY VARIABLES *(Continued)*

Personality Variable	Middle-class Males vs. Lower-class Males	Middle-class Females vs. Lower-class Females	Group Interaction Males vs. Lower-class Males	Group Interaction Females vs. Lower-class Females
Belief in fate	−4.17*	−0.70	−2.22†	−0.34
Belief that events clearly are either good or bad	−1.62	−0.29	−1.07	−0.24
Belief that actions have many consequences	−0.01	2.29†	0.16	1.24
Optimism (belief that bad things won't happen)	−2.60†	0.15	−2.00	−0.14
Belief that events are probable or improbable	−1.01	−0.33	−2.30†	0.52
Belief in trying many actions in solving problems	−0.26	0.84	0	0.27
Independence of judgment	2.32†	2.43†	1.71	0.34

* Significant at .01 or less.   † Significant at .05 or less.   ‡ Dots mean test not used.

TABLE 34. HUSBAND-WIFE CORRELATIONS ON PERSONALITY CHARACTERISTICS*

Personality Characteristics		Middle-class Subjects	Lower-class Subjects	Group Interaction Subjects
Husband	Wife			
Same Variables				
General Satisfaction	General Satisfaction	0.41	0.53	0.51
Independence of judgment	Independence of judgment	0.54	0.39	0.41
Belief that good things will happen	Belief that good things will happen	0.36	0.16	0.43
PARI: Dominance	PARI: Dominance	0.38	0.36	0.53
Verbal I.Q.	Verbal I.Q.	0.39	0.28	0.59
Belief in trying many actions	Belief in trying many actions	0.32	−0.24	0.13
Belief in fate	Belief in fate	0.43	0.30	0.14
Taylor Manifest Anxiety Scale	Taylor Manifest Anxiety Scale	0.40	0.11	0.22
Belief that bad things won't happen	Belief that bad things won't happen	0.35	−0.42	−0.07
Dissimilar Variables				
Verbal I.Q.	PARI: Dominance	−0.39	−0.33	−0.43
Verbal I.Q.	Independence of judgment	0.34	0.23	0.39
PARI: Dominance	Verbal I.Q.	−0.41	−0.15	−0.45
PARI: Dominance	PARI: (Wife's ascendancy)	0.40	0.31	0.42
PARI: Dominance	Belief in thinking before acting	−0.37	−0.37	−0.44
PARI: Dominance	Belief that events clearly are either highly probable or highly improbable	0.50	0.21	0.41
Taylor Manifest Anxiety Scale	Belief that bad things will happen	0.29	−0.03	0.43
Belief in multiple causation of events	Belief that events clearly are either highly probable or highly improbable	0.35	−0.07	0.49
Belief in supernatural causes	Verbal I.Q.	−0.29	−0.03	−0.55
Belief in supernatural causes	PARI: Dominance	0.34	0.06	0.62
Belief in supernatural causes	Belief in fate	0.46	0.13	0.46
Belief in supernatural causes	Independence of judgment	−0.43	−0.44	−0.38
Belief in fate	Independence of judgment	−0.46	−0.42	−0.18
Belief in fate	PARI: (Wife's ascendancy)	0.34	0.24	0.54
Belief in trying many actions	PARI: Dominance	−0.31	0.15	−0.62
Belief in trying many actions	PARI: (Wife's ascendancy)	−0.29	0.11	−0.56
Future time orientation	Belief in thinking before acting	0.32	0.28	0.42

* We report only those cases where the correlations are significant for middle-class couples and either one of two conditions is met; (1) the correlation is also significant for one of the other groups, or (2) the middle-class correlation is on one of the variables which load personality factors of autonomy-dependency or anxiety noted in Chapter 6. Note: there is no instance of a correlation between dissimilar variables being significant for all three groups.

TABLE 35. MEAN SCORE ON NUMBER OF OUTCOMES

Decision Situation	Middle-class Subjects		Lower-class Subjects		Group Interaction
	Male	Female	Male	Female	
Masturbation	1.53	1.39	1.23	1.32	1.39
Homework	1.66	1.59	1.32	1.46	1.51
Obedience	1.67	1.55	1.35	1.45	1.47
Stealing	1.70	1.58	1.33	1.58	1.50
Mean of situations	1.64	1.53	1.31	1.45	1.47

TABLE 36. MEAN SCORE ON PROBABILITY DIRECTION

Decision Situation	Middle-class Subjects		Lower-class Subjects		Group Interaction
	Male	Female	Male	Female	
Masturbation	.76	.78	.76	.73	.79
Homework	.77	.78	.78	.74	.80
Obedience	.77	.78	.78	.77	.78
Stealing	.77	.76	.77	.75	.77
Mean of situations	.77	.78	.77	.75	.78

TABLE 37. MEAN SCORE ON PROBABILITY EXTREMITY

Decision Situation	Middle-class Subjects		Lower-class Subjects		Group Interaction
	Male	Female	Male	Female	
Masturbation	1.26	1.30	1.13	1.25	1.34
Homework	1.30	1.30	1.24	1.19	1.37
Obedience	1.27	1.25	1.25	1.25	1.28
Stealing	1.22	1.21	1.24	1.18	1.28
Mean of situations	1.26	1.27	1.20	1.22	1.32

TABLE 38. MEAN SCORE ON DESIRABILITY DIRECTION*

Decision Situation	Middle-class Subjects		Lower-class Subjects		Group Interaction
	Male	Female	Male	Female	
Masturbation	1.90	2.07	1.85	2.22	2.09
Homework	2.01	1.85	2.08	2.24	2.13
Obedience	1.49	1.53	1.76	1.66	1.85
Stealing	1.84	1.76	2.06	2.20	2.07
Mean of situations	1.81	1.80	1.94	2.08	2.04

* Constant of 2 added to all scores.

TABLE 39. MEAN SCORE ON DESIRABILITY EXTREMITY

Decision Situation	Middle-class Subjects		Lower-class Subjects		Group Interaction
	Male	Female	Male	Female	
Masturbation	1.44	1.56	1.58	1.56	1.62
Homework	1.62	1.61	1.64	1.65	1.61
Obedience	1.61	1.64	1.68	1.62	1.64
Stealing	1.68	1.67	1.70	1.81	1.67
Mean of situations	1.59	1.62	1.65	1.66	1.64

TABLE 40. MEAN SCORE ON TIME DIRECTION*

Decision Situation	Middle-class Subjects		Lower-class Subjects		Group Interaction
	Male	Female	Male	Female	
Masturbation	3.57	3.84	4.02	4.30	4.10
Homework	4.19	4.07	4.11	4.16	4.21
Obedience	4.11	4.11	4.04	4.40	4.27
Stealing	4.10	4.05	4.10	4.25	4.27
Mean of situations	3.99	4.02	4.07	4.28	4.21

* High score indicates present time orientation.

TABLE 41. MEAN SCORE ON TIME EXTREMITY

Decision Situation	Middle-class Subjects		Lower-class Subjects		Group Interaction
	Male	Female	Male	Female	
Masturbation	1.20	1.17	1.29	1.41	1.35
Homework	1.31	1.28	1.22	1.38	1.31
Obedience	1.28	1.32	1.34	1.60	1.40
Stealing	1.29	1.23	1.32	1.38	1.39
Mean of Situations	1.27	1.25	1.29	1.44	1.36

TABLE 42. MEAN SCORE ON NUMBER OF ACTIONS CHOSEN

Decision Situation	Middle-class Subjects		Lower-class Subjects		Group Interaction
	Male	Female	Male	Female	
Masturbation	1.83	2.09	1.95	2.14	1.86
Homework	2.48	2.45	2.17	2.75	2.46
Obedience	2.14	2.00	1.96	2.25	2.17
Stealing	1.87	1.79	2.15	2.30	1.92
Mean of situations	2.08	2.08	2.06	2.36	2.10

TABLE 43. MEAN S-SCORE*

Decision Situation	Middle-class Subjects		Lower-class Subjects		Group Interaction
	Male	Female	Male	Female	
Masturbation	24.54	24.27	22.29	24.58	25.79
Homework	24.56	23.31	23.83	24.13	24.71
Obedience	23.77	23.17	22.58	22.42	24.42
Stealing	23.38	23.85	23.13	22.29	24.58
Mean of situations	24.06	23.65	23.05	23.40	24.88

* Constant of 15 added to all scores.

TABLE 44. TYPE OF STRATEGY SELECTION

Type of Strategy	Situation			
	Masturbation	Homework	Obedience	Stealing
	% in each category			
Middle-class Males				
Do all actions together	78	66	40	68
Do one at a time until success	14	19	30	8
Do all actions, but in *set* order	0	0	0	0
Set order, but 1st action must work first ..	0	6	0	0
Set order, but go on *only* if 1st doesn't work	7	9	30	24
N*	(28)	(32)	(30)	(25)
Middle-class Females				
Do all actions together	83	64	54	80
Do one at a time until success	7	10	14	4
Do all actions, but in *set* order	0	3	4	4
Set order, but 1st action must work first ...	0	3	0	0
Set order, but go on *only* if 1st doesn't work	10	19	28	12
N*	(29)	(31)	(28)	(25)
Lower-class Males				
Do all actions together	38	50	14	71
Do one at a time until success	23	14	36	0
Do all actions, but in *set* order	8	0	0	0
Set order, but 1st action must work first ...	0	7	0	0
Set order, but go on *only* if 1st doesn't work	31	29	50	29
N*	(13)	(14)	(14)	(14)
Lower-class Females				
Do all actions together	81	56	10	53
Do one at a time until success	6	17	40	29
Do all actions, but in *set* order	0	10	5	0
Set order, but 1st action must work first ...	0	17	5	6
Set order, but go on *only* if 1st doesn't work	13	11	40	12
N*	(16)	(18)	(20)	(17)
Group Interaction Subjects				
Do all actions together	75	85	35	81
Do one at a time until success	8	10	41	6
Do all actions, but in *set* order	8	5	0	12
Set order, but 1st action must work first..	8	0	0	0
Set order, but go on *only* if 1st doesn't work	0	0	24	0
N*	(12)	(20)	(17)	(16)

* N's differ because the data are applicable only to those subjects who choose more than one action for performance.

TABLE 45. STANDARD DEVIATIONS ON NUMBER OF OUTCOMES

Decision Situation	Middle-class Subjects		Lower-class Subjects		Group Interaction
	Male	Female	Male	Female	
Masturbation	.56	.52	.45	.46	.51
Homework	.64	.65	.48	.59	.60
Obedience	.67	.59	.53	.53	.58
Stealing	.63	.59	.48	.58	.63
Standard Deviation of the Mean Score	.57	.52	.46	.50	.54

TABLE 46. STANDARD DEVIATIONS ON PROBABILITY DIRECTION

Decision Situation	Middle-class Subjects		Lower-class Subjects		Group Interaction
	Male	Female	Male	Female	
Masturbation	.11	.11	.10	.11	.07
Homework	.11	.09	.10	.11	.08
Obedience	.11	.09	.10	.11	.08
Stealing	.11	.10	.10	.09	.07
Standard Deviation of the Mean Score	.09	.16	.08	.10	.06

TABLE 47. STANDARD DEVIATIONS ON PROBABILITY EXTREMITY

Decision Situation	Middle-class Subjects		Lower-class Subjects		Group Interaction
	Male	Female	Male	Female	
Masturbation	.36	.43	.35	.41	.23
Homework	.36	.36	.39	.36	.31
Obedience	.41	.36	.40	.45	.30
Stealing	.42	.40	.42	.36	.22
Standard Deviation of the Mean Score	.31	.31	.30	.30	.19

TABLE 48. STANDARD DEVIATIONS ON DESIRABILITY DIRECTION

Decision Situation	Middle-class Subjects		Lower-class Subjects		Group Interaction
	Male	Female	Male	Female	
Masturbation	.45	.62	.64	.57	.63
Homework	.61	.61	.56	.48	.57
Obedience	.61	.57	.79	.51	.72
Stealing	.56	.60	.70	.78	.58
Standard Deviation of the Mean Score	.41	.47	.51	.37	.50

TABLE 49. STANDARD DEVIATIONS ON DESIRABILITY EXTREMITY

Decision Situation	Middle-class Subjects		Lower-class Subjects		Group Interaction
	Male	Female	Male	Female	
Masturbation	.43	.44	.32	.53	.30
Homework	.28	.35	.32	.35	.27
Obedience	.31	.37	.31	.39	.30
Stealing	.30	.33	.27	.24	.31
Standard Deviation of the Mean Score	.28	.32	.22	.33	.23

TABLE 50. STANDARD DEVIATIONS ON TIME DIRECTION

Decision Situation	Middle-class Subjects		Lower-class Subjects		Group Interaction
	Male	Female	Male	Female	
Masturbation	.62	.61	.55	.33	.53
Homework	.49	.59	.48	.59	.45
Obedience	.61	.58	.70	.50	.53
Stealing	.53	.55	.60	.33	.56
Standard Deviation of the Mean Score	.45	.46	.44	.30	.44

TABLE 51. STANDARD DEVIATIONS ON TIME EXTREMITY

Decision Situation	Middle-class Subjects		Lower-class Subjects		Group Interaction
	Male	Female	Male	Female	
Masturbation	.36	.39	.41	.26	.34
Homework	.37	.42	.38	.37	.39
Obedience	.47	.40	.41	.31	.40
Stealing	.41	.37	.45	.24	.40
Standard Deviation of the Mean Score	.30	.29	.30	.20	.30

TABLE 52. STANDARD DEVIATIONS ON NUMBER OF ACTIONS CHOSEN

Decision Situation	Middle-class Subjects		Lower-class Subjects		Group Interaction
	Male	Female	Male	Female	
Masturbation	.80	.91	.79	.88	.78
Homework	1.02	1.10	1.11	1.09	.87
Obedience	.86	.79	.93	.66	.67
Stealing	.93	.69	.83	.84	.86
Standard Deviation of the Mean Score	.65	.66	.78	.56	.62

TABLE 53. STANDARD DEVIATIONS ON *S*-SCORE (UTILITY ORDERING)

Decision Situation	Middle-class Subjects		Lower-class Subjects		Group Interaction
	Male	Female	Male	Female	
Masturbation	3.25	3.73	4.61	3.28	2.35
Homework	3.21	3.07	3.62	2.67	2.42
Obedience	2.85	3.44	4.20	4.44	3.39
Stealing	4.18	3.53	3.61	3.91	2.97
Standard Deviation of the Mean Score	1.87	2.25	3.04	2.32	1.99

TABLE 54. VALUES OF *t* FOR DIFFERENCES IN MEANS BETWEEN GROUPS
OF SUBJECTS ON NUMBER OF OUTCOMES

Group of Subjects	Decision Situation				
	Mastur-bation	Home-work	Obedi-ence	Steal-ing	Mean
Middle-class male vs. lower-class male....	2.44*	2.47*	2.19*	2.65†	2.54*
Middle-class female vs. lower-class female.	0.53	0.88	0.67	0.80	0.68
Middle-class male vs. middle-class female..	1.62	0.63	1.20	1.20	1.52
Lower-class male vs. lower-class female...	−0.80‡	−1.27	−0.97	−1.10	−1.10
Middle-class male vs. group interaction....	1.08	0.95	1.26	1.21	1.20
Middle-class female vs. group interaction..	0.00	0.52	0.51	0.49	0.30

* Significant at .05 or less.
† Significant at .01 or less.
‡ In Tables 54–62, a negative *t* value indicates the first group has a lower mean than the second group.

TABLE 55. VALUES OF *t* FOR DIFFERENCES IN MEANS BETWEEN GROUPS
OF SUBJECTS ON PROBABILITY DIRECTION

Group of Subjects	Decision Situation				
	Mastur-bation	Home-work	Obedi-ence	Steal-ing	Mean
Middle-class male vs. lower-class male....	0.00	−0.10	−0.10	0.10	0.00
Middle-class female vs. lower-class female.	1.65	1.88	0.33	0.43	1.99*
Middle-class male vs. middle-class female..	−0.96	−0.49	−0.43	0.41	−1.06
Lower-class male vs. lower-class female...	0.75	1.19	0.30	0.62	1.27
Middle-class male vs. group interaction....	−1.40	−1.29	−0.18	0.00	−0.74
Middle-class female vs. group interaction..	−0.41	−1.09	0.20	−0.44	0.60

* Significant at .05 or less.

TABLE 56. VALUES OF *t* FOR DIFFERENCES IN MEANS BETWEEN GROUPS
OF SUBJECTS ON PROBABILITY EXTREMITY

	Decision Situation				
Group of Subjects	Mastur-bation	Home-work	Obedi-ence	Steal-ing	Mean
Middle-class male vs. lower-class male....	1.45	0.73	0.14	−0.19	0.74
Middle-class female vs. lower-class female.	0.55	1.26	0.00	0.37	0.66
Middle-class male vs. middle-class female..	−0.53	0.00	0.19	0.13	−0.11
Lower-class male vs. lower-class female...	−1.03	0.48	0.00	0.61	−0.17
Middle-class male vs. group interaction....	−1.10	−0.77	−0.12	−0.75	−0.89
Middle-class female vs. group interaction..	−0.43	−0.76	−0.32	−0.92	−0.77

TABLE 57. VALUES OF *t* FOR DIFFERENCES IN MEANS BETWEEN GROUPS
OF SUBJECTS ON DESIRABILITY EXTREMITY

	Decision Situation				
Group of Subjects	Mastur-bation	Home-work	Obedi-ence	Steal-ing	Mean
Middle-class male vs. lower-class male....	−1.56	−0.23	−0.87	−0.30	−0.65
Middle-class female vs. lower-class female.	0.00	−0.39	0.18	−2.01*	−0.01
Middle-class male vs. middle-class female..	−1.39	0.35	−0.33	0.18	−0.58
Lower-class male vs. lower-class female...	0.24	−0.15	0.64	−1.33	−0.01
Middle-class male vs. group interaction....	−2.00*	0.08	−0.34	0.12	−0.49
Middle-class female vs. group interaction..	−0.59	0.00	0.00	0.00	−0.14

* Significant at .05 or less.

TABLE 58. VALUES OF *t* FOR DIFFERENCES IN MEANS BETWEEN GROUPS
OF SUBJECTS ON DESIRABILITY DIRECTION

	Decision Situation				
Group of Subjects	Mastur-bation	Home-work	Obedi-ence	Steal-ing	Mean
Middle-class male vs. lower-class male....	0.34	−0.50	−1.43	−1.35	−1.09
Middle-class female vs. lower-class female.	−0.01	−2.92*	−0.97	−2.40†	−2.83*
Middle-class male vs. middle-class female..	−1.62	2.66*	−0.41	0.81	0.27
Lower-class male vs. lower-class female...	−1.80	−0.89	0.50	−0.70	−1.04
Middle-class male vs. group interaction....	−1.29	−0.78	−2.03†	−1.58	−1.91
Middle-class female vs. group interaction..	−0.12	−1.84	−1.82	−2.07†	−1.99†

* Significant at .01 or less.
† Significant at .05 or less.

TABLE 59. VALUES OF *t* FOR DIFFERENCES IN MEANS BETWEEN GROUPS
OF SUBJECTS ON TIME DIRECTION

| | Decision Situation | | | | |
Group of Subjects	Mastur-bation	Home-work	Obedi-ence	Steal-ing	Mean
Middle-class male vs. lower-class male....	−1.85	0.58	0.39	0.00	−0.34
Middle-class female vs. lower-class female.	−4.08*	−0.61	−2.13†	−1.91	−2.83*
Middle-class male vs. middle-class female..	−0.69	1.23	0.00	0.52	−0.21
Lower-class male vs. lower-class female...	−2.45†	−0.30	−2.08†	−1.07	−2.28†
Middle-class male vs. group interaction....	−2.49†	−0.19	−1.17	−1.21	−1.57
Middle-class female vs. group interaction..	−1.87	−1.08	−1.13	−1.57	−1.71

* Significant at .01 or less.
† Significant at .05 or less.

TABLE 60. VALUES OF *t* FOR DIFFERENCES IN MEANS BETWEEN GROUPS
OF SUBJECTS ON TIME EXTREMITY

| | Decision Situation | | | | |
Group of Subjects	Mastur-bation	Home-work	Obedi-ence	Steal-ing	Mean
Middle–class male vs. lower-class male....	−0.89	0.89	−0.53	−0.27	−0.39
Middle-class female vs. lower-class female.	−3.14*	−1.00	−3.29*	−2.00†	−3.24*
Middle-class male vs. middle-class female..	0.37	0.34	−0.44	0.82	0.38
Lower-class male vs. lower-class female...	−1.54	−1.76	−2.46†	−0.55	−2.28†
Middle-class male vs. group interaction....	−1.72	0.30	−1.09	−0.97	−1.17
Middle-class female vs. group interaction..	−2.00†	−0.29	−0.79	−1.64	−1.49

* Significant at .01 or less.
† Significant at .05 or less.

TABLE 61. VALUES OF *t* FOR DIFFERENCES IN MEANS BETWEEN GROUPS
OF SUBJECTS ON NUMBER OF ACTIONS CHOSEN

| | Decision Situation | | | | |
Group of Subjects	Mastur-bation	Home-work	Obedi-ence	Steal-ing	Mean
Middle-class male vs. lower-class male....	−0.67	1.28	0.70	−1.53	0.14
Middle-class female vs. lower-class female.	−0.21	−0.19	−1.39	−2.56*	−1.78
Middle-class male vs. middle-class female..	−1.30	0.14	0.92	0.62	0.00
Lower class male vs. lower-class female...	−0.63	−1.81	−1.07	−0.74	−1.34
Middle-class male vs. group interaction....	−0.14	0.08	−0.13	−0.20	−0.12
Middle-class female vs. group interaction..	1.08	−0.05	−0.92	−0.63	−0.12

* Significant at .05 or less.

TABLE 62. VALUES OF *t* FOR DIFFERENCES IN MEANS BETWEEN GROUPS
OF SUBJECTS ON *S*-SCORE (UTILITY ORDERING)

	Decision Situation				
Group of Subjects	Mastur-bation	Home-work	Obedi-ence	Steal-ing	Mean
Middle-class male vs. lower-class male....	2.10*	0.82	1.23	0.26	1.45
Middle-class female vs. lower-class female.	−0.36	−1.14	0.71	1.62	0.39
Middle-class male vs. middle-class female..	0.40	2.06*	0.97	−0.58	0.93
Lower-class male vs. lower-class female...	−1.96	−0.33	0.16	0.96	−0.57
Middle-class male vs. group interaction....	−1.84	−0.21	−0.79	−1.39	−1.67
Middle-class female vs. group interaction..	−2.08*	−2.07*	−1.44	−0.90	−2.36

* Significant at .05 or less.

TABLE 63. EFFECTS OF FAMILIARITY WITH DECISION SITUATION
UPON DECISION PROCESS VARIABLES

	Decision Situation			
Decision Variable	Masturbation	Homework	Obedience	Stealing
Middle-class Males (N = 48)				
Number of Outcomes	−.29*	−.26	.08	−.06
Probability Direction	−.07	.30*	−.18	.12
Probability Extremity	−.23	.20	−.08	.16
Desirability Direction	.17	.14	.08	.17
Desirability Extremity	.44†	−.09	−.06	−.11
Time Direction	−.09	.06	−.03	.26
Time Extremity	−.11	.05	−.05	.29*
Number of Actions Chosen	.13	−.12	−.18	−.27
S-scores (Utility Ordering)	−.08	−.13	.04	−.04
Middle-class Females (N = 48)				
Number of Outcomes	.01	.10	.05	−.27
Probability Direction	.07	−.03	−.09	.07
Probability Extremity	−.14	−.04	−.17	−.02
Desirability Direction	.25	.16	.31*	.08
Desirability Extremity	.18	.15	−.20	−.17
Time Direction	−.19	−.06	−.35*	−.07
Time Extremity	−.41†	.02	−.49†	−.08
Number of Actions Chosen	.00	.07	−.17	.20
S-scores (Utility Ordering)	−.04	.05	−.11	.23
Group Interaction Subjects (N = 24)				
Number of Outcomes	−.10	−.44*	−.51*	(a)
Probability Direction	.01	−.12	−.04	
Probability Extremity	.20	−.01	−.31	
Desirability Direction	.41*	.22	.15	
Desirability Extremity	.00	−.08	−.28	
Time Direction	.07	.25	.44*	
Time Extremity	.10	.28	.33	
Number of Actions Chosen	.35	−.64†	−.34	
S-scores (Utility Ordering)	−.18	−.14	−.43*	

* Significant at .05 or less.
† Significant at .01 or less.
(a) Effects of familiarity with the stealing situation are not presented here because no group subjects reported familiarity with this situation.

TABLE 64. EFFECTS OF HUSBAND-WIFE DISCUSSION ABOUT DECISION
SITUATIONS UPON DECISION PROCESS VARIABLES

Decision Variable	Decision Situation			
	Masturbation	Homework	Obedience	Stealing
Middle-class Males (N = 48)				
Number of Outcomes	−.16	−.20	−.01	−.17
Probability Direction	−.04	.06	−.18	.36*
Probability Extremity	−.23	−.05	−.14	.41†
Desirability Direction	.03	.11	.10	.19
Desirability Extremity	.39†	−.31*	−.22	−.05
Time Direction	.04	−.02	−.10	.31*
Time Extremity	−.01	−.08	−.18	.33*
Number of Actions Chosen	.00	−.09	−.18	−.16
S-scores (Utility Ordering)	−.09	−.12	.08	.07
Middle-class Females (N = 48)				
Number of Outcomes	−.22	−.03	−.10	−.12
Probability Direction	.11	.05	−.03	−.12
Probability Extremity	−.15	.10	−.10	−.12
Desirability Direction	.26	.20	.39†	.20
Desirability Extremity	.07	.16	−.07	−.12
Time Direction	−.12	−.03	−.29*	−.06
Time Extremity	−.36*	.04	−.41†	−.08
Number of Actions Chosen	.01	.04	.00	.22
S-scores (Utility Ordering)	−.04	.11	.07	.22
Group Interaction Subjects (N = 24)				
Number of Outcomes	−.16	−.60†	−.42*	(a)
Probability Direction	.05	−.10	.14	
Probability Extremity	.32	.02	−.18	
Desirability Direction	.25	.15	.18	
Desirability Extremity	.09	−.15	−.19	
Time Direction	.27	−.12	.20	
Time Extremity	.33	−.03	.06	
Number of Actions Chosen	.26	−.66†	−.38	
S-scores (Utility Ordering)	−.25	−.10	−.31	

* Significant at .05 or less.
† Significant at .01 or less.
(a) Effects of husband-wife discussion about the stealing situation are not presented
here since subjects who reported that they were unfamiliar with a situation were not asked
whether they had discussed it.

TABLE 65. EFFECTS OF ORDER OF PRESENTATION OF DECISION SITUATION
UPON DECISION PROCESS VARIABLES: MIDDLE-CLASS MALES

Decision Variable		Decision Situation			
		Masturbation	Homework	Obedience	Stealing
Number of Outcomes	Ma	−.33*	.18	.01	.07
	Hw	−.17	−.12	.07	.20
	Ob	−.18	.10	−.08	.11
	St	−.22	.19	.04	−.06
Probability Direction	Ma	−.23	−.02	.19	.03
	Hw	−.12	.07	.14	−.10
	Ob	−.11	−.27	.31*	.08
	St	−.15	−.07	.20	.00
Probability Extremity	Ma	−.20	−.05	.14	.08
	Hw	−.09	.09	.07	−.08
	Ob	−.01	−.21	.18	.05
	St	−.07	.00	.19	−.13
Desirability Direction	Ma	.07	.12	−.27	.06
	Hw	.10	.30*	−.16	−.25
	Ob	.09	.16	−.22	−.04
	St	.14	.12	−.07	−.16
Desirability Extremity	Ma	−.18	−.37†	.20	.34*
	Hw	−.35*	−.08	.14	.23
	Ob	−.20	−.24	.11	.30*
	St	−.09	.00	−.01	.08
Time Direction	Ma	−.19	.23	.14	−.22
	Hw	.15	−.14	.06	−.03
	Ob	.04	−.13	.10	.01
	St	−.02	.10	.25	−.31
Time Extremity	Ma	−.15	.18	.05	−.11
	Hw	.10	−.19	.12	.01
	Ob	.00	−.07	.00	.07
	St	.00	.05	.22	−.25
Number of Actions Chosen	Ma	−.05	−.28	−.02	.35*
	Hw	−.09	−.07	−.06	.19
	Ob	.07	−.32*	−.01	.28
	St	.04	−.05	−.17	.17
S-scores (Utility Ordering)	Ma	.08	−.10	−.16	.18
	Hw	−.06	.12	−.05	−.04
	Ob	.24	.00	−.10	−.10
	St	.16	.00	−.04	−.10

* Significant at .05 or less.
† Significant at .01 or less.

TABLE 66. EFFECTS OF ORDER OF PRESENTATION OF DECISION SITUATION
UPON DECISION PROCESS VARIABLES: MIDDLE-CLASS FEMALES

Decision Variable		Decision Situation			
		Masturbation	Homework	Obedience	Stealing
Number of Outcomes	Ma	−.26	.28	−.07	.08
	Hw	−.14	.21	−.15	.11
	Ob	.01	.24	−.30*	.08
	St	−.10	.37†	−.06	−.19
Probability Direction	Ma	.17	−.18	−.06	.05
	Hw	.24	−.20	.08	−.16
	Ob	.09	−.13	.07	−.04
	St	.38†	−.28	.17	−.34*
Probability Extremity	Ma	.16	−.14	−.10	.07
	Hw	.08	−.07	.04	−.06
	Ob	.06	−.09	.03	.00
	St	.34*	−.23	.12	−.28
Desirability Direction	Ma	.09	.10	.07	−.26
	Hw	−.14	.20	.16	−.22
	Ob	−.03	−.17	.29*	−.12
	St	.02	−.11	.05	.04
Desirability Extremity	Ma	−.08	.06	.19	−.17
	Hw	−.08	.06	.14	−.13
	Ob	.07	.10	.04	−.23
	St	.12	.14	.07	−.34*
Time Direction	Ma	.13	−.06	.08	−.17
	Hw	.12	−.25	.33*	−.24
	Ob	.07	−.09	.15	−.15
	St	.32*	−.11	.09	−.34*
Time Extremity	Ma	−.04	−.10	.11	.02
	Hw	.22	−.28	.29*	−.28
	Ob	−.07	−.01	.21	−.14
	St	.32*	−.07	.01	−.30*
Number of Actions Chosen	Ma	−.07	.00	.23	−.17
	Hw	.05	.02	.17	−.26
	Ob	−.07	−.32*	.28	.10
	St	−.05	−.02	.10	−.03
S-scores (Utility Ordering)	Ma	−.09	.15	−.25	.23
	Hw	−.08	.15	−.16	−.07
	Ob	.02	.09	−.14	.05
	St	−.34*	.25	−.05	.19

* Significant at .05 or less.
† Significant at .01 or less.

TABLE 67. EFFECTS OF ORDER OF PRESENTATION OF DECISION SITUATION
UPON DECISION PROCESS VARIABLES: GROUP INTERACTION SUBJECTS

Decision Variable		Decision Situation			
		Masturbation	Homework	Obedience	Stealing
Number of Outcomes	Ma	.31	.04	.12	−.47*
	Hw	.40*	.00	−.11	−.28
	Ob	.36	.19	−.14	−.42*
	St	.31	.23	.05	−.58†
Probability Direction	Ma	−.31	.36	.07	−.11
	Hw	−.63†	.27	.35	.01
	Ob	−.22	.28	−.07	.01
	St	−.12	.16	.12	−.16
Probability Extremity	Ma	−.19	.12	.32	−.25
	Hw	−.60†	.08	.54†	−.01
	Ob	−.28	.09	.04	.16
	St	−.14	.20	.26	−.33
Desirability Direction	Ma	−.37	−.27	.05	.59†
	Hw	−.21	−.28	.07	.42*
	Ob	−.15	−.27	.07	.35
	St	−.28	−.28	.10	.46*
Desirability Extremity	Ma	−.29	−.07	−.06	.30
	Hw	.06	−.12	.21	−.15
	Ob	−.09	−.16	.06	.19
	St	.04	−.01	.10	−.14
Time Direction	Ma	−.05	.04	.14	−.13
	Hw	.12	−.10	.18	−.20
	Ob	.06	−.19	.13	.01
	St	.14	.17	.02	−.33
Time Extremity	Ma	−.19	.15	.22	−.19
	Hw	.01	−.23	.30	−.08
	Ob	.05	−.06	.14	−.13
	St	.12	.14	.10	−.36
Number of Actions Chosen	Ma	−.14	−.30	−.08	.52†
	Hw	−.06	.02	−.06	.11
	Ob	−.26	.07	.04	.15
	St	−.17	.00	−.22	.39
S-scores (Utility Ordering)	Ma	.12	.09	−.25	.04
	Hw	.16	.39	−.36	−.19
	Ob	.22	.14	−.06	−.31
	St	−.15	.54†	−.09	−.30

* Significant at .05 or less.
† Significant at .01 or less.

TABLE 68. VALUES OF *t* FOR DIFFERENCES IN MEANS BETWEEN DECISION SITUATIONS: NUMBER OF OUTCOMES

Decision Situation	Middle-class Males	Middle-class Females	Lower-class Males	Lower-class Females	Group Interaction Subjects
Masturbation vs. homework...	−2.05*	−3.16†	−1.54	−2.03	−1.37
Masturbation vs. obedience....	−2.59*	−2.14*	−1.54	−1.99	−1.23
Masturbation vs. stealing......	−3.54†	−3.27†	−1.65	−1.62	−1.52
Homework vs. obedience......	−0.14	0.70	−0.41	0.09	0.50
Homework vs. stealing........	−0.51	0.29	−0.23	−0.00	0.13
Obedience vs. stealing.........	−0.44	−0.45	0.18	−0.07	−0.57

* Significant at .05 or less.
† Significant at .01 or less.

TABLE 69. VALUES OF *t* FOR DIFFERENCES IN MEANS BETWEEN DECISION SITUATIONS: PROBABILITY DIRECTION

Decision Situation	Middle-class Males	Middle-class Females	Lower-class Males	Lower-class Females	Group Interaction Subjects
Masturbation vs. homework...	−1.37	0.21	−1.00	−0.20	−0.79
Masturbation vs. obedience....	−0.83	0.01	−1.12	−1.20	0.68
Masturbation vs. stealing......	−0.92	1.13	−0.66	−0.64	1.01
Homework vs. obedience......	0.12	0.31	0.21	−1.11	1.55
Homework vs. stealing........	0.15	1.84	0.37	−0.52	1.84
Obedience vs. stealing.........	0.00	1.34	0.83	0.81	0.25

TABLE 70. VALUES OF *t* FOR DIFFERENCES IN MEANS BETWEEN DECISION SITUATIONS: PROBABILITY EXTREMITY

Decision Situation	Middle-class Males	Middle-class Females	Lower-class Males	Lower-class Females	Group Interaction Subjects
Masturbation vs. homework...	−0.77	0.00	−0.12	0.73	−0.42
Masturbation vs. obedience....	−0.14	0.95	−1.62	0.03	0.84
Masturbation vs. stealing......	0.63	1.46	−1.64	0.82	1.18
Homework vs. obedience......	0.63	1.12	−0.21	−0.62	1.30
Homework vs. stealing........	1.59	1.88	0.06	0.16	1.40
Obedience vs. stealing.........	0.82	0.78	0.16	0.91	0.03

TABLE 71. VALUES OF *t* FOR DIFFERENCES IN MEANS BETWEEN DECISION
SITUATIONS: DESIRABILITY DIRECTION

Decision Situation	Middle-class Males	Middle-class Females	Lower-class Males	Lower-class Females	Group Interaction Subjects
Masturbation vs. homework....	−1.12	2.46*	−1.69	−0.15	−0.29
Masturbation vs. obedience....	5.00†	6.69†	0.78	3.79†	2.04
Masturbation vs. stealing......	0.73	3.78†	−1.23	0.13	0.19
Homework vs. obedience......	5.42†	3.80†	2.25*	4.87†	1.96
Homework vs. stealing........	1.86	0.91	0.13	0.25	0.51
Obedience vs. stealing.........	−4.00†	−2.45*	−2.28*	−3.46†	−1.56

* Significant at .05 or less.
† Significant at .01 or less.

TABLE 72. VALUES OF *t* FOR DIFFERENCES IN MEANS BETWEEN DECISION
SITUATIONS: DESIRABILITY EXTREMITY

Decision Situation	Middle-class Males	Middle-class Females	Lower-class Males	Lower-class Females	Group Interaction Subjects
Masturbation vs. homework...	−3.11†	−0.96	−0.63	−1.40	0.05
Masturbation vs. obedience....	−3.17†	−1.50	−1.47	−0.93	−0.34
Masturbation vs. stealing......	−4.20†	−1.78	−1.50	−2.42*	−0.75
Homework vs. obedience......	0.13	−0.68	−0.62	0.80	−0.43
Homework vs. stealing........	−1.60	−1.58	−1.20	−2.14*	−1.00
Obedience vs. stealing.........	−1.12	−0.86	−0.36	−2.23*	−0.97

* Significant at .05 or less.
† Significant at .01 or less.

TABLE 73. VALUES OF *t* FOR DIFFERENCES IN MEANS BETWEEN DECISION
SITUATIONS: TIME DIRECTION

Decision Situation	Middle-class Males	Middle-class Females	Lower-class Males	Lower-class Females	Group Interaction Subjects
Masturbation vs. homework...	−5.08†	−2.55*	−0.85	0.95	−1.20
Masturbation vs. obedience....	−4.24†	−3.40†	−0.18	−0.93	−2.21*
Masturbation vs. stealing......	−4.21†	−2.29*	−0.51	0.74	−1.85
Homework vs. obedience......	1.08	−0.53	0.68	−1.83	−0.60
Homework vs. stealing	1.01	0.23	0.12	−0.77	−0.65
Obedience vs. stealing.........	0.03	0.85	−0.33	1.42	0.01

* Significant at .05 or less.
† Significant at .01 or less.

TABLE 74. VALUES OF *t* FOR DIFFERENCES IN MEANS BETWEEN DECISION
SITUATIONS: TIME EXTREMITY

Decision Situation	Middle-class Males	Middle-class Females	Lower-class Males	Lower-class Females	Group Interaction Subjects
Masturbation vs. homework...	−2.11*	−1.70	0.72	0.43	0.57
Masturbation vs. obedience....	−1.20	−2.63†	−0.74	−2.61*	−0.71
Masturbation vs. stealing......	−1.49	−0.99	−0.36	0.68	−0.52
Homework vs. obedience......	0.45	−0.49	−1.36	−2.69†	−1.01
Homework vs. stealing........	0.21	0.80	−0.84	0.05	−0.90
Obedience vs. stealing.........	−0.20	1.46	0.12	2.86†	0.05

* Significant at .05 or less.
† Significant at .01 or less.

TABLE 75. VALUES OF *t* FOR DIFFERENCES IN MEANS BETWEEN DECISION
SITUATIONS: NUMBER OF ACTIONS CHOSEN

Decision Situation	Middle-class Males	Middle-class Females	Lower-class Males	Lower-class Females	Group Interaction Subjects
Masturbation vs. homework...	−4.36†	−2.13*	−1.14	−2.35*	−3.89†
Masturbation vs. obedience....	−2.64†	0.70	−0.07	−0.54	−2.28*
Masturbation vs. stealing......	−0.26	2.36*	−1.58	−0.69	−0.35
Homework vs. obedience......	2.40*	3.18†	1.26	2.30*	1.74
Homework vs. stealing........	3.62†	4.58†	0.14	1.66	2.77*
Obedience vs. stealing.........	1.77	1.89	−1.24	−0.26	1.32

* Significant at .05 or less.
† Significant at .01 or less.

TABLE 76. VALUES OF *t* FOR DIFFERENCES IN MEANS BETWEEN DECISION
SITUATIONS: *S*-SCORES (UTILITY ORDERING)

Decision Situation	Middle-class Males	Middle-class Females	Lower-class Males	Lower-class Females	Group Interaction Subjects
Masturbation vs. homework...	−0.04	1.52	−1.80	0.54	1.66
Masturbation vs. obedience....	1.18	1.94	−0.33	2.02	1.91
Masturbation vs. stealing......	1.44	0.67	−0.90	2.56*	1.80
Homework vs. obedience......	1.33	0.31	1.20	1.52	0.35
Homework vs. stealing........	1.85	−0.85	0.81	2.30*	0.24
Obedience vs. stealing.........	0.57	−0.93	−0.60	0.10	−0.20

* Significant at .05 or less.

TABLE 77. VALUES OF *r* FOR MEANS BETWEEN DECISION SITUATIONS: NUMBER OF OUTCOMES

	Middle-class Males	Middle-class Females	Lower-class Males	Lower-class Females	Group Interaction Subjects
Masturbation and homework.....	.75*	.72*	.81*	.84*	.68*
Masturbation and obedience......	.84*	.58*	.72*	.81*	.81*
Masturbation and stealing........	.86*	.78*	.79*	.73*	.81*
Homework and obedience........	.77*	.71*	.81*	.88*	.78*
Homework and stealing..........	.72*	.82*	.85*	.87*	.77*
Obedience and stealing...........	.80*	.66*	.75*	.80*	.92*

* *r* is significant at .05 or less.

TABLE 78. VALUES OF *r* FOR MEANS BETWEEN DECISION SITUATIONS: PROBABILITY DIRECTION

	Middle-class Males	Middle-class Females	Lower-class Males	Lower-class Females	Group Interaction Subjects
Masturbation and homework.....	.66*	.37*	.56*	.46*	.68*
Masturbation and obedience......	.51*	.54*	.49*	.12	.81*
Masturbation and stealing........	.61*	.50*	.65*	−.01	.81*
Homework and obedience........	.62*	.45*	.55*	.23	.46*
Homework and stealing..........	.69*	.67*	.51*	.16	.46*
Obedience and stealing...........	.63*	.66*	.78*	.45*	.66*

* *r* is significant at .05 or less.

TABLE 79. VALUES OF *r* FOR MEANS BETWEEN DECISION SITUATIONS: PROBABILITY EXTREMITY

	Middle-class Males	Middle-class Females	Lower-class Males	Lower-class Females	Group Interaction Subjects
Masturbation and homework.....	.60*	.39	.68*	.54*	.22
Masturbation and obedience......	.53*	.54*	.52*	.28	.13
Masturbation and stealing........	.44*	.43*	.65*	.44*	.45*
Homework and obedience........	.45*	.59*	.51*	.36	.38
Homework and stealing..........	.59*	.59*	.56*	.43*	.36
Obedience and stealing...........	.57*	.55*	.60*	.56*	.59*

* *r* is significant at .05 or less.

TABLE 80. VALUES OF *r* FOR MEANS BETWEEN DECISION SITUATIONS: DESIRABILITY DIRECTION

	Middle-class Males	Middle-class Females	Lower-class Males	Lower-class Females	Group Interaction Subjects
Masturbation and homework.....	.21	.50*	.39	.12	.46*
Masturbation and obedience......	.47*	.56*	.72*	.15	.64*
Masturbation and stealing........	.30*	.56*	.24	.27	.57*
Homework and obedience........	.41*	.52*	.52*	.30	.45*
Homework and stealing..........	.39*	.29*	.26	.13	.53*
Obedience and stealing...........	.49*	.43*	.64*	.40	.46*

* *r* is significant at .05 or less.

TABLE 81. VALUES OF *r* FOR MEANS BETWEEN DECISION SITUATIONS: DESIRABILITY EXTREMITY

	Middle-class Males	Middle-class Females	Lower-class Males	Lower-class Females	Group Interaction Subjects
Masturbation and homework.....	.44*	.58*	.24	.80*	.12
Masturbation and obedience......	.52*	.65*	.49*	.78*	.44*
Masturbation and stealing........	.45*	.43*	.19	.38	.34
Homework and obedience........	.50*	.79*	.42*	.89*	.47*
Homework and stealing..........	.58*	.77*	.62	.34	.53*
Obedience and stealing...........	.58*	.77*	.50*	.32	.86*

* *r* is significant at .05 or less.

TABLE 82. VALUES OF *r* FOR MEANS BETWEEN DECISION SITUATIONS: TIME DIRECTION

	Middle-class Males	Middle-class Females	Lower-class Males	Lower-class Females	Group Interaction Subjects
Masturbation and homework.....	.44*	.46*	.45*	—.07	.65*
Masturbation and obedience......	.55*	.55*	.61*	.23	.75*
Masturbation and stealing........	.49*	.40*	.18	.57*	.67*
Homework and obedience........	.60*	.48*	.66*	.33	.44*
Homework and stealing..........	.38*	.52*	.17	.34	.57*
Obedience and stealing...........	.54*	.57*	.21	.31	.50*

* *r* is significant at .05 or less.

TABLE 83. VALUES OF *r* FOR MEANS BETWEEN DECISION SITUATIONS:
TIME EXTREMITY

	Middle-class Males	Middle-class Females	Lower-class Males	Lower-class Females	Group Interaction Subjects
Masturbation and homework.....	.53*	.36*	.24	.40	.60*
Masturbation and obedience......	.42*	.51*	.17	.69*	.59*
Masturbation and stealing........	.35*	.37*	.40	.39	.42*
Homework and obedience........	.50*	.24	.34	.47*	.45*
Homework and stealing..........	.30*	.39*	.55*	.05	.38
Obedience and stealing...........	.39*	.43*	.07	.13	.44*

* *r* is significant at .05 or less.

TABLE 84. VALUES OF *r* FOR MEANS BETWEEN DECISION SITUATIONS:
NUMBER OF ACTIONS

	Middle-class Males	Middle-class Females	Lower-class Males	Lower-class Females	Group Interaction Subjects
Masturbation and homework.....	.38*	.34*	.54*	.20	.59*
Masturbation and obedience......	.52*	.46*	.62*	.17	.60*
Masturbation and stealing........	.28	.41*	.71*	.08	.56*
Homework and obedience........	.48*	.51*	.69*	.38	.45*
Homework and stealing..........	.29*	.45*	.66*	.13	.39*
Obedience and stealing...........	.30*	.45*	.65*	.11	.31*

* *r* is significant at .05 or less.

TABLE 85. VALUES OF *r* FOR MEANS BETWEEN DECISION SITUATIONS:
S-SCORES (UTILITY ORDERING)

	Middle-class Males	Middle-class Females	Lower-class Males	Lower-class Females	Group Interaction Subjects
Masturbation and homework.....	.20	.18	.52*	.07	.10
Masturbation and obedience......	.11	.39*	.53*	.14	.28
Masturbation and stealing........	.13	.30*	.43*	.30	.25
Homework and obedience........	.07	.51*	.19	−.09	.02
Homework and stealing..........	.30*	.11	.33	.38	.57*
Obedience and stealing...........	.11	.08	.39	−.01	.15

* *r* is significant at .05 or less.

TABLE 86. CORRELATIONS BETWEEN HUSBANDS AND WIVES ON
DECISION PROCESS CHARACTERISTICS

Decision Characteristic	Middle-class Subjects					Lower-class Subjects				
	Mastur-bation	Home-work	Obedi-ence	Steal-ing	Mean	Mastur-bation	Home-work	Obedi-ence	Steal-ing	Mean
Number of Outcomes.	.36*	.37†	.38†	.39†	.43†	.20	.55†	.51*	.48*	.54†
Probability Direction.	.01	.14	.05	.08	−.09	.01	.02	.14	.24	.08
Probability Extremity	.09	.24	.11	.04	−.25	.01	.11	.18	.11	.07
Desirability Direction	.10	.40†	.27	.30*	.39†	.33	.36	.04	.21	−.06
Desirability Extremity	.00	.26	.21	.16	−.25	.16	.16	.17	.11	.34
Time Direction	.06	.28	.05	.12	.15	.30	.41*	.07	.06	.38
Time Extremity	.10	.09	.08	.08	.07	.36	.33	.01	.14	.37
Number of Actions Chosen	.26	.01	.15	.32*	.07	.48*	.03	.32	.28	−.18
S-score (Utility Ordering)	.09	.05	.06	.10	−.14	.02	.13	.30	.39	.40

* Significant at .05 or less.
† Significant at .01 or less.

TABLE 87. COMPARISON OF ACTUAL HUSBAND-WIFE CORRELATIONS WITH
MAXIMUM POSSIBLE HUSBAND-WIFE CORRELATIONS

Decision Variable	Husband $\sqrt{r}$	×	Wife $\sqrt{r}$	=	Maximum Possible Husband-Wife r	Actual Husband-Wife r
Number of Outcomes............	.88	×	.85	=	.75	.43
Probability Direction	.79	×	.72	=	.57	−.09
Probability Extremity	.74	×	.74	=	.55	−.25
Desirability Direction	.63	×	.72	=	.45	.39
Desirability Extremity	.72	×	.84	=	.60	−.25
Time Direction	.72	×	.71	=	.51	.15
Time Extremity	.64	×	.62	=	.40	.07
Number of Actions Chosen.......	.58	×	.67	=	.39	.07
S-score	.74	×	.76	=	.56	−.14

All values of $\sqrt{r}$ are based on the median value of inter-situational correlations (see Table 1), except the $\sqrt{r}$ value for S-score, which is based on the median h^2 values from Tables 107 and 108.

TABLE 88. COMPARISON OF HUSBAND-WIFE CORRELATIONS: COUPLES WHO AGREE
THEY HAVE DISCUSSED OBEDIENCE VS. COUPLES WHO AGREE THEY
ARE UNFAMILIAR WITH THE OBEDIENCE PROBLEM

Decision Variable	Couple Have Discussed (N = 23)	Couple Unfamiliar (N = 7)
Number of Outcomes	.45*	.61
Probability Direction	.14	.56
Probability Extremity	−.07	−.10
Desirability Direction	.61†	.38
Desirability Extremity	−.19	−.04
Time Direction	−.29	.27
Time Extremity	−.07	.34
Number of Actions Chosen	.23	.34
S-score (Utility Ordering)	.13	.05

* Significant at .05 or less.
† Significant at .01 or less.

TABLE 89. MEANS FOR GROUP INTERACTION SUBJECTS, AND FOR HIGH-SCORING
SPOUSES, LOW-SCORING SPOUSES, AND AVERAGE JOINT SCORE OF
MIDDLE-CLASS INDIVIDUAL HUSBANDS AND WIVES

Decision Variable	Group Interaction Subjects	High-Scoring Spouse	Low-Scoring Spouse	Average Husband-Wife Joint Score
Number of Outcomes	1.47	1.80	1.34	1.57
Probability Direction	.78	.84	.73	.78
Probability Extremity	1.31	1.47	1.06	1.26
Desirability Direction	2.04	1.99	1.62	1.81
Desirability Extremity	1.64	1.82	1.43	1.62
Time Direction	4.21	4.27	3.78	4.03
Time Extremity	1.36	1.44	1.09	1.26
Number of Actions Chosen	2.10	2.42	1.74	2.08
S-scores (Utility Ordering)	2.49	2.51	2.26	2.38

Scores represent means across the four decision situations.

TABLE 90. COMPARISON OF GROUP INTERACTION SUBJECTS WITH HIGH-SCORING SPOUSES, LOW-SCORING SPOUSES, AND AVERAGE JOINT SCORE OF MIDDLE-CLASS INDIVIDUAL HUSBANDS AND WIVES

Decision Variable	High vs. Group t	Low vs. Group t	Average vs. Group t
Number of Outcomes	2.33*	−1.08	0.74
Probability Direction	2.26*	−3.27†	0.09
Probability Extremity	2.96†	−4.75†	1.04
Desirability Direction	0.46	−3.51†	2.04*
Desirability Extremity	3.37†	−3.34†	0.20
Time Direction	0.60	−3.94†	1.78
Time Extremity	1.11	−4.07†	1.43
Number of Actions Chosen	2.06*	−2.38*	0.13
S-scores (Utility Ordering)	0.51	−4.67†	2.25*

* Significant at .05 or less.
† Significant at .01 or less.

TABLE 91. NUMBER OF CORRECT AND INCORRECT PREDICTIONS BASED ON THE EXPECTED UTILITY HYPOTHESIS

Decision Situation	Husbands		Wives	
	Right	Wrong	Right	Wrong
Masturbation	23	15	15	13
Homework	24	13	17	16
Obedience	24	12	20	12
Stealing	21	18	23	10
Mean	23.0	14.5	18.8	12.8

As discussed in the text, by chance (1/6) N correct predictions should be expected in each decision situation. By x^2 with 1 d.f., all predictions are significantly better than chance ($p < .001$). The N varies because certain subjects failed to respond to all decision situations; also, in some cases, two alternatives were tied for highest expected utility: these were eliminated from the tabulation.

TABLE 92. NUMBER OF CORRECT AND INCORRECT PREDICTIONS BASED ON THE MODIFIED EXPECTED UTILITY HYPOTHESIS

Decision Situation	Husbands		Wives	
	Right	Wrong	Right	Wrong
Masturbation	24	19	17	16
Homework	27	13	23	17
Obedience	25	13	23	15
Stealing	21	20	27	11
Mean	24.3	16.3	22.5	14.8

By chance (1/6) N correct predictions should be expected in each decision situation. By x^2 with 1 d.f., all predictions are significantly better than chance ($p < .001$). The N varies because certain subjects failed to respond to all decision situations; also, in some cases, two alternatives were tied for highest modified expected utility: these were eliminated from the tabulation.

TABLE 93. NUMBER OF CORRECT AND INCORRECT PREDICTIONS
BASED ON DESIRABILITY (UTILITY)

Decision Situation	Husbands		Wives	
	Right	Wrong	Right	Wrong
Masturbation	15	10	6	11
Homework	13	10	10	13
Obedience	20	9	12	12
Stealing	15	10	14	8
Mean	15.8	9.8	10.5	11.0

By chance (1/6) N correct predictions would be expected in each decision situation. By χ^2 with 1 d.f., all predictions (including mean predictions) are significantly better than chance ($p < .05$). The N varies because certain subjects failed to respond to all decision situations.

TABLE 94. NUMBER OF CORRECT AND INCORRECT PREDICTIONS
BASED ON SUBJECTIVE PROBABILITY

Decision Situation	Husbands		Wives	
	Right	Wrong	Right	Wrong
Masturbation	5	28	1	19
Homework	3	22	1	24
Obedience	3	23	0	31
Stealing	4	20	2	18
Mean	3.8	23.3	1.0	23.0

By chance (1/6) N correct predictions should be expected in each decision situation. By χ^2 with 1 d.f., all predictions were not significant ($p > .05$). The N varies because certain subjects failed to respond to all decision situations.

TABLE 95. COMPARISON OF THE THEORETICAL DISTRIBUTION OF S-SCORES WITH THE OBTAINED DISTRIBUTION OF S-SCORES, HUSBAND DATA

| S-scores | Expected Distribution | | Obtained Frequency Distribution | | | |
	Probability Values	Frequency	Mastur- bation	Homework	Obedience	Stealing
+15	.0014	.05	3	0	0	1
+13, 14	.0069	.34	5	10	3	8
+11, 12	.0197	.96	10	14	13	8
+9, 10	.0400	1.92	17	8	11	10
+7, 8	.068	3.26	6	9	11	4
+5, 6	.099	4.75	3	4	7	9
+3, 4	.125	6.00	3	1	2	3
+1, 2	.140	6.72	0	3	1	3
−1, 2	.140	6.72	1	0	0	1
−3, 4	.125	6.00	0	0	0	1
−5, 6	.099	4.75	0	0	0	0
−7, 8	.068	3.26	0	0	0	0
−9, 10	.040	1.92	0	0	0	0
−11, 12	.0197	.96	0	0	0	0
−13, 14	.0069	.34	0	0	0	0
−15	.0014	.05	0	0	0	0

$N = 48$. By x^2 with 7 d.f., the observed distribution of S-scores is significantly different from the theoretical distribution at less than the .001 level.

TABLE 96. COMPARISON OF THE THEORETICAL DISTRIBUTION OF S-SCORES WITH THE OBTAINED DISTRIBUTION OF S-SCORES, WIFE DATA

| S-scores | Expected Distribution | | Obtained Frequency Distribution | | | |
	Probability Values	Frequency	Mastur- bation	Homework	Obedience	Stealing
+15	.0014	.05	2	0	2	0
+13, 14	.0069	.34	6	3	3	1
+11, 12	.0197	.96	11	7	10	3
+9, 10	.040	1.92	12	17	11	14
+7, 8	.068	3.26	11	12	8	9
+5, 6	.099	4.75	1	4	8	9
+3, 4	.125	6.00	2	2	4	8
+1, 2	.140	6.72	1	2	0	2
−1, 2	.140	6.72	1	1	2	0
−3, 4	.125	6.00	1	0	0	2
−5, 6	.099	4.75	0	0	0	0
−7, 8	.068	3.26	0	0	0	0
−9, 10	.040	1.92	0	0	0	0
−11, 12	.0197	.96	0	0	0	0
−13, 14	.0069	.34	0	0	0	0
−15	.0014	.05	0	0	0	0

$N = 48$. By x^2 with 7 d.f., the observed distribution of S-scores is significantly different from the theoretical distribution at less than the .001 level.

TABLE 97. COMPARISON OF THE THEORETICAL DISTRIBUTION OF *S*-SCORES (BASED ON *E'* VALUES) WITH THE OBTAINED DISTRIBUTION OF *S*-SCORES (BASED ON *E'* VALUES), HUSBAND DATA

	Expected Distribution		Obtained Frequency Distribution			
S-scores	Probability Values	Frequency	Mastur-bation	Homework	Obedience	Stealing
+15	.0014	.05	5	1	1	2
+13, 14	.0069	.34	5	6	3	5
+11, 12	.0197	.96	7	13	12	6
+9, 10	.040	1.92	16	14	8	11
+7, 8	.068	3.26	6	5	14	8
+5, 6	.099	4.75	5	4	7	9
+3, 4	.125	6.00	2	2	2	3
+1, 2	.140	6.72	1	3	1	1
−1, 2	.140	6.72	1	0	0	2
−3, 4	.125	6.00	0	0	0	1
−5, 6	.099	4.75	0	0	0	0
−7, 8	.068	3.26	0	0	0	0
−9, 10	.040	1.92	0	0	0	0
−11, 12	.0197	.96	0	0	0	0
−13, 14	.0069	.34	0	0	0	0
−15	.0014	.05	0	0	0	0

$N = 48$. By χ^2 with 7 d.f., the observed distribution of *S*-scores is significantly different from the theoretical distribution at less than the .001 level.

TABLE 98. COMPARISON OF THE THEORETICAL DISTRIBUTION OF *S*-SCORES (BASED ON *E'* VALUES) WITH THE OBTAINED DISTRIBUTION OF *S*-SCORES (BASED ON *E'* VALUES), WIFE DATA

	Expected Distribution		Obtained Frequency Distribution			
S-scores	Probability Values	Frequency	Mastur-bation	Homework	Obedience	Stealing
+15	.0014	.05	0	0	2	1
+13, 14	.0069	.34	11	8	4	7
+11, 12	.0197	.96	10	4	10	10
+9, 10	.040	1.92	10	13	12	10
+7, 8	.068	3.26	10	12	9	9
+5, 6	.099	4.75	3	4	4	7
+3, 4	.125	6.00	2	2	5	1
+1, 2	.140	6.72	1	3	0	1
−1, 2	.140	6.72	0	2	2	2
−3, 4	.125	6.00	0	0	0	0
−5, 6	.099	4.75	1	0	0	0
−7, 8	.068	3.26	0	0	0	0
−9, 10	.040	1.92	0	0	0	0
−11, 12	.0197	.96	0	0	0	0
−13, 14	.0069	.34	0	0	0	0
−15	.0014	.05	0	0	0	0

$N = 48$. By χ^2 with 7 d.f., the observed distribution of *S*-scores is significantly different from the theoretical distribution at less than the .001 level.

TABLE 99. COMPARISON OF THE THEORETICAL DISTRIBUTION OF S-SCORES (BASED ON SUBJECTIVE PROBABILITY ALONE) WITH THE OBTAINED DISTRIBUTION OF S-SCORES (BASED ON SUBJECTIVE PROBABILITY ALONE), HUSBAND DATA

S-scores	Expected Distribution		Obtained Frequency Distribution			
	Probability Values	Frequency	Mastur-bation	Homework	Obedience	Stealing
+15	.0014	.05	0	0	0	0
+13, 14	.0069	.34	0	0	0	0
+11, 12	.0197	.96	0	2	0	0
+9, 10	.040	1.92	0	1	0	4
+7, 8	.068	3.26	4	3	0	2
+5, 6	.099	4.75	7	2	2	3
+3, 4	.125	6.00	2	8	4	5
+1, 2	.140	6.72	7	0	8	8
−1, 2	.140	6.72	9	11	6	8
−3, 4	.125	6.00	4	5	9	5
−5, 6	.099	4.75	5	8	7	3
−7, 8	.068	3.26	4	6	4	7
−9, 10	.040	1.92	5	0	4	1
−11, 12	.0197	.96	1	1	2	2
−13, 14	.0069	.34	0	1	2	0
−15	.0014	.05	0	0	0	0

$N = 48$. By χ^2 with 7 d.f., the observed distribution of S-scores is significantly different from the theoretical distribution only for the masturbation and stealing situations, at less than the .05 level.

TABLE 100. COMPARISON OF THE THEORETICAL DISTRIBUTION OF S-SCORES (BASED ON SUBJECTIVE PROBABILITY ALONE) WITH THE OBTAINED DISTRIBUTION OF S-SCORES (BASED ON SUBJECTIVE PROBABILITY ALONE), WIFE DATA

S-scores	Expected Distribution		Obtained Frequency Distribution			
	Probability Values	Frequency	Mastur-bation	Homework	Obedience	Stealing
+15	.0014	.05	0	0	0	0
+13, 14	.0069	.34	0	1	0	0
+11, 12	.0197	.96	0	0	0	0
+9, 10	.040	1.92	2	0	0	1
+7, 8	.068	3.26	2	1	2	2
+5, 6	.099	4.75	5	1	2	2
+3, 4	.125	6.00	3	7	1	3
+1, 2	.140	6.72	10	13	6	13
−1, 2	.140	6.72	6	7	6	9
−3, 4	.125	6.00	7	10	8	5
−5, 6	.099	4.75	8	4	12	10
−7, 8	.068	3.26	4	3	4	2
−9, 10	.040	1.92	1	1	4	1
−11, 12	.0197	.96	0	0	3	0
−13, 14	.0069	.34	0	0	0	0
−15	.0014	.05	0	0	0	0

$N = 48$. By χ^2 with 7 d.f., the observed distribution of S-scores is significantly different from the theoretical distribution for all decision situations except masturbation, at less than the .05 level.

TABLE 101. COMPARISON OF THE THEORETICAL DISTRIBUTION OF S-SCORES (BASED ON UTILITY ALONE) WITH THE OBTAINED DISTRIBUTION OF S-SCORES (BASED ON UTILITY ALONE), HUSBAND DATA

	Expected Distribution		Obtained Frequency Distribution			
S-scores	Probability Values	Frequency	Mastur-bation	Homework	Obedience	Stealing
+15	.0014	.05	0	0	0	0
+13, 14	.0069	.34	5	5	3	3
+11, 12	.0197	.96	14	10	4	7
+9, 10	.040	1.92	12	13	15	14
+7, 8	.068	3.26	9	7	12	12
+5, 6	.099	4.75	2	4	9	7
+3, 4	.125	6.00	2	4	1	1
+1, 2	.140	6.72	2	4	3	3
−1, 2	.140	6.72	2	1	1	0
−3, 4	.125	6.00	0	0	1	1
−5, 6	.099	4.75	0	0	0	0
−7, 8	.068	3.26	0	0	0	0
−9, 10	.040	1.92	0	0	0	0
−11, 12	.0197	.96	0	0	0	0
−13, 14	.0069	.34	0	0	0	0
−15	.0014	.05	0	0	0	0

$N = 48$. By χ^2 with 7 d.f., the observed distribution of S-scores is significantly different from the theoretical distribution at less than the .001 level.

TABLE 102. COMPARISON OF THE THEORETICAL DISTRIBUTION OF S-SCORES (BASED ON UTILITY ALONE) WITH THE OBTAINED DISTRIBUTION OF S-SCORES (BASED ON UTILITY ALONE), WIFE DATA

	Expected Distribution		Obtained Frequency Distribution			
S-scores	Probability Values	Frequency	Mastur-bation	Homework	Obedience	Stealing
+15	.0014	.05	0	0	0	0
+13, 14	.0069	.34	3	0	1	0
+11, 12	.0197	.96	10	9	9	11
+9, 10	.040	1.92	12	12	17	11
+7, 8	.068	3.26	10	15	7	12
+5, 6	.099	4.75	7	8	8	9
+3, 4	.125	6.00	1	1	1	3
+1, 2	.140	6.72	2	1	3	0
−1, 2	.140	6.72	1	1	1	2
−3, 4	.125	6.00	1	1	0	0
−5, 6	.099	4.75	0	0	1	0
−7, 8	.068	3.26	1	0	0	0
−9, 10	.040	1.92	0	0	0	0
−11, 12	.0197	.96	0	0	0	0
−13, 14	.0069	.34	0	0	0	0
−15	.0014	.05	0	0	0	0

$N = 48$. By χ^2 with 7 d.f., the observed distribution of S-scores is significantly different from the theoretical distribution at less than the .001 level.

TABLE 103. MEANS AND STANDARD DEVIATIONS OF THE TIME ESTIMATES
IN THE FOUR DECISION SITUATIONS*

Subjects†	Masturbation		Homework		Obedience		Stealing	
	Mean	S.D.	Mean	S.D.	Mean	S.D.	Mean	S.D.
Husbands	3.75	.62	4.18	.49	4.11	.61	4.10	.53
Wives	3.84	.61	4.07	.58	4.11	.59	4.05	.55

* High score indicates present time orientation.
† There were 48 males and 48 females in this analysis.

TABLE 104.
INTERCORRELATIONS OF E AND E' BY DECISION SITUATION, HUSBAND DATA

	E			
	Masturbation	Homework	Obedience	Stealing
Masturbation, E'	.86			
Homework, E'		.87		
Obedience, E'			.92	
Stealing, E'				.94

$N = 48$. All values of r significant at less than .01.

TABLE 105. INTERCORRELATIONS OF E AND E' BY DECISION SITUATION, WIFE DATA

	E			
	Masturbation	Homework	Obedience	Stealing
Masturbation, E'	.88			
Homework, E'		.96		
Obedience, E'			.95	
Stealing, E'				.94

$N = 48$. All values of r significant at less than .01.

TABLE 106. VARIABLES USED IN FACTOR ANALYSES OF PERSONALITY VARIABLES
AND *S*-SCORES: MIDDLE–CLASS MALES AND FEMALES

Number	Variable.
1	*S*-score: Masturbation Decision
2	*S*-score: Homework Decision
3	*S*-score: Obedience Decision
4	*S*-score: Stealing Decision
5	Independence of judgment
6	Parental concern with child rearing: Sex
7	Parental concern with child rearing: Honesty
8	Parental concern with child rearing: Work
9	Parental concern with child rearing: Obedience
10	Verbal I.Q.
11	Manifest Anxiety
12	PARI: Dominance
13	PARI: Rejection
14	PARI: Complaint over wife's ascendancy; Wife's ascendancy
15	Age
16	Religion
17	Autism
18	Cycloid tendencies
19	Emotionality
20	Nervousness
21	Self-sufficiency
22	Future time orientation
23	Optimism (belief that good things will happen)
24	Belief in thinking before acting
25	General satisfaction (total score)
26	Anti-traditionalistic orientation
27	Self-confidence
28	Belief in predictability of life
29	Belief in multiple causation of events
30	Belief in animism
31	Belief in supernatural causes
32	Belief in fate
33	Belief that events clearly are either good or bad
34	Optimism (belief that bad things won't happen)
35	Belief in trying many actions in solving problems
36	Mean Expected Utility: Masturbation
37	Mean Expected Utility: Homework
38	Mean Expected Utility: Obedience
39	Mean Expected Utility: Stealing
40	Interest in philosophizing and puzzles

TABLE 107. ROTATED FACTORS; PERSONALITY VARIABLES AND S-SCORES MIDDLE-CLASS MALES ($N = 48$)

Variable	1	2	3	4	5	6	7	8	9	10	11	12	h^2
1	-.30	.08	.04	-.54	-.15	-.09	.21	-.18	.11	-.03	.31	.00	.60
2	-.08	-.20	-.14	-.20	.01	.18	-.27	-.11	.53	-.23	-.01	.04	.55
3	-.20	.19	-.04	.22	.56	.04	-.08	-.09	.16	-.01	.05	-.16	.51
4	.15	.12	.13	.20	-.04	.05	-.16	-.02	.61	.06	.01	.18	.54
5	-.53	.18	.20	-.30	.18	.19	.03	-.53	-.08	.01	.13	-.25	.87
6	.08	.05	-.53	-.04	.05	-.11	.13	.16	-.03	-.41	.12	-.07	.53
7	.32	-.02	-.71	.06	-.15	-.07	-.08	.06	.06	.01	.19	-.01	.69
8	.02	-.14	-.73	-.16	-.05	.10	-.12	-.06	.11	.20	-.11	-.08	.68
9	.09	.37	-.77	.06	.13	.15	.11	-.05	-.10	.01	.00	-.01	.80
10	-.44	-.11	.19	.17	.40	.13	.12	-.25	.23	.01	.11	-.03	.58
11	.15	.81	-.08	-.12	.03	-.18	.10	.31	.01	.17	.03	-.01	.86
12	.68	.13	-.19	.10	.00	.10	.26	.26	-.07	.10	-.19	-.22	.76
13	.10	.17	.00	-.03	-.04	-.09	.84	.07	-.08	.07	.03	-.02	.77
14	.08	.13	-.32	-.07	-.29	.21	.59	-.01	-.05	-.25	-.16	.02	.69
15	.13	.14	.00	.72	-.03	-.13	-.07	.03	.01	.03	.17	.13	.62
16	-.07	.15	.01	-.46	.09	.22	.12	-.11	-.25	.18	.18	.17	.47
17	-.05	.70	.00	.17	.00	.21	.10	-.24	-.10	.37	-.01	-.01	.79
18	.02	.67	-.17	.04	-.07	-.06	.25	-.04	.12	-.19	.13	-.22	.66
19	.05	.95	-.10	.03	-.02	.02	-.06	-.01	-.17	-.10	-.09	.03	.98
20	.02	.87	.00	.06	-.01	.12	-.02	.03	.18	-.12	.02	.13	.83
21	.02	-.04	-.16	.07	.05	.07	-.09	-.01	-.17	-.11	-.42	.08	.27
22	-.44	.02	-.03	-.14	.18	-.18	.33	.09	.20	-.01	.20	.25	.53
23	.64	.03	.14	-.19	.05	.18	.12	.22	-.02	-.06	-.19	-.35	.72
24	-.38	-.14	-.06	.05	.07	-.07	-.09	-.05	.21	-.07	-.09	.59	.60
25	.32	-.20	.19	.09	.05	.08	-.08	.22	.08	-.47	-.13	.08	.50
26	-.08	-.10	.15	.15	.16	.00	-.07	-.14	-.25	-.17	.33	-.08	.32
27	.02	-.62	-.28	.18	.01	.43	.14	.16	-.01	.01	.06	.21	.76
28	-.05	.05	.05	-.20	.54	.01	-.14	-.20	-.12	-.11	-.20	.24	.52
29	.27	.09	-.33	.11	.25	.02	.43	-.11	.03	.10	-.08	.23	.52
30	.45	.23	-.09	.19	-.14	.22	.00	-.07	-.06	.01	.52	-.01	.64
31	.77	.17	-.07	-.33	.11	-.07	-.06	.01	.05	.10	.03	.14	.79
32	.96	.14	-.09	.06	.04	-.01	.05	-.06	.10	-.09	.12	.01	.99
33	.35	-.10	-.08	-.04	.39	.08	-.02	.36	-.11	-.01	.10	.06	.45
34	.49	.12	-.26	.21	-.23	-.33	-.09	.04	-.12	.12	.08	-.01	.57
35	-.46	.08	.46	-.10	-.12	.08	-.02	-.34	.11	.12	.10	-.11	.62
36	.25	.06	.12	-.04	-.05	.10	.10	.73	-.10	-.19	.05	-.02	.68
37	.19	.20	-.17	-.24	.05	.60	-.25	.08	-.05	-.01	-.03	-.15	.62
38	.27	-.01	-.10	.17	-.05	.39	.11	.46	.15	.15	.07	-.26	.60
39	.32	.23	.08	.25	-.05	.26	.04	.44	.11	.31	.00	-.19	.63
40	-.07	-.21	.12	.09	.25	-.49	.02	-.05	-.17	.00	-.02	-.17	.43

TABLE 108. ROTATED FACTORS; PERSONALITY VARIABLES AND S-SCORES
MIDDLE-CLASS FEMALES ($N = 48$)

Variable	1	2	3	4	5	6	7	8	9	10	11	h^2
1	−.20	.01	.05	.80	−.06	−.06	.03	−.08	−.13	.06	.08	.72
2	−.06	−.03	−.03	.02	−.01	.03	.04	−.03	−.75	−.05	.04	.58
3	.06	.12	−.06	.38	−.02	.03	−.07	−.10	−.58	.02	−.20	.56
4	−.07	−.22	.01	.25	.09	−.13	.47	−.01	.05	.11	.03	.38
5	−.60	−.06	.29	.25	.20	.27	−.01	−.01	−.11	.21	−.07	.68
6	−.06	−.10	−.76	.03	−.06	.01	.10	.13	−.06	−.07	−.09	.64
7	.15	−.06	−.76	−.14	.01	−.30	−.02	.12	−.07	−.04	.03	.73
8	.34	.10	−.62	.10	.11	.14	−.03	.00	.12	.09	.28	.65
9	−.16	−.14	−.55	.10	−.28	.23	.05	.12	.01	.13	.29	.60
10	−.38	−.35	.08	−.25	.01	−.16	.15	.19	−.09	.24	.00	.48
11	−.05	.88	.05	.01	−.02	−.03	−.06	−.02	.10	−.13	.03	.81
12	.59	.07	−.32	−.17	−.17	.10	.44	−.03	.16	.01	−.20	.78
13	−.10	.41	−.01	−.44	−.02	−.10	.47	−.08	.10	.02	−.08	.62
14	.50	.03	−.10	−.14	−.03	.26	.61	−.09	−.13	−.01	−.07	.75
15	.21	.17	.05	−.44	.11	.28	.06	−.19	−.22	.14	.19	.51
16	−.06	.18	−.03	.24	.01	.07	−.01	.11	.20	−.24	−.15	.23
17	.19	.58	.00	.10	−.01	.02	.10	−.06	−.15	.39	.24	.63
18	.13	.70	.16	−.06	.05	.01	−.05	−.21	−.23	.12	.05	.66
19	−.06	.22	−.26	.07	−.13	−.11	−.05	.01	.03	.01	.64	.57
20	.03	.49	−.13	−.22	−.03	−.62	.07	−.05	−.01	−.20	.05	.74
21	.06	.00	.03	−.19	.05	.66	.16	−.08	−.02	−.10	−.02	.52
22	−.23	−.08	.07	.11	−.11	.16	−.10	−.15	.25	.50	.05	.46
23	.36	−.29	−.04	.24	.00	.05	.29	.11	−.20	−.22	.15	.48
24	−.19	.25	.26	−.28	−.01	.29	−.34	.21	.11	.07	−.06	.50
25	.13	−.52	−.11	.19	−.33	−.22	−.08	−.05	−.08	.16	.20	.57
26	.07	.00	.28	.00	.52	.01	.15	−.03	.14	−.05	.14	.42
27	.10	−.53	.10	−.29	.15	.35	−.07	.09	.07	−.33	−.02	.65
28	.13	−.08	.09	.13	−.42	.02	−.25	.09	−.21	−.01	.07	.34
29	−.18	.21	−.02	.08	.02	−.01	.31	.30	−.42	.04	.38	.59
30	.00	.08	.09	.01	.01	.03	−.01	−.97	−.06	.04	−.01	.95
31	.03	.06	.05	.02	−.04	−.01	.03	−.95	.04	.00	.01	.92
32	.31	.01	−.39	.10	.07	−.41	.18	−.01	.13	−.18	.21	.56
33	.24	.21	.19	.33	−.48	−.02	.14	−.18	.05	.10	.10	.56
34	.26	.06	−.25	.11	−.06	−.05	.42	.17	−.06	−.38	.27	.58
35	−.63	−.21	.15	−.02	.16	.01	.00	.21	−.10	.28	−.25	.68
36	.78	−.12	−.08	−.11	.23	.04	−.03	.06	−.06	.17	.03	.74
37	.74	−.03	.18	.18	−.17	.01	−.07	−.03	−.16	.09	−.26	.75
38	.68	.02	.22	−.10	−.01	−.06	.00	.09	.07	−.07	.09	.56
39	.43	−.19	−.05	.23	.33	−.34	.13	−.06	.16	.05	−.12	.56
40	−.33	.12	.21	.03	.57	.09	−.15	.14	−.12	.06	−.13	.58

APPENDIX B

DECISION PROCESS TEST

INTRODUCTION
(Read Carefully)

This part of the study is concerned with how parents decide what child-rearing practices to use. In each of the four booklets which follow a decision problem is presented. Each problem involves the behavior of a boy about ten years old. You may feel that some of the problems are more serious than others. However, in every case the problems can be handled by the parents without outside assistance. The boy is a normal healthy child without any symptoms of maladjustment. There is no need to seek psychiatric assistance.

This will be the longest part of the study. You should plan to spend about 15 minutes on each of the four decision problems.

This is a study of parent decision-making.

You are asked to fill out a series of questionnaires. It will take between 2½–3 hours to finish, allowing for a 15-minute coffee break.

You are one of many groups of parents who are taking part in this study. Your co-operation is appreciated.

Please feel free to criticize any questions, or set of questions, by writing in the margin. However, be sure to *answer* all questions.

For some time now in a certain family a boy about 10 years old has been masturbating occasionally and in private. The parents know about the behavior.

Suppose that *you* were the parent faced with this situation. On the following pages are six different actions which you as a parent might take. Each action is listed on a separate page.

You are asked to do two things:

1. First, you are asked to evaluate each action by filling in the boxes on that page.
2. Second, when you have evaluated all six actions, you are asked to decide which of the actions are best.

It is very important for us to know how familiar you are with this situation. Therefore, will you please check one of the following:

1. This situation has happened in my family...................._____
2. This situation is happening right now in my family.............._____
3. This situation has never happened in my family................_____

Answer only if you checked 1 or 2 above:

If this situation has happened or is happening, to what extent have you discussed it with your husband or wife?

(Circle only one number)

A Great Deal	Quite a Bit	Some	Not Much	Not at All
1	2	3	4	5

(Please turn the page and begin)

This is an ACTION a parent might take →   NUMBER 2. TELL HIM IT IS A DIRTY AND SHAMEFUL PRACTICE

	i)	ii)	iii)
A) What would be some of the *results* if you took this action? Space is provided on the right to write in as many as three results if you wish to. Write only one result in each box.			
B) What are the *chances* that the results written in above would happen?	___Highly probable ___Probable ___About half and half ___Improbable ___Highly improbable	___Highly probable ___Probable ___About half and half ___Improbable ___Highly improbable	___Highly probable ___Probable ___About half and half ___Improbable ___Highly improbable
C) How much would you *want* these results to happen?	___Strongly desire ___Desire ___Don't care either way ___Do not desire ___Strongly do not desire	___Strongly desire ___Desire ___Don't care either way ___Do not desire ___Strongly do not desire	___Strongly desire ___Desire ___Don't care either way ___Do not desire ___Strongly do not desire
D) How soon would these results *begin to happen?*	___Within a week ___A week to 6 months ___6 months to 1 year ___1 to 5 years ___5 years or more	___Within a week ___A week to 6 months ___6 months to 1 year ___1 to 5 years ___5 years or more	___Within a week ___A week to 6 months ___6 months to 1 year ___1 to 5 years ___5 years or more

---

THESE LAST QUESTIONS ASK YOU TO CHOOSE AMONG THE
ACTIONS YOU HAVE JUST EVALUATED

---

1. Now, suppose that a parent could take only one of these actions. Look back over the six actions and *rank* them below from the best to the worst single action a parent might take. You may feel that none is any good or worth doing, but rank them anyway according to which is the best of the group, second best, and so on.

Write in
Number of Action

i) Single best action	_____
ii) Second best action	_____
iii) Third best action	_____
iv) Fourth best action	_____
v) Fifth best action	_____
vi) Worst action	_____

2. Now, write in the number, or numbers, of the action(s) from among the six that *you would take* in this situation.

    Write number(s) here_____

    I can't decide what I'd do................☐

    I wouldn't do any of the six............☐

3. If for question 2 above you have listed *more than one* action which you would take, check the one statement below which best describes the way you would do these.

    a) I would start doing all of these together at about the same time..............☐

    b) I would try one first, and then another, until I found one of them that worked....☐

    c) I would try these in a special, planned order; that is, I would try a particular one first and

        i) it would not matter whether it works or doesn't before I would begin the next...☐

        ii) if the first one worked, then I would go on to the next...............☐

        iii) if the first one didn't work, I would go on to the next...............☐

TAYLOR MANIFEST ANXIETY SCALE (MAS)

The following is a list of statements some of which may be true of you, some of which may not be true of you.

If the statement is true of you, circle the word "True" at the right of that statement.
If the statement is not true of you, circle the word "False" at the right of that statement.

Work rapidly; don't spend a lot of time on any statement.

1.	I do not tire quickly.	True	False
2.	I am often sick to my stomach.	True	False
3.	I am about as nervous as other people.	True	False
4.	I have very few headaches.	True	False
5.	I work under a great deal of strain.	True	False
6.	I cannot keep my mind on one thing.	True	False
7.	I worry over money and business.	True	False
8.	I frequently notice my hand shakes when I try to do something.	True	False
9.	I blush as often as others.	True	False
10.	I have diarrhea ("the runs") once a month or more.	True	False
11.	I worry quite a bit over possible troubles.	True	False
12.	I practically never blush.	True	False
13.	I am often afraid that I am going to blush.	True	False
14.	I have nightmares every few nights.	True	False
15.	My hands and feet are usually warm enough.	True	False
16.	I sweat very easily even on cool days.	True	False
17.	When embarrassed I often break out in a sweat which is very annoying.	True	False
18.	I do not often notice my heart pounding and I am seldom short of breath.	True	False
19.	I feel hungry almost all the time.	True	False
20.	Often my bowels don't move for several days at a time.	True	False
21.	I have a great deal of stomach trouble.	True	False
22.	At times I lose sleep over worry.	True	False
23.	My sleep is restless and disturbed.	True	False
24.	I often dream about things I don't like to tell other people.	True	False
25.	I am easily embarrassed.	True	False
26.	My feelings are hurt easier than most people.	True	False
27.	I often find myself worrying about something.	True	False
28.	I wish I could be as happy as others.	True	False
29.	I am usually calm and not easily upset.	True	False
30.	I cry easily.	True	False
31.	I feel anxious about something or someone almost all of the time.	True	False
32.	I am happy most of the time.	True	False
33.	It makes me nervous to have to wait.	True	False
34.	At times I am so restless that I cannot sit in a chair for very long.	True	False
35.	Sometimes I become so excited that I find it hard to get to sleep.	True	False
36.	I have often felt that I faced so many difficulties I could not overcome them.	True	False
37.	At times I have been worried beyond reason about something that really did not matter.	True	False
38.	I do not have as many fears as my friends.	True	False
39.	I have been afraid of things or people that I know could not hurt me.	True	False
40.	I certainly feel useless at times.	True	False
41.	I find it hard to keep my mind on a task or job.	True	False
42.	I am more self-conscious than most people.	True	False
43.	I am the kind of person who takes things hard.	True	False
44.	I am a very nervous person.	True	False
45.	Life is often a strain for me.	True	False
46.	At times I think I am no good at all.	True	False
47.	I am not at all confident of myself.	True	False
48.	At times I feel that I am going to crack up.	True	False
49.	I don't like to face a difficulty or make an important decision.	True	False
50.	I am very confident of myself.	True	False

GENERAL SATISFACTION SCALE

Indicate your satisfaction or dissatisfaction with the following by circling the S if you are satisfied, and D if you are dissatisfied, and the N if you are neutral (have no particular feeling about the matter one way or another).

1. The city in which you live. S D N	21. Your name. S D N
2. The house or apartment in	22. The people you know. S D N
which you live. S D N	23. TV programs. S D N
3. The area of the city or town	24. The way people drive. S D N
in which you live. S D N	25. The way you were raised. S D N
4. The high school you attended. S D N	26. Income taxes. S D N
5. The climate where you live. S D N	27. Public transportation in your
6. The movies being produced. S D N	town. S D N
7. The local political situation. S D N	28. Women's clothing styles S D N
8. The national political situa-	29. The school your child is at-
tion. S D N	tending. S D N
9. Our foreign policy. S D N	30. Telephone service. S D N
10. Your last job. S D N	31. Yourself. S D N
11. Present food prices. S D N	32. Popular music. S D N
12. Today's cars. S D N	33. Movie censorship. S D N
13. Opportunities to get ahead in	34. Advertising methods. S D N
this country. S D N	35. Most of the books being pub-
14. Your local newspapers. S D N	lished nowadays. S D N
15. Car prices. S D N	36. The way most people act to
16. The amount of time you have	me. S D N
for recreation. S D N	37. What my child learns in
17. Your last boss. S D N	school. S D N
18. The college you attended. S D N	38. Young people's behavior. S D N
19. The kind of education you	39. The people I live with. S D N
had. S D N	40. Dogs, pets. S D N
20. The way children are raised	
nowadays. S D N	

TEST OF PARENTAL CONCERN WITH CHILD REARING

The following statements of opinion refer to a number of issues about which people disagree. To the right of each statement are five categories: Strongly Agree (SA), Agree (A), Uncertain (?), Disagree (D), and Strongly Disagree (SD). Please circle the category which reflects your opinion.

There are no right or wrong answers, so answer according to your own opinion. It is very important to the study that all questions be answered. Many of the statements will seem alike but all are necessary to show slight differences of opinion.

1. It's bad for a 10-year-old boy to argue with his parents about what television programs to watch. SA A ? D SD
2. It's bad for a 10-year-old boy to play sex games with girls in the neighborhood. SA A ? D SD
3. It's bad for a 10-year-old boy to eat between meals. SA A ? D SD
4. It's all right for a 10-year-old boy to borrow things from his friends without telling them. SA A ? D SD
5. It's wrong for a 10-year-old boy to show a lot of love for his parents. SA A ? D SD
6. It's not good when a 10-year-old boy is easily led by his friends. SA A ? D SD
7. It's very important that a 10-year-old boy belong to his church choir. SA A ? D SD
8. It's wrong for a 10-year-old boy not to do "chores" around the house. SA A ? D SD
9. It's wrong for a 10-year-old boy to hit his brothers and sisters. SA A ? D SD
10. It's wrong for a 10-year-old boy to keep asking for a bigger allowance. SA A ? D SD
11. It's all right for a 10-year-old boy to argue with his teacher in the classroom. SA A ? D SD
12. It's all right if a 10-year-old boy likes to play with dolls, play keeping house, and the like. SA A ? D SD
13. It's important for a 10-year-old boy not to play too hard. SA A ? D SD
14. It's important for a 10-year-old boy to learn that there is never any excuse at all for dishonesty. SA A ? D SD
15. It's bad that a 10-year-old boy takes so much of his parents' time. SA A ? D SD
16. It's important for a 10-year-old boy to have a lot of friends. SA A ? D SD
17. It's important that a 10-year-old boy always say his prayers before going to bed at night. SA A ? D SD
18. It's good for a 10-year-old boy to spend most of his free time working at some useful hobby. SA A ? D SD
19. It's bad for a 10-year-old boy to argue a lot with his brothers and sisters. SA A ? D SD
20. It's wrong for a 10-year-old boy to act as though he had a right to his parents' money. SA A ? D SD
21. It's important that a 10-year-old boy always do what his parents tell him to. SA A ? D SD
22. It's all right for a 10-year-old boy never to ask questions about sex. SA A ? D SD
23. It's bad for a 10-year-old boy to always be tired when he goes to bed at night. SA A ? D SD
24. It's all right for a 10-year-old boy to sneak into the movies without paying if it's only done in fun. SA A ? D SD
25. It's good for a 10-year-old boy to feel that his parents love him no matter what he does. SA A ? D SD
26. It's all right for a 10-year-old boy to have arguments and fights with his friends. SA A ? D SD
27. It's important that a 10-year-old boy go to the church that his parents go to. SA A ? D SD
28. It's bad for a 10-year-old boy not to finish a task once he has started it. SA A ? D SD
29. It's wrong for a 10-year-old boy to try to outdo his brothers and sisters. SA A ? D SD
30. It's bad for a 10-year-old boy to save almost all the money he gets from his parents. SA A ? D SD

31. It's wrong for a 10-year-old boy to ask for an explanation every time his parents tell him to do something.   SA A ? D SD
32. It's all right for a 10-year-old boy to sleep in the same bed with his 6-year-old sister.   SA A ? D SD
33. It's important that a 10-year-old boy always take some kind of medicine whenever he doesn't feel well.   SA A ? D SD
34. It's very bad for a 10-year-old boy ever to take money from his mother's pocketbook without her knowledge.   SA A ? D SD
35. It's important that a 10-year-old boy's ideas be seriously considered in making family decisions   SA A ? D SD
36. It's all right for a ten-year-old boy to keep to himself and rarely make any friends.   SA A ? D SD
37. It's important that a 10-year-old boy always observe religious holidays.   SA A ? D SD
38. It's important for a 10-year-old boy to do his work very carefully.   SA A ? D SD
39. It's all right for a 10-year-old boy not to share his things with his brothers and sisters.   SA A ? D SD
40. It's bad for a 10-year-old boy to get every toy and game he wants.   SA A ? D SD
41. It's wrong for a 10-year-old boy to have friends his parents don't like.   SA A ? D SD
42. It's all right for a 10-year-old boy to sleep in the same room as his parents.   SA A ? D SD
43. It's all right if a 10-year-old boy is underweight.   SA A ? D SD
44. It's wrong for a 10-year-old boy to keep something he has found when he knows who the owner is.   SA A ? D SD
45. It's wrong that a 10-year-old boy be treated by his parents as an equal.   SA A ? D SD
46. It's wrong for a 10-year-boy to take the attitude that he can't trust any of his friends.   SA A ? D SD
47. It's important that a 10-year-old boy attend church services regularly.   SA A ? D SD
48. It's important for a 10-year-old boy to work as hard as he can on every task he does.   SA A ? D SD
49. It's important that a 10-year-old boy always take care of his younger brothers and sisters.   SA A ? D SD
50. It's bad for a 10-year-old boy to have all the money he wants.   SA A ? D SD

PARENTAL ATTITUDE RESEARCH INSTRUMENT (PARI)

INVENTORY OF ATTITUDES ON FAMILY LIFE AND CHILDREN (FATHER)

Read each of the statements below and then rate them as follows:

A	a	d	D
strongly agree	mildly agree	mildly disagree	strongly disagree

Indicate your opinion by drawing a circle around the "A" if you strongly agree, around the "a" if you mildly agree, around the "d" if you mildly disagree, and around the "D" if you strongly disagree.

There are no right or wrong answers, so answer according to your own opinion. It is very important to the study that all questions be answered. Many of the statements will seem alike, but all are necessary to show slight differences of opinion.

	Agree		Disagree	
1. A good father should shelter his child from life's little difficulties.	A	a	d	D
2. People who think they can get along in marriage without arguments just don't know the facts.	A	a	d	D
3. A young father feels "held down" because there are lots of things he wants to do while he is young.	A	a	d	D
4. More parents should teach their children to have unquestioning loyalty to them.	A	a	d	D
5. A parent should never be made to look wrong in a child's eyes.	A	a	d	D
6. The things wives and children ask of a man after his hard day's work are enough to make anyone lose his temper at times.	A	a	d	D
7. When a wife gets the idea she has to outdo the husband, the whole family is in for it.	A	a	d	D
8. An alert parent should try to learn all his child's thoughts.	A	a	d	D
9. A father should do his best to avoid any disappointment for his child.	A	a	d	D
10. Sometimes it's necessary for a husband to tell off his wife in order to get his rights.	A	a	d	D
11. After a man has lived a life of his own it's hard to be tied down by a family.	A	a	d	D
12. A child soon learns that there is no greater wisdom than that of his parents.	A	a	d	D
13. There is no excusing someone who upsets the confidence a child has in his parents' ways of doing things.	A	a	d	D
14. It's no wonder men reach their boiling point when they come home and run right into family problems as soon as they come in the door.	A	a	d	D
15. The biggest mistake a man can make is marrying a woman who always wants to wear the pants in the family.	A	a	d	D
16. A father should make it his business to know everything his children are thinking.	A	a	d	D
17. A child should be protected from jobs which might be too tiring or hard for him.	A	a	d	D
18. No matter how well a married couple love one another, there are always differences which cause irritation and lead to arguments.	A	a	d	D
19. Men don't know how much they enjoy being free to do as they please until they begin raising a family.	A	a	d	D
20. Parents deserve the highest esteem and regard of their children.	A	a	d	D
21. It's best for the child if he never gets started wondering whether his father's views are right.	A	a	d	D
22. There are times when any husband or father gets to the point where he feels he can't stand his family a moment longer.	A	a	d	D
23. The old fashioned family was best because the wife kept in her place.	A	a	d	D
24. It is a father's duty to make sure he knows a child's innermost thoughts.	A	a	d	D
25. Parents should know better than to allow their children to be exposed to difficult situations.	A	a	d	D

26. It's natural to have quarrels when two people who both have minds of their own get married.   A a d D
27. Before marriage most men don't realize how much of a burden the responsibility of a family can be.   A a d D
28. A child should always love his parents above everyone else.   A a d D
29. The child should not question the thinking of his parents.   A a d D
30. A man has a right to be angry and irritated when the family doesn't give him a chance to relax at home.   A a d D
31. Most wives would do better if they would quit trying to look smarter than their husbands.   A a d D
32. A father has a right to know everything going on in his child's life because his child is a part of him.   A a d D
33. A child is most lovable when he is small and helpless.   A a d D
34. Even in marriage a person must fight for his rights at times.   A a d D
35. Most young fathers are bothered more by the feeling of being tied to the home than by anything else.   A a d D
36. Loyalty to parents comes before everything else.   A a d D
37. A child's trust in his parent should be safeguarded better by not having so many people with different ideas around him.   A a d D
38. A man may need to "blow his top" once in a while around the home just to clear the air a bit.   A a d D
39. The main thing wrong with today's homes is the wife tries too much to run everything.   A a d D
40. If a father is not careful a child may be thinking things he does not know about.   A a d D

INVENTORY OF ATTITUDES ON FAMILY LIFE AND CHILDREN (MOTHER)
Read each of the statements below and then rate them as follows:

A	a	d	D
strongly agree	mildly agree	mildly disagree	strongly disagree

Indicate your opinion by drawing a circle around the "A" if you strongly agree, around the "a" if you mildly agree, around the "d" if you mildly disagree, and around the "D" if you strongly disagree.

There are no right or wrong answers, so answer according to your own opinion. It is very important to the study that all questions be answered. Many of the statements will seem alike, but all are necessary to show slight differences of opinion.

        Agree Disagree

1. An alert parent should try to learn all her child's thoughts.   A a d D
2. Parents deserve the highest esteem and regard of their children.   A a d D
3. Parents should know better than to allow their children to be exposed to difficult situations.   A a d D
4. It's natural to have quarrels when two people who both have minds of their own get married.   A a d D
5. It's natural for a mother to "blow her top" when children are selfish and demanding.   A a d D
6. Children should never learn things outside the home which make them doubt their parents' ideas.   A a d D
7. Having to be with the children all the time gives a woman the feeling her wings have been clipped.   A a d D
8. A married woman knows that she will have to take the lead in family matters.   A a d D
9. A mother should make it her business to know everything her children are thinking.   A a d D
10. More parents should teach their children to have unquestioning loyalty to them.   A a d D
11. A mother should do her best to avoid any disappointment for her child.   A a d D

			Agree		Disagree	

12. Sometimes it's necessary for a wife to tell off her husband in order to get her rights. — A a d D

13. Children will get on any woman's nerves if she has to be with them all day. — A a d D

14. The child should not question the thinking of his parents. — A a d D

15. One of the worst things about taking care of a home is a woman feels that she can't get out. — A a d D

16. The whole family does fine if the mother puts her shoulder to the wheel and takes charge of things. — A a d D

17. It is a mother's duty to make sure she knows a child's innermost thoughts. — A a d D

18. A child soon learns that there is no greater wisdom than that of his parents. — A a d D

19. A child should be protected from jobs which might be too tiring or hard for him. — A a d D

20. People who think they can get along in marriage without arguments just don't know the facts. — A a d D

21. It's a rare mother who can be sweet and even tempered with her children all day. — A a d D

22. A parent should never be made to look wrong in a child's eyes. — A a d D

23. A young mother feels "held down" because there are lots of things she wants to do while she is young. — A a d D

24. If a mother doesn't go ahead and make rules for the home the children and husband will get into troubles they don't need to. — A a d D

25. A mother has a right to know everything going on in her child's life because her child is a part of her. — A a d D

26. Loyalty to parents comes before everything else. — A a d D

27 Children should be kept away from all hard jobs which might be discouraging. — A a d D

28. No matter how well a married couple love one another, there are always differences which cause irritation and lead to arguments. — A a d D

29. A small child's wild play ties a mother's nerves in knots. — A a d D

30. There is nothing worse than letting a child hear criticisms of his mother. — A a d D

31. Most young mothers are bothered more by the feeling of being shut up in the home than by anything else. — A a d D

32. A mother has to do the planning because she is the one who knows what's going on in the home. — A a d D

33. If a mother is not careful, a child may be thinking things she does not know about. — A a d D

34. A child should always love his parents above everyone else. — A a d D

35. A child is most lovable when he is small and helpless. — A a d D

36. There are some things which just can't be settled by a mild discussion. — A a d D

37. It's a mother's right to refuse to put up with a child's annoyances. — A a d D

38. There is no excusing someone who upsets the confidence a child has in his parents' ways of doing things. — A a d D

39. One of the bad things about raising children is that you aren't free enough of the time to do just as you like. — A a d D

40. A mother's duty is to see to it that the whole family does what she knows is best. — A a d D

TEST OF PERSONALITY FACTORS

The following is a list of statements, some of which may be true for you and some of which may not be true for you.

If the statement is true for you, circle the word *True* at the right of that statement.

If the statement is not true for you, circle the word *False* at the right of that statement.

If you cannot decide whether the statement is true or false for you, circle the *?*. You should circle the *?* only when it is quite impossible to say *True* or *False*.

Work rapidly; don't spend a lot of time on any statement.

There are no right or wrong answers, as everyone is different.

1. Books have been more entertaining to me than companions.	True	?	False
2. I have ups and downs in mood.	True	?	False
3. I do not keep my head in excitement.	True	?	False
4. I like to discuss more the serious questions of life with friends.	True	?	False
5. In general, I usually get my own way with people.	True	?	False
6. I am often in a state of excitement.	True	?	False
7. I am a steady worker.	True	?	False
8. I get discouraged easily.	True	?	False
9. I prefer to be alone at times of emotional distress.	**True**	**?**	**False**
10. The systematic way of doing things in science appeals to me.	True	?	False
11. There is little point in having things done just so.	True	?	False
12. I often feel lonesome with other people.	True	?	False
13. My feelings alternate between happiness and sadness without reason.	True	?	False
14. I do not indulge in self-pity.	True	?	False
15. I am more interested in intellectual things than other things.	True	?	False
16. I usually do not plan out work carefully before beginning it.	True	?	False
17. I am a dominant person.	True	?	False
18. My interests change rapidly.	True	?	False
19. I do not hesitate to put my abilities to the test.	True	?	False
20. I prefer to work things out my own way rather than accept suggestions.	True	?	False
21. "A place for everything and everything in its place" describes one of my habits very well.	True	?	False
22. I like a task in which there are many detailed operations that must be done just so.	True	?	False
23. I daydream instead of doing work.	True	?	False
24. I frequently have spells of the blues without reason.	True	?	False
25. I am a nervous person.	True	?	False
26. I am inclined to analyze the motives of others.	True	?	False
27. I often say things on the spur of the moment and then regret it.	True	?	False
28. I am easily startled by unexpected things.	True	?	False
29. I would complain if I were served bad food in a restaurant.	True	?	False
30. I'm self-confident about my ability to succeed.	True	?	False
31. I get myself out of difficult situations without help.	True	?	False
32. It is a waste of time to try to keep everything in its place all the time.	True	?	False
33. When I write a report, I reread it many times to make sure it is free of errors.	True	?	False
34. Ideas run through my head so as to prevent sleep.	True	?	False
35. I am inclined to worry over possible misfortunes.	True	?	False
36. I cannot stand criticism.	True	?	False
37. I enjoy thinking out complicated problems.	True	?	False
38. I am impulsive.	True	?	False
39. I get rattled easily in exciting situations.	True	?	False
40. I prefer a job that offers constant change, travel and variety.	True	?	False
41. I like to express my own ideas even though other people may not like them.	True	?	False
42. I usually understand a problem better alone than with discussion.	True	?	False
43. I would like to classify specimens for a museum.	True	?	False
44. I would prefer to work on the broad aspects of a problem and leave the small details to others.	True	?	**False**
45. I often feel worried or tense without cause.	True	?	False

46. I am often just miserable for no sufficient reason.	True	?	False
47. I am more emotional than average.	True	?	False
48. I like to try my wits in solving puzzles.	True	?	False
49. I am happy-go-lucky.	True	?	False
50. I keep my emotions under good control.	True	?	False
51. I like to change from one type of work to another frequently.	True	?	False
52. I worry about being successful in life.	True	?	False
53. I like to get other people to see things my way.	True	?	False
54. I hang up my clothes each night before going to bed.	True	?	False
55. It is a waste of time trying to see that everything is "just so."	True	?	False
56. Through tenseness I use up more energy than most people.	True	?	False
57. I am talkative.	True	?	False
58. I have difficulty making up my own mind.	True	?	False
59. My feelings are easily hurt.	True	?	False
60. I am ordinarily carefree.	True	?	False
61. I plan alone, without suggestions or discussion.	True	?	False
62. I am easily moved to tears.	True	?	False
63. I become so absorbed in creative work that I do not mind lack of friends.	True	?	False
64. I like to travel alone rather than with a guide.	True	?	False
65. I am not inclined to stop and think before acting.	True	?	False
66. I am easily disturbed by distractions while doing mental work.	True	?	False
67. I crave excitement.	True	?	False
68. In general, I'm self-confident about my abilities.	True	?	False
69. I usually face troubles alone without seeking help.	True	?	False

TEST OF EPISTEMOLOGICAL AND INSTRUMENTAL BELIEFS

These are proverbs and statements about life. You will find you agree with some, and disagree with others.

For each of these sayings, circle the answer at the right which best expresses how you feel about it.

	Strongly Agree	Agree	?	Disagree	Strongly Disagree
1. Happiness comes from living day to day.	SA	A	?	D	SD
2. It's easy to get what one wants out of life.	SA	A	?	D	SD
3. Nothing is less in our power than the heart, and far from commanding it we are wiser to obey it.	SA	A	?	D	SD
4. Into each life some rain must fall.	SA	A	?	D	SD
5. Originality is the noblest end of life.	SA	A	?	D	SD
6. The greater the prize, the greater the risk.	SA	A	?	D	SD
7. Nothing happens without a cause.	SA	A	?	D	SD
8. The more we learn, the more we see that everything in the world is related to everything else.	SA	A	?	D	SD
9. Every object—man, animal, plant and stone—has its own soul.	SA	A	?	D	SD
10. Many strange things are caused by spirits who influence the fortunes of men.	SA	A	?	D	SD
11. There is a divinity that shapes our ends, roughhew them as we will.	SA	A	?	D	SD
12. One of the most important things in life is to be absolutely sure of what you want.	SA	A	?	D	SD
13. In deciding whether or not to do something it's wise to make as long a list as you can of all the outcomes.	SA	A	?	D	SD
14. One often expects misery in vain.	SA	A	?	D	SD
15. One of the saddest things is that we never know what tomorrow may bring.	SA	A	?	D	SD
16. To try to do many things is to do none of them well.	SA	A	?	D	SD
17. The world moves in an orderly fashion.	SA	A	?	D	SD
18. Everything in life has its own unique and special cause, could we but find it.	SA	A	?	D	SD
19. Only the foolish believe in spirits.	SA	A	?	D	SD
20 A river overflows its banks when nature is angry with man.	SA	A	?	D	SD
21. If one is faithful to the duties of the present, the future will take care of itself.	SA	A	?	D	SD
22. To fear the worst is to go through life with an unnecessary burden.	SA	A	?	D	SD
23. Impulse rarely works ; thought is the key to success.	SA	A	?	D	SD
24. Forewarned is forearmed.	SA	A	?	D	SD
25. The tried and true ways are the best.	SA	A	?	D	SD
26. One's fondest hopes rarely come true.	SA	A	?	D	SD
27. Things that seem mysterious and unpredictable now will one day be predicted by science.	SA	A	?	D	SD
28. No matter how little or unimportant what we do may seem, the effects spread outward and onward through eternity.	SA	A	?	D	SD
29. Trees can't feel the wind pass, no matter how hard it blows.	SA	A	?	D	SD
30. Not a leaf falls from a tree but is plucked by the hand of God.	SA	A	?	D	SD
31. Nothing comes to pass but what fate wills.	SA	A	?	D	SD
32. It is easy to classify most things as either good or bad.	SA	A	?	D	SD
33. A man who tries to figure out everything that will happen can never decide anything.	SA	A	?	D	SD
34. There's no reason to anticipate trouble, or worry about what may never happen.	SA	A	?	D	SD

	Strongly Agree	Agree	?	Disagree	Strongly Disagree
35. Certainty alone brings peace of mind.	SA	A	?	D	SD
36. Life is best handled by having a whole bag of tricks, not by a simple rule or two.	SA	A	?	D	SD
37. Where men feel sure, they are bound to be mistaken.	SA	A	?	D	SD
38. Few things have but a single cause; for most the "cause" is really a multitude of little things happening together.	SA	A	?	D	SD
39. The unlighted match feels its own heat when lighted.	SA	A	?	D	SD
40. The volcano erupts to show its power over man.	SA	A	?	D	SD
41. To live each day as if it were the last would soon lead one to disaster.	SA	A	?	D	SD
42. It is worth a thousand dollars a year to have the habit of looking on the bright side of things.	SA	A	?	D	SD
43 Happiness comes from impulse, rather than reason.	SA	A	?	D	SD
44. Trouble is inevitable.	SA	A	?	D	SD
45. To live by custom is a foolish thing.	SA	A	?	D	SD
46. The best laid plans of mice and men go oft astray.	SA	A	?	D	SD
47. There is an order to existence although we often may not see it.	SA	A	?	D	SD
48. Most things are easily explained when we have the time to think about them.	SA	A	?	D	SD
49. Old houses, like old people, feel very tired at times.	SA	A	?	D	SD
50. As God created the world, so He can change or end it as He pleases.	SA	A	?	D	SD
51. Man's existence is completely under the control of destiny.	SA	A	?	D	SD
52. Sometimes it's hard to tell whether one likes something or not.	SA	A	?	D	SD
53. The more results you can think of ahead of time, the better off you'll be.	SA	A	?	D	SD
54. It is madness to be expecting evil before it comes.	SA	A	?	D	SD
55. To know what may happen tomorrow is one of the dullest things in life.	SA	A	?	D	SD
56. Each important thing that happens to man can be traced to a single cause.	SA	A	?	D	SD
57. The world is a seething chaos.	SA	A	?	D	SD
58. We can never find the one ultimate cause of everything.	SA	A	?	D	SD
59. Flowers know where the sun is, and feel its warmth.	SA	A	?	D	SD
60. Lady Luck decides the turn of the card.	SA	A	?	D	SD
61. Our grand business is not to see what lies dimly at a distance, but to do what lies clearly at hand.	SA	A	?	D	SD
62. The highest wisdom is continual cheerfulness.	SA	A	?	D	SD
63. Thinking is a luxury, sometimes useless, sometimes fatal.	SA	A	?	D	SD
64. Life often presents us with a choice of evils rather than of good.	SA	A	?	D	SD
65. When ancient opinions and rules of life are taken away, the loss to people cannot possibly be estimated.	SA	A	?	D	SD
66. He that lives on hope will die starving.	SA	A	?	D	SD
67. People try to find order in the world when in fact there is none.	SA	A	?	D	SD
68. For any event there are an infinite number of results.	SA	A	?	D	SD
69. The sea, moving restlessly, knows where the sunken ships are on its floor.	SA	A	?	D	SD
70. God is powerless in the face of natural laws and to ask Him for help is to shout at the wind.	SA	A	?	D	SD

	Strongly Agree	Agree	?	Disagree	Strongly Disagree
71. A childlike and abiding trust in destiny is anxiety's best preventive and remedy.	SA	A	?	D	SD
72. It's best not to get too excited about anything.	SA	A	?	D	SD
73. You can only confuse yourself by thinking of all that might happen.	SA	A	?	D	SD
74. Nothing is so wretched or foolish as to anticipate misfortunes.	SA	A	?	D	SD
75. Uncertainty and expectation are the joys of life.	SA	A	?	D	SD
76. You can spend so much time trying different ways of handling a situation that none of them is given a fair trial.	SA	A	?	D	SD
77. Like a morning dream, life becomes more and more bright the longer we live and the reason of everything appears more clear.	SA	A	?	D	SD
78. The causes of any event are so intertwined that it is difficult to know how important each may be.	SA	A	?	D	SD
79. The sun, although warm and powerful, cannot be called alive.	SA	A	?	D	SD
80. Every human problem can be solved and every hunger satisfied and every promise can be fulfilled if God so wills.	SA	A	?	D	SD
81. The pleasures of one today are worth those of two tomorrows.	SA	A	?	D	SD
82. In the lottery of life there are more prizes drawn than blanks.	SA	A	?	D	SD
83. Our first impulses are good; thought usually weakens them.	SA	A	?	D	SD
84. To fear the worst often cures the worst.	SA	A	?	D	SD
85. All truly wise thoughts have been thought already by others.	SA	A	?	D	SD
86. He who never hopes can never despair.	SA	A	?	D	SD
87. There are more things in heaven and earth than are dreamt of in your philosophy.	SA	A	?	D	SD
88. From one action many outcomes will result.	SA	A	?	D	SD
89. Trees feel no pain when they are cut with an axe.	SA	A	?	D	SD
90. The Devil lurks constantly, waiting to push those over who wander too close to the precipice of temptation.	SA	A	?	D	SD
91. Whatever may happen to thee, it was prepared for thee from all eternity.	SA	A	?	D	SD
92. In striving for the goals of life, when things go bad they're very very bad.	SA	A	?	D	SD
93. For every action there's a limited number of outcomes; it's smart to consider them all beforehand.	SA	A	?	D	SD
94. To forecast our sorrows is only to increase the suffering without increasing our strength to bear them.	SA	A	?	D	SD
95. Of all the conditions to which the heart is subject, suspense is one that most gnaws and cankers into the frame.	SA	A	?	D	SD
96. It's important to decide upon one thing and stick to it.	SA	A	?	D	SD
97. There is no such thing as chance, and what seems to us the merest accident springs from the deepest source of nature.	SA	A	?	D	SD
98. Life is like a rich tapestry, each strand woven together in delicate detail.	SA	A	?	D	SD
99. The ocean feels the pull of the moon which causes its high tides.	SA	A	?	D	SD
100. God's in His heaven, all's right with the world.	SA	A	?	D	SD

TEST OF INDEPENDENCE OF JUDGMENT

Please circle either True (T) or False (F) for each of the following statements.

		True	False
1.	I would enjoy the experience of living and working in a foreign country.	T	F
2.	I prefer team games to games in which one individual competes against another.	T	F
3.	The unfinished and the imperfect often have greater appeal for me than the completed and the polished.	T	F
4.	Disobedience to the government is never justified.	T	F
5.	I could cut my moorings . . . quit my home, my parents and my friends . . . without suffering great regrets.	T	F
6.	Things seem simpler as you learn more about them.	T	F
7.	When a person has a problem or worry, it is best for him not to think about it, but to keep busy with more cheerful things.	T	F
8.	Perfect balance is the essence of all good compositions.	T	F
9.	Politically I am probably something of a radical.	T	F
10.	Kindness and generosity are the most important qualities for a wife to have.	T	F
11.	An invention which takes jobs away from people should be suppressed until new work can be found for them.	T	F
12.	I think I take primarily an esthetic view of experience.	T	F
13.	It is a pretty callous person who does not feel love and gratitude toward his parents.	T	F
14.	When someone talks against certain groups of nationalities, I always speak up against such talk, even though it makes me unpopular.	T	F
15.	It is the duty of a citizen to support his country, right or wrong.	T	F
16.	Barring emergencies, I have a pretty good idea what I'll be doing for the next ten years.	T	F
17.	Many of my friends would probably be considered unconventional by other people.	T	F
18.	I don't like modern art.	T	F
19.	Some of my friends think that my ideas are impractical, if not a bit wild.	T	F
20.	I much prefer symmetry to asymmetry.	T	F
21.	Straightforward reasoning appeals to me more than metaphors and the search for analogies.	T	F
22.	I enjoy discarding the old and accepting the new.	T	F

STATISTICAL QUESTIONNAIRE

FOR STATISTICAL PURPOSES, WILL YOU KINDLY SUPPLY THE FOLLOWING INFORMATION

1. Please check whether you are: Mother ☐   Father ☐

2. (a) What is your occupation?

   (b) What do you actually do in your work?

   (c) For husband only: In your *main* work do you

   work for someone else.............................☐

   have your own business or practice................☐

3. What was your age on your last birthday?_____

4. (a) What was the name of the last school or college you attended?

   (b) What was the last grade you completed in that school or college? (Circle one)

Grammar	High School	College	More than College
0– 6 7 8	9 10 11 12	1 2 3 4	1 2 3

5. What is your religious preference?

   Protestant_____   Catholic_____   Jewish_____

   Other (specify)_____ None_____

6. Please list the age and sex of your children:

Age at last birthday	Boy	Girl
_____	____	____
_____	____	____

7. Check the country of birth for *each* of the persons listed below:

	Your Mother	Your Father	Your Mother's Mother	Your Mother's Father	Your Father's Mother	Your Father's Father
United States or Canada						
England or Scotland						
Ireland						
Norway, Sweden or Denmark						
Roumania or Bulgaria						
Hungary or Galicia						
Poland						
Germany or Austria						
Italy						
Russia						
France						
Other (please name)						
Do not know						

How many sisters do you have? .... Older than you_____

Younger than you_____

How many brothers do you have? .... Older than you_____

Younger than you_____

ADDITIONAL TESTS USED

In addition to the tests listed in the preceding pages, the following were also used in the study.

Name of Test	Source
Vocabulary Screening Test of Verbal Intelligence, I.E.R. Intelligence Scale CAVD.	Thorndike, Edward L., "Two Screening Tests of Verbal Intelligence," *Journal of Applied Psychology*, 26 (1942), 128–35.
	Thorndike, Edward L., and George Gallup, "Verbal Intelligence of American Adults," *Journal of Genetic Psychology*, 30 (1944), 75–85.
	Thorndike, Robert L., *Research Problems and Techniques*, AAF Aviation Psychology Prog. Res. Rep., No. 3, Government Printing Office, Washington, D.C., 1947, pp. 102–3.
Desire for Certainty Test	Brim, Orville G., Jr., "Attitude Content-Intensity and Probability Expectations," *American Sociological Review*, 59 (1954), 556–64.
	Brim, Orville G., Jr., and David B. Hoff, "Individual and Situational Differences in Desire for Certainty," *Journal of Abnormal and Social Psychology*, 54 (1957), 225–29.

REFERENCES

INTRODUCTION

1. Brim, Orville G., Jr., *Education for Child Rearing,* New York: Russell Sage Foundation, 1959.
2. Gerard, Ralph W., "Biological Roots of Psychiatry," *Science,* 122, No. 3162 (1955), 225–30.
3. Kardiner, Abram, *The Individual and His Society,* New York: Columbia Univ. Press, 1945.
4. Kluckhohn, Florence R. and Fred L. Strodtbeck, *Variations in Value Orientations,* Evanston, Ill.: Row, Peterson, 1961.
5. Linton, Ralph, *The Cultural Background of Personality,* New York: Appleton-Century-Crofts, 1945.

CHAPTER 1

1. Adams, Edward, and Robert Fagot, "A Model of Riskless Choice," *Behavioral Science,* 4 (1959), 1–10.
2. Beal, George M., and Joseph M. Bohlen, *The Diffusion Process,* Special Report No. 18, Agricultural Extension Service, Ames, Iowa: Iowa State College, March 1957, pp. 1–6.
3. Becker, Howard S., "The Implications of Research on Occupational Careers for a Model of Household Decision-Making," in *Household Decision-Making,* Consumer Behavior, Vol. IV, Nelson N. Foote (Ed.), New York: New York Univ. Press, 1961, pp. 239–54.
4. Barnard, Chester I., *The Functions of the Executive,* Cambridge, Mass.: Harvard Univ. Press, 1938.
5. Brim, Orville G., Jr., *Education for Child Rearing,* New York: Russell Sage Foundation, 1959.
6. Bruner, Jerome S., Jacqueline J. Goodnow, and George A. Austin, *A Study of Thinking,* New York: Wiley, 1957.
7. Conant, James B., *On Understanding Science,* New Haven, Conn.: Yale Univ. Press, 1947.
8. Coombs, Clyde H., and David Beardslee, "On Decision Making Under Uncertainty," in *Decision Processes,* R. M. Thrall, C. H. Coombs, and R. L. Davis (Eds.), New York: Wiley, 1954, pp. 255–87.
9. Coombs, Clyde H., Howard Raiffa, and Robert M. Thrall, "Mathematical Models and Measurement Theory," in *Decision Processes,* R. M. Thrall, C. H. Coombs, and R. L. Davis (Eds.), New York: Wiley, 1954, pp. 19–39.
10. Copeland, Melvin T., *The Executive at Work,* Cambridge, Mass.: Harvard Univ. Press, 1951.
11. Cronbach, Lee J., "Personality and Intellectual Functioning in Graduate Students," in *Growing Point in Educational Research,* 1949, pp. 89–95. (Official report of the American Educational Research Association.)

12. Cronbach, Lee J., and Goldine C. Gleser, *Psychological Tests and Personnel Decisions,* Urbana, Ill.: Univ. of Illinois Press, 1957, pp. 13–15.

13. Dewey, John, *How We Think,* New York: Heath, 1910.

14. Dollard, John, and Neal E. Miller, *Personality and Psychotherapy,* New York: McGraw-Hill, 1950.

15. Duncker, K., "A Qualitative (Experimental and Theoretical) Study of Productive Thinking (Solving of Comprehensible Problems)," *Journal of Genetic Psychology,* 33 (1926), 642–708.

16. Edwards, Ward, "The Theory of Decision Making," *Psychological Bulletin,* 51 (1954), 380–417.

17. Flood, M. M., "Game-Learning Theory and Some Decision Making Experiments," in *Decision Processes,* R. M. Thrall, C. H. Coombs, and R. L. Davis (Eds.), New York: Wiley, 1954, pp. 139–59.

18. Foote, Nelson N., and Leonard S. Cottrell, *Identity and Interpersonal Competence,* Chicago, Ill.: Univ. of Chicago Press, 1955.

19. Gagné, Robert M., "Problem-Solving and Thinking," *Annual Review of Psychology,* Paul R. Farnsworth and Quinn McNemar (Eds.), Palo Alto, Calif.: Annual Reviews, 1959, pp. 147–73.

20. Getzels, Jacob W., and Philip W. Jackson, "Family Environment and Cognitive Style: A Study of the Sources of Highly Intelligent and of Highly Creative Adolescents," *American Sociological Review,* 1961, pp. 351–59.

21. Ghiselin, B., *The Creative Process,* A Symposium, Berkeley, Calif.: Univ. of California Press, 1952.

22. Glaser, Edward M., "An Experiment in the Development of Critical Thinking," *Teachers College Contributions to Education,* New York: Columbia Univ., Teachers College, Bureau of Publications, 1941, No. 843.

23. Glaser, Robert, D. E. Damrin, and F. M. Gardner, *The Tab Item Technique for the Measurement of Proficiency in Diagnostic Problem-Solving Tasks,* Champaign, Ill.: Univ. of Illinois, College of Education, Bureau of Research and Service, 1952.

24. Guilford, J. Paul, "Creative Abilities in the Arts," *Psychological Review,* 64 (1957), 110–18.

25. Guilford, J. Paul, "The Structure of Intellect," *Psychological Bulletin,* 53 (1956), 267–93.

26. Hurwicz, L., "Game Theory and Decisions," *Scientific American,* February 1955, pp. 78–83.

27. Janis, Irving, and Fredrick Frick, "The Relationship Between Attitudes Toward Conclusions and Errors in Judging Logical Validity in Syllogism," *Journal of Experimental Psychology,* 33 (1943), 73–77.

28. Johnson, Donald M., *The Psychology of Thought and Judgment,* New York: Harper, 1955.

29. Katona, George, "Business Expectations in the Framework of Psychological Economics," in *Expectations, Uncertainty and Business Behavior,* Mary J. Bowman (Ed.), New York: Social Science Research Council, 1958, pp. 59–74.

30. Katona, George, and Eva Mueller, "A Study of Purchase Decisions," in *Consumer Behavior,* Lincoln H. Clark (Ed.), New York: New York Univ. Press, 1954, pp. 30–87.

31. Katz, Elihu, and Paul F. Lazarsfeld, *Personal Influence: The Part Played by People in the Flow of Mass Communications,* Glencoe, Ill.: Free Press, 1955.

32. Kawin, Ethel, *Middle Childhood,* Chicago, Ill.: Univ. of Chicago Press, 1957.

33. Kochen, Manfred, and Marion J. Levy, Jr., "The Logical Nature of an Action Scheme," *Behavioral Science,* 1 (1956), 265–89.

34. Kohler, Wolfgang, *The Mentality of Apes* (Trans. E. Winter), New York: Harcourt, Brace, 1927.

35. Lazarsfeld, Paul F., "Sociological Reflections on Business: Consumers and Managers," in *Social Science Research on Business: Product and Potential,* Robert A. Dahl, Mason Haire, and Paul F. Lazarsfeld (Eds.), New York: Columbia Univ. Press, 1959.

36. Lorge, Irving, David Fox, Joel Davitz, and M. Brenner, "A Survey of Studies Contrasting the Quality of Group Performance and Individual Performance, 1920–1957," *Psychological Bulletin* 55, (1958) 337–72.

37. Luce, R. Duncan, and Howard Raiffa, *Games and Decisions,* New York: Wiley, 1957.

38. Marks, Melvin R., "Problem Solving as a Function of the Situation," *Journal of Experimental Psychology* 41 (1951), 74–80.

39. Marschak, Jacob, "Norms and Habits of Decision Making Under Uncertainty," *Mathematical Models of Human Behavior,* Stamford, Conn.: Dunlap, 1955, pp. 45–54.

40. Marschak, Jacob, "Probability in the Social Sciences," *Mathematical Thinking in the Social Sciences,* Glencoe, Ill.: Free Press, 1954, pp. 166–205.

41. Marschak, Jacob, "Value, Amount and Structure of Information, and the Cost of Decision Making," *Behavioral Science,* 1 (1956), 69–78.

42. Merton, Robert K., "The Unanticipated Consequences of Purposive Social Action," *American Sociological Review,* 1 (1936), 894–904.

43. Miller, George A., Review of *Thinking: The Adventurous Skill,* by Sir Frederic Bartlett, *Contemporary Psychology,* 3, No. 9 (1958), 241–43.

44. Newell, Allen, J. C. Shaw, and Herbert A. Simon, "Elements of a Theory of Human Problem Solving," *Psychological Review,* 65, No. 3 (1958), 151–66.

45. Parsons, Talcott, "The Professions and Social Structure," in *Essays in Sociological Theory,* rev. ed., Glencoe, Ill.: Free Press, 1954, pp. 34–49.

46. Rainwater, Lee, Asst. by Karol Kane Weinstein, *And the Poor Get Children: Sex, Contraception, and Family Planning in the Working Class,* Chicago, Ill.: Quadrangle Books, 1960.

47. Ray, Wilbert S., "Complex Tasks for Use in Human Problem-Solving Research," *Psychological Bulletin,* 52, No. 2, (1955), 134–49.

48. Rimoldi, Horacio J. A., "A Technique for the Study of Problem Solving," *Educational and Psychological Measurement,* 15 (1955), 450–61.

49. Rose, Arnold M., "The Adequacy of Women's Expectations for Adult Roles," *Social Forces,* 30, No. 1 (1951), 69–77.

50. Russell, David H., *Children's Thinking,* New York: Ginn, 1956.

51. Siegel, Sidney S., "Level of Aspiration and Decision Making," *Psychological Review,* 64 (1957), 253–62.

52. Simon, Herbert A., *Administrative Behavior,* New York: Macmillan, 1957.

53. Snyder, Richard C., H. W. Bruck, and Burton Sapin, *Decision Making as an Approach to the Study of International Politics,* Foreign Policy Analysis Project, Organizational Behavioral Section, Princeton University, June 1954.

54. Stryker, Sheldon, "Relationships of Married Offspring and Parent: A

Test of Mead's Theory," *American Journal of Sociology,* 62, No. 3 (1956), pp. 308–19.

55. Super, Donald E., *The Psychology of Careers,* New York: Harper, 1957.

56. Travers, Robert M. W., Joseph E. Marron, and Andrew J. Post, *Some Conditions Affecting Quality, Consistency, and Predictability of Performance in Solving Complex Problems,* Project No. 7703, Task Nos. 77071 and 77073, Air Force Personnel and Training Research Center, Lackland Air Force Base, San Antonio, Tex., September 1955.

57. Vinacke, W. Edgar, *The Psychology of Thinking,* New York: McGraw-Hill, 1952.

58. Von Neumann, John, and Oskar Morgenstern, *Theory of Games and Economic Behavior,* 2d ed., Princeton, N.J.: Princeton Univ. Press, 1947.

59. Wallas, Graham, *The Art of Thought,* New York: Harcourt, Brace, 1926.

60. Welford, Alan T., *Skill and Age,* New York: Oxford Univ. Press, 1951.

61. Wells, Frederic L., "Instruction Time in Certain Multiple-Choice Tests; Cases XCVI–CII," *Journal of Genetic Psychology,* 77 (1950), 267–81.

62. Westoff, Charles, Robert G. Potter, Jr., Philip Sagi, and Elliot G. Mishler, *Family Growth in Metropolitan America,* Princeton, N.J.: Princeton Univ. Press, 1961.

63. Williams, Jack D., *The Compleat Strategyst,* New York: McGraw-Hill, 1954

64. Woodworth, Robert S., and Saul B. Sells, "An Atmosphere Effect in Formal Syllogistic Reasoning," *Journal of Experimental Psychology,* 18 (1935), 451–60.

CHAPTER 2

1. Brim, Orville G., Jr., and Raymond Forer, "A Note on the Relation of Values and Social Structure to Life Planning," *Sociometry,* 19 (1956), 54–60.

2. Brim, Orville G., Jr., and Fred Koenig, "Subjective Probability Among College Students," *Journal of Communications,* 9 (1959), 19–26.

3. Campbell, Donald Thomas, "Recommendations for APA Test Standards Regarding Construct, Trait or Discriminant Validity," *American Psychologist,* 15 (1960), pp. 546–54.

4. Edwards, Ward, "The Theory of Decision Making," *Psychological Bulletin,* 51 (1954), 380–417.

5. Fiske, Donald W., and Laura Rice, "Intra-Individual Response Variability," *Psychological Bulletin,* 52 (1955), 217–50.

6. Guilford, J. Paul, *Psychometric Methods,* New York: McGraw-Hill, 1954.

7. Gulliksen, Harold, *Theory of Mental Tests,* New York: Wiley, 1950.

8. Guttman, Louis, "Problems of Reliability," in *Measurement and Prediction,* S. Stouffer, *et al.* (Eds.), Princton, N.J.: Princeton Univ. Press, 1950, p. 311.

9. Hull, Clark L., *Principles of Behavior,* New York: Appleton-Century-Crofts, 1943.

10. Kendall, Maurice G., *Rank Correlation Methods,* London: Charles Griffin, 1948, pp. 173–74.

11. Kluckhohn, Florence, "Dominant and Variant Value Orientation," *Personality in Nature, Society, and Culture,* C. Kluckhohn and H. A. Murray (Eds.), rev. ed., New York: Knopf, 1953, pp. 342–57.

12. Leeper, Robert, "Cognitive Processes," in *Handbook of Experimental Psychology,* S. S. Stevens (Ed.), New York: Wiley, 1951, pp. 730–57.

13. Luce, R. Duncan, and Howard Raiffa, *Games and Decisions,* New York: Wiley, 1957.

14. Miller, George A., "The Magical Number Seven, Plus or Minus Two: Some Limits on Our Capacity for Processing Information," *Psychological Review,* 1956, 63, pp. 81–97.

15. Strodtbeck, Fred L., "Family Interaction, Values and Achievement," in *Talent and Society,* D. C. McClelland, *et al.* (Eds.), Princeton, N.J.: D. Van Nostrand, 1958, pp. 135–95.

16. Taylor, Janet A., "A Personality Scale of Manifest Anxiety," *Journal of Abnormal and Social Psychology,* 48 (1953), pp. 285–90.

17. Thorndike, Robert L., *Research Problems and Techniques,* AAF Aviation Psychology Prog. Res. Rep., No. 3, Washington, D.C.: Government Printing Office, 1947, pp. 102–3.

18. Tolman, Edward C., "A Psychological Model," in *Toward a General Theory of Action,* T. Parsons and E. A. Shils (Eds.), Cambridge, Mass.: Harvard Univ. Press, 1954, pp. 279–361.

19. Travers, Robert M. W., Joseph E. Marron, and Andrew J. Post, *Some Conditions Affecting Quality, Consistency, and Predictability of Performance in Solving Complex Problems,* Project No. 7703, Task Nos. 77071 and 77073, Air Force Personnel and Training Research Center, Lackland Air Force Base, San Antonio, Tex., September, 1955.

20. Von Neumann, John, and Oskar Morgenstern, *Theory of Games and Economic Behavior,* 2d ed., Princeton, N.J.: Princeton Univ. Press, 1947.

CHAPTER 3

1. Adorno, Theodore W., Else Frenkel-Brunswik, Daniel J. Levinson, and R. Nevitt Sanford, *The Authoritarian Personality,* New York: Harper, 1950.

2. Atkinson, John W., "Towards Experimental Analysis of Human Motivation in Terms of Motives, Expectancies, and Incentives," *Motives in Fantasy, Action, and Society,* John W. Atkinson (Ed.), New York: Van Nostrand, 1958, pp. 288–306.

3. Atkinson, John W., and Walter R. Reitman, "Motive Strength, Goal Expectancy, and Performance," *Journal of Abnormal and Social Psychology,* 53, No. 3 (1956), 361–66.

4. Atkinson, John W., and Walter R. Reitman, "Performance as a Function of Motive Strength and Expectancy of Goal-Attainment," in *Motives in Fantasy, Action, and Society,* New York: Van Nostrand, 1958, pp. 278–88.

5. Barnes, Charles A., "A Statistical Study of the Freudian Theory of Levels of Psychosexual Development," Unpublished Ph.D. Dissertation, University of Southern California, 1952.

6. Barron, Frank, "Complexity-Simplicity as a Personality Dimension," *Journal of Abnormal and Social Psychology,* 48 (1953), 163–73.

7. Barron, Frank, "The Psychology of Imagination," *Scientific American,* 199 (1958), 151–66.

8. Barron, Frank, "Some Personality Correlates of Independence of Judgment," *Journal of Personality,* 21 (1953), 287–97.

9. Barron, Frank, and George S. Welsh, "Artistic Perception as a Possible Factor in Personality Style: Its Measurement by a Figure Preference Test," *Journal of Psychology,* 33 (1952), 199–203.

10. Brim, Orville G., Jr., "Personality Development as Role-Learning," in *Personality Development in Children,* I. Iscoe, and H. Stevenson (Eds.), Austin, Tex.: Univ. of Texas Press, 1960.

11. Brim, Orville G., Jr., and Raymond Forer, "A Note on the Relation of Values and Social Structures to Life Planning," *Sociometry,* 19 (1956), 54–61.

12. Brim, Orville G., Jr., and David B. Hoff, "Individual and Situational Differences in Desire for Certainty," *Journal of Abnormal and Social Psychology,* 54 (1957), 225–29.

13. Brim, Orville G., Jr., and Fred Koenig, "Subjective Probability Among College Students," *Journal of Communications,* 9 (1959), 19–26.

14. Cohen, John, and Mark Hansel, *Risk and Gambling: The Study of Subjective Probability,* New York: Philosophical Library, 1956.

15. Edwards, Ward, "Probability-Preferences in Gambling," *American Journal of Psychology,* 66 (1953), 349–64.

16. Estes, William K., "Learning," *Annual Review of Psychology,* Paul R. Farnsworth and Quinn McNemar (Eds.), Vol. 7, Palo Alto, Calif.: Annual Reviews, 1956, pp. 1–39.

17. Fenichel, Otto, *The Psychoanalytic Theory of Neurosis,* New York: Norton, 1945.

18. French, Elizabeth G., "Effects of Interaction of Achievement, Motivation, and Intelligence on Problem-Solving Success," *American Psychologist,* 1957, pp. 400–401.

19. French, John W., *The Description of Personality Measurements in Terms of Rotated Factors,* Educational Testing Service, Princeton, N.J.: Princeton Univ. Press, 1953.

20. Frenkel-Brunswik, Else, "Personality Theory and Perception," in *Perception: An Approach to Personality,* R. R. Blake and G. V. Ramsey (Eds.), New York: Ronald Press, 1951, pp. 356–421.

21. Gillin, John, *The Ways of Men: An Introduction to Anthropology,* New York: Appleton-Century-Crofts, 1948.

22. Gross, P. K., and Eugene L. Gaier, "Techniques in Problem-Solving as a Predictor of Educational Achievement," *Journal of Educational Psychology,* 46 (1955), 193–206.

23. Henry, William E., "Personality Factors in Managerial Reaction to Uncertainty," in *Expectations, Uncertainty, and Business Behavior,* M. J. Bowman (Ed.), New York: Social Science Research Council, 1958, pp. 86–93.

24. Hull, Clark L., *Principles of Behavior,* New York: Appleton-Century-Crofts, 1943.

25. Hyman, Ray, and Noel S. Jenkin, "Involvement and Set as Determinants of Behavioral Stereotype," Southern Universities Press, *Psychological Reports,* 2 (1956), 131–46.

26. Irwin, Francis W., "Motivation," in *Theoretical Foundations of Psychology,* Harry Helson (Ed.), New York: Van Nostrand, 1951, Ch. 5, pp. 200–53.

27. Jackson, Douglas N., and Samuel Messick, "Content and Style in Personality Assessment," *Psychological Bulletin,* 55 (1958), 243–52.

28. Kantor, Mildred B., John C. Glidewell, Ivan N. Mensh, Herbert R. Domke, M.D., and Margaret C. L. Gildea, M.D., "Socio-Economic Level and Maternal Attitudes Toward Parent-Child Relationships," *Human Organization*, 16, No. 4, (1957), 44–48.

29. Katona, George, "Business Expectations in the Framework of Psychological Economics," in *Expectations, Uncertainty, and Business Behavior*, M. J. Bowman (Ed.), New York: Social Science Research Council, 1958, pp. 59–74.

30. Kluckhohn, Florence, and Fred L. Strodtbeck, *Variations in Value Orientations*, Evanston, Ill.: Row, Peterson, 1961.

31. LeShan, Lawrence L., "Time Orientation and Social Class," *Journal of Abnormal and Social Psychology*, 47 (1952), 589–92.

32. McClelland, David C., *Personality*, New York: Dryden Press, 1951.

33. Miller, E. H., "A Study of Difficulty Levels of Selected Types of Fallacies in Reasoning and Their Relationships to the Factors of Sex, Grade Level, Mental Age, and Scholastic Standing," *Journal of Educational Research*, October 1955, pp. 123–29.

34. Murphy, Gardner, *Personality: A Biosocial Approach to Origins and Structure*, New York: Harper, 1947.

35. Newcomb, Theodore M., *Social Psychology*, New York: Dryden Press, 1950.

36. Ojeman, Ralph H., "Investigations Upon the Effects of Teaching and Understanding and Appreciation of Behavior Dynamics," in *Prevention of Mental Disorders in Children: Initial Explorations*, Gerald Caplan (Ed.), New York: Basic Books, 1961, Ch. 17.

37. Rainwater, Lee, Asst. by Karol Kane Weinstein, *And the Poor Get Children: Sex, Contraception, and Family Planning in the Working Class*, Chicago, Ill.: Quadrangle Books, 1960.

38. Schaefer, Earl S., and Richard Q. Bell, "Development of a Parental Attitude Research Instrument," *Child Development*, 29, (1958), 339–61.

39. Scodel, Alvin, Philburn Ratoosh, and J. Sayer Minas, "Some Personality Correlates of Decision Making Under Conditions of Risk," *Behavioral Science*, 4, (1959), 19–29.

40. Spence, Kenneth W., "A Theory of Emotionally Based Drive (D) and Its Relation to Performance in Simple Learning Situations," *American Psychologist*, 13 (1958) 131–41.

41. Strodtbeck, Fred L., "Family Interaction, Values and Achievement," in *Talent and Society*, D. C. McClelland, *et al.* (Eds.), Princeton, N.J.: D. Van Nostrand, 1958, pp. 135–95.

42. Taylor, Janet A., "Drive Theory and Manifest Anxiety," *Psychological Bulletin*, 53 (1956), 303–21.

43. Taylor, Janet A., "A Personality Scale of Manifest Anxiety," *Journal of Abnormal and Social Psychology*, 48 (1953), 285–90.

44. Taylor, Janet A., "The Relationship of Anxiety to the Conditioned Eyelid Response," *Journal of Experimental Psychology*, 14 (1951), 81–92.

45. Taylor, Janet A., and Kenneth W. Spence, "The Relationship of Anxiety Level to Performance in Serial Learning," *Journal of Experimental Psychology*, 44 (1952), 61–64.

46. Thrall, Robert M., Clyde H. Coombs, and Robert L. Davis, *Decision Processes*, New York: Wiley, 1954.

47. Tolman, Edward C., "A Theoretical Analysis of the Relations Between

Sociology and Psychology," *Journal of Abnormal and Social Psychology,* 47 (1952), 291–98.

48. Tolman, Edward C., "A Psychological Model," in *Toward a General Theory of Action,* Talcott Parsons and Edward A. Shils (Eds.), Cambridge, Mass.: Harvard Univ. Press, 1954, pp. 279–361.

49. Travers, Robert M. W., "Individual Differences," *Annual Review of Psychology,* Calvin P. Stone and Quinn McNemar (Eds.), Vol. 6, Palo Alto, Calif.: Annual Reviews, 1955, 137–60.

50. Volkart, Edmund H., *Social Behavior and Personality,* Contributions of W. I. Thomas, Social Science Research Council, 1951.

CHAPTER 4

1. Barnes, Charles A., "A Statistical Study of the Freudian Theory of Levels of Psycho-sexual Development," Unpublished Ph.D. Dissertation, Univ. of Southern California, 1952.

2. Barron, Frank, "Complexity-Simplicity as a Personality Dimension," *Journal of Abnormal and Social Psychology,* 48 (1953), 163–73.

3. Barron, Frank, "Some Personality Correlates of Independence of Judgment," *Journal of Personality,* 21 (1953), 287–97.

4. Barron, Frank, "The Psychology of Imagination," *Scientific American,* 199 (1958), 151–66.

5. Barron, Frank, and George S. Welsh, "Artistic Perception as a Possible Factor in Personality Style: Its Measurement by a Figure Preference Test," *Journal of Psychology,* 33 (1952), 199–203.

6. Brim, Orville G., Jr., "Attitude Content-Intensity and Probability Expectations," *American Sociological Review,* 59 (1954), 556–64.

7. Brim, Orville G., Jr., and David B. Hoff, "Individual and Situational Differences in Desire for Certainty," *Journal of Abnormal and Social Psychology,* 54 (1957), 225–29.

8. French, John W., *The Description of Personality Measurements in Terms of Rotated Factors,* Princeton, N.J.: Educational Testing Service, 1953.

9. Hollingshead, August B., "Two Factor Index of Social Position," New Haven, Conn.: Yale Univ. (Dittoed).

10. Holtzman, W. H., Allen D. Calvin, and Morton E. Bitterman, "New Evidence for the Validity of Taylor's Manifest Anxiety Scale," *Journal of Abnormal and Social Psychology,* 47 (1952), 853–54.

11. Jensen, Arthur R., "Personality," *Annual Review of Psychology,* Paul R. Farnsworth and Quinn McNemar (Eds.), Vol. 9, Palo Alto, Calif.: Annual Reviews, 1958, pp. 295–323.

12. Jessor, Richard, and Kenneth R. Hammond, "Construct Validity and the Taylor Anxiety Scale," *Psychological Bulletin,* 54 (1957), 161–70.

13. Kendall, Edward, "The Validity of Taylor's Manifest Anxiety Scale," *Journal of Consulting Psychology,* 18 (1954), 429–32.

14. Matarazzo, Joseph D., S. B. Guze, and Ruth G. Matarazzo, "An Approach to the Validity of the Taylor Anxiety Scale: Scores of Medical and Psychiatric Patients," *Journal of Abnormal and Social Psychology,* 51 (1955), 276–80.

15. Miner, John B., *Intelligence in the United States: A Survey—with Conclusions for Manpower Utilization in Education and Employment,* New York: Springer, 1957.

16. Schaefer, Earl S., and Richard Q. Bell, "Parental Attitude Research Instrument (PARI), Normative Data," Unpublished manuscript, Bethesda, Md.: Library, National Institute of Mental Health, 1955.

17. Schaefer, Earl S., and Richard Q. Bell, "An Adaptation of the Parental Attitude Research Instrument for Fathers," Unpublished Manuscript, 1957 (Mimeo.).

18. Schaefer, Earl S., and Richard Q. Bell, "Development of a Parental Attitude Research Instrument," *Child Development,* 29 (1958), 339–61.

19. Spence, Kenneth W., "A Theory of Emotionally Based Drive (D) and its Relation to Performance in Simple Learning Situations," *American Psychologist,* 13 (1958), 131–41.

20. Spence, Kenneth W., and Janet A. Taylor, "The Relation of Conditioned Response Strength to Anxiety in Normal, Neurotic, and Psychotic Subjects," *Journal of Experimental Psychology,* 45 (1953), 265–72.

21. Taylor, Janet A. "The Relationship of Anxiety to the Conditioned Eyelid Response," *Journal of Experimental Psychology,* 41 (1951), 81–92.

22. Taylor, Janet A., "A Personality Scale of Manifest Anxiety," *Journal of Abnormal and Social Psychology,* 48 (1953), 285–90.

23. Taylor, Janet A., "Drive Theory and Manifest Anxiety," *Psychological Bulletin,* 53 (1956), 303–21.

24. Thorndike, Edward L., "Two Screening Tests of Verbal Intelligence," *Journal of Applied Psychology,* 26 (1942), 128–35.

25. Thorndike, Edward L., and George Gallup, "Verbal Intelligence of American Adults," *Journal of Genetic Psychology,* 30 (1944), 75–85.

26. Thorndike, Robert L., *Research Problems and Techniques,* AAF Aviation Psychology Prog. Res. Rep., No. 3, Washington, D.C.: Government Printing Office, 1947, pp. 102–3.

CHAPTER 5

1. Axelrod, Morris, "Urban Structure and Social Participation," *American Sociological Review,* 21 (1956), 13–18.

2. Barber, Bernard, *Social Stratification,* New York: Harcourt, Brace, 1957.

3. Bell, Wendell, and Maryanne T. Force, "Urban Neighborhood Types and Participation in Formal Associations," *American Sociological Review,* 21 (1956), 25–34.

4. Bendix, Reinhard, and Seymour M. Lipset (Eds.), *Class, Status and Power: A Reader in Social Stratification,* Glencoe, Ill.: Free Press, 1953.

5. Hollingshead, August B., and Fredrich C. Redlich, *Social Class and Mental Illness: A Community Study,* New York: Wiley, 1958.

6. Scott, John C., Jr., "Membership and Participation in Voluntary Associations," *American Sociological Review,* 22 (1957), 315–26.

7. Sklare, Marshall (Ed.), *The Jews: Social Patterns of An American Group,* Glencoe, Ill.: Free Press, 1958.

8. Wright, Charles R., and Herbert H. Hyman, "Voluntary Association Memberships of American Adults: Evidence from National Sample Surveys," *American Sociological Review,* 23 (1958), 284–94.

CHAPTER 6

1. Cattell, Raymond B., *Factor Analysis,* New York: Harper, 1952.
2. French, John W., *The Description of Personality Measurements in Terms of Rotated Factors,* Educational Testing Service, Princeton, N.J.: Princeton Univ. Press, 1953.
3. Neuhaus, Jack O., and Charles Wrigley, "The Quartimax Method," *British Journal of Statistical Psychology,* 7, Part 2 (1954), 81–91.
4. Strodtbeck, Fred L., "Family Interaction, Values and Achievement," in *Talent and Society,* D. C. McClelland, *et al.* (Eds.), Princeton, N.J.: D. Van Nostrand, 1958, pp. 135–95.
5. Thurstone, L. L., *Multiple Factor Analysis,* Chicago, Ill.: Univ. of Chicago Press, 1947.

CHAPTER 7

1. Auld, B. Franklin, Jr., "Influence of Social Class on Personality Test Response," *Psychological Bulletin,* 49 (1952), 318–32.
2. Bedell, Ralph C., "The Relationship Between the Ability to Recall and the Ability to Infer in Specific Learning Situations," *Bulletin of the Northeast Missouri State Teachers College,* 34, No. 9 (1934).
3. Bennett, Edward M., and Larry R. Cohen, "Men and Women: Personality Patterns and Contrasts," *Genetic Psychology Monographs,* 59 (1959), 101–55.
4. Bieri, James, "Parental Identification, Acceptance of Authority and Within-Sex Differences in Cognitive Behavior," *Journal of Abnormal and Social Psychology,* 60 (1960), 76–80.
5. Bieri, James, and Robin Lobeck, "Self-Concept Differences in Relation to Identification, Religion and Social Class," *Journal of Abnormal and Social Psychology,* 62 (1961), 94–98.
6. Billings, M. L., "Problem Solving in Different Fields of Endeavor," *American Journal of Psychology,* 2 (1934), 259–72.
7. Brim, Orville G., Jr., and Raymond Forer, "A Note on the Relation of Values and Social Structure to Life Planning," *Sociometry,* 19 (1956), 54–61.
8. Brown, F., "Comparative Study of the Influence of Race and Locale Upon Emotional Stability of Children," *Journal of Genetic Psychology,* 49 (1936), 325–42.
9. Carey, Gloria L., "Sex Differences in Problem-Solving Performance as a Function of Attitude Differences," *Journal of Abnormal and Social Psychology,* 56 (1958), 256–60.
10. Cattell, Raymond B., "The Cultural Functions of Social Stratification: II. Regarding Individual and Group Dynamics," *Journal of Social Psychology,* 21 (1948), 25–56.
11. Edwards, Ward, "Behavioral Decision Theory," *Annual Review of Psychology,* Paul R. Farnsworth, Olga McNemar, and Quinn McNemar (Eds.), Vol. 12, Palo Alto, Calif.,: Annual Reviews, 1961, 473–99.
12. Eells, Kenneth, Allison Davis, Robert Havighurst, Virgil E. Herrick, and Ralph Tyler, *Intelligence and Cultural Differences,* Chicago, Ill.: Univ. of Chicago Press, 1951.
13. Eysenck, Sybill B. G., "Social Class, Sex, and Response to a Five-Part

Personality Inventory," *Educational and Psychological Measurement,* 20 (1960), 47–54.

14. Freidman, Milton, and Leonard J. Savage, "The Utility Analysis of Choices Involving Risk," *Journal of Political Economy,* 56 (1948), 279–304.

15. Glazer, Nathan, "The American Jew and the Attainment of Middle-Class Rank: Trends and Explanations," in *The Jews: Social Patterns of an American Group,* Marshall Sklare (Ed.), Glencoe, Ill.: Free Press, 1958.

16. Green, Arthur, "The Middle-Class Male Child and Neurosis," in *Class, Status and Power: A Reader in Social Stratification,* R. Bendix and S. M. Lipset (Eds.), Glencoe, Ill.: Free Press, 1953.

17. Havighurst, Robert J., "Social Class and Personality," paper read before the Society for the Psychological Study of Social Issues, Chicago, September 1951.

18. Hollingshead, August B., and Fredrich C. Redlich, *Social Class and Mental Illness: A Community Study,* New York: Wiley, 1958.

19. Kagan, Jerome, Howard A. Moss, and Irving E. Sigel, "Conceptual Style and the Use of Affect Labels," *Merrill-Palmer Quarterly,* 6 (1960), 261–79.

20. Kelly, E. Lowell, "Consistency of the Adult Personality," *American Psychologist,* 10 (1955), 659–82.

21. Lipset, Seymour M., "Democracy and Working-Class Authoritarianism," *American Sociological Review,* 24 (1959), 482–501.

22. Miller, Seymour M., and Frank Riessman, "The Working Class Subculture: A New View," Paper read before the American Sociological Association, New York City, August 1960.

23. Milton, G. Alexander, "The Effects of Sex Role Identification Upon Problem Solving Skill," *Journal of Abnormal and Social Psychology,* 55 (1957), 209–12.

24. Milton, G. Alexander, "Sex Differences in Problem-Solving as a Function of Role Appropriateness of the Problem Content," *Psychological Reports,* 5 (1959), 705–8.

25. Morgan, Antonia B., "Sex Differences in Adults on a Test of Logical Reasoning," *Psychological Reports,* 2 (1956), 227–30.

26. Patterson, Cecil H., "The Relationship of Bernreuter Scores to Parent Behavior, Child Behavior, Urban–Rural Residence, and Other Background Factors in 100 Normal Adult Parents," *Journal of Social Psychology,* 24 (1946), 3–50.

27. Rainwater, Lee, Asst. by Karol Kane Weinstein, *And the Poor Get Children: Sex, Contraception, and Family Planning in the Working Class,* Chicago, Ill.: Quadrangle Books, 1960.

28. Rainwater, Lee, "A Study of Personality Differences Between Middle and Lower Class Adolescents: The Szondi Test in Culture-Personality Research," *Genetic Psychology Monographs,* 54 (1956), 3–86.

29. Rosenberg, Morris, "The Social Roots of Formalism," *Journal of Social Issues,* 5 (1949), 14–23.

30. Schneider, Leonard, and Sverre Lysgaard, "The Deferred Gratification Pattern: A Preliminary Study," *American Sociological Review,* 18 (1953), 142–49.

31. Sewell, William H., and Archie O. Haller, "Social Status and the Personality Adjustment of the Child," *Sociometry,* 19 (1956), 114–25.

32. Sheriffs, Alex C., and James B. McKee, "Qualitative Aspects of Beliefs About Men and Women," *Journal of Personality,* 25 (1957), 451–64.

33. Sklare, Marshall, "Aspects of Religious Worship in the Contemporary Conservative Synagogue," in *The Jews: Social Patterns of an American Group,* M. Sklare (Ed.), Glencoe, Ill.: Free Press, 1958.

34. Strodtbeck, Fred L., "Family Interaction, Values and Achievement," in *Talent and Society,* David C. McClelland, *et al.* (Eds.), Princeton, N.J.: D. Van Nostrand, 1958, pp. 135–95.

35. Terman, Lewis M., "Psychological Sex Differences," in *Manual of Child Psychology,* Leonard Carmichael (Ed.), New York: Wiley, 1946, pp. 1064–1114.

36. Winch, Robert F., *Mate-Selection: A Study of Complementary Needs,* New York: Harper, 1958.

37. Zborowski, Mark, "Children of the Covenant," in *Studies in Motivation,* David C. McClelland (Ed.), New York: Appleton-Century-Crofts, 1955, pp. 352–74.

CHAPTER 8

1. Brim, Orville G., Jr., *Education for Child Rearing,* New York: Russell Sage Foundation, 1959.

2. Kinsey, Alfred C., Wardell B. Pomeroy and Clyde E. Martin, *Sexual Behavior in the Human Male,* Philadelphia, Pa.: Saunders, 1948.

3. Kohn, Melvin L., "Social Class and Parental Values," *American Journal of Sociology,* 54, No. 3 (1959), 337–51.

4. Stouffer, George A. W., Jr., "Behavior Problems of Children as Viewed by Teachers and Mental Hygienists," *Mental Hygiene,* 36, No. 2 (1952), 271–85.

5. Stouffer, George A. W., Jr., "The Attitudes of Parents Toward Certain Behavior Problems of Children," State Teachers College, Indiana, Pa., *Teachers College Bulletin,* 5, No. 1 (1959), 11–22.

CHAPTER 9

1. Allport, Floyd H., "The Influence of the Group upon Association and Thought," *Journal of Experimental Psychology,* 3 (1920), 152–82.

2. Arrow, Kenneth J., *Social Choice and Individual Values,* New York: Wiley, 1951.

3. Baldwin, James M., *Social and Ethical Interpretations in Mental Development,* New York: Macmillan, 1897; or reprinted in *Sociological Theory,* Edgar F. Borgatta and Henry J. Meyer (Eds.), New York: Knopf, 1956, pp. 16–34 and 62–70.

4. Barnlund, Dean C., "A Comparative Study of Individual, Majority, and Group Judgment," *Journal of Abnormal and Social Psychology,* 58 (1959), 55–60.

5. Bavelas, Alex, "Communication Patterns in Task-Oriented Groups," *Journal of Acoustical Sociology of America,* 22 (1950), 725–30.

6. Brim, Orville G., Jr., "Family Structure and Sex Role Learning by Children: A Further Analysis of Helen Koch's Data," *Sociometry,* 21 (1958), 1–16.

7. Cooley, Charles H., *Human Nature and the Social Order,* New York: Scribner's, 1922; or reprinted in *Sociological Theory,* Edgar F. Borgatta and Henry J. Meyer (Eds.), New York: Knopf, 1956, pp. 34–49.

8. Cottrell, Leonard S., "The Analysis of Situational Fields in Social Psychology," *American Sociological Review,* 7 (1942), 370–82.

9. Faust, William L., "Group Versus Individual Problem Solving," *Journal of Abnormal and Social Psychology,* 59 (1959), 68–72.

10. Fawcett Publications, *Male vs. Female: Influence on the Purchase of Selected Products as Revealed by an Exploratory Depth Interview Study With Husbands and Wives,* New York, 1958.

11. Hare, A. Paul, Edgar F. Borgatta, and Robert F. Bales (Eds.), *Small Groups,* New York: Knopf, 1955, pp. 194–225.

12. Herbst, P. G., "Task Differentiation of Husband and Wife in Family Activities," in *A Modern Introduction to the Family,* Norman W. Bell and Ezra F. Vogel (Eds.), Glencoe, Ill.: Free Press, 1960, pp. 339–46.

13. Jenness, Arthur, "The Role of Discussion in Changing Opinion Regarding a Matter of Fact," *Journal of Abnormal and Social Psychology,* 27 (1932), 279–96.

14. Kelley, Harold H., and John W. Thibaut, "Experimental Studies of Group Problem Solving and Process," in *Handbook of Social Psychology,* Gardner Lindzey (Ed.), Cambridge, Mass.: Addison-Wesley, 1954.

15. Kenkel, William F., "Influence Differentiation in Family Decision-Making," *Sociology and Social Research,* 42 (1957), 18–25.

16. Kenkel, William F., and Dean K. Hoffman, "Real and Conceived Roles in Family Decision-Making," *Marriage and Family Living,* 28 (1956), 311–16.

17. Lorge, Irving, David Fox, Joel Davitz, and Marlin Brenner, "A Survey of Studies Contrasting the Quality of Group Performance and Individual Performance, 1920–1957," *Psychological Bulletin,* 55 (1958), 337–72.

18. Lorge, Irving, Joel Davitz, David Fox, Kenneth Herrold, and Paula Weltz, "Evaluation of Instruction in Staff Action and Decision-Making," *USAF Human Resources Research Institute Technical Report,* 1953, No. 16.

19. Maccoby, Eleanor E., "Role-Taking in Childhood and its Consequence for Social Learning," *Child Development,* 30 (1959), 239–52.

20. March, James G., "Husband-Wife Interaction Over Political Issues," *Public Opinion Quarterly,* 27 (1953–54), 461–70.

21. Marquart, Dorothy I., "Group Problem Solving," *Journal of Social Psychology,* 41 (1955), 103–13.

22. Mead, George H., *Mind, Self, and Society,* Chicago, Ill.: Univ. of Chicago Press, 1934.

23. Mussen, Paul, and Luther Distler, "Masculinity, Identification, and Father-Son Relationships," *Journal of Abnormal and Social Psychology,* 59 (1959), 350–56.

24. Parsons, Talcott, *The Social System,* Glencoe, Ill.: Free Press, 1951.

25. Parsons, Talcott, and Edward A. Shils (Eds.), *Toward a General Theory of Action,* Cambridge, Mass.: Harvard Univ. Press, 1952.

26. Shaw, Marvin E., "Comparison of Individuals and Small Groups in the Rational Solution of Complex Problems," *American Journal of Psychology,* 44 (1932), 491–504.

27. Strodtbeck, Fred L., "Husband-Wife Interaction Over Revealed Differences," *American Sociological Review,* 16 (1951), 468–73.

28. Taylor, Donald W., and William L. Faust, "Twenty Questions: Efficiency in Problem Solving as a Function of Size of Group," *Journal of Experimental Psychology,* 44 (1952), 360–68.

29. Thomas, Edwin J., and C. J. Fink, *Models of Group Problem-Solving, Journal of Abnormal and Social Psychology,* 63 (1961), 53–63.

30. Timmons, William M., "Can the Product Superiority of Discussors Be Attributed to Averaging or Majority Influences?" *Journal of Social Psychology,* 15 (1942), 23–32.

31. Timmons, William M., "Decisions and Attitudes as Outcomes of the Discussion of a Social Problem," *Contributions to Education,* No. 777, New York: Columbia University, Teachers College, Bureau of Publications, 1939.

32. Watson, Goodwin B., "Do Groups Think More Efficiently Than Individuals?" *Journal of Abnormal and Social Psychology,* 23 (1928), 328–36.

33. Wolgast, Elizabeth H., "Economic Decisions in the Family," *Survey Research Center Economic Program,* Ann Arbor, Mich., 1957 (Mimeo.).

CHAPTER 10

1. Guilford, J. Paul, *Psychometric Methods,* New York: McGraw-Hill, 1954, pp. 350–54.

2. Kluckhohn, Clyde, "Values and Value-Orientations in the Theory of Action," in *Toward a General Theory of Action,* Talcott Parsons and Edward A. Shils (Eds.), Cambridge, Mass.: Harvard Univ. Press, 1951.

3. Kenkel, William F., "Influence Differentiation in Family Decision Making," *Sociology and Social Research,* 42 (1957), 18–25.

4. Kenkel, William F., and Dean K. Hoffman, "Real and Conceived Roles in Family Decision Making," *Marriage and Family Living,* 28 (1956), 311–16.

5. McNemar, Quinn, *Psychological Statistics,* New York: Wiley, 1955, pp. 160–61.

CHAPTER 11

1. Atkinson, John W., "Motivational Determinants of Risk-Taking Behavior," *Psychological Review,* 64 (1957), 359–72.

2. Atkinson, John W., and Walter R. Reitman, "Performance as a Function of Motive Strength and Expectancy of Goal Attainment," in *Motives in Fantasy, Action, and Society,* John W. Atkinson (Ed.), New York: Van Nostrand, 1958.

3. Bernard, Jessie, "The Theory of Games of Strategy as a Modern Sociology of Conflict," *American Journal of Sociology,* 59 (1954), 411–24.

4. Brim, Orville G., Jr., and Raymond Forer, "A Note on the Relation of Values and Social Structure to Life Planning," *Sociometry,* 19 (1956), 54–60.

5. Davidson, Donald, Patrick Suppes, and Sidney Siegel, *Decision Making,* Stanford, Calif.: Stanford Univ. Press, 1957.

6. Edwards, Ward, "Probability Preferences in Gambling," *American Journal of Psychology,* 66 (1953), 349–64.

7. Edwards, Ward, "Probability Preferences Among Bets with Differing Expected Values," *American Journal of Psychology,* 67 (1954), 56–67.

8. Edwards, Ward, "The Reliability of Probability Preferences," *American Journal of Psychology,* 67 (1954), 68–95.

9. Edwards, Ward, "The Theory of Decision Making," *Psychological Bulletin,* 51 (1954), 380–417.

10. Edwards, Ward, "An Attempt to Predict Gambling Decisions," in *Mathematical Models of Human Behavior*, Stamford, Conn.: Dunlap, 1955, pp. 83–96.

11. Edwards, Ward, "Behavioral Decision Theory," *Annual Review of Psychology*, Paul R. Farnsworth, Olga McNemar, and Quinn McNemar (Eds.), Vol. 12, Palo Alto, Calif.: Annual Reviews, 1961.

12. Hull, Clark L., *Principles of Behavior*, New York: Appleton-Century-Crofts, 1943.

13. Kendall, Maurice G., *Rank Correlation Methods*, London: Charles Griffin, 1948.

14. Kluckhohn, Florence, "Dominant and Variant Value Orientations," in *Personality in Nature, Society, and Culture*, Clyde Kluckhohn, Henry A. Murray, and David M. Schneider (Eds.), rev. ed., New York: Knopf, 1953, pp. 342–57.

15. Lewin, Kurt, *et al.*, "Level of Aspiration," in *Personality and the Behavior Disorders*, Vol. 1, J. McV. Hunt (Ed.), New York: Ronald Press, 1944, pp. 333–78.

16. Liverant, Shephard, and Alvin Scodel, "Internal and External Control as Determinants of Decision Making Under Conditions of Risk," *Psychological Reports, 7* (1960), 59–67.

17. Luce, R. Duncan, and Howard Raiffa, *Games and Decisions*, New York: Wiley, 1957.

18. Luce, R. Duncan, *Individual Choice Behavior*, New York: Wiley, 1959.

19. Von Neumann, John, and Oskar Morgenstern, *Theory of Games and Economic Behavior*, 2d ed., Princeton, N.J.: Princeton Univ. Press, 1947.

20. Schubert, Glendon A., *Quantitative Analysis of Judicial Behavior*, Glencoe, Ill.: Free Press, 1959.

21. Scodel, Alvin, Philburn Ratoosh, and J. Sayer Minas, "Some Personality Correlates of Decision Making Under Conditions of Risk," *Behavioral Science*, 4 (1959), 19–29.

22. Shubik, Martin, *Readings in Game Theory and Political Behavior*, Garden City, N.Y.: Doubleday, 1954.

23. Siegel, Sidney, "Level of Aspiration and Decision Making," *Psychological Review*, 64 (1957), 253–62.

24. Strodtbeck, Fred L., "Family Interaction, Values, and Achievement," in *Talent and Society* by D. C. McClelland, *et al.* (Eds.), New York: D. Van Nostrand, 1958, pp. 135–94.

25. Tolman, Edward C., "A Psychological Model," in *Toward a General Theory of Action*, Talcott Parsons and Edward A. Shils (Eds.), Cambridge, Mass.: Harvard Univ. Press, 1954, pp. 279–361.

26. Wallach, Michael A., and Nathan Kogan, "Aspects of Judgment and Decision Making: Interrelationships and Changes with Age," *Behavioral Science*, 6 (1961), (in press).

CHAPTER 12

1. Atkinson, John W., "Motivational Determinants of Risk-Taking Behavior," *Psychological Review*, 64 (1957), 359–72.

2. Brim, Orville G., Jr., *Education for Child Rearing*, New York: Russell Sage Foundation, 1959.

3. Kinsey, Alfred C., Wardell B. Pomeroy, and Clyde E. Martin, *Sexual Behavior in the Human Male*, Philadelphia, Pa.: Saunders, 1948.

4. Neuhaus, Jack, and Charles Wrigley, "The Quartimax Method," *British Journal of Statistical Psychology, 7,* Part II (1954), 81–91.

5. Siegel, Sidney S., "Level of Aspiration and Decision Making," *Psychological Review, 64* (1957), 253–62.

6. Scodel, Alvin, Philburn Ratoosh, and J. Sayer Minas, "Some Personality Correlates of Decision Making Under Conditions of Risk," *Behavioral Science, 4* (1959), 19–29.

7. Thurstone, L. L., *Multiple-Factor Analysis,* Chicago, Ill.: Univ. of Chicago Press, 1947.

INDEX

INDEX

Allport, Floyd H., 167
Anxiety, as personality factor, 119–21; *see also* Taylor Manifest Anxiety Scale
Asch-type conformity experiments, 57
Autonomy-dependency, correlations between spouses, 128–29; as personality decision process factor, 105–10; and *S*-scores, 221

Baldwin, James M., 176
Barnard, Chester I., 19
Barron, Frank, 57, 74–76
Barron-Welsh Art Scale, 57–58
Bartlett, Sir Frederic, 12
Bavelas, Alex, 167
Beardslee, David, 16
Beliefs, as personality component, 54–58; tests of, 71–76
Bell, Richard Q., 67, 68–69
Bentham, Jeremy, 24
Bieri, James, 133
Brim, Orville G., Jr., 33, 179

Cattell, Raymond B., 103 n.
Certainty, defined, 15
Child-rearing decisions, characteristics of, 24–26
Choice, prediction of first choices among alternatives, 207–11
Columbia University, Institute of Educational Research, 63
Conant, James B., 19
Complementary needs, between spouses, 131–32
Conflict, in decisions, 13–16; effect on *S*-scores, 214–16
Concept formation, 14
Cooley, Charles H., 176
Coombs, Clyde H., 16
Copeland, Melvin T., 18
Correlations, between spouses on decision process variables, 188–91; between spouses on personality

characteristics, 128–32; curvilinear relationships, 94–95
Cottrell, Leonard S., 13, 22, 177
Creativity, 13, 57–58
Critical thinking, 13
Cronbach, Lee J., 18
Culture, and beliefs, 54–58; Jewish, 136–38, 221–22; Protestant ethic, 27; proverbs, 22; and rationality, 22

Decisions, and social roles, 17–20; characteristics of child-rearing decisions, 24–26; formal properties of, 14–17; substantive properties of, 16–20; types of, 14–20
Decision problem: *see* Situational effects
Decision processes, acquiring information phase, 12–13; correlations between spouses, 188–91; descriptive variables, 27–28; evaluation and strategy-selection phases, 13–14, 26–27; factor structure, 95–103; methodological issues in studying, 26–27; performance and learning phase, 14; phases of, 9–14; producing solutions phase, 13; recognition of problem, 12; sex differences in, 132–39; social class differences in, 132–39; tests of, 21
Decision Process Test, general description, 29–45; description of problems, 29–32; evaluation variables, 32–36; range of scores, 190; reliability, 39–44, 189–90; strategy-selection variables, 36–39; validity, 44–45
Desirability direction, correlations between spouses, 128–29; as decision profess factor, 97–100; as decision process variable, 34; as personality decision process factor, 105–10
Desirability extremity, as decision